German History 1789–1871

From the Holy Roman Empire to the Bismarckian Reich

GERMAN HISTORY 1789–1871

From The Holy Roman Empire To The Bismarckian Reich

ERIC DORN BROSE

Berghahn Books
Providence • Oxford

First published in 1997 by

Berghahn Books

Library of Congress Cataloging-in-Publication Data

Brose, Eric Dorn, 1948-
German history, 1789-1871 : from Holy Roman Empire to Bismarckian Reich / Eric Dorn Brose.
p. cm.
Includes bibliographical references and index.
ISBN 1-57181-055-2 (alk. paper). -- ISBN 1-57181-056-0 (pbk. : alk. paper)
1. Germany--Politics and government--1789-1900. 2. Germany--Intellectual life. 3. France--History--Revolution, 1789-1799. 4. Germany--Economic conditions--19th century. 5. Conservatism--Germany. 6. Holy Roman Empire--History--Francis II, 1792-1806. I. Title.
DD197.5.B76 1997
944.04--dc21 97-11757
CIP

British Library Cataloguing in Publication Data

A catalogue record for this book is available
from the British Library.

Printed in the United States on acid-free paper.

Contents

List of Illustrations and Maps

Illustrations

Maps

Preface

Historians always take liberties with the starting and ending dates of their studies. In order to explain developments fully as well as to assess their long-term significance, it is necessary to wander backwards and forwards beyond the chronological parameters set in the title. Nevertheless, there should be good reasons why an author chooses one specific period over another, for, despite the natural liberties taken, the underlying constraints imposed by the time period limit him.

This book is set between 1789 – the outbreak of the French Revolution – and 1871 – the formation of the Second German Empire. Both years were meaningful turning points in the history of Germany and Europe. In 1789, the numerous states of German Europe were still organized into the Holy Roman Empire. While there was much discussion of reforming this medieval hold-over, there was no reason to assume that the Empire would end in the foreseeable future. The Enlightenment of the eighteenth century had generated much discussion and debate about reforming monarchy, similarly, but none of the hundreds of German rulers was constrained by an elected political body. Socially and economically, moreover, Germany was already experiencing change as serfdom and the corporate world of the guilds began to yield to newer institutional forms. Yet there was no reason at all to believe that serfdom would soon begin to disappear or that a nascent modern industry and mechanical technology would spread from England and inundate the continent. By 1806, however, the French Revolution and the wars it sparked had terminated the Holy Roman Empire, prompting six decades of discussion, controversy, and finally, war, over what would replace it. Between 1815 and 1820, the first constitutions and representative assemblies appeared on German soil, opening a long period of experimentation and learning as state after state groped its way toward something approaching a working party system – and provoking a half century of struggle over parliamentary challenges to the authority of monarchs. And during the 1810s and 1820s, industrialism began to accelerate, leading to intense debates over whether or not to put barriers in its path. By 1871, all three of these issues were resolved. How they were settled is the subject of the chapters that follow.

In pursuing this story, we will notice that the German view of the past changed. By the late eighteenth century, many educated men and women began to turn to the history of previous eras for inspiration in the present. Ancient Greece, in particular, was held up as a model for opening the state to intellectuals and wealthy commoners previously excluded from participation in government. During the Napoleonic Wars this yearning for antiquity as an expression of dissatisfaction with present times became more widespread. By the 1820s and 1830s, the Middle Ages emerged as a competing backward-looking vision of the future. Conservatives turned to the medieval epoch as a pattern for reactionary measures, while, in contrast, nationalists expropriated the same period to generate excitement for German unification. Significantly enough, these political issues spilled over into music, art, architecture, literature, and academic history. Only with the resolution of the German Question in 1871 did this political and cultural engagement with the past begin to lose intensity.

* * * *

As many readers will know, the decades from 1789 to 1871 – or the greater part of this period – have been the subject of many previous works. Indeed it is humbling to consider the names of just some of these authors: Heinrich von Treitschke, Franz Schnabel, Thomas Nipperdey, Hans Ulrich Wehler, and James Sheehan. The publishers were correct in believing, however, that another rendering was justified. For one thing, even the most recent works – those of Wehler and Sheehan – are now a decade old. And scholarship has raced forward, generating many significant new publications that produce new insights into this complex period of transition and transformation in German History. Secondly, the previous renderings listed above are prodigious accomplishments approaching or easily passing a thousand pages, and all except Sheehan's impressive tome are in German. The present work strives to be more accessible to students and historians in the English-speaking world without losing the interest of German scholars.

Like previous studies, this is a work of synthesis and interpretation. During the last thirty years, scholarship has deepened in the traditional areas of political, diplomatic, military, and economic history while simultaneously widening and deepening to include the history of work, gender, religion, race, and the various branches of art or culture. The scholar's focus has also broadened from Prussia and Austria, Germany's feuding giants, to include the rich diversity of the rest of German Europe. The approach taken in the present work is to consider, select, and combine evidence from older and newer studies in these many fields to produce a composite image of Germany between 1789 and 1871. Let us put many of the available pieces together, step back, and see what the mosaic looks like.

All readers need to know the source of the evidence. For this reason the bibliography is limited to those works actually used in writing the book. There are frequent quotations from the literature, moreover, making it easy to determine which works from the bibliography have been most influential. To enhance readability, on the other hand, only direct quotes are cited. Finally, a word about the book's scenes or vignettes. I employ these literary devices to accustom readers in an artful way to the subject matter and themes which follow, but they are factual – and documented – not fictional. In these ways the present work stays within the accepted limits of historical scholarship without crossing over the boundary to literature.

* * * *

I want to thank Marion Berghahn for giving me an opportunity to write this book; the readers at Berghahn Books for insightful comments that improved the manuscript; as well as persons close to me who patiently and lovingly waited for it to appear.

Eric Dorn Brose, Philadelphia, April 1997

Part I

A REVOLUTIONARY CHALLENGE

The brightly colored houses, steeply angled roofs, and imposing stone ramparts of the Imperial City of Aachen sparkled in the sunlight as the travelers ascended a bumpy road which led westward. Near the Austrian territory of Limburg the coaches turned onto a more comfortable paved highway traversing a ridge. Occasionally, the discussion of the gentlemen inside yielded to silence as they peered reverently through the hedges which lined their way. Below them a collage of red and white farm house walls, blue slate roofs, golden meadows, and shady copses stretched southeast to the dark green of the Ardennes and the gray walls of Limburg. Finally they halted for a late lunch at the Gasthof Bel Oeil, appropriately named for the beautiful panorama around it.[1]

One of the six seated around the inn's largest wooden table was Joachim Heinrich Campe, a journalist and educational reformer from Brunswick. As the others returned to the debate which had raged since the previous evening, he busied himself with notes for his travel journal. Campe's campanion, Wilhelm von Humboldt, a gifted young scholar from Berlin, implored his former teacher, Chris-

1. For a detailed description of the trip to the Bel Oeil, and the conversation there, see *Wilhelm von Humboldts Tagebücher*, ed. Albert Leitzmann, (Berlin, 1916), 14:90-91, 94; and Joachim Heinrich Campe, "Reise des Herausgebers von Braunschweig nach Paris im Heumonat 1789," *Sämmtliche Kinder- und Jugendschriften* (Brunswick, 1831), 24:52-53.

tian Wilhelm Dohm, to listen. That the state's sole function should be to provide military and police security for a people, as Dohm was arguing, was mistaken. For in reality, the provision of security often endangered a person's freedom. True prosperity, welfare, and enlightenment had to be fostered and promoted by progressive state institutions and policies. In this way states could facilitate personal growth and enable individuals to realize their fullest capacities.

The older man leaned forward, knowing that Humboldt had mistaken him for an enemy of the individual. Famous for his advocacy of Jewish emancipation and assimilation without religious conversion, Dohm believed that governments should promote freedoms and champion rights. But all means that individuals employed to attain physical, intellectual, and moral well-being were more likely to succeed *without* state intervention. So it was with manufacture, trade, commerce, education, and morality, where individual initiative was crucial. This is why he felt so strongly that the function of states should be limited mainly to security. Humboldt, somewhat more impressed, but not entirely satisfied, reclined in his chair.

The mid-summer sun of 1789 was just beginning its descent in the western sky as Campe and Humboldt parted company with their friends outside the Bel Oeil. They watched and waved as Dohm's coach returned to Aachen, standing silently until it became indistinguishable from the hedges on either side. A moment later they too seated themselves in a coach and headed back onto the highway which, ten days later, would bring them to the revolutionary metropolis of Paris.

Each was drawn for different reasons to the great city that was the intense focus of European attention. Campe could not resist the urge to be an eyewitness to the "stirring victory of humanity over tryanny" and the glorious political achievements of "the new Greeks and Romans."[2] Humboldt was attracted more by the Sorbonne, Notre Dame, and the architectural delights of Paris than its teeming masses and political dramas. Thus the ongoing demolition

2. Cited in Campe, *Kinder- und Jugendschriften*, 24:3; and Thomas P. Saine, *Black Bread – White Bread: German Intellectuals and the French Revolution* (Columbia, SC, 1988), 23.

Caspar David Friedrich's *Ruins of Eldena,* 1824-25.
Friedrich often employed ruins as symbols of the old order.

of the Bastille, a "beautiful medieval building", saddened him. But the young, sophisticated opponent of state tyranny also appreciated the historic, progressive scene which was unfolding before him. Six days a week the work crews swung their hammers, hurrying to remove the massive prison and make way for a freedom memorial on the same site. "Yes," he admitted to his diary, "the destruction of the Bastille was necessary. It was the real bulwark of despotism."[3] Avid defenders of individual rights like Humboldt naturally preferred a freedom memorial to the Bastille.

3. *Wilhelm von Humboldts Tagebücher,* 14:120.

Chapter 1

Germany before the French Revolution

Campe and his friends began their journey that historic summer in Brunswick, capital of the Duchy of Brunswick-Wolfenbüttel, a small but prominent territory located in the north-central portion of the Holy Roman Empire of the German Nation. There were 350 of these secular states in the Reich of 1789, ranging in size from the tiny County of Lippe to large dynastic powers like Prussia, Saxony, Bavaria, and the imperial heartland of Austria. The first days of their trip took them through the Bishoprics of Hildesheim and Paderborn, two of 61 church-held, ecclesiastical territories scattered throughout the central, western, and southern parts of the empire. Within a week, Campe and Humboldt had reached Aachen, one of 51 imperial city-states. Before they crossed into France on the twelfth day, the travelers had entered and exited six duchies, four bishoprics, and one free city. This was a mere fraction, however, of the 462 largely sovereign political entities of the Holy Roman Empire.

While in Aachen days before their luncheon at the Bel Oeil, our travelers noted signs of tension between forces of change in society and the old traditional ways. Like many other free city-states, the ancient capital of Charlemagne was a citadel of the guilds. These medieval craft corporations had controled urban economic, social, and political life in former centuries. A boy of twelve or thirteen aspiring to the status of master baker, butcher, weaver, or jeweler embarked on this path by paying a fee to enter the master's household as an apprentice. After years of hard work and training, there followed "tramping days" as a journeyman moving from town to town to work with other masters and acquire more skills. If all proceeded well, a journeyman completed a "masterpiece" carefully evaluated by guild authorities for proper workmanship. Graduation to guild master was still not guaranteed, however, for one had to purchase the legal right to establish a shop. These so-called "real rights" *(Realrechte)* represented a sizable investment – 2, 500 florins for an apothecary in Augsburg around 1800, for instance – and usually required considerable negotiation with guild and town authorities.

They brought entrée, however, to the quaint, exclusionary world of the German home towns. Mack Walker's research has uncovered about four thousand of these guild-run communities. Rarely exceeding 10,000 inhabitants, they more typically contained only a few thousand people. With the purchase of shop rights came the right to reside and marry in such a town. At home the successful master provided food, shelter, and the emotional security that accompanies survival in an uncertain world. His was a patriarchal household where wife, journeymen, sons, apprentices, daughters, and servants lived and worked in a hierarchy of age and gender. The craftsman also had a seat on guild councils that regulated the entry of new masters into the guild, the quantity of wares produced, the quality and price of final products, and the social behavior of members. Guildmasters usually dominated town government, moreover, passing offices back and forth over the decades between closely related families – a kind of "regime of uncles."[1] It was a much-idealized world of quality workmanship, fulfilling labor, and high status in the community. Thus Christian Wilhelm Dohm wrote in 1781 that the mastercraftsman "enjoys the present with a pure and perfect joy and expects tomorrow to be exactly like today."[2]

The guilds had guaranteed many qualified journeymen entry to a trade during the best economic periods of former centuries, but

1. Mack Walker, *German Home Towns: Community, State, and General Estate 1648-1871* (Ithaca, 1971), 106.

2. Cited in James J. Sheehan, *German History 1770-1866* (Oxford, 1989), 109.

Western Germany 1789 12353

idealism such as Dohm's was inappropriate by the 1780s because foreign competition and warfare had ended this golden era two centuries earlier. With markets shrinking, corporate masters began to exploit their hierarchical advantages. Hometown birth became almost a prerequisite for guild membership and related rights. Widows were often forbidden from continuing to run their husbands' crafts, while towns like Göttingen and Leipzig barred female workers from weaving. Although male weavers benefitted from this practice, young journeymen also found their path to establishing independent shops blocked by oppressive guild controls. The result

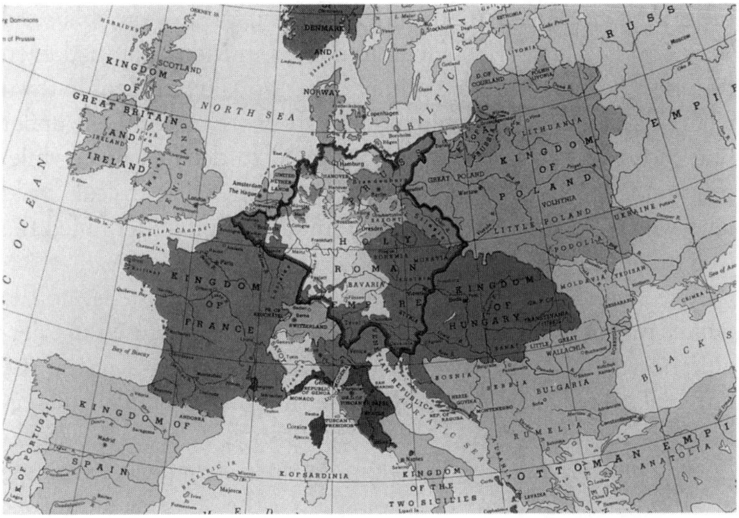

Europe 1763 12353

was a wave of strikes which accelerated in the eighteenth century despite an imperial ordinance of 1731 designed to restore order. One of the worst uprisings occurred in Aachen in 1786. Angry woolen artisans stormed city hall and did not disband until troops from the neighboring Duchy of Jülich entered the gates. The empire appointed a commission headed by Dohm to rewrite the city's constitution. Sobered on the subject of the guilds, he was in the process of recommending a dismantling of most corporate controls when Campe and his friends visited him in 1789.

Guild abuses stood behind another significant challenge to the old ways. Frustrated by stifling corporate restrictions, renegade woolen and linen producers began as early as the sixteenth century to move a portion of their operations beyond city walls. Raw materials like wool were distributed to poor rural families for inexpensive spinning, collected by agents (factors), then returned to town for weaving and finishing. By the late eighteenth century this so-called putting out system had spread throughout the Reich. In some regions, villages and small towns in the vicinity of guild-controlled cities grew into impressive centers of cottage handicraft production. Crefeld, Elberfeld, and Barmen were classic examples of this new type of town, while west of Aachen, pre-industrial textile output multiplied in Burtscheid, Düren, Vaels, Monschau, and Verviers. The firm of Scheibler and Sons in Monschau had even begun to re-assemble the spinning of high-quality woolens in town where factory foremen could monitor the work more closely under one roof. Aachen's prosperity continued to decline, meanwhile, prompting an observant Campe to castigate "non-sensical" guild laws which "killed entrepreneurial initiative and undermined the welfare of the city."[3]

The states of the Reich represented another challenge to the guilds' way of life. Thus larger powers like Prussia refused to tolerate the waning authority of the urban corporations, using the imperial decree of 1731 to undermine the guilds' political and regulatory autonomy. Other rulers established orphanages, workhouses, prisons, and lunatic asylums where a great deal of spinning and weaving was completed for sale by the state or its lessors. States also began to enter business themselves in order to enhance revenues and shelter their lands from imports. Of the roughly 1,000 large-scale manufacturing establishments in German Europe by the late 1700s, for instance, about sixty were fully state-owned. They were concentrated mainly in luxury areas like porcelain, carpets and tapestries, and hats and lace, but also included food processing industries like sugar, coffee, and chocolate. The states' role in the economy of eighteenth century Germany was further enhanced through monopoly charters, tax exemptions, and subsidies granted to private businesses. Although they were an important source of income for princes usually strapped for funds, few of these mercantilistic ventures were efficiently run, nor should we look here for the origins of modern industrialism. A more fertile seed was the above-mentioned putting-out system, which constituted about 43 percent of German manufacturing production of all kinds and was gradually evolving toward factories, as in Monshau.

Cottage industry was just one way that urban well-being in German Europe was linked to the surrounding countryside. Most of a city's food was grown outside the walls. Much of its production was sold in those rural areas where almost three-quarters of the population lived and worked. From the country came hops and barley for

3. Campe, *Kinder- und Jugendschriften*, 24:46-47.

brewers, flax seeds for linen spinners, raw wool for woolen manufacturers, moad and madder for dye works, leather for harnesses, pulleys, and the first machine belts, wood and stone for construction, and charcoal for iron makers. Germany's manufacturing establishments represented a mere 2 percent of net investment in the late eighteenth century, while about 70 percent went into agriculture. Land was undoubtedly the most important means of production.

These circumstances help to explain the great influence wielded in state and society by landowners. The largest tracts were usually possessed by territorial princes. The ruling Wittelsbachs owned about an eighth of the land in Bavaria, while the Hohenzollerns of Prussia held title to a third of Brandenburg and over half of the province of East Prussia. Although it made up a mere 1 or 2 percent of the population, the Catholic hierarchy was also a significant landowner, witness its control over roughly half of the property in Bavaria. In almost every secular and ecclesiastical state, moreover, families of noble rank (representing an even slighter 1 percent of the people) possessed the lion's share of real estate. This ensured them easy access to the ruler and a privileged status in the state. Thus Frederick the Great, King of Prussia from 1740 until 1786, chose all of his generals and 95 percent of his ministers from the Junker nobility. Indeed these inequities were so deeply entrenched in time that the law had come to reflect them. Noblemen answered to a different set of statutes and were tried in different courts from the common people. Noble rank was so important that it still guaranteed these legal privileges if a noble family lost its land.

The inverse was true for serfs. Generally speaking, the status of these peasant commoners on the land amounted to semi-slavery. Men of aristocratic blue-blood usually administered justice to peasants in country courts, collected the small farmer's state taxes, and enlisted him in the king's army. Peasants under serfdom paid to grind grain in an aristocrat's mill and could not hunt or cut wood in the forest without payment or permission from the local potentate. Serfs were not free to leave the land, moreover, for they had to pay cash rent or else work two or three days a week in the nobleman's fields in return for access to lands he allowed them to farm. It is a generalization, but rent in western and southern Germany typically took monetary form by the mid-to-late 1700s, while labor and other service obligations to noblemen usually remained the norm in Habsburg territories and on the Junker lands of eastern Prussia, Mecklenburg, and Pomerania. Only a small number of small farmers actually held title and thus escaped serfdom: some along the French border; some in the Alps; and others in the eastern borderlands of the Reich. A somewhat greater number enjoyed the hereditary right to lease property from a nobleman – and thus technically were not serfs – but the majority of peasants in German lands had neither land nor rights, and lived in hereditary subjection to a seigneurial lord who charged them for rights to the soil. Aside from the freeholders and hereditary lessors, writes James Sheehan, "the quality of [land] tenure declined through a scale of gradations, each one shading off into the next: lifetime leaseholds, leaseholds for a given period of time, sharecropping, [and] annual renting at the whim of the lord or his agent."[4]

Regardless of one's tenure, however, the ugliest reality for most peasants was the small combined size of their scattered holdings. In the Hochberg region of Baden, for example, 40 percent of the peasantry farmed less than seven acres, while 45 percent was totally without access to land. Whether or not they actually owned a farm, in other words, few peasants worked enough land to be secure. The putting-out of the spinning of women and children, the husband's hired labor in a nearby town or more prosperous estate, and the good fortune to avoid fire, pestilence, and war often meant the margin of survival.

The only significant force working to ameliorate the lot of the common man was the peasant protection policy of some German states. We must be careful here not to generalize. Many of the worst abuses occurred in ecclesiastical territories where the state was essentially the landlord, while the duchies of Mecklenburg and Pomerania were notorious for catering to the often cruel whims of their noblemen. Led by Saxony and Brandenburg Prussia, on the other hand, many states in central and northwestern Germany sought to prevent abuses, increase overall prosperity, and maximize tax revenues. Decrees and ordinances spoke out against physical mistreatment of peasants, encroachment by nobles on land rented

4. Sheehan, 96.

by peasants, violation of tenure rights, and oppressive labor obligations. Joseph II of the House of Habsburg was undoubtedly the most ambitious of these so-called enlightened princes. In a series of controversial decrees after 1781, he abolished hereditary personal servitude in Austria, Bohemia, Galicia, and Hungary, fixed the portion of a peasant's income that could be paid out in rents at 30 peercent and taxes at 20 percent, and encouraged the commutation of labor obligations into money rents. Not all of this legislation survived his death in 1790, but the peasants would remain personally free from the worst legal aspects of serfdom.

Pressing against the institutional barriers that assured people of survival in the late 1700s – and thereby protected the equilibrium of traditional society – was the ominous and freightening threat of population growth. Demographers cannot supply a definitive explanation, but it seems likely that numerous factors were converging to reduce mortality: the virtual disappearance of bubonic plague; slight increases in nutrition; and thirty years of uninterrupted peace in central Europe after 1763. Consequently, the population in German Europe increased between 30 percent and 50 percent in the second half of the century. Significantly enough, the level of misery also lurched upward as families already living close to the margin were forced to support new members. Shrinking inheritances and more landlessness, beggary, infanticide, and illegitimacy affected the countryside, especially in southwestern Germany, while towns and cities suffered through an alarming increase in the number of thieves, prostitutes, country drifters, and the homeless.

Many schemes to bolster the public order through moral improvement and enhanced police controls came under consideration. It stands to reason, moreover, that the period saw an intensified discussion of how to improve agricultural productivity. "By the 1760s and 1770s this literature had achieved the status of a cottage industry in itself," observes John Gagliardo, "and its exhortations and suggestions were eagerly discussed in many newly-founded agricultural societies patronized by a mixture of princes, nobles, officials, academics, clerics and ordinary burghers."[5]

5. John Gagliardo, *Germany under the Old Regime 1600-1790* (London, 1991), 131.

It was significant that no one looked to the Holy Roman Empire of the German Nation for answers to this new complex of social and economic problems. As much as our guests around the table at the Gasthaus Bel Oeil appreciated the "peculiar freedoms" of the empire, they, like most men of the Enlightenment, expected either the private sector or the most enlightened rulers and bureaucracies in the myriad German territories to find solutions, not the Reich itself. In order to understand why, we turn now to a more detailed explanation of the precarious state of the empire in the late 1700s.

* * * *

Contemporaries were well aware that Germany was not an empire in the usual sense of the word. It had been over half a millennium since German emperors wielded extensive power in their vast domains. Over the centuries a complex web of institutions had evolved to protect the special rights of hundreds of petty rulers and more ambitious potentates from the once mighty emperor – and from one another. A Council of Electors, consisting of eight of the greatest secular and ecclesiastical princes, selected the person who would head the empire for life. Although it was not a hereditary position, the imperial title had gone to the Habsburgs of Austria almost without exception since 1438. The Emperor's decision-making powers were constrained by three bodies which jointly made up an Imperial Diet. These were: the Council of Electors, mentioned above; the Council of Princes, an unwieldy assembly which represented the remaining secular and religious rulers; and the Council of Cities, which spoke for the city-states. The privileges and immunities of the cities and smaller states were further guarded by two autonomous legal bodies, the Aulic Council and the Imperial Cameral Tribunal. Thus most of these rulers had a vested interest in a decentralized imperial structure. "The empire is an ill-cohering, clumsy mass," complained Swiss jurist Johannes von Müller, but the imperial states, he added, were "free through its fragmentation."[6] And considerable historical inertia worked toward maintenance of the status quo.

6. Cited in Sheehan, 23, 236.

The empire of 1789 also enjoyed a precarious peace between Catholics and Protestants who had once slaughtered one another in the sixteenth century Reformation and the Thirty Years War (1618-1648). The Council of Princes, for example, set aside majority voting (which had favored the Catholic states) in favor of consensual agreements between separate caucuses of Protestant and Catholic delegates. The religious carnarge of earlier centuries finally yielded after 1648, moreover, to the somewhat more tolerant practice of allowing each ruler to determine the official religion of his land. Such compromises did little, unfortunately, to temper deep-seated religious prejudice. Thus we find Campe in the Bishopric of Paderborn railing against Catholicism as "the crudest, most superstitious forced religion."[7] Such narrow-mindedness could have tragic consequences when translated into policy, as witnessed by the expulsion of 20,000 Protestants from the Archbishopric of Salzburg in 1731. It is important to note, however, that most of the abject victims of Salzburg's persecution found new homes and occupations in the Protestant lands of the German North. Indeed the Holy Roman Empire became a haven for persecuted religious groups from other parts of Europe, most notably for tens of thousands of Huguenots expelled from France after the revocation of the Edicts of Nantes in 1685. It is significant, moreover, that litigants of all social classes who believed they were the victims of religiously or politically biased justice possessed the right (guaranteed by imperial ordinances of 1570 and 1600) to refer the case to a university law faculty which sat as an impartial appeals committee. Such circumstances only strengthened the arguments of champions of the empire's decentralized territorial structure like Karl August, Duke of Saxe-Weimar, who touted this peculiar German sort of freedom.

Thus by the late eighteenth century the political equilibrium of the Holy Roman Empire was no longer threatened by the emperors, whose *imperial* powers had eroded, or by religious antagonists, whose hatreds had found less violent outlets. The deepening feud between Austria and Prussia, on the other hand, was a definite source of destabilization. Precipitated by Prussia's growing power, the rivalry worsened after 1648 as the House of Hohenzollern

7. Campe, 24:19.

steadily consolidated and expanded its holdings at the expense of small states in the north-western and north-central portions of the empire. In 1701 the brash rulers from Brandenburg flagrantly exposed the fiction of Habsburg imperial sovereignty by titling themselves "Kings in Prussia." Injury followed insult in 1740 when Frederick the Great seized Austria's rich and populous province of Silesia, thereby triggering warfare that lasted intermittently until 1763. The following quarter-century was peaceful, but tensions continued as the Habsburgs, painfully aware that territories under their direct control were a more important power base than the waning authority of the Holy Roman Emperors, schemed unsuccessfully to acquire Bavaria.

Such acquisitiveness was shocking to smaller states in the empire that feared for their autonomy. The petty duchies and fiefdoms had even more reason now to value a reform of imperial structures, for this seemed to be the only way of preventing absorption by Austria or Prussia. Thus while some critics of the empire lamented "the misery of polycentrism," bemoaned the regimes of "princelings who would not be competent to rule over twelve chickens,"[8] or joked about the "ruling prince who accidentally dropped his realm out of his pocket and lost it forever on an afternoon's stroll,"[9] others, like Johann Jacob Moser of Württemberg and Johann Stephan Pütter of Göttingen (Hanover), both legal theorists, searched for the right political and legal formulas that would strengthen the empire's ability to preserve the peace and ensure internal harmony.

It was somewhat ironic that Austrian and Prussian self-interest led them to similar conclusions regarding the future of the Reich. For, despite all of its drawbacks, the Holy Roman Empire was still a useful mechanism for mobilizing support. The Habsburgs could usually play the small ecclesiastical and city-states off against the threatening Hohenzollerns, and imperial conscripts, although largely ineffective, occasionally took the field against Prussia, as they did at Rossbach in 1757. Prussia also used the empire to thwart Austria, as witnessed by the League of Princes, a union of

8. Cited in Holger H. Herwig, *Hammer or Anvil: Modern Germany 1648-Present* (Lexington, 1994), 3.

9. Cited in Murray B. Peppard, *Paths Through the Forest: A Biography of the Brothers Grimm* (New York, 1971), 1.

seventeen German states formed by Berlin in 1785 to save Bavaria from Austria's clutches. In a way, then, the Austro-Prussian rivalry was not exclusively harmful to the empire, but also served as an unusual kind of insurance against further disintegration – which explains why the small states, as well as writers like Moser and Pütter, watched warily for any sign of *rapprochement* between the feuding German powers.

Added insurance – and probably a more effective one – was a French, Swedish, and Russian pledge of 1648 to guarantee the empire's survival. Indeed their interests were served by German imperial institutions which kept their rivals, Austria and Prussia, in check. Thus there was political equilibrium in central Europe in 1789 – but it was an unstable one, dependent on a fortuitous combination of too many forces beyond the control of most Germans.

* * * *

Campe and his circle of friends participated in the vibrant "literary culture"[10] of late eighteenth-century Germany. They recorded their impressions in diaries, exchanged thoughts with correspondents in faraway towns, contributed articles to a burgeoning number of scholarly journals, browsed in Germany's rapidly proliferating bookstores for recent works of literature, science, and philosophy, and read book reviews in periodicals like Friedrich Nicolai's *General German Library*, devoted specifically to this purpose. Indeed the opportunity afforded by their Parisian journey for *personal* interaction between learned men from different parts of the Reich was very rare. Whether it was advanced by the pen or spoken word, however, theirs was a culture of progress. They sought to promote enlightenment and affect intelligent change in German countries still largely unaccustomed to it.

Individuals express their feelings, impressions, world views, and politics in many ways. Because such expression can take the form of culture – that is, literature, painting, architecture, music, entertainment, and so on – culture can therefore become political. "[Culture] orients us to reality as much as to life," writes Thomas Nipperdey. "It explains, conciliates, analyzes, discovers, presents,

10. The term is used by Sheehan, 144ff.

and discusses – culture interprets meaning, or creates it."[11] Thus aesthetic expression, although less threatening than subversive political activity or less obviously manipulative than state propaganda, can easily cross over into the realm of the politically controversial when it attempts overtly to shape the perceptions that others have of reality. Whether we are referring to powerful state authorities, wealthy aristocrats, town magistrates, men of the Enlightment like Campe and his friends – or just simple folk – their culture usually assumes a meaningful political dimension.

Progressive literary culture was taking its place in the late 1700s beside older forms of popular culture. This plebian means of expression, which had dominated Europe for centuries, manifested itself in the minstrels, magicians, jugglers, and traveling troupes of actors who frequented local fairs, festivals, and holiday celebrations, performing in the country market place or town square. According to Peter Burke, there were two significant characteristics of Europe's popular culture: first, it was a societal phenomenon which brought all classes together in a celebratory atmosphere; and second, it was *distinctly* political. Undoubtedly the best example of the politics of early modern popular culture was Carnival, the annual topsy-turvy party of February. This wild time of year emphasized excesses of food, sex, and violence which would, if regularly tolerated, have meant chaos. In Carnival parades, "the son is shown beating his father, the pupil beating his teacher, servants giving orders to their masters, the poor giving alms to the rich, the laity saying Mass or preaching to the clergy, the king going on foot while the peasant rides, the husband holding the baby and spinning while his wife smokes and holds a gun."[12] During Carnival, suppressed men and women vented their emotions and feelings. Riots and violence were frequently the result, but authorities looked anxiously askance, grudgingly permitting cultural forms that had the potential for greater disorder. For, as one clergymen put it, "once a year the foolishness innate in us can come out … Don't wine skins and barrels burst very often if the air-hole is not opened from time to time?"[13]

11. Thomas Nipperdey, *Deutsche Geschichte 1800-1866: Bürgerwelt und starker Staat* (Munich, 1983), 533.

12. Peter Burke, *Popular Culture in Early Modern Europe* (New York, 1978), 189.

13. Ibid., 202.

Excesses could not always be controlled by the authorities, and famous examples of revolt like the Peasants' Rebellion of 1525 had a marked carnivalesque quality. Invading the Order of the Teutonic Knights in Heilbronn, for instance, rebellious serfs turned the world upside down by making the nobles wait table. "Today, little Junker," said one of the rebels, "*we* are the knights."[14] But "bread and circus" reasons of state allowed such traditions to continue.

Generally speaking, the upper classes of Europe and Germany lost their tolerance for the excesses of popular culture in the 1700s. The previous two centuries had featured war and disorder so disruptive that ruling secular and religious authorities were determined to reinstitute calm and order. By the eighteenth century, moreover, there was substantial economic recovery and an accompanying advance in science, learning, and art. The result was an intensive (but only partially successful) effort by the upper classes to repress a persistent popular culture. More importantly for our purposes, there was also a marked cultural withdrawal of the cadres of well-to-do from their social inferiors. Kings and other secular and ecclesiastical rulers, noblemen and town magistrates, and educated bourgeois types like our conversationalists at the Gasthaus Bel Oeil, eager to prove themselves, repaired to their "[with]drawing rooms" to pursue there a more refined and dignified culture. In Germany, the growing cultural separation was evident, according to Burke, with Friedrich Friese's work of 1703 on "the remarkable ceremonies of the peasants of Altenburg"[15] in Saxony. It was the first time that popular culture had been distinguished from culture in general.

The literary culture mentioned above must be placed in the context of this upper class reaction. For many decades in the late 1600s and early 1700s, however, it paled in significance to another aspect of withdrawal. For the seventeenth and eighteenth centuries were an unfolding age of official state culture in German Europe. These cultural expressions were designed to celebrate the power and prestige of the secular and ecclesiastical princes and to strengthen the social, economic, and political hierarchy they

14. Ibid., 189.
15. Ibid., 282.

headed. The completion of Versailles in the 1680s, for instance, stimulated architectural imitation throughout central Europe. The Habsburg palace at Schönbrunn, finished in 1730, is the best illustration on German soil of this ornate, monumental, Baroque style, but lavish royal residences were also constructed in Berlin, Stuttgart, Mannheim, Karlsruhe, Salzburg, Prague, and other capitals. Music was another favorite means of patronage of the empire's many rulers, best exemplified, perhaps, by the Prince-Archbishop of Salzburg's support for Wolfgang Amadeus Mozart. Most courts also boasted exquisite private theaters for the production of plays and operas composed and performed by state artists. One of the favorite arguments used by defenders of the Holy Roman Empire, in fact, was the cultural flowering which seemed to have resulted in the 1700s from Germany's political fragmentation. The complex, multi-part harmonies of the Brandenburg Concertos undoubtedly reflected the Enlightenment's belief in science and mathematical precision – and were therefore part of the emerging progessive culture of the middle class – but they must also be seen as Johann Sebastian Bach's musical salute to the Hohenzollerns of Prussia.

For decades, bourgeois culture was part of this general withdrawal of clerical and secular elites from the lower classes. But, as noted earlier, a distinct artistic milieu was forming by the late 1700s. "The fine arts broke the fetters binding them to court, church, estatist circles, and to representative and liturgical functions and traditions," writes Nipperdey. Bourgeois culture "ended its role of being a decorative accessory subsidiary to courtly and noble sociability."[16] This new culture possessed a different and more critical function than official culture. Disseminated mainly by writers with humble or bourgeois backgrounds, it was a decidedly unofficial commentary on the world designed to educate the literate public. Thus Gotthold Ephraim Lessing, son of a poor Saxon pastor, produced in *Nathan the Wise* a moving theatrical plea for religious tolerance, while Christoph Martin Wieland, a poet and essayist whose father was a Swabian preacher, wrote *The Golden Mirror* as an educational program to enlighten princes.

16. Nipperdey , 533.

Younger playwrights and poets like Johann Wolfgang Goethe, born into a prosperous Frankfurt family, and Friedrich Schiller, son of a junior officer in Württemberg, continued this tradition. Goethe's *The Sorrows of Young Werther* was a passionate exploration of the conflict between a sensitive youth and the harsher reality surrounding him. In plays like *The Robbers* and *Don Carlos* , Schiller presented tragedies of youthful rebellion that served as indictments against tyranny and the misuse of power. Both artists were committed to the notion that human reason, once unchained from injurious institutions, could lead to individual refinement, social progress, and harmony between peoples.

A similar preference for enlightenment stood behind much of the movement's fascination with the art and science of antiquity. Johann Joachim Winckelmann, a cobbler's son from Brandenburg who became the era's most prominent art historian, selected Periclean Athens as the source of true beauty. Greek sculpture had surpassed the Baroque and achieved the ideal, he believed, because it was created on political free soil. The same longing for harmony between political and artistic life moved Goethe to write *Iphigenia on Taurus* and Schiller to praise Greek drama, infused as it was with "the Greek spirit, the great interests of the state and of a better humanity."[17] Later Wilhelm von Humboldt would deprecate the importance of the present and glorify antiquity as a model for the future when he wrote that "our new world is actually nothing at all. It consists of nothing more than a yearning for the past and an always uncertain groping for that which is yet to be created."[18]

The Freemasons also revered antiquity in their quest to improve life in the present. An English import, Freemasonry in its modern form appeared in Hamburg in 1737, spreading thereafter to Göttingen, Königsberg, Berlin, Frankfurt, and many other German towns. Like their English brothers, German Freemasons believed that the ancients had possessed scientific and philosophical secrets which, if properly deciphered, could unlock the mysteries of nature, lighten man's burden, and create harmony on earth. As one historian writes, the brothers "sought valiantly, in the ruin of time, for

17. Cited in Sheehan, 173.

18. Humboldt to Wolf, 20 July 1805, in Karl August Varnhagen von Ense, *Vermischte Schriften* (Leipzig, 1875), 18:242.

the lost keys to the sacred sciences."[19] Lodge names like Hippocrates in Magdeburg, Pythagoras in Berlin, and Minerva in Cologne reflected this noble mission. It should come as no surprise, therefore, that the ranks of the Freemasons included many scientists, engineers, businessmen, as well as philosophical and historical giants of the Enlightenment like Immanuel Kant, Johann Gottfried Herder, and Johann Gottlieb Fichte. Lessing, Wieland, Goethe, and Friedrich Gottlieb Klopstock, a well-known poet, were also freemasons. One outgrowth of the Masonic movement, the so-called Order of the Illuminati, schemed to place its most illustrious brethren in positions of power in a more overtly political attempt to advance progressive goals. Later reformers of the Napoleonic era like Maximilian von Montgelas of Bavaria and Karl August von Hardenberg of Prussia had been members of this secret order.

Freemasonry was just one part of a vast organizational web which spread across Germany's literary culture by the late 1700s, giving it a certain cohesion and semi-political significance. There were about a dozen scientific societies and academies that pursued research, published proceedings, offered prizes, and communicated with scientists in other parts of Germany and Europe. One of the most active was the Erfurt Academy of Useful Sciences. Founded in 1754, it maintained a library, observatory, anatomical amphitheater, chemical laboratory, and botanical garden, and awarded four prizes a year in utilitarian subjects. The Erfurt Academy also kept in close contact with many of the dozens of so-called patriotic or utilitarian societies scattered throughout German Europe. As their names implied, these groups sought to develop and disseminate information on farming, animal husbandry, mechanical technologies, and even poor relief. In addition, there were over three hundred reading and discussion clubs in Germany which afforded an opportunity to become familiar with developments in all fields. The very existence of this network of lodges, societies, and clubs, meeting privately, germinating ideas, and discussing proposals for action on specific projects, was potentially unsettling to rulers accustomed to absolute rule. Hence censorship was strict and, occasionally, retribution swift. Thus the Iluminati and Freemasons

19. Manly P. Hall, *Freemasonry of the Ancient Egyptians* (Los Angeles, 1937), 6.

were banned in Bavaria in 1785, while legal scholar Johann Jacob Moser suffered five years of arbitrary imprisonment under Duke Karl Eugen of Württemberg.

It would be misleading to convey the impression, however, that the German Enlightenment was radical or revolutionary. Most of its leading figures were, as explained, divorced from popular currents and believed that absolutism, rescued from tyranny, possessed the greatest potential of all political systems to reform society. Schiller's *Don Carlos* and Wieland's *The Golden Mirror* both offered this message. The American Revolution made few converts to revolutionary activism, nor did Klopstock's call for a return to the allegedly democratic practices of the early German tribes move many to follow. Rather, most sympathized with Herder's condemnation of "the rabble of the streets which never sings or creates, but roars and mutilates."[20]

We would also search in vain for many leaders of the Enlightenment who extended their reformist thinking to women. Most agreed with Wieland's desire for a wife who "fits in ... with my taste, my mood, and my way of life." He did not require "a grain of intellect" from her. "I have plenty of that in my books."[21] His comments reflected the generally low status of women at this time. Some, of course, managed to rise to an exceptional level. A few wives of aristocrats, important bureaucrats, and rich bourgeois attained intellectual prominence in their own right in salons throughout Germany famous for their witty exchanges, artistic performances, sophisticated discussion of contemporary culture and politics, and sexual, religious, and class tolerance. The Jewess Rahel Levin – Rahel Varnhagen after her marriage – fondly described the "beauty, grace, coquetry, taste, romance, wit, elegance, cordiality, drive to develop ideas, serious talk, open company, [and] good-hearted fun"[22] of her salon life. But most women of the upper classes were relegated increasingly to the separate sphere of domestic family life, while men conducted a public life in the state or private economic sector. As we shall explore in more detail in Part 2,

20. Cited in Sheehan, 203.

21. Cited in Herwig, 11.

22. Cited in Petra Wilhelmy, *Der Berliner Salon im 19. Jahrhundert (1780-1914)* (Berlin, 1989), 133.

moreover, women of the lower strata of urban and rural society had *at best* a life of hard work and demanding maternal responsibilities beside a struggling handicraftsman or small farmer. But the late eighteenth century was not the best of times. Gender relations suffered as a result.

* * * *

There were forces of change at work everywhere in the German state and society on the eve of the French Revolution, but none had progressed to the point of upsetting Germany's balance. The Holy Roman Empire survived in altered form despite the ravages of the Reformation, the Thirty Years War, and Austro-Prussian rivalry. Traditional social institutions and time-honored means of production still predominated in the countryside amidst much discussion of ways to improve output. By creating paid work, moreover, the putting-out system provided a buffer against greater misery on the land. The guilds were more seriously threatened by this development, but far from defeated. Uprisings like the one that shook Aachen in 1786 could be contained with the small army of a petty state. Finally, absolutism found no serious, far-reaching challenges from the private discussions, correspondence, and partly underground culture of the cultivated bourgeoisie. The phenomenal occurences which Campe and Humboldt journeyed westward to observe, however, would soon change this.

Chapter 2

The Decline of the Holy Roman Empire

German interest in French developments approached monomaniac proportions during the summer of 1789. Thus Johann Wilhem Archenholtz, a historian and journalist in Berlin, lamented that "the tremendous interest aroused by the French Revolution crowds out all other concerns; the best poems remain unread, men are interested only in newspapers and in writings which satisfy their voracious political appetite."[1] Within a year Archenholtz himself became so caught up in the excitement that he moved his family to Paris. Like Campe, Archenholtz had gone west to report on events firsthand. Not surprisingly, he too greeted the toppling of the old regime and the apparent triumph of constitutionalism, equality before the law, and religious toleration.

Indeed the overwhelming weight of enlightened opinion in Germany stood behind the initial French attempt to reconstruct government and society in accordance with rational principles. So it was with poets like Klopstock and Wieland and philosophers such as Kant, Herder, and Fichte. Giants of the Protestant Enlightenment like Nicolai and Ludwig von Schlözer, an innovative historian at Göttingen, applauded the first act on the revolutionary stage. Early developments across the Rhine were also welcomed by young,

1. Cited in Klaus Epstein, *The Genesis of German Conservatism* (Princeton, New Jersey, 1966), 435.

discontented Catholic intellectuals like Joseph Görres of Coblenz as well as Elector-Archbishop Maximilian Franz of Cologne, a champion of reforming the Catholic church. In Hamburg, radical republicans went to extra lengths to demonstrate their feelings, gathering in the garden of Georg Heinrich Sieveking, a successful merchant, to celebrate the first anniversary of the storming of the Bastille. Following French fashion, the women wore Tricolor gowns and toasts were made to the heroes of freedom. This optimistic, magnanimous response to the French Revolution prevailed in Germany well into the early 1790s.

There were many reasons for this generally positive reception. A few reacted out of hatred for the Holy Roman Empire. But most, like Humboldt and Dohm, preferred Germany's plethora of small states to the centralized regime of the Bourbons. The collapse of absolutist France was a chance for Frenchmen to acquire the same freedom from tyrannical concentrations of power that existed in most parts of Germany. Similarly, while some humanists used France's Civil Constitution of the Clergy (1790) to sermonize against Germany's religious intolerance or Bavaria's suppression of the Illuminati, many more were relieved that France was finally attaining the measure of religious toleration allegedly introduced in Germany after 1648. There were also Germans like the young Prussian publicist, Friedrich Gentz, who were sufficiently troubled by social problems to hope that the French Revolution "provides consolation to men elsewhere who continue to groan under the weight of age-old evils."[2] And in Königsberg, Theodor Hippel, a city magistrate, pointed to the efforts of French women to participate equally in social, economic, and political life. Hippel urged both French and German men to demolish "the Bastilles of gallantry, the prisons of domesticity, and the civic dungeons in which the fair sex continues to find itself."[3] But the majority of enlightened upper-class thinkers were less concerned about social and gender issues. They greeted French events with the smug assurance that the Revolution was something good for humanity and for France, but was generally unnecessary in the Germanies. "We can

2. Ibid., 436
3. Ibid., 230.

watch the French Revolution," noted Herder, "as we watch a shipwreck at sea from the safety of the shore."[4]

Not all Germans reacted with pleasure or indifference, however, to the outbreak of revolution in France. The Enlightenment had also found conservative critics and determined opponents in the German states, and so it was now with the events of 1789. Justus Möser, a conservative social theorist and opponent of the Enlightenment from Osnabrück, was far too attached to the entrenched traditions of his hometown to react with anything but disgust to the far-reaching changes threatening in the West. Johann August Starck, court pastor in Hesse-Darmstadt, and his colleague in the ducal ministries, Ludwig Grolman, also opposed the revolution from the outset. Taking the cure together in Schwalbach when they heard the news, the two concluded instinctively that Freemasons and Illuminati were to blame. Only an energetic counteroffensive in print and press could combat this conspiratorial danger. In Augsburg, ex-Jesuits Alois Merz and Felix Franz Hofstaeter reacted with equal alarm to the perceived threat to order, religion, and morality. But these anti-revolutionaries remained distinctly in the minority during 1789 and 1790. Even moderate conservatives like August Wilhelm Rehberg, a Hanoverian publicist, mocked the notion of a Masonic plot, while in the chancelleries of Berlin and Vienna, the truly powerful saw no reason to worry about the apparent weakening of a dangerous rival like France.

The warnings of these Cassandras of the political Right began to receive added impetus with the influx of the émigrés. Fleeing France for the haven of friendly ecclesiastical states in the Rhineland, these aristocrats and clergymen grew steadily in numbers until their ranks had swelled to around 40,000 by late 1791. Among them were prominent members of the royal family like the Counts of Provence and Artois, Louis XVI's younger brothers. The two indignant, affronted princes settled into a palace in Coblenz provided by Clemens Wenceslaus, Archbishop-Elector of Trier, then attempted to foment a counterrevolutionary crusade. This campaign registered its first noteworthy success in August, 1791

4. Cited in Koppel Pinson, *Modern Germany: Its History and Civilization* (New York, 1966), 28

when Leopold II of Austria and Frederick William II of Prussia declared themselves in favor of concerted European action to restore monarchical government in France. Meeting at a hunting lodge near Pillnitz, Saxony, the two agreed to mobilize their armies if the other powers, especially England, would cooperate.

The Declaration of Pillnitz was a carefully worded diplomatic compromise. The Count of Artois, present at the negotiations, received a very sympathetic hearing from the Prussian king of five years. Although filled with the ardor of the Rosicrucians, an anti-revolutionary, anti-Masonic order, Frederick William II also had practical reasons for wanting military action. The nephew of Frederick the Great wanted the West German duchies of Jülich and Berg to fall to Prussia after a victorious incursion into France. Although Leopold was basically more supportive of the enlightened principles which French moderates were trying to implement, he too was capable of anti-revolutionary outbursts. But reasons of state constantly led him away from the brink. Austria's finances were in a shambles, her rear threatened by the Turks, her new-found Prussian ally of questionable loyalty, and her interests served by a continuation of France's enervated status. Leopold signed the declaration as a gesture to the émigrés and his unhappy sister, Marie Antoinette, the Queen of France. For he knew that England was opposed to an invasion, and consequently, that the likelihood of concerted European action was extremely low. The gesture at Pillnitz was largely an empty one.

Yet only eight months would pass before Austria and Prussia were at war with France. The war party in Paris bristled with anger after Pillnitz. Was this not solid evidence, they argued, of collusion between the émigrés and Europe's eastern monarchs? The National Assembly agreed, demanding the dispersal of émigré armies training in Trier and Mainz. When this produced a curt Austrian warning that it would defend the two archbishoprics, the French Assembly resolved in January 1792 that unless Leopold renounced all aggressive designs against France, a state of war would exist. March brought the death of Leopold and the ascension to the throne of his belligerent son, Francis II. Within weeks Austria had mobilized 50,000 troops and issued orders for an invasion of France. In Prussia, Frederick William II instructed army contractors to make ready.

Simultaneously, France declared war on Austria and sent an army into the Austrian Netherlands. After this first revolutionary offensive of troops without training and discipline quickly disintegrated, Francis and Frederick William assembled a punitive expedition near Coblenz, headed by Duke Karl Ferdinand of Brunswick.

The deterioration of relations with France caused considerable controversy in Germany. Reactionaries naturally cheered the Duke of Brunswick as a champion who would purge France of its insubordination and anarchy. On the other hand, moderates and republicans like Archenholtz in Berlin and Adolph von Knigge, a former Iluminati from Hamburg, expressed dismay that the same countries which had produced enlightened monarchs like Frederick the Great and Joseph II could now serve the dark cause of suppressing progress. They also warned that the Revolution had transformed France into a nation which would not be easily conquered. Enlightened thinkers assumed optimistically that their rulers would eventually listen to reason, avert revolution at home, and avoid disaster abroad.

The number of educated Germans who agreed with the Archenholtzes and Knigges had declined considerably, however, since the first sanguine summer of 1789. The rise of the Jacobins, the advent of the Parisian mob, and the threat of an impending European war induced many early supporters of the Revolution to turn away in disgust. So it was with Schlözer in Göttingen, while in nearby Hanover, a center of moderate opposition formed around Rehberg. The conservative tract of Rehberg's English friend, Edmund Burke, also appeared in German translation that year. Well before the Duke of Brunswick moved his forces westward toward Paris, Rehberg and Burke were using the old arguments about the benefits of Germany's peculiar imperial institutions to contrast France unfavorably with Germany and turn former adherents of France's revolutionary regime into its enemies.

The shocking outcome of the Duke's campaign strengthened this trend. With the approach of his armies, mob violence in Paris increased, the hapless king and queen were arrested, and a republic declared. Archenholtz's warning about the virility of revolutionary France also proved true. After Longwy and Verdun fell quickly that summer, French troops under General Charles-Francois Dumouriez stood their ground at Valmy. The brief artillery battle, together with heavy rains, dysentery, and supply problems, convinced Karl Ferdinand to retreat. His orderly march turned into a desperate scramble to regain Coblenz safely, however, when a French army under Adam-Philippe de Custine struck north from Metz and threatened to surround the allied columns. By October, the Tricolor flew over Mainz, Speyer, Worms, and Frankfurt. Dumouriez had marched north in the meantime to occupy the Austrian Netherlands. Advance French units entered the gates of Aachen and Crefeld in December 1792. What was to be a glorious promenade to Paris had turned into one of the greatest military debacles in history.

Friends of the Enlightenment in Germany who had opposed the Austro-Prussian invasion were angered when French troops refused to halt at the frontier. For the occupation of German lands and cities seemed to violate the Assembly's promise never to use its power against the liberty of any other people. These worries were heightened in January 1793 when Louis XVI was beheaded. All but the most ardent defenders of the Revolution now deserted a cause whose promise of human progress seemed to have been betrayed by a new breed of revolutionary leaders who had abandoned all reason and moderation. To Archenholtz, the Jacobins were "monsters,"[5] while to Humboldt, the despotism of the Bourbons had been replaced by a more frightening tyranny. Klopstock, who had celebrated the first Bastille Day with Sieveking in 1790, mourned the turnaround in France as if he had lost a beloved son. Campe, too, was deeply disappointed. In a pamphlet of May 1793, he differentiated between Paris "then" and Paris "now." Repelled by the bloody "cannibals" who were engineering the Reign of Terror, he shed "bitter tears of unhappiness over the fate of humanity."[6]

The tide of anti-French feeling was accompanied by stricter anti-revolutionary measures in many German states. Censorship, already prevalent in the empire before 1789, was tightened. Some governments went even farther. Thus Bavaria began to publish a weekly register of banned books, while Austria opened mail, closed

5. Cited in Saine, *Black Bread – White Bread* , 365.
6. Ibid., 363.

lending libraries, inspected professors' bookshelves, and curbed publishing activity. Hesse-Kassel established a surveillance committee to spy on professors at the University of Giessen and joined Austria, Hanover, and the bishoprics of Regensburg and Augsburg as the latest to ban Freemasonry. Suppression also characterized policies in Prussia, where reactionary, narrow-minded zealots like Johann Christoph Wöllner headed censorship efforts which were not strict enough for a worried king.

Initially it seemed unlikely that the Holy Roman Empire would join the fighting. Austria and Prussia paid no attention to the imperial diet when war broke out, not wishing to complicate the anticipated distribution of spoils. When Austria finally asked the diet to subsidize allied operations in September 1792, moreover, the cautious councillors refused due to lingering suspicions that Prussia and Austria would exploit the war to absorb German territory. With the French threat growing later that autumn, the diet finally acted. There would be no levies for Austria and Prussia, however, only funds for a defensive force of 120,000 imperial troops. This decision reflected worries that the two German powers were still unreliable and might even go to war against each other. There were also doubts about Prussia's willingness to fight in the west when annexation of Polish territory beckoned in the east (see below). In March 1793, renewed French attacks in the Rhineland finally moved the diet to a formal declaration of war. France's revolutionary challenge would not be met with timely reforms, as advocated by Freemasons like Knigge, but rather with oppressive internal policies and military force.

At first it appeared this would fully suffice. Prussian troops lessened the danger to central Germany by recapturing Frankfurt in December. An Austrian army under the Duke of Coburg retook Aachen in March 1793, then pushed into the Netherlands where Dumouriez's victorious soldiers awaited. At Neerwinden Austrian regulars demonstrated their superiority over a revolutionary army of roughly equal strength. The talented Archduke Charles, brother of Emperor Francis, crashed through Dumouriez's left flank, routing the French and forcing them to evacuate the entire province. After the French garrison at Mainz succumbed to siege in June 1793, the Duke of Brunswick prepared to move west again and salvage his sagging military reputation. The French tide now receded from the middle Rhine as quickly as it had come in.

Indeed France now faced a serious crisis. The execution of Louis XVI in January 1793 ignited an internal revolt in the Vendée and brought England, Holland, Spain, and Sardinia into the war on the side of Prussia, Austria, and the Holy Roman Empire. With armies totaling over 450,000 soldiers, these countries were pressing on or over France's borders by spring. In response, the dictatorial Committee of Public Safety introduced mass conscription – the famous *levée en masse* – and raised the most capable officers to positions of command. It was at this time that a young Major of Artillery, Napoleon Bonaparte, began his remarkable ascent from obscurity to glory.

By the summer of 1793 France's forces had doubled to 650,000 and by the fall of that year her armies were on the offensive once again. As the number of Frenchmen under arms rose to about 850,000 during 1794, they were able to smash the rebels in the Vendée and sweep the invaders back through the Netherlands into Westphalia and across the Rhine to Mannheim. Although there were allied victories against the French that year, the momentum had clearly changed. By the summer of 1795 Austrian and Imperial armies readied their defenses for a French incursion across the Rhine. And they stood alone, for the once-imposing coalition had dissolved.

Of particular interest to our story is the withdrawal of Prussia from the war. Since the early stages, Frederick William II had concerned himself with territorial acquisitions. The war against France presented opportunities of this sort, but increasingly, the king turned his efforts toward the East. In January 1793, Prussia seized Danzig, Thorn, Posen, and Kalish from a defenceless Poland, while Russia took Lithuania and other lands. The desperate uprising of Thaddeus Kosciuszko drew another 20,000 Prussian soldiers east in 1794, helping to deplete what remained of Frederick the Great's massive war chest. Frederick William now demanded British subsidies to continue operations along the Rhine. When negotiations broke down over the use of Prussian troops for English and Dutch strategic goals in November 1794, the Prussians withdrew their armies and signed an armistice with France. Two months later,

Prussia, Russia, and Austria crushed the Poles and divided the rump country among themselves.

Finalized in April 1795, the Peace of Basel between Prussia and France sparked considerable controversy in Germany. For the treaty conceded scores of ecclesiastical and secular states in the Rhineland to France and stipulated that Prussia would be the guarantor of a "neutral" zone north of the Main River. Although relieved that the ravages of war would not spread into their territories, few states in northern Germany harbored illusions about the naked self-interest which would color Prussian neutrality. South of the river, ecclesiastical rulers deeply resented Prussian collaboration with France, the power whose mighty legions were spreading secularization and anti-clericalism eastward. Throughout Germany, moreover, critics exposed Prussia's desertion of the Holy Roman Empire. Indeed, the delicate equilibrium of the empire was threatened by the temptation to acquire set loose by the impending French invasion. Smaller secular states like Baden, Hesse-Kassel, and Nassau were considering pooling military resources to place themselves in a better bargaining position to acquire church lands during negotiations following a likely French victory. The pragmatic reverence for the empire shown by Prussia's critics helps to explain the spate of publications which appeared in 1794 and 1795 advocating a revitalization of imperial military institutions. Only in this way could the empire avoid its debilitating dependency on Austria and Prussia. Traditional aversions to centralization were overlooked with French troops on German soil.

Unlike Prussia, Austria had little choice but to continue the fight against France. For a war with Prussia would merely strengthen Paris, while peace talks with the French could not be conducted from a position of strength until Austria won military victories. Thus the Austrians were still in the field when revolutionary armies crossed the Rhine in the autumn of 1795. French columns were halted in the Taunus, and by Christmas, Austrian units had swung over to an offensive which pushed west of Mainz. Napoleon's string of victories against Austrian armies in Italy, however, forced Archduke Charles to shift troops south and abandon an offensive into Alsace planned for the spring of 1796. This allowed the French to strike into southern Germany that summer with two powerful armies. In a series of brilliant engagements, the Archduke forced the French back across the Rhine by October. But again it was Napoleon who prevented the Habsburgs from capitalizing at the bargaining table. Seemingly invincible, he routed his opponents, crossed the Alps into the Tyrol, and drove relentlessly on to Vienna in early 1797. Not even Archduke Charles, recalled from Germany, could rally Austria's shattered forces. With Bonaparte only 130 kilometers from the capital, Austria accepted a cease-fire.

The Treaty of Campo Formio followed in October 1797. Austria was ceded Venice and Venetia while France received the Ionian Islands, Lombardy, Belgium, and formal possession of almost the entire left bank of the Rhineland. Prussia's Rhenish possessions were exempted as part of an Austrian scheme to prevent its rival from attempting to acquire right bank territory as compensation. Austria and France agreed, on the other hand, that the other secular princes who lost lands west of the Rhine would later receive territory east of the Rhine. Austria sanctioned the start of this process at Campo Formio by taking the Archbishopric of Salzburg and a sliver of Bavaria east of the Inn River as payment for the loss of Freiburg-Breisgau, which was transferred to a dispossessed duke. This was a dubious precedent, for rumors of the deal spread, prompting other secular states in the empire to clamor for cession of church territory.

The treaties of Basel and Campo Formio were symptoms of a Holy Roman Empire in the throes of death. For a century and a half prior to 1789, the Germans had carefully maintained an unstable equilibrium. Protestants and Catholics, small states and large, secular potentates and princes of the church – all tended to regard the institutions of the empire as a form of protection from threatening rivals and therefore as an acceptable alternative to change. As we have seen, even the wars between Prussia and Austria had not shredded the fabric of the empire. The German balance, however, depended on a balance of power in Europe. Wary of one another and their German rivals, France, Sweden, and Russia had agreed to guarantee the empire's integrity. Once the Wars of the French Revolution disrupted this arrangement, some German states gravitated toward France, while others took advantage of new, highly attractive alternatives to the empire which war had usherd into existence. Now lack of equilibrium led to self-destruction.

The process began at the Congress of Rastatt in November, 1797. Representatives from France, Austria, Prussia, and the various imperial states met to formulate a treaty between France and the Holy Roman Empire. The deputies approved the cession of the *whole* Rhineland to France in March 1798, thus undermining Austria's plot to exclude Prussia from right bank compensation. The congress also considered a proposal favored by Prussia and the larger secular states to expropriate every ecclesiastical state in the empire. Austria fought this plan in an attempt to preserve church territories which had often voted with the Habsburgs in the diet. But the motion passed in April 1798.

With control of the empire slipping away at the peace table, Austria once again began to regard war as a more attractive alternative. Vienna concluded an alliance with Russia in July 1798, and in December, Tsar Paul signed a treaty of friendship with England. With the deliberations still ongoing in Rastaat on New Year's Day 1799, the powerful Second Coalition came into being to overthrow all of Rastatt's arrangements and check French expansion elsewhere in Europe.

Preempting her enemies, France struck in February 1799. A flanking force under Jean Baptiste Bernadotte moved over the Rhine to Mannheim, while the main army under Jean Baptiste Jourdan, the foe of Archduke Charles in 1795 and 1796, invaded the upper Rhine at Basel. The unfortunate people of the Rhineland braced themselves for a repetition of the unpleasantly familiar experience of revolutionary warfare.

* * * *

The population of the Rhineland paid dearly for its liberation from the Old Regime. For, unlike the conventional armies of the eighteenth century, France's revolutionary forces were compelled to live largely off the land. Her armies were also much larger. Bernadotte and Jourdan marched with a combined strength of about 60,000 soldiers in 1799, but this force, large by Old Regime standards, was the smallest to cross the Rhine in years. Earlier in the decade, the French had annually deployed two armies of around 80,000 men each. With dependents, camp-followers, and support personnel, the total number of Frenchmen operating in the province annually between 1793 and 1797 approached 250,000. Horses and draft animals were not as numerous, but ate incomparably more.

Payment took many harsh forms. When Custine's columns reached Frankfurt in October 1792 they took hostages until the town paid an indemnity of two million livres. Dumouriez forced the burghers of Crefeld to pay 212,000 gulden that first December. By the end of the decade French commanders had exacted about 150 million livres from the left bank area. This rate of spontaneous taxation was ten to twenty times higher than it had been under the Old Regime. Foraging parties took much more. When the French reached Zweibrücken in November 1793, for instance, they seized all food, clothing, raw materials, horses, and livestock – "virtually everything,"[7] bemoaned the town council. By late 1796, French armies had crossed and retreated across the middle Rhine three times. One French general described the stretch between Mülheim and the Sieg River as "a hideous desert."[8] The country between the Sieg and Lahn rivers was even worse. "There is nothing to be found of any description, not even a piece of straw."[9] The situation was exacerbated by wanton pilfering, vandalism, and wreckage unrelated to the supply needs of the army.

Forced labor was a curse of wartime for the Rhinelanders. Thus 4,000 construction workers were required at the fortifications around Coblenz in 1796; 3,500 in the Düsseldorf area in 1797; and 6,000 at the fortress of Mainz in 1799. Peasants and rural laborers were herded away from their own fields and vineyards, marched for miles, and subjected to hard labor, corporal punishment, and prison-like housing. Such miseries were often compounded by violent crimes at home as women left without husbands were victimized by marauding soldiers. The billeting of French soldiers was another pervasive and extremely unpopular fact of life during the 1790s. Every single house in Oppenheim in 1793, for instance, had to quarter and feed eight to ten soldiers. All

7. Cited in T.C.W. Blanning, *The French Revolution in Germany: Occupation and Resistance in the Rhineland 1792-1802* (Oxford, 1983), 106.

8. Ibid., 87.

9. Ibid., 87.

too often, moreover, the guests had to be "entertained." Thus one family in Cologne in 1798 was greeted by six drunken gunners who yelled "come out whores!"[10] Managing with the help of neighbors to drive them off, the unfortunate defenders had to endure beating and rape when a stronger force of artillerymen returned hours later.

Indeed the incidence of atrocities by French soldiers was alarmingly high during the 1790s, especially when retreating French armies vented their anger and humiliation on the local inhabitants. Retiring from Mainz before the Austrians in 1796, for instance, French soldiers cut a swathe of murder, rape, and looting across the unfortunate Palatinate. "Atrocities were committed the like of which have never been seen before," observed a liberating Austrian soldier. "Not a village was passed, neither to the right nor to the left, which was not brutally pillaged."[11]

To these woes were added a war-related economic blight. The flight of petty princes and church potentates left destitute large numbers of townsmen who had lived off the business of court. One-third of the labor force in Bonn, for instance, had depended on orders from the Archbishop Elector. Commerce was disrupted, moreover, as boats were destroyed, boatsmen avoided Cologne and Coblenz for safer ports of call in right bank towns, and armies marched back and forth. One historical analysis of Mainz, for example, found that trade during the war years of 1792-1797 sank to 39 percent of the Old Regime level. Business and commerce were further undermined by the inflation that came with French paper currency, while the left bank's embryonic factories suffered immediately after annexation (1798) when prohibitive tariffs severed the flow of raw materials from the right bank. Adding to urban misery was a veritable epidemic of prostitution and venereal disease in the area's many garrison towns.

The fabric of Rhenish society unraveled as the numbers of dispossessed, homeless, jobless, and victimized increased. Because the welfare and law enforcement mechanisms of churches and local governments were too disrupted and overburdened to alleviate or contain the situation, a wave of banditry soon gripped the land. By

10. Ibid., 90.
11. Ibid., 98.

1796 the inaccessible forests of the Hunsrück, Eifel, and Westerwald had become hideaways for robbers and highwaymen who made travel by night or day extremely hazardous in the surrounding areas. The boldest gangs also struck back against small French patrols and wandering soldiers, thereby acquiring tremendous popularity with peasants and villagers who themselves could only dream of revenge.

The most notorious of these social bandits was Johannes Bückler, the *Schinderhannes* ("Hans the Knacker"). His defiance of French authority and seeming immunity from capture reached legendary proportions well before his final arrest in 1802. Another measure of Bückler's popularity – and of the tenor of Rhenish society – was his band's hatred of Jews. On one occasion, *Schinderhannes* and his men broke into a shop in Sötern owned by Moses and Mendel Löb. Moses ran out, but could not persuade the villagers to come to his aid. Appealing to the church verger to ring the alarm, he was told that the bells were only rung for peasants, not Jews. Horrified, Moses returned home to find Mendel dying of gunshot wounds. In 1801, left-bank Jews made a formal plea to French authorities for protection against this murderous gang. To xenophobic anti-semities who glorified *Schinderhannes*, this was evidence that *both* foreign enemies – the Frenchman and, allegedly, the Jew – were responsible for the accursed hard times.

The blight of military exploitation, vandalism, and violent crime overshadowed the significant positive contributions which the early stages of the French Revolution brought to the Rhineland. With French annexation, for instance, came the abolition of serfdom. Thus seemingly with the stroke of a pen, serfs became small farmers with the freedom to try a new life. Similarly, French rule brought an end to guild monopolies which had benefitted only a privileged few. Manufacturers on the left bank welcomed the Revolution's abolition of the guilds, but shared with ex-guildsmen the anger associated with threatened livelihoods as wartime disruption and financial levies undermined their businesses. Initially, some peasants saw promise in the new regime's abolition of serfdom, but the excruciating tax burden of the French, combined with the terror of war, quickly dispelled favorable thoughts. The new secularization policies and extreme anti-clerical attacks against the church, moreover, proved highly unpopular with fundamentally devout Rhenish Catholics. Parish priests quickly emerged as organizers of passive resistance and anti-French politics. Even radicals like Joseph Görres grew disillusioned with the cruelty of French soldiers and perceived corruption of French administrators. "It is terrible to see the entire splendid house [of liberty] in ruins and its grounds laid waste," he complained in November 1799. "And now in place of that magnificent monument designed for all eternity there is a pestilential swamp in which salamanders and toads crawl through the stinking mud."[12]

* * * *

We have seen that Johann Wolfgang Goethe and Friedrich Schiller offered their novels and plays of the 1770s and 1780s as assertions of enlightened values. Neither Goethe nor Schiller believed that the French Revolution of 1789 disproved the validity of these values as much as it challenged society to implement them in a new and dynamic setting. The writer could face this challenge by gradually educating, improving, and arousing the public. This was one purpose of the Court Theater which Duke Karl August of Saxe-Weimar established under Goethe's directorship in 1791. By the time Schiller moved to Weimar in 1794, Goethe had become somewhat disillusioned with the educative function of the theater, and was turning more toward poems and novels. Schiller, however, would continue to put his poetry on the stage. Just as the art of ancient Greece was in harmony with a virtuous society, so German art would eventually blend with a better world.

Like all great artists, obviously, Goethe and Schiller were unusually sensitive to the currents and undercurrents of the era. This sensitivity enabled them to render valuable assistance to contemporaries struggling to perceive the rhythm of the times. By interpreting and defining reality with their imagery, however, artists enter a political dimension, especially during anxious and frightening periods of rapid change or when oppressive regimes stifle other means of expression. With its succession of wars, political upheaval, and censorship, the revolutionary era was such a time.

12. Ibid., 284.

Written by Goethe in 1796, *Wilhelm Meister's Apprenticeship* initiated a genre of German novels which took as their central theme the gradual formation of the protagonist's character, personality, and philosophy of life. Goethe moved his hero, Wilhelm Meister, through a series of environments and experiences in order to educate readers to the many obstacles barring the way to self-fullfilment. An arrogant and boorish aristocracy which concerned itself with life's superficialities and a subjugated bourgeois class preoccupied with money and economic specialization – in short, a degraded social order in Germany – could destroy or compromise a person. In the end, Wilhelm steers clear of these fates, but settles for the unheroic role of husband, father, and productive citizen. The novel expresses Goethe's faith in man's ability to rise above society's constraining circumstances, but also warns against ineffectual revolts against entrenched forces.

Goethe expanded upon this theme in his great poem of the contemporary revolutionary era, *Hermann and Dorothea.* Shortly before he penned this work, Saxe-Weimar narrowly averted a French invasion by choosing to desert Austria's self-interested struggle and adhere to the terms of neutrality guaranteed to North Germany under the Peace of Basel. Set against the backdrop of similar threatening circumstances, Goethe's epic poem can be seen as a defense of Karl August's cautious foreign policy. Hermann, namesake of the famous Arminius, conqueror of the Romans at the ancient Battle of Teutoburg Forest, longs for an opportunity to defend his homeland against French forces which have crossed the Rhine. He also wishes to marry Dorothea, a refugee from the Rhineland whose determination and physical strength have saved her from the perils of French marauders. Dorothea's fiancé has not been as fortunate, dying a martyr's death in Paris at the hands of revolutionaries he traveled there to support. Hermann's mother eventually cools her son's martial passion and convinces him to stay home and devote himself to a life of marital bliss and personal self-improvement. Before the betrothal, Dorothea praises the memory of her dead fiancé; afterwards, she wears his ring along with Hermann's. With this literary device, Goethe expressed his lasting sympathy for the cosmopolitan idealism of the Enlightenment and the early stages of the French Revolution. But the contrasting fates of Hermann and Dorothea's first fiancé also conveyed Goethe's disdain for imprudent and untimely action.

When *Hermann and Dorothea* appeared in 1797, Schiller was embarking upon the most fruitful and productive years of his career. The great *Wallenstein* trilogy was performed in Weimar that year, followed by *Mary Stuart* in 1800 and *The Maid of Orleans* in 1802. Like *The Robbers* and *Don Carlos*, these later masterpieces were guided by the motif of revolt against authority. Unlike the earlier plays, which featured an adolescent sort of rebellion, these turn-of-the-century productions elevated the theme into the realm of high political drama. Thus Schiller, in the prologue to *Wallenstein*, identified the political imperative facing artists. At the "climactic end of a century" which saw "life rising to the level of poetry," he wrote, when humanity struggled over issues as great as power and freedom, artists had to seek out a higher level "lest what art puts on stage shame the stage of life."[13] Given these bold words of introduction, it is surprising that Schiller's artistic message to Germans seems to be, like Goethe's, one of prudence and caution. For the stories of these heroes and heroines end tragically: Wallenstein is betrayed; Mary Stuart beheaded; and Joan of Arc burned at the stake. Preoccupied with Greek drama, Schiller allows a cruel fate to undermine the revolts, struggles, and intrigues of his characters – a destiny which individual action cannot avoid or alter. "In the end," observes Martin Malia, "rebellion is invariably punished by failure."[14]

To Schiller, in fact, the times were not ripe for revolt because the people were imperfect. The deterioration of the French Revolution – ending, as he predicted in 1794, with the advent of "a strong man" (like Napoleon) who would restore order and become "the unlimited lord" of France and "much of the rest of Europe" – had demonstrated that freedom was not attained through reason alone. The greatness of French philosophy could not compensate for the corrupt overrefinement of the nobility and the brutality and indifference of the masses. "What we lack is not so much knowledge of the truth and of justice, as the effective use of this knowledge to influence the will,

13. Cited in Walter Löhde, *Friedrich Schiller im politischen Geschehen seiner Zeit* (Munich, 1959), 334-35.

14. Martin Malia, *Alexander Herzen and the Birth of Russian Socialism* (New York, 1965), 40.

not so much light as warmth, not so much philosophical as aesthetic cultivation." By the "formation" or education of a people's feelings, the artist could create an inner beauty that would, in turn, prepare the way for freedom. "Drive the arbitrary, the frivolous, the coarse, out of their pleasures, and you will imperceptibly banish these things from their actions, and finally from their habit of mind."[15]

We must listen carefully to Schiller's tragedies, in other words, to hear his underlying call to action. His heroes fail, but the artistic rendering of an ineluctable fate could help to reshape a people. Unlike Wallenstein or Joan, Germans could affect their destiny by moving closer to inner beauty. Only in Schiller's last completed work, *Wilhelm Tell*, do we find a hero who strikes a successful blow for freedom. Every aspect of the play, from the pastoral musical accompaniment and the beautiful painted backdrops of Switzerland, to Tell's rousing soliloquy in defiance of tryanny, was consciously designed to manipulate the emotions of his audience. And successfully: when *Wilhelm Tell* moved from Weimar to Berlin in July 1804, the company had to perform three times in eight days to excited theatergoers in the Hohenzollern capital. Interestingly, the censors had tried to expunge Tell's monologue, but the cultural giant from Weimar stood his ground and the play was performed without cuts. The politics of culture naturally gave rise to political controversy.

By this time, Ludwig van Beethoven was already making friends and enemies with a bold new musical style. Some listeners praised the young Rhinelander's accomplishments. Thus one Viennese critic observed in 1799 that "Beethoven in time can effect a revolution in music like Mozart's. He is hastening towards it with great strides." Others, attuned to traditional sounds, covered their ears. Hearing the Violin Sonatas, Opus 12, for instance, an angry writer bemoaned the "heaping up of difficulties on difficulties until one loses all patience and enjoyment." Another critic commented on the "awkward passages" in Beethoven's piano variations where "harsh tirades in continuous semitones create an ugly relationship."[16]

Beethoven began his career in the 1780s as a teenage prodigy in Bonn under the patronage of Elector-Archbishop Maximilian Franz

15. Ibid., 307, 311.

16. Cited in Frida Knight, *Beethoven and the Age of Revolution* (London, 1973), 48.

of Cologne. Most of Beethoven's early works remained within the symmetrical, undynamic pattern of eighteenth-century official classical culture, but there were occasional passages that evidenced a new style – a musical sound characterized by glaring discords, unexpected rhythms, tremendous technical complexity, and emotional feeling. The Funeral Cantata for Emperor Joseph (1790) was one such piece. Johannes Brahms later described "the intensity, perhaps violence, in [the Cantata's] expression ... all characteristics which we may observe and associate with his later works."[17] During his years of apprenticeship in Vienna after 1792, Beethoven began to depart from the staid genre of the chamber piece, shifting to piano and violin sonatas which allowed for a much greater expressive flexibility. It was only toward the end of the decade, however, that the complicated and energetic style of the mature Beethoven became more evident and dominant. By 1800, he was indeed moving "with great strides" toward a new music.

It is tempting to argue that the increasing turbulence and upheaval of the 1790s imparted a certain dynamism and controversy to Beethoven's music. The great composer, in other words, recorded the tenor and tone of the revolutionary era. While this was undoubtedly true, there was also conscious political statement in much of his music. We know that the young man was deeply committed to and caught up in the political progression of his age. A member of the radical Enlightenment tolerated by Archbishop Maximilian Franz, Beethoven later sympathized with the French Revolution and remained its advocate long after other cultural leaders had turned against it. His republican and anticlerical tendencies were well known and closely observed in Vienna, as were his frequent visits to the home of Marshal Bernadotte, the French ambassador after 1798. The famous soldier brought Beethoven into closer contact with the grandiose, serious, and militaristic music of revolutionary France. These influences helped to push Beethoven away from classical works, styles, and genres which no longer interested him and toward a cultural revolution which was both a passive reflection and an active statement about the times.

17. Ibid., 21-22.

It was also Bernadotte who encouraged Beethoven to compose a symphony in honor of republican principles, victories, and heroes. The famous result was the Third Symphony – better known as the *Eroica* Symphony. The first movement has suggested to many listeners the sound of battle or the conflict between the old and the new in Europe, while the second clearly expresses the sad dignity of a funeral – for soldiers, or perhaps for the Old Regime. The quicker tempo and syncopated rhythm of the third movement, or Scherzo, conveys the excitement of a victory parade or triumphal entry. And in the finale, Beethoven celebrates the human triumph of Napoleon, the "hero" whose tyrannical bent would eventually disappoint and disillusion Beethoven before the work was finally performed.

There was, however, another level of meaning in the *Eroica*. The principles of the revolution triumph in the end, but the furious forces of change require a steadying hand. Beethoven expressed this thought *musically*:

> Because of its sheer size and intensity [writes Michael Broyles], the first movement of the *Eroica* constantly verges on structural disaster, appearing at any moment ready to spin apart, a victim of its own centrifugal momentum. Centrifugal tendencies are held in check, however, primarily through an emphasis upon meter and elemental tonal forces ... The newness of the *Eroica* is due to the boldness and the scale of the [structural] departures, but the success of the movement depends upon those elements – melodic simplicity, tonal clarity, metric drive, and phrase continuity – that were at the very core of the Classical symphony style.

By controlling its structural departures with elements of older stylistic traditions, the first movement symbolizes Napoleon's consolidation of the Revolution. The recurring hero theme in the finale, presented in the older sonata form, serves the same function of balancing the symphony's revolutionary opening. "Beethoven had blown the old world apart with the first movement," concludes Broyles, "and in the last movement we have one final look over our shoulder at what it was about."[18]

18. Michael Broyles, *Beethoven: The Emergence and Evolution of Beethoven's Heroic Style* (New York, 1987), 51.

Small wonder that the tempermental composer flew into a rage when Napoleon finally proclaimed himself emperor, ripping up the cover page with its dedication to the hero. For, unlike the symphony, Napoleon had gone too far. "It's a pity I don't understand the art of war as well as I do the art of music," blurted Beethoven. "I would conquer him!"[19]

* * * *

Like their native son and famous composer a few years later, Rhinelanders in 1799 wanted the armies of the Second Coalition to trounce France. A string of allied victories during the spring of that year sent village priests throughout the Rhineland into the streets to spread the good news. By autumn, Jourdan had been defeated in Switzerland, Archduke Charles had recaptured northern Italy, and Napoleon's Egyptian expedition had failed. Over the angry protest and dissent of northern states in Prussia's neutral zone, the Imperial Diet also approved a huge war levy that September.

In 1800, however, the French proved stronger. Advancing along a broad front between Strassburg and Zurich, Jean Victor Moreau's 120,000 troops pushed the Austrians and imperial recruits out of Baden, Württemberg, and western Bavaria, ravaging the countryside and population as they went. Napoleon's Egyptian fiasco worked against the coalition too, for in June 1800, the master tactician was present to crush Austria's Italian forces at Marengo. When the French routed Austrian forces at Hohenlinden east of Munich, Francis II called Archduke Charles out of an untimely retirement prompted by disputes over war policy. His presence helped Austria obtain an armistice before Vienna was threatened, but all knew the peace terms would be unfavorable. The Second Coalition had dissolved and Austria's lackluster military performance would not permit her to negotiate from strength.

The Peace of Lunéville between Austria and France in February 1801 opened the door to vast changes within the Holy Roman Empire. The treaty confirmed many of the terms of Campo Formio and Rastatt. Thus France would receive the Netherlands and the entire left bank of the Rhineland. Territorial compensation to dis-

19. Cited in Knight , 66.

possessed secular rulers, moreover, would take the form of expropriation of ecclesiastical territories and imperial city-states in central Germany. It was a measure of its defeat that Austria agreed to sacrifice or dismantle a number of strategic fortresses east of the Rhine and yielded claims to recently acquired Salzburg and eastern Bavaria.

Emperor Francis II also accepted the Treaty of Lunéville for the Holy Roman Empire. Reflecting the numerical strength of the secular states in the Council of Electors and the Council of Princes, the Imperial Diet ratified Lunéville in March 1801 over the objections of the Elector-Archbishops and the outmaneuvered Council of Cities. Later that year, the diet constituted an Imperial Deputation to formulate a specific plan for the exchange of German territories.

Hoping for larger and quicker acquisitions, Prussia and the southern states negotiated their own treaties with Bonaparte. Tsar Alexander, courted by Napoleon and eager to protect the interests of his German relatives below the Main River, joined the talks. Before the Deputation held its first meeting in August 1802, the major annexations were already arranged. Without even waiting for the Deputation to convene, in fact, Prussia occupied its territorial allotment. The bishoprics of Hildesheim, Paderborn, and parts of Münster fell to the Hohenzollerns, plus other lands in the Harz and northern Thuringia – a net gain of 2,300 square kilometers. Baden, Württemberg, Bavaria, and the smaller states demonstrated more patience, allowing the Deputation to complete formal work in February 1803 before occupying their new lands. Altogether, 112 imperial states, representing 10,000 square kilometers and a population of over three million people changed hands.

These takeovers altered the Holy Roman Empire beyond recognition. Nine secular states now sat on the Council of Electors next to the sole ecclesiastical surviver, the Elector-Archbishop of Mainz, who was forced to accept Regensburg as his new see. Protestants also dominated the Council of Princes two-to-one, reversing the old Catholic majority and eliminating the system of consensus between caucuses. The Council of Cities, moreover, was gutted – only Bremen, Hamburg, Lübeck, Frankfurt, Nürnberg, and Augsburg remained. The emperor's influence, so often dependent on the goodwill of the ecclesiastical states and imperial cities, was undermined. The old balance, always precarious, was now thoroughly upset. Not surprisingly, the storm of protests which had begun at the time of Rastatt now grew to torrential proportions as scores of dispossessed rulers found champions to pen their causes. The revolution set in motion at Lunéville also found critics in the educated population who mourned the imminent passing of imperial institutions and practices which had facilitated religious tolerance, cultural diversity and flowering, individual autonomy, and the rule of law. It was not the first time – nor would it be the last – that German cohesion and unity had dissolved in a welter of internal discord exacerbated by the intervention of external forces.

Indeed France was the real gainer in 1803. Napoleon had rubbed salt in Austria's wounds by fostering the expansion of Baden, Württemberg, and Bavaria – three Austrian rivals who were not strong enough to stand against the Habsburgs without French aid. Prussia, although less dependent than the southern states on military backing from Bonaparte, had also played into his hands by expanding in the North at Austria's expense. Indeed by keeping the old dynastic duel with Vienna alive, Prussia had greatly benefitted the new Alexander who ruled in Paris. Like the ancient Macedonian warrior he respected so much, in fact, Napoleon dreamed of further conquests. It was no coincidence that he left the strategic passes of the upper Rhine in the hands of a weak vassal state like Baden and insisted on Austrian evacuation of right-bank fortresses at Mannheim and Coblenz-Ehrenbreitstein. Ominously, his invasion routes to the east were open. All that Napoleon needed was some assurance that he would not face a *united* coalition of the absolute monarchs. The eastern remnant of Old Regime Europe – Austria, the Holy Roman Empire, Prussia, and Russia – would not survive intact the revolutionary challenge it was about to face.

Chapter 3

Napoleonic Conquests and the Era of Reform in German Europe

Mikhail Kutuzov, commander of the Tsar's forces in Austria, squinted through the frosty window of Olmütz castle at the spectacle below. As the cheers and hurrahs of the regular troops rose up and around the cold walls, the aged veteran gently rubbed his left eye, strained from an old wound that had left his right eye nearly permanently shut. For almost an hour now Alexander had kept the hideous-looking Field Marshall waiting in the hall. Inside, the young, handsome sovereign and his entourage stood with noble bearing on the balcony to greet the arriving columns of the Russian Imperial Guard. Ten battalions of foot, eighteen squadrons of horse, ten thousand warriors – on marched the green and white clad giants of the famous Semenovski and Preobrajenski regiments. Depressed, sensing the hopelessness of his cause, Kutuzov turned away from the window and continued pacing.

For two days that late autumn of 1805, Field Marshall Kutuzov had tried to talk sense to Alexander. "My troops are bereft of physical strength,"[1] he had said. "Fall back to the Carpathians," he had counseled. Alexander had replied angrily: "Just where *do* you propose to fight, Kutuzov?" "Wherever we will be able to join the

1. The quotations in this scene are cited in Christopher Duffy, *Austerlitz 1805* (London, 1977), 73-74, and Claude Manceron, *Austerlitz: The Story of a Battle* (New York, 1966), 153, 155, 298.

Prussians," was Kutuzov's answer. "The further we entice Napoleon," he continued, "the weaker he will become and the greater will be the distance that separates him from his reserves." But others had the ear of the Tsar. "We have only a few days left in which to secure *our* victory," urged Prince Dolgoruki. "Will you let the Prussians rob us of the glory and the fruit of it?" Alexander was eager to be the first to defeat Napoleon. Francis of Austria, also present at Olmütz, desperately wanted to expel the French from Vienna. Kutuzov knew that the mood of wild euphoria and overconfidence created by the arrival of the Imperial Guard would end the strategic debate in Dolgoruki's favor.

Finally the dandies of the imperial entourage streamed out of the Tsar's chambers and Kutuzov was ushered in. Although he assumed that orders were already being drawn up for a westward advance to Austerlitz, Kutuzov again counseled caution. "Archduke Charles and 80,000 men are only two weeks' march from Vienna, Your Majesty." Alexander had heard, but turned his good ear to the general and asked him to repeat. Exasperated, Kutuzov gave up. "May I ask Your Highness his intentions for the movement of my troops?" The Tsar straightened up. "That, Kutuzov, is none of your business." Kutuzov smiled nervously. "As Your Majesty wishes," he said, and left the room.

* * * *

Europe's respite from war after the Peace of Lunéville had not lasted long. In May 1803, only one month after the Imperial Diet accepted a radical restructuring of the empire, war broke out between France and England. Germans were affected immediately as French troops occupied Hanover and closed the ports of the Weser and Elbe to English commerce. The British prime minister, William Pitt, worked assiduously to convince the eastern powers that the Corsican's military ambitions had to be checked. When Napoleon offended royal sensitivities in 1804 and 1805 by successively proclaiming himself Emperor of the French and King of Italy, Austria and Russia agreed to join Europe's Third Coalition against France. Prussia remained neutral, thus fulfilling Napoleon's conditions for war in the East. 200,000 strong, his new *Grand Armeé* amassed on the Rhine in September 1805.

The events of that autumn explained Kutuzov's counsel for caution and delay. In late September, eight French army corps had exploded into southern Germany along a broad front stretching from Hanover to the Black Forest. Eleven days later his converging forces crossed the Danube west and east of Ulm, completely surrounding an Austrian army led by Baron Karl von Mack, one of the hawks in Vienna. Kutuzov's Russians were bloodied and pushed back in their turn, permitting Napoleon to enter Vienna in mid-November. But Bonaparte's position was untenable. Archduke Charles was rushing north from Italy with a sizeable contingent; Alexander and Francis were gathering an allied army of 80,000 northeast of Vienna at Olmütz, and the Prussians were concentrating their forces around Erfurt – a sign that Berlin was leaning toward a declaration of war. Foolishly, however, the two monarchs could not wait.

The two armies met at Austerlitz on 2 December 1805. The Russians and Austrians attacked Napoleon's weak right flank with 30,000 men early in the day, but their assault soon deteriorated. The defenders refused to surrender against great odds. Moreover, Austrian and Russian line officers became confused when the commander of the attack, inebriated by mid-morning, failed to issue further orders. Meanwhile, with the bulk of his 70,000 troops, Bonaparte overran the allied center on the Pratzen Heights and refused to yield before a furious counterattack of the Russian Imperial Guard. Split into three fragments, the Russian-Austrian army was now routed, suffering 25,000 casualties. "Mikhail Illarionovich [Kutusov] certainly anticipated events more than [my advisers]," said Alexander that night as his decimated forces fled eastwards. Francis met Napoleon on 4 December. The humiliated monarch agreed to the cession of Austria's Italian lands to France and additional German territories to Bavaria, Württemberg, and Baden.

Prussia was the next pillar of the Old Regime to collapse. Prepared in November to join Alexander and Francis, Frederick William III, Prussia's indecisive, unhappy young king of eight years, agreed after Austerlitz to sign the unfavorable Treaty of Paris. Prussia would receive Hanover, a British possession, and join Napoleon's continental blockade of English goods, thus triggering war with Great Britain. The Hohenzollerns also sacrificed their southern holding of Ansbach-Bayreuth and the Rhenish property of Cleve, with its important right-bank fortress at Wesel. Furthermore, Prussia agreed to assist France against Russia. Such an agreement was too one-sided to endure, especially with England enticing Prussia and Russia with subsidies to form a fourth coalition. When the French emperor concentrated armies on Prussia's western and southern frontiers in August 1806, Frederick William III finally realized that Napoleon could not be trusted. The king mobilized his own forces and a state of war soon followed.

The aged Duke of Brunswick joined the melancholy king in a kind of dual command. Although many still regarded the Prussian army as the best in Europe, discipline would prove no substitute for intelligent leadership. Splitting their forces, the Prussians advanced into Saxony to give battle. They opted foolishly not to wait for the slow-moving Russians who were concentrating another army in Poland. Bonaparte's troops burst through the Thuringian forests, overran the Prussian advance guard at Saalfeld, and cut off supply lines to Berlin. On 14 October 1806, the divided, outmaneuvered Prussians were crushed at the twin battles of Jena and Auerstädt. Napoleon swept all before him, entering Berlin thirteen days later. Frederick William fled to the northeastern border town of Memel with 20,000 men, humbled but still hopeful that Alexander would rescue him and his kingdom.

A Russian army of about 150,000 was assembling in central Poland. An even larger French force stripped the Prussian countryside bare as it moved east. The two titanic hoards clashed at Eylau in early February 1807. After bloody fighting, another Austerlitz was narrowly averted when fresh Prussian soldiers arrived late in the day to bolster the Russians' crumbling left flank. After a lengthy truce, both armies met again at Friedland on 14 June. This time Napoleon trapped the allies against the Alle River, inflicting 40,000 casualties on them.

Defeated again, Alexander sued for peace and withdrew from the coalition. Like Prussia earlier, Russia now acceded to France's continental blockade of England. A worse fate befell helpless Prussia as it was compelled to swallow the crushing treaty which Napoleon and Alexander negotiated at Tilsit. The once-mighty kingdom sacrificed all territories west of the Elbe River to the new kingdom of Westphalia, headed by Jerome Bonaparte, and all Polish provinces to a new Grand Duchy of Warsaw, headed by the King of Saxony. Napoleon would occupy rump Prussia until reparations of 311 million francs – a sum equal to Prussia's prewar budget – were paid. Broken and embarrassed, Frederick William III would not return to Berlin until French troops left in December 1809.

The string of disasters which began at Austerlitz and ended at Friedland was a phenomenon far too complex to be attributed solely to the military genius of Napoleon. It is more useful to view these debacles as a product of the relatively backward social and political systems of Austria, Prussia, and Russia. While Napoleon, Ney, Davout and other top French generals had advanced to their positions because of unusual abilities, the eastern armies were commanded or influenced by hereditary monarchs of limited talent who were surrounded by officers selected exclusively from the narrow ranks of the nobility. Sometimes the system produced a Frederick the Great, an Archduke Charles, or a Kutuzov; more often, however, it advanced anachronisms and mediocrities like the Duke of Brunswick, the unfortunate General Mack of Ulm, or General Buxhöwden, the drunkard of Austerlitz. This relative dearth of talent was not only a battlefield liability, but also affected the crucial maneuvering stage of a campaign. Thus Napoleon could trust the capable leaders of his mobile, semi-autonomous army corps to move under general orders in a general direction before converging to give battle. The relatively inept, class-bound army leadership of the Old Regime was usually unable to do this.

The comparative ineffectiveness of Austrian, Prussian, and Russian armies was related in other ways to the backwardness of these societies. Another reason for French mobility, for instance, was their willingness to live off the land. German and Russian armies occasionally resorted to this practice, but usually avoided it for fear that serf-peasant recruits, unpatriotic victims of the society they were forced to defend, would desert while foraging. France's citizen soldier would sometimes desert, but the problem was not systemic in nature. Similarly, French commanders could allow their troops to chase a defeated army and rout it; eastern generals knew that thousands of their serf infantrymen would never return to camp. Fear of armed peasant revolt also prevented serious consideration of the *levée en masse*. Unless a united coalition faced him, therefore, Napoleon entered campaigns with numerical superiority. Repeatedly, however, the overconfident monarchs refused to coordinate their movements, convinced, as they were, that no illegitimate upstart from Corsica could defeat sovereigns chosen by God.

For a variety of reasons, moreover, Bonaparte could rely on the holders of wealth in France to lend money to his ambitious regime. The mechanism of lending was institutionalized in 1800 with the creation of the Bank of France. In Austria, Prussia, and Russia, no modern institutions of public finance existed. This inadequacy reflected not only the relative commercial and industrial backwardness of Germany and Russia *vis à vis* the West, but more importantly, the fact that merchants and bankers who possessed funds had less incentive to lend money to an absolutist state which neither respected them nor desired their participation in government. The relative limits which politics placed on government borrowing were a great liability in this long era of unlimited warfare.

This one-sided military conflict of the modern and the backward determined the ultimate fate of the Holy Roman Empire. In December 1805 Napoleon compelled Francis II to recognize Württemberg, Bavaria, and Saxony as sovereign kingdoms. In July 1806 he forced Bavaria, Württemberg, Baden, Hesse-Darmstadt, the Duchy of Berg, and eleven lesser dukes and princes in western Germany to join a newly formulated Confederation of the Rhine. The member states became allies of France and pledged themselves to raise an army of 63,000 men. With Napoleon as their "Protector," the confederate governments were not permitted to remain in the Holy Roman Empire. The involuntary secession of the sixteen was followed in August 1806 by the inevitable abdication of Francis as Holy Roman Emperor. An empire of a thousand years passed away with him. The imperious nature of these changes – and the shifting balance of power – had nudged Frederick William III toward war later that year. But the armies of the Fourth Coalition failed in their stipulated mission of pushing the French out of Germany. Rather, the battles of Jena, Auerstädt, and

Friedland confirmed the political rearrangements begun in the aftermath of Austerlitz.

* * * *

The defeat of Prussian and Russian arms encouraged most German states to join the Confederation of the Rhine. There were twenty-three *new* members by 1808, including Westphalia, the Thuringian states, Saxony, and Mecklenburg – making the new union of thirty-nine states something of a misnomer. In fact, with the exception of Austria, Prussia, Swedish Pomerania, the Hanseatic cities, and Danish Holstein, all German lands belonged. Napoleon saw the Confederation primarily as a source of tribute and soldiers. In addition, he valued it as a *cordon sanitaire* between France and the eastern monarchies. The great conqueror sought to guarantee French influence in this buffer zone by encouraging the adoption of French laws and institutions. "What people would want to return to the rule of Prussia," he wrote his brother Jerome in November 1807, "once it had tasted the benefits of a wise and liberal administration?" By promoting progressive rule in the Confederation, Jerome could contribute more to the defense of central Germany "than the Elbe River, the fortresses and the protection of

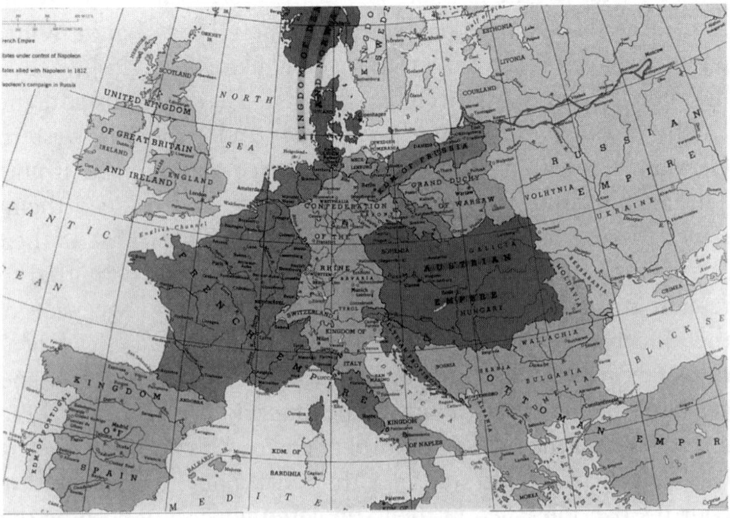

Europe 1812 12353

France."[2] Like its armies over the past decade, France's revolution should finally cross the Rhine.

French political machinations in the Confederation touched off an intense struggle between the advocates of change and the defenders of tradition. In peripheral territories like Saxony and Mecklenburg where French influence was less immediate, reform parties and factions ventured little and gained next to nothing. The political dynamics were quite different, however, in South German states closer to France. Cliques around progressive bureaucrats either strengthened their positions – as was the case in Bavaria under Maximilian von Montgelas – or outmaneuvered their opponnents and came to the fore – as occurred in Baden under Johann Friedrich Brauer, and later, Sigismund von Reitzenstein. In Württemberg, an autocratic, modernizing King Frederick took the reins of reform.

The motives for change were complex. In principle, all of the reformers were true to the Enlightenment. But philosophical preferences mixed with pragmatic considerations of greater weight. Prompt initiation of reform could preserve a country's autonomy by obviating the need for French legislative fiats and deflecting Napoleon from his scheme of creating a more unitary – and easily controllable – German state based in Frankfurt. The southern states were also new, largely artificial creations with little or no legitimacy in recently annexed areas. Bavaria and Württemberg had roughly doubled in area since 1803, while Baden now stretched to ten times its former size. Enlightened legal, social, and economic reforms, it was hoped, could win popularity for the new governments among the unprivileged classes. Certain South German leaders also favored representative institutions. Parliaments would draw local notables to the capital city, thereby integrating peoples and lands of very heterogenous character. By providing an advisory voice to the holders of wealth, moreover, parliaments would help states bent under the burden of Napoleon's wars to raise loans. Finally, bureaucrats wanted to reorganize their own agencies and improve their own status and security. Such measures would create

2. Napoleon to Jerome, 15 November 1807, printed in A. du Casse (ed.), *Mèmoires et correspondance du roi Jèrome* (Paris, 1862), 71, 73.

the efficient and elite mechanism of state required to implement ambitious, controversial policies.

Programs designed to further the French principles of liberty and equality experienced success everywhere below the Main River. Censorship was abolished and freedom of the press introduced. Religous freedom for Catholics and Protestants was proclaimed, while in Baden and Bavaria, the legal status of Jews was greatly improved. Public education became available to greater numbers as gymnasiums and universities received added governmental attention and funding. The most striking change occurred, however, in the privileged status of the nobility. Egalitarian legislation eliminated the aristocracy's tax exemption, monopoly of government positions, legal privileges, and control of local justice. Only Bavaria was unable to break the nobility's exclusive legal status and hold over the courts. On the other hand, the Bavarian Edict on the Nobility of July 1808 angered and humiliated noble families by forcing them to show documentation of their titles and heritage in order to enjoy privileges.

The transformation to parliamentary monarchy proceeded more haltingly. Napoleon was particularly adamant for financial reasons that constitutions accompany the introduction of his Civil Code, pressing his arguments personally before South German leaders at Milan in November 1807. The constitution of the Kingdom of Westphalia, completed that month, was to serve as a model. Bavaria produced a document in May 1808 which called for indirect male election of deputies who met property and education qualifications. The Diet could not initiate legislation, but could advise the king on laws which he presented to them for review. Montgelas saw the need for democratic improvements, however, with the result that elections scheduled for 1810 were postponed, then finally cancelled amidst the confusion of Napoleon's last wars. In Baden, Brauer and Reitzenstein exploited the unsettled times to delay establishment of a representative body which did not fit their bureaucratic vision, while in Württemberg, Frederick balked when advisers suggested that he share power. For the most part, constitutionalism in South Germany would await the postwar period.

The introduction of free enterprise made even less headway. Both Baden and Würtemberg refused to follow the French example of abolishing guild controls, thereby making it easier to found a new business. Continuation of the old guild legislation, plus the widespread popular perception – often quite accurate – that guild shops produced the best merchandise, enabled them to survive well into the postwar era in both states. In Bavaria, Montgelas showed more willingness initially to challenge medieval structures. Between 1804 and 1808, licensing was transferred to state authorities and the sale or inheritance of guild privileges abolished. He envisioned a freer, more prosperous economy which would expand along familiar artisanal lines – there was no futuristic vision, in other words, of a great urban-technological transformation. Although limited, these programs nevertheless failed, for guild protests grew so intense by 1811 that Montgelas retreated and largely abandoned his efforts.

Agrarian reforms also stagnated. As explained earlier, the seigneurial system in southern Germany had yielded almost entirely by the eigtheenth century to a system of peasant rent payments to absentee landlords. After 1806, governments attempted to transfer land title to the peasantry with compensation to former owners. These efforts foundered, however, on the bitter opposition of beleaguered noblemen. Peasants on former church properties also encountered difficulty in becoming free landholders. In this case, ironically, it was the states themselves which erected barriers to freedom. The massive secularization of church lands and absorption of ecclesiastical states in southern Germany after 1803 transformed the secular states into major landlords. In Bavaria, for example, 76 percent of the peasantry now farmed government property. Unable to afford a termination of rent payments which comprised 15 to 25 percent of total revenue, officials in Munich, Stuttgart, and Karlsruhe often denied peasant applications for purchase of rented land.

Bureaucratic reforms, not surprisingly, were implemented quickly in all three states. Ministries were organized along French lines according to functions like war, foreign affairs, or interior affairs, sweeping away the old regional offices which combined all functions. Attempts were made to bring formerly independent hometown officials under central control. By the end of the Napoleonic era, moreover, civil servants in the south had acquired higher salaries, impressive pensions, and tenure rights to lifetime employment as well as a variety of special privileges. The creation of modern bureaucracies and the introduction of ambitious programs affecting almost every aspect of society would assure the southern governmental systems a leasehold in the less favorable era following their Protector's final defeat. Indeed, the Old Regime had expired beyond the point of resuscitation.

The Kingdom of Westphalia was not as fortunate as the new states of the south. Constructed in 1807 from Hanover, Brunswick, Electoral Hesse, and Prussian lands west of the Elbe, Jerome Bonaparte's fiefdom was a microcosm of Napoleonic France which was designed to be popular with his subjects and inspirational to his fellow rulers in the Confederation. These goals did not entirely elude Jerome. His peasants welcomed the abolition of serfdom and the end of aristocratic privileges. There can be no doubt, moreover, that Westphalia had a great influence on the thinking of German statesmen – even beyond the Elbe in Prussia. But the regime was never popular. Jerome's extravagant life style in Kassel, an exorbitant tax burden, and the constant threat of military conscription prevented widespread acceptance of the new regime. Baron von Dornberg commanded more loyalty in April 1809 when he led a revolt of Hessians which French troops suppressed with great difficulty. Nor were Hanoverians and Prussians willing to forget former allegiances. Until it collapsed in 1814, the Kingdom of Westphalia was seen as a foreign creation and an alien state.

* * * *

The Rhenish perception of French administration, meanwhile, had improved. Memories of the worst years of the 1790s were not forgotten, nor were the new rulers forgiven for past crimes. But the Rhineland ceased to be an "ungovernable"[3] province, as T. C. W. Blanning described the earlier situation. Formal annexation to France after the Treaty of Lunéville in 1801 brought a definite end to financial and military exploitation. Although the left bank would be a staging ground for offensives in 1805 and 1809, war's destruction would not return until early 1814 – and then, the

3. Blanning, *French Revolution in Germany* , 286.

French treated the Rhinelanders as citizens, not an enemy people. The intervening years of peace brought a return to social normalcy and allowed the benefits of egalitarian French legislation to be widely felt and appreciated. Master craftsmen still dreamed of reviving their guilds, and many Rhinelanders continued to pray for the Holy Roman Emperor – but the opposition of devout Catholics and the open resistance of priests came to an end after a pragmatic condordat which Napoleon negotiated with the Vatican in 1801.

The Rhenish business community grew particularly content with French rule. The prefects of the four Rhenish departments welcomed the participation of chambers of commerce and city councils in decisions affecting economic and political life. As a result, manufacturers, traders, and bankers became accustomed to a form of interest group politicing which gave them real influence. In fact, this mode of operating under the prefects facilitated a smooth transition to authoritarian Prussian rule after 1815. Factory owners also benefitted from access to French markets which were internally free of tolls and externally well-protected by tariffs. Moreover, expanded sales opportunities combined with Napoleonic subsidies and war-related labor shortages to accelerate the transition from labor-intensive putting-out methods of production to mechanized textile manufacture. By 1811, spinning mules, fly shuttles, self-acting looms, and a panoply of novel machines were beginning to appear in the woolen and silk works of Aachen, Crefeld, and Cologne. Finally, Rhenish business leaders appreciated the Napoleonic Code with its recognition of inviolable rights of private property, strict penal statutes, and Draconian labor control measures.

French reforms proved popular with Rhenish businessmen in yet another way. The emergence of the propertied and cultivated bourgeoisie during the late eighteenth century was accompanied by significant changes in relations between men and women. As we shall see in Part II, the closely integrated and mutually dependent work routines of the workshop and farm were yielding in the early 1800s to separate spheres of influence for the two sexes. Men conducted a public life in the bureaucracy, barrister's office, classroom, or factory, while wives were relegated to the private sphere of household management and childcare. The Code Napolèon reinforced and institutionalized this trend by declaring that a husband "owes protection to his wife" and a wife "obedience to her husband"; that a wife "cannot give, convey, mortgage or acquire property without the husband joining in the instrument or giving his written consent"; that a wife "cannot sue in court"; and that "married women are incapable of making contracts."[4] Just as Theodor Hippel's call to demolish "the prisons of domesticity" had found few male friends in the early 1790s, so now few men in the Rhineland came forward to speak against statutes that protected "separate spheres" and made the man's home his castle.

* * * *

Francis of Austria was not a cruel man. News of an epidemic, a natural calamity, or the slaughter of Austrian soldiers greatly saddened him. But he was neither capable nor desirous of peering beneath the surface of ordinary events to examine the structure of his state and society for any inherent flaws which might exist. The gauntlet that revolutionary France hurled before Austria in the 1790s triggered no such self-assessment – only an instinctive reaction to hold tightly onto the present system. Francis neither rescinded nor advanced the agrarian reforms of Joseph II that had begun to commute peasants' labor obligations into money rents. Intellectual life was not freed; on the contrary, it became more stultifying. Austria's internal spy network was extended and the police given charge of censorship. Censors were asked to be wary of all praise of France and criticism of the homeland, even to the point of scrutinizing mottos on fans, snuffboxes, monuments, and toys. In 1803, a new commission reexamined published works that had passed the censors before 1792, laboring assiduously to ban 2,500 of them in two years.

Francis also ignored the arguments of mercantilists who wanted to expand manufacturing as envisioned by the great reformist kaiser, Joseph II. Reactionary advisers argued successfully that new industries and technologies, like subversive literature, were tangible symbols of change which could corrupt a country's morals and lead to urban rioting. In 1794, accordingly, police officials forbade new factories in Vienna. In 1802, the state barred importation of

4. Cited in *The Code Napolèon* , trans. by Bryant Barrett, (London, 1811).

flax-spinning machinery and widened the ban on the establishment of factories. New ventures were only permitted in the countryside where it was felt industries could be safely dispersed. After a few years, the ban was lifted for towns with surplus labor, but not for Vienna – the memory of Parisian mob politics was still too fresh.

Archduke Charles was the only partially effective voice for change. After Lunéville, for instance, Francis allowed his brother to reorder the top administration. All department heads reported to ministers who presided over foreign affairs, internal affairs, and defense, which Charles took himself. This new cabinet would meet with Francis on a frequent basis to tender advise on critical matters of state. Within a few years, however, the new ministerial system had deteriorated and Francis, ever suspicious of the Archduke, reemerged with his old absolutist habits.

Charles was able to register some progress with the army before administrative stagnation returned. Thus he introduced a Quartermaster General Staff to develop operational plans and attempted to popularize the army by reducing the period of conscription from life to ten to fourteen years depending on the branch of service. Charles had wanted a uniform term of eight years, but was told by conservatives at court that shorter terms would train too many soldiers who, after release, would have the expertise to lead insurrections.

The magnitude of the disaster at Austerlitz prompted Charles to beg his brother to purge government of "the obscure quacks gathered round the deathbed of the monarchy."[5] These protestations led to the appointment of new men like Count Philipp Stadion in foreign affairs. The Archduke himself was promoted to "generalissimo" and given relatively free reign with the army. Twenty-five generals were dismissed, army discipline made more humane, and an army reserve and people's militia introduced. The regular army was also organized into army corps, somewhat like the French. But the general rhythm of Austrian society remained unchanged. Expression of thought and opinion remained unfree, frustrating Stadion's efforts to rally the intelligentsia behind the crown. Charles' desire for an unfettering of economic life was also foiled.

5. Cited in C. A. Macartney, *The Habsburg Empire 1790-1918* (New York, 1969), 181.

Stadion himself feared "the influence of the [bourgeois] Third Estate and the power of money," while Count Ratschky, a conservative at court, warned against "the spirit of commerce." This debilitating mindset would create a people "greedy only for profitable speculation, emasculated by soft living and sedentary work and at last quite unserviceable for defence."[6]

Indeed the country's energies were devoted far more to defense than to reform. Stadion dreamed of revenge against Napoleon and the South German states that had humiliated the Habsburgs. He assumed that Russia and Prussia would be eager to join a new coalition and that the German people would rise up to oust the hated foreigner and overthrow their artificial regimes. Bonaparte's invasion of Spain in 1808, the overthrow of the Spanish Bourbons, Joseph Bonaparte's ascension to the Spanish throne, and the fierce guerrilla resistance which resulted supplied added encouragement. How long would it be before Napoleon tired of the Habsburgs and moved to enthrone another member of his family in Vienna? With Francis again firmly behind the hawks, the war party planned hostilities for the spring of 1809. Before this time, the massive recruiting drive would be unfinished; afterwards, there would not be enough money in the treasury.

The Austrian uprising of 1809 was another debacle. Archduke Charles and the main army crossed the Inn River into Bavaria with no assurance that Russia and Prussia wanted to risk another war with France. With the exception of the Hessians and Tyroleans, moreover, no guerrilla forces rose up to harry the French. After defeating his great Austrian rival at Regensburg in April, Napoleon advanced on Vienna in May. Charles repulsed the French at Aspern later that month, but in the plodding fashion of Old Regime combat, failed to capitalize on his victory. The third battle of the campaign, for example, was not fought until early July at Wagram. For two days, 180,000 French, Bavarian, and Saxon troops struggled to dislodge 130,000 Austrians from their positions. Finally, a cautious Archduke gave the order to retreat. For his less than dynamic performance in a war he regarded as foolhardy, Charles was removed from public life by an ungrateful

6. Ibid., 161, 181.

brother. Francis' anger stemmed from the resulting treaty terms of Schönbrunn that sacrificed Austria's Polish and remaining Italian provinces, reduced the army and militia to 150,000 men, imposed an indemnity of 85 million gulden, and forced Austria into the Continental Blockade and an unwanted alliance with France.

Even now Austria did not venture to introduce reforms. Francis ruled more absolutely than ever before and was supported in this stance by a new chief minister with impeccable conservative credentials: Clemens von Metternich. The social and political stagnation was accompanied, however, by a slightly new approach to industry. In order to enhance the kingdom's finances and exploit the exclusion of British imports to Europe, guild restrictions were lifted for textile firms producing goods for export. Francis also consented to open his domains to machine imports and to lift the ban on new factories in Vienna. These decrees represented a victory for a school of pragmatic bureaucrats who were eager to continue the reforming tradition of Joseph II. But the industrial boomlet was cut abruptly short in 1811 by Draconian monetary measures introduced to end Austria's raging inflation. The defenders of traditional society shed no tears as one textile mill after another closed its doors. Thus Europe's revolutionary era produced remarkably little change in Austria.

* * * *

It was a largely unchanged Old Regime that Prussian soldiers left behind as they marched to their fate at Jena and Auerstädt. The country's king, Frederick William III, was a moody pragmatist who had meant well since ascending the throne in 1797. In stark contrast to Francis in Austria, the Hohenzollern's administration had discussed ambitious reforms such as reorganization of the bureaucracy along French lines, peasant emancipation, a popular militia, termination of guild restrictions, and other measures to liberalize the economy. But Frederick William possessed neither the self-assurance to trust his instincts and his enlightened advisers, nor the audacity to challenge conservatives entrenched in the bureaucracy, army, and nobility. Consequently, the social, governmental, and military system of Frederick the Great came crashing down in 1806, a victim of France's spreading revolution.

The totality of the defeat shocked everyone. Prussia's finest were thoroughly routed on the battlefield; many of her fortress towns, including Berlin, were captured without a shot; the country from Jena to Eylau was ravaged; and the peasants remained indifferent to everything but French foraging parties at harvest time. Further campaigning brought the ignominious Treaty of Tilsit. The kingdom that previous Hohenzollerns had forged into a great European power was halved in size, compelled to support a French army of occupation, and forced to pay a huge indemnity. Prussian ports were closed to English commerce and a decade of lucrative agricultural exports to the booming industrial island halted. The subsequent recession in an already devastated countryside quickly spread to the towns, where many artisans and manufacturers had to close shop. Prussia's tax base was demolished, making it doubly difficult to pay the French. It is no wonder that Frederick WIlliam sank into a deep depression during his first months in Memel and Königsberg.

Discredited and politically paralyzed by this disaster, Prussian conservatives were pushed into the wings by advocates of change who had languished politically during the long, frustrating years of peace. In the army, reformers grouped around the new minister of war, Gerhard Scharnhorst, an innovative Hanoverian who had transferred into Prussian service in 1801. Allied with his circle were two groups of talented civilians around Karl August von Hardenberg, chief minister during the gloomy spring of 1807, and Baron Karl vom Stein, Hardenberg's successor until the fall of 1808. Hardenberg returned to the chancellery in 1810 to continue the work of reform and revitalization. Still relatively young and idealistic, these men envisioned a thoroughgoing overhaul of state and society which would charge the Prussian nation with energies untapped by the outmoded institutions of Frederick the Great. Thus Prussia met France's revolutionary challenge with strategies strikingly different from the business as usual approach of the Austrians.

Scharnhorst set to work in the summer of 1807. Above all, he wanted to end the aristocratic privileges encouraged in the past. The officer corps should be opened to all social classes with admission based on education and competitive examination. Promotion should be based on merit. Alongside the regular army, moreover, would arise a national guard to lend popular fervor to a war of liberation against Napoleon. With the exception of the national guard, these recommendations were approved by Frederick William and implemented in 1808 and 1809. The king feared that an overtly aggressive institution like the national guard might alarm the French. He also doubted whether the Prussian people would rally to the colors. This reform would wait until March 1813.

Like Scharnhorst, Stein and Hardenberg strove to transform a country of dejected subjects into a nation of inspired citizens. One of Stein's early edicts in 1807 eliminated the personal duties that serfs owed to lords, abolished legal distinctions between noblemen and commoners, eliminated the nobility's exclusive right to own land, and proclaimed the right of all citizens – not just guild shops in towns – to practice a trade. The latter decree had added significance because Prussia had enforced the old law in order to facilitate tax collection inside city walls, thus retarding the spread of putting-out industry to Prussian lands. Another decree of 1808 granted towns and cities far-reaching rights of self-governance. Stein also borrowed the system of functional ministries introduced by the French, Westphalians, and South Germans. Before he could make proposals for a central representative body, however, Stein became implicated in a military conspiracy against the French that forced him from office. His immediate successors, Alexander von Dohna and Karl von Altenstein, were unable to maintain Stein's political momentum.

Hardenberg's second ministry picked up the cudgel of reform in the autumn of 1810. Preceding his first acts – and enhancing the atmosphere of rebirth – came the dual inaugurations of the University of Berlin and the War School. The former was the crowning accomplishment of Wilhelm von Humboldt, head of the new Ministry of Culture until June 1810. For over two decades, Humboldt had favored individual intellectual growth in a free political atmosphere, but recognized the benefits which state institutions could provide to individuals. The liberal regime of the University of Berlin with its far-reaching academic freedom for professors and students was the realization of Humboldt's dream. Scharnhorst's War School offered a much more regimented curriculum of science and the humanities, but here too the aim was the intellectual growth of each officer candidate. From these two institutes, the officers and civil servants of the new Prussia were to spring forth.

Stein's Emancipation Edict of 1807 terminating the legal subordination of peasants did not become effective until November 1810. This fact necessitated some of Hardenberg's first agrarian legislation, for there were loop-holes in Stein's decree and the crucial question of the property rights of lords and peasants remained unresolved. One of the first ordinances therefore suspended local laws sanctioning the servitude of peasant children in noble households. In 1811, moreover, an edict granted to 161,000 peasant households – about 10 percent of all farming families – the right to land title in return for a compensatory payment to the lord of a third or a half of the peasant's land. Capping Hardenberg's rural legislation was an ordinance promoting rural transportation, animal husbandry, and new farming techniques.

Agriculture, however, was just one part of a greater economic whole in the minds of Hardenberg and his economic experts. Thus the agrarian edicts of 1810 and 1811 were accompanied by others designed to cultivate agricultural side-industries close to cheap water power, abundant rural labor, and the farmer-consumers which, it was hoped, the agrarian laws would spawn. Rural industries possessed the added advantage of being removed from cities and towns that were more prone to riots and revolutions. All of these considerations led to decrees eliminating the exclusive rights and privileges of the guilds, abolishing the manufacturing monopoly of towns, ending wage and price supports for chartered companies, and granting tax preferences to rural factories. Prussia's legislation borrowed a great deal from the Rhenish Confederation, but there was a radical, rebellious aspect to the East Elbian programs which was missing in the west. By substituting economic freedom and rural industries for the Frederickian system of state subsidies, monopolistic companies, and guilds, Hardenberg's team gambled that the state's coffers would fill quickly enough to finance Scharnhorst's dreams of liberation from the French. It was this military agenda that gave the Prussian reforms their distinctive flavor.

Hardenberg was also impressed by the progress made in France, Westphalia, and Bavaria with advisory representative institutions.

He hoped that "democratic principles in a monarchical government" would strengthen the state politically, and ultimately, financially. The Chancellor convened an Assembly of Notables in 1811 to make a "democratic" beginning in Prussia, but the birthing effort miscarried when the aristocratic majority launched an assault upon proposals to tax noble estates and eliminate the nobility's local police powers. Hardenberg modified his tactics shrewdly in 1812, calling a Provincial National Assembly to Berlin consisting of eighteen noblemen, twelve burghers, and nine peasant farmers. Town criticism of the government's anti-guild legislation combined with continued noble opposition, however, to dampen enthusiasm in bureaucratic circles for parliamentary institutions which seemed to threaten further progressive reforms. Wary of popular experiments in the first place, Frederick William, not surprisingly, was even less enthused. The Provincial National Assembly continued its deliberations until 1815, but the country's leaders and its people were distracted long before this time by the final act of Europe's struggle to unseat Napoleon.

Chapter 4

Patriotism, Nationalism, and the Liberation of Germany

The paintings of Caspar David Friedrich evoked an emotional response in his contemporaries. Born in the Pomeranian town of Greifswald in 1774, Friedrich grew up near the sea, the countryside, and the Protestant world of thrift, hard work, and religious devotion. The sensitive young artist studied at the Copenhagen Academy of Art before moving permanently to Dresden in 1798, but the early impressions of Greifswald stayed with him, shaping the visual images and spiritual messages of his life's work. Nature dominated all of his paintings and served a variety of purposes. Friedrich's nature motifs are a fitting introduction to this chapter, for he often employed them as artistic symbols of yearning for better times during the last years of Napoleon's rule. Like much of the culture we will encounter in this study, his art possessed a political message.

Unlike some romantics, Friedrich did not long for a resuscitation of medieval institutions or a return to universal Catholicism. A devout Protestant and political progressive, he believed that spiritual renewal and vibrant forms of government had to supplant an old order which God had punished with military defeat and humiliation. In *Winter*, painted in 1808, and *Abbey in the Eichenwald*, painted in 1809 and 1810, Friedrich placed Gothic ruins in frozen forest settings. Like the medieval world, the stone walls are demolished and inorganic; yet they stand in stark contrast to the surrounding trees which, like contemporary Germany, will bear leaves when springtime arrives. Other works from these years show Christ on a cross amidst the organic wintry splendor of the forest. In *Winter Landscape*, finished around 1811, he added a Neo-Gothic church to this scene. The crucifix and a cripple praying for recovery in the foreground seem to offer hope for a religious-political revival, symbolized by spires rising from a dark and distant fog.

By 1813, Friedrich's paintings began to demonstrate a more overt patriotism and nationalism. In *The Grave of Arminius*, for instance, a French cuirassier, or heavy cavalryman, stands before a stone grave that is miracuously opening. Huge bolders and rocky crags tower above the tomb. Rising past the grave and the stone walls are tall pines whose tops are beyond the frame of the picture. Borrowed from religious art, the strong vertical lines of the painting symbolize a resurrection which the hapless Frenchman will not survive. *Cuirassier in the Forest* contains a similar message. Alone and seemingly lost, a weary warrior stands on snow-covered ground before a frightening and menacing forest which almost closes around him. Friedrich evokes the feeling of impending doom by making the forest thicker, darker, and taller than usual. Behind the cuirassier, blocking his rear, sits a predatory eagle. Few Germans in 1814 would have failed to appreciate the meaning behind this depiction of wintry death and disastrous retreat. Indeed, like Friedrich's cuirassier, France's fortunes in Germany were on the wane by 1813 and 1814.

Such themes abounded in German culture during the last decade of the Napoleonic era. Ludwig van Beethoven's sentiments were anti-Napoleonic after the *Eroica* Symphony, and occasionally this feeling worked its way into the great composer's music. Thus *Wellington's Victory* was a celebration of French setbacks in Spain. Friedrich Schiller, too, adopted patriotic motifs in later plays like *Wilhelm Tell*. Indeed, the goal of freeing Central Europe from French tyranny was shared by those Germans who did not support the Rhenish Confederation. This patriotic yearning to defeat France should not be confused, however, with more overtly nationalistic efforts to found a modern, unified German state. While *both* impulses can be found in Friedrich's work, far more frequently, patriotic Germans longed for a return to the Holy Roman Empire

– a goal that admittedly had nationalistic overtones even though it was backward-looking – or pledged themselves to support existing governments, or both. The sometimes blurry distinction between patriotism and nationalism is important to keep in mind as we discuss the final stage of the Napoleonic era in Germany.

Caspar David Friedrich's *Cuirassier in the Forest,* 1813.
Art serves the cause of national liberation.

Patriotic intellectuals leaned toward either Austria or Prussia as champions against France. This was quite logical, for both retained a degree of power and neither was constrained by membership in the Rhenish Confederation. By 1808, publicists like Friedrich von Gentz and the brothers August Wilhelm and Friedrich Schlegel were extolling Austria as the country that would save Germany and the continent. Europe would regain freedom beneath Austrian standards, proclaimed Friedrich Schlegel on the eve of Austria's uprising in 1809. Its victories would loose Europe's bonds. After the Habsburg defeat at Wagram, Berlin began to rival Vienna as a mecca of patriots. This trend was reinforced by the disappointing return to conservatism in Vienna and a promising reform movement in Prussia that attracted northern activists. Of the many names which adorn all heroic historical accounts of this period, two stand out: Friedrich Schleiermacher, a professor of theology at the university and popular preacher at Berlin's Trinity Church, and Friedrich Ludwig Jahn, a writer and school teacher.

Schleiermacher left Halle during the turbulence of 1806 and found his way to Berlin. There he moved into the circle of Baron Stein and other reforming bureaucrats. Schleiermacher's Protestant faith and political liberalism prevented any romantic yearning for medieval times or the Habsburg-dominated Holy Roman Empire. Instead he poured himself into passionate sermons which warned against a mistaken attachment to the past, criticized inequality and privilege, and recognized the necessity of general renewal. Like Stein, Schleiermacher believed deeply that social and political reforms were the prerequisite for success in any Prussian campaign against Napoleon. But Prussia, he preached in 1808, was obligated to rise up. For no country could remain true to God's laws if it tolerated foreign domination.

Jahn founded his famous gymnastics club in 1811 with similar motives. The youth of the capital were encouraged to join in physical exercise and sing patriotic songs on the Hasenheide outside Berlin in order to prepare their bodies and souls for Prussia's final reckoning with France. With Jahn, however, there was a tinge of nostalgia for the defunct empire which, paradoxically, brought him close to modern nationalism. The old Reich had maintained autonomy for the different ways, customs, and governments of the

German people. Thus it had represented a "world state in microcosm." But now that the empire had disappeared, he wrote in 1810, German revival depended on Prussia, a country where the "lineage of the overwhelming majority of the people is German," not on Austria, a land with only a "mix of peoples." Prussia was "the youngest and quickest-growing off-shoot of the old imperial root."[1] All that was needed before Prussia was ready to carry Germany's sword were steps to include "the people" in the government of this most German and ethnically pure of states. Reflecting Jahn's royalism, he left the determination and implementation of these measures to the Hohenzollerns.

The patriotic ideas of Schleiermacher and Jahn were very similar to those of official Prussian circles. Both the civilians around Stein and Hardenberg and the military reformers under Scharnhorst envisioned their work leading to a great Prussian uprising that would free Germany from the yoke of French subjugation. Frederick William III, however, refused to give serious consideration to a policy which could lead, like the Austrian debacle of 1809, to a tightening of Napoleon's hold on the kingdom, or possibly, Prussia's outright elimination as a state. The prudent monarch's timidity eventually drove Prussian patriots into the service of Russia. "It is very difficult to reconcile the duties of the citizen," wrote Stein in March 1812, "with those of a moral man."[2] Joining Stein in St. Petersburg to continue the struggle against France were Carl von Clausewitz, a brilliant protégé of Scharnhorst, and Hermann von Boyen, minister of war under Stein and Hardenberg. As we shall see, the break from Prussia and the move east unleashed more genuinely nationalistic feelings in these men.

There were spokesmen in Berlin, however, whose views had been more nationalistic from the beginning. One of these was Johann Gottlieb Fichte, a leading Freemason and professor of philosophy at the university. Fichte, who had originally welcomed the French Revolution, sympathized neither with the Holy Roman Empire nor with old states like Prussia which by 1806 had demonstrated their uselessness. In his "Addresses to the German Nation"

1. Cited in Rudolf Ibbeken, *Preussen 1807-1813: Staat und Volk als Idee und Wirklichkeit* (Cologne, 1970), 322.

2. Cited in Sheehan, *German History*, 310.

delivered in Berlin during the Winter of 1807-08, Fichte praised Germans as a people bound together by a common language and a mission to redeem human culture. Foreign domination, which had already weakened German independence, now threatened to hamper Germany's cultural mission by undermining this unique language. He therefore asked Germans to devote themselves to "the devouring flame of higher patriotism which embraces the nation as the vesture of the eternal."[3] Fichte's concept of cultural-linguistic unity lacked only a more definite political shape. Creation of a unitary state was in his opinion a task for future generations.

Ernst Moritz Arndt, a popular writer, pointed the way toward this political structure. Like Jahn, he lamented the passing of the Holy Roman Empire. But, unlike Jahn, Arndt held states like Prussia directly responsible for the loosening of common imperial ties "between north and south." He reserved most of his wrath, however, for the French. "In the name of God and my people, I hate all Frenchmen without exception. I will teach my son this hate."[4] Arndt hoped that passions like his would erupt in a great war of liberation and unification. Although his formulations were vague, the fiery nationalist wanted to dismantle most existing German states and incorporate them into Austria and Prussia. Somehow, then, these two rival giants would join hands in a new German empire. Arndt made no attempt to reconcile the contradiction between his nationalistic ideal of unification and the reality of Austro-Prussian animosity.

Linking Jahn's Prussian-German patriotism and Arndt's German nationalism was an emotional attachment to imperial institutions which had disappeared in 1806 and a deep resentment against the guilty parties. In Arndt's case there was also a willingness to replace the older forms of union with a new state. Mixed together with these patriotic and nationalistic sentiments, however, was a xenophobic anti-Semitism similar to what we have observed in the Rhineland. Jahn's emphasis on ethnic purity would soon burst forth into "hatred for Jews,"[5] as Hans-Ulrich Wehler

3. Cited in Pinson, *Modern Germany*, 35.

4. Cited in Hans-Ulrich Wehler, *Deutsche Gesellschaftsgeschichte* ... (Munich, 1987), 1:523.

5. Ibid., 2:335.

describes it, while Arndt preached openly against the Jews and the alleged Jewishness of the French Enlightenment. These were troubling traditions against which the newer, more tolerant trends of the German Enlightenment progressed with great difficulty. Unfortunately, the violence and warfare that returned to Germany after 1812 brought progress toward tolerance to a standstill.

* * * *

Napoleon stood at the height of his power in 1812. Belgium, the Rhineland, Holland and the Hanseatic coast were annexed to France, while Bonaparte, his loyal generals, or family members ruled in Italy and Spain. The Rhenish Confederation extended French power and influence into central Europe, contributing greatly to the involuntary subordination of Prussia and Austria. Napoleon had never succeeded in taming the Russian eagle, however, and during 1810 and 1811, relations steadily deteriorated. Alexander knew that cooperation with Bonaparte was disliked by his people and that participation in the Continental Blockade was against Russian economic interests. When France violated the Treaty of Tilsit by annexing the North German Duchy of Oldenburg, whose heir was married to Alexander's sister, both countries began to prepare for war.

The Grand Army crossed the River Nieman into Russian Poland in late June 1812. Comprised of 450,000 soldiers in the principal army groups, 1,200 cannon, and 150,000 troops in reserve, it was the largest and most intimidating invasion force in history. Included in this "army of twenty nations," as it was called, were 180,000 Germans from the Rhenish Confederation, Austria, and Prussia. The Russians could field only 180,000 men and were therefore forced into a strategy of evasion and orderly retreat. This proved to be surprisingly successful. Desertion among the non-French contingents, disease, and casualties had reduced the Grand Army by a third when Smolensk fell in August, and at Borodino in September, Napoleon could concentrate only 130,000 soldiers. A bloody victory there led to the occupation and burning of Moscow, inescapable supply problems, and the beginning of Napoleon's catastrophic withdrawal in October. Snow, partisans, and Kutuzov's pursuing soldiers exacted a terrible revenge. Hardly 60,000 men straggled out of Russia in December.

The high military drama of 1812 initiated a series of events in 1813 which successively weakened Napoleon's hold on Germany. After months of characteristic indecision, Frederick William III announced his belligerency in March. It is significant that his ministers had first secured an alliance with Russia which guaranteed Prussian acquisitions in eastern and northern Germany in return for cession of Polish lands to Russia. In April 1813, Austria withdrew from the French camp into a sort of armed neutrality. Saxony and Bavaria quickly appealed to Vienna for support. Napoleon's victories against Russo-Prussian forces at Lützen and Bautzen in May shored up French influence in the Rhenish Confederation, but these were Bonaparte's last conquests. Although Metternich continued to worry about substituting Russian for French hegemony in Europe, he abandoned negotiations with Napoleon in August. Austria's entry into the coalition set the stage for the climactic "Battle of the Nations."

In early October 1813, Napoleon had stationed approximately 200,000 soldiers around Leipzig. Faulty reconnaissance from cavalry units unable to recover completely from the Russian debacle blinded the still-dangerous victor of Austerlitz. But he knew that several allied armies of combined superior strength were converging on his position from the north and south. The obvious strategy was to move in one direction or the other and defeat the allies in separate engagements. He waited four days in the old fortress of Bad Düben, north of the city, in a foul mood brought on by uncharacteristic indecision. Finally, Napoleon decided to march toward Leipzig.

On the morning of 16 October, the French and their German allies were battle-ready with about 130,000 soldiers along a four-mile front south of the city. Orders were dispatched at first light to Marshals Marmont and Ney, still a half-day's march north of the city, to move quickly south. Three Austrian, Prussian, and Russian armies attacked in the morning hours with all units available in advance positions – around 90,000 troops. The goal was to break through the center of Napoleon's line. One hundred French canons, placed side by side, brutally decimated the attackers. Sensing a smashing success as in former times, the French Emperor ordered the church bells in Leipzig to ring victory. His left flank, under Marshal MacDonald, swung over to the offensive, piercing one mile into the allies's right. Simultaneously, about 9,000 cavalrymen under Marshal Murat, the King of Naples, counterattacked in the center. The thundering horsemen and their impetuous commander overran the allied forward lines and galloped wildly forward. It seemed to be the moment of glory for Napoleon. But reinforcements were moving north to stop MacDonald, and in the center, 10,000 cavalrymen counterattacked in what became one of the greatest horse engagements of modern times. The frustrated French emperor waited vainly for Marmont – pinned down, he would later learn, by powerful allied forces under General Blücher which had assaulted from the north in the late morning. Ney had marched promptly south as ordered, but, inexplicably, never reached the battlefield. The moment of victory was lost.

The seventeenth of October was a necessary day of rest. On 18 October, however, 300,000 Austrian, Prussian, and Russian soldiers resumed the battle. Napoleon, with 160,000 effectives, fought bravely and wisely, but had no chance. As rear guard units defended Leipzig unsuccessfully on 19 October, Napoleon and the main army retreated westwards. In the succeeding weeks, French units retreated to the Rhine, the Kingdom of Westphalia teetered, and the Rhenish Confederation collapsed. By Christmas 1813, Germany was "liberated" after two decades of French domination.

* * * *

The battles of 1813 produced an interesting mix of modern nationalism and traditional patriotism in Germany. In Berlin, the excitement of the liberation from Napoleon transformed many Prussian patriots into nationalists. Thus Jahn spoke out for a Greater Germany built upon the foundations of existing Austria and Prussia, but including Switzerland, Denmark, Holland, and a new capital city of Teutonia on the Elbe. Although his goals were less ambitious, Schleiermacher nevertheless envisioned the creation of "one true German Empire, powerfully representing the entire German folk and territory to the outside world, while internally allowing the various states and their princes a great deal of freedom."[6] Stein,

6. Cited in Sheehan, 379.

Clausewitz, and Boyen also returned from Russia with hopes for a united Germany. "I have but one Fatherland, and that is Germany," wrote Stein. "You may do with Prussia what you like."[7] "All of Germany" is what motivated Boyen. "If the princes do not want this, the people will know how to follow us."[8] It is doubtful, however, that many common people shared these dreams. Recent research on the free corps units – which always figured prominently in later nationalistic accounts of the period – reveals that these colorful voluntary detachments which fought alongside the regular army were not a vanguard of German unification. To be sure, as explained in Part II, there were many enthusiastic students and young civil servants who joined up, ready to fight in war and peace for their ideals. But Jahn, who wore the black blouse of the famous Lützow Corps, was disappointed in the small number of nationalistic young men who joined him. In fact, of the approximately 30,000 free corps fighters, most were artisans (41 percent) or peasant sons and servants (30 percent). These figures reflected the traditional allegiance of handicraftsmen to the Hohenzollern crown and the loyalty of many noblemen who, as in centuries past, were able to dragoon their peasants into military service for Prussia.

Trends elsewhere in Germany were even more disappointing to the small but growing number of ardent nationalists in Berlin. For instance, less than a third of the Lützow Corps, whose founders wanted to attract an all-German following, was recruited from lands outside Prussia. Lower class adherence to the status quo in southern and western Germany was matched by governmental actions there which dashed the hopes of Prussian nationalists for a new German state. In October 1813, Metternich negotiated an agreement with Bavaria which guaranteed this state full sovereignty in return for abandoning the Rhenish Confederation and rendering military assistance to the allies. Austria signed similar treaties in November and December with Württemberg, Baden, Hesse-Darmstadt, Hesse-Kassel, Nassau, and Saxe-Coburg. These deals not only contributed to Bonaparte's surrender in April 1814, but also assured Austria a significant degree of influence in postwar

7. Ibid., 320.
8. Cited in Wehler, 1:529.

Germany. With the backing of Russia, meanwhile, Prussia was prepared to present its list of territorial demands at peace talks scheduled to begin at Vienna in September. As we shall see in Part II, the reemergence of Austria and Prussia as great powers left no room for a nationalistic agenda.

* * * *

There would be one more round of bloodshed before the revolutionary era passed. Unable to accept defeat, Bonaparte escaped from Elba in March 1815, returned triumphantly to Paris, and raised another army. English and Prussian armies brought an end to Napoleonic ambition at Waterloo in June, thereby avoiding another destructive campaign in the Rhineland where Austrian and Russian armies were concentrating. Germans would be spared the ravages of war, for the most part, until 1866.

The Germany which looked forward to peace in 1815, however, was vastly different from the Germany which Campe and Humboldt traveled through in 1789. The Holy Roman Empire and the plethora of small ecclesiastical and city states were gone. Austria, which had fought to restore the old imperial order in 1809, had no plans to do so under a more pragmatic Metternich in 1815. As the empire disintegrated, new states with ambitious reform policies emerged in southern Germany and managed to survive the final turbulent years of the era. Prussia and Austria had also withstood the challenge of revolutionary France. Prussia faced this challenge, however, by embarking upon social, economic, and political reforms similar to those undertaken in the Rhenish Confederation, whereas Austria persevered with most of its traditional institutions. These contrasting responses to the gauntlet thrown down by France would effect the outcome of the Austro-Prussian rivalry as each came to see in the other its major challenger in the new age.

Part II

THE VIEW FROM VIENNA

The bright autumn morning had already reduced the mountain fog to a silvery ring which clung reverently to the parapets and outer buildings of the castle. To the hundreds of university students assembling below in the market square of Eisenach, the famous Wartburg, towering above them in its historic majesty, seemed to be rising from the fragrant incense of a religious ceremony. Indeed the political mission which had brought them to the heart of Saxe-Weimar on the eighteenth of October 1817 was rife with religious overtones. Almost three hundred years earlier, Martin Luther had translated the Bible from Greek into German on this sacred spot, thus facilitating the cultural unification of Germany. Four years earlier to the day, Germany had freed itself from Napoleonic hegemony outside Leipzig. Now the students would march to the Wartburg to demonstrate their longing for political unification in a new Reich free of despotism. They set off with every church bell ringing. Strolling in double file into the woods, their long column of black coats and oak-leaved hats soon stretched toward the holy summit.[1]

1. For detailed desriptions of the Wartburgfest of 1817, see Dietrich Georg Kieser, *Das Wartburgfest am 18. October 1817: Seiner Entstehung, Ausführung und Folgen nach Aktenstücken und Augenzeugnissen (Jena, 1818)*; Günther Steiger, *Aufbruch: Urburschenschaft und Wartburgfest* (Leipzig, 1967); and Lutz Winckler, *Martin Luther als Bürger und Patriot: Das Reformationsjubiläum von 1817 und der politische Protestantismus des Wartburgfestes* (Lübeck, 1969).

A greeting party of town magistrates, professors, and guests of honor waited in the Wartburg's long, narrow inner courtyard, busying themselves with the final preparations. Shortly they noticed the sounds of patriotic singing. Its youthful resonance rolled upward, reverberating ever louder between the walls as the lead group made the final steep ascent to the gate. The first student to enter carried the sword of the host fraternity from Jena. Next came four "men of the castle" from faraway towns to symbolize German unity. Behind them marched a party with a large flag derived, it was said, from the colors of the old Reich, and the same colors worn by the Lützow Free Corps: horizontal red and black bars, gold fringe, and an oak-leave cluster in the center. After circling the courtyard, the procession entered the musty medieval darkness of the huge rectangular Knight's Hall, opened by town officials especially for this occasion after decades of neglect. Once the banner was secure in its standard, there was a benediction and rousing singing of Luther's "A Mighty Fortress." Now Heinrich Hermann Riemann, a theology student from Jena who had fought with Lützow and the Prussian militia, mounted the speaker's platform. His long, narrow face, Iron Cross, and soldierly bearing were in perfect harmony with the serious mood of the assemblage.

Riemann knew that his brothers expected an oration from the heart, not a stiff and formal recitation from a prepared text. He gave them what they wanted. They were gathered within the Wartburg's holy walls to seek inspiration from the past for "living action in the present." Four long years had passed since the glories of Leipzig. "Then the German people had high hopes. Now these hopes have all been frustrated. Everything turned out differently than we expected. Many grand and noble dreams that could have happened – that had to happen! – were left undone. Many pure and holy emotions have been treated with scorn and derision! Of all the princes in Germany, only one has kept his word – the one whose free land is the site of our celebration."

Many Germans, Riemann continued, had retreated from political life into business or academia as some kind of compensation for the dashing of their ideals. Some had even withdrawn across the sea to another world in America. Was this, he asked them, what they wanted? "No! Not now, not ever! In times of danger we recognized God's will and followed him. We must now hold fast to that which we came to know then – hold fast as long as a drop of blood flows in our veins! The spirit which brought us all together here – the spirit of truth and justice – should guide us all our lives so that we, all brothers and sons of one and the same Fatherland, may build a brazen wall against every internal and external enemy of this Fatherland!"

"Thou, Luther, God and man, thou solid rock of Christ's church, thou who hast fought with iron courage against the darkness, thou who hast subdued the devil in this very castle: hear our solemn promise. Ye, ghosts of our fallen heroes Schill and Scharnhorst ... and all of ye others who shed thy hearts' blood for the glory and freedom of the Fatherland, ye who float above us in eternal clarity and peer clearly into the future: we appeal to thee to bear witness to our vow. Thoughts of thee shall give us strength in every struggle and make us able for every sacrifice. Hate of the righteous and damnation to those who forget in their lowly, dirty selfishness the common good!"[2]

Riemann's peroration left few eyes in the hall dry. His stirring words stayed with the students as they filed back into the open air for an intermission before the midday banquet. Suddenly one of the fraternity brothers standing near the wall noticed a column of troops passing through the valley far below. Closer inspection disclosed that it bore the colors of the Second Pomeranian Regiment, finally returning home from the wars. As every patriot knew, this was the same unit which had defended the Fortress of Kolberg in 1807 against overwhelming odds. A great cheer went up from the young men packed onto the parapet. Here, surely, was a good omen for the cause they had just vowed to uphold.

2. Riemann's speech is in Kieser, 104-10.

Chapter 5

The German Confederation and Conservatism Triumphant

The resolution of the German question which so upset the students, professors, and dissidents who assembled on the Wartburg began at Paris three years earlier. The victorious allies pledged themselves in the Treaty of Chaumont to a "Germany composed of sovereign princes unified by a federal bond that shall assure and guarantee the independence of Germany."[1] The agreement reflected joint anxieties about security in the event of a resurgent France as well as the particular concern of Austria's chancellor, Clemens von Metternich, that Prussian expansionism be checked within a German league controlled by Austria. In fact, Prussian policy discussions prior to the Congress of Vienna veered between the schemes of statesmen like Baron Stein and Wilhelm von Humboldt, who were genuinely committed to the notion of a German union as some kind of replacement for the old Reich, and the pragmatic preference of Chancellor Karl August von Hardenberg for Prussian domination of North Germany. Although many discussions took place, Vienna and Berlin had not proceeded beyond the general wording of Chaumont when the congress opened in September 1814.

The Prussian delegation headed by Hardenberg and Humboldt arrived with a fully developed plan. The states of German Europe

1. Cited in Enno E. Kraehe, *Metternich's German Policy: The Congress of Vienna, 1814-1815* (Princeton, New Jersey, 1983), 16.

would be grouped into seven districts or circles. Two of the circles (Brandenburg and Westphalia) were to be under Prussian control; two under the Habsburgs (Bohemia and Austria); and one each under Hanover, Württemberg, and Bavaria. An upper Council of Circle Chiefs, a lower diet for all other states within the circles, a court system, and a military mechanism gave the proposal a facade similar to the Holy Roman Empire. But appearances could not disguise the fact that Prussia was essentially offering Austria joint control of a new Reich. Metternich sought to allay Bavarian fears by castigating the plan as "so bizarre" that he "rejected it on the spot."[2]

Characteristically, the Austrian counterproposal was more subtle. Like Prussia's, it sought to accommodate England, whose king ruled Hanover, and Russia, whose tsar was the nephew of King Frederick of Württemberg. But the wily Austrian diplomat hoped to mollify Hanover, Württemberg, and Bavaria – and to contain Prussia – by reducing the number of circles to five and giving each of these three states, Prussia, and Austria one vote in the council. Austria, moreover, would have executive power in this upper chamber. Although Hanover and Prussia agreed, Bavaria and Württemberg balked, Frederick asserting that "there could be no thought of decreasing or limiting the existing sovereign power now held by his supreme majesty."[3] The plan was obviously unacceptable to the remaining German princes whose sovereignty was more blatantly threatened. During the winter, negotiations deteriorated to seemingly interminable wrangling among the states. Prussia and its patron Russia almost went to war with the other powers in early 1815 over the division of Saxony and Poland.

Napoleon's escape from Elba in the spring of 1815 provided the external stimulus for ending the bickering and agreeing to a looser form of union. Indeed with the South German states refusing to mobilize unless significant concessions were made to them, and Austria worried that Prussia was again considering a consolidation of its position in North Germany, compromises seemed imperative. By late May, Austria was able to present a draft. Within weeks, thirty-nine "sovereign princes and free cities of Germany" –

2. Ibid., 144.
3. Cited in James J. Sheehan, *German History 1770-1866* (Oxford, 1989) , 400.

all that were left after the Napoleonic Era – had agreed to join a German Confederation.

The system of circles that would have allowed a few large kingdoms to dominate whole regions of Germany was discarded. The statutes called for a federal diet which could meet in full session or in a more streamlined council chaired by Austria. Delegates to these bodies were appointed by the sovereign princes, not elected by the people or upper classes. When the diet met in full session, either a two-thirds majority or, in important matters, unanimity, was required for decisions. Austria, Prussia, Hanover, Württemberg, Bavaria, and Saxony had four votes each, enabling the larger states, if they could unite, to defeat any proposal with over a third of the ballots – but never to force their will on the others which also had more than enough votes to defeat any proposal. The Small Council gave one vote each to the six states above, plus Baden, Hesse-Kassel, Hesse-Darmstadt, Denmark (as ruler in Holstein), and Holland (as ruler in Luxemburg). The remaining duchies and city-states were grouped into six blocs with one vote per bloc. Reflecting its confederate nature, the diet's competency was limited to common German matters like defense and trade, but even here the details were left to future deliberations. Small

Germany 1815-71 12353

wonder that German nationalists who wanted a more unitary state were deeply disappointed.

The federal document stipulated, however, that "in all German states there will be estatist *(landständische)* constitutions."[4] Here was a concession that raised the spirits of the crestfallen, for patriots and nationalists alike saw political participation as just reward for helping the princes oust Napoleon. The proposal originated with the Prussian plan of September 1814. As we know, Hardenberg's faction in Prussia was promoting parliamentary reform. With the extension of "estatist constitutions" to other German lands "we will win for ourselves the good opinion of Germany,"[5] said Prussian General Neidhardt von Gneisenau, especially in South Germany where discussion of parliamentarism had been underway since the days of the Rhenish Confederation of 1806. Within the Hohenzollern monarchy, Stein was another persistent advocate of such ideas. During the summer he had convinced Duke Frederick William of his native Nassau to promulgate an English-style constitution which gave the nobility – the first estate of the realm – an upper chamber, while the lower estates were elected to a representative assembly with some power of the purse. From there the scheme spread to Baden where Minister of State Karl Wilhelm Marschall von Bieberstein, whose brother Ernst Franz had advised the Duke of Nassau on his constitution, circulated a plan for parliamentary institutions in the German states. Significantly enough, the Austrians played along, even agreeing to grant these parliaments "special rights regarding taxes."[6] As Enno Kraehe writes, Metternich was willing to approve a plan so opposed to Austria's reactionary political culture in order to beat the Prussians at their own game. He "did not intend to challenge Prussia with it; rather he desired to provide a common program among the [southern] states he was trying to align against her, but without destroying all possibility of a later reconciliation, for in the long run only by entangling Prussia in the nets of the [Confederation] could she be even partially drawn away from an exclusive

4. Cited in Kraehe, 379.

5. Gneisenau to Arndt, 28 August 1814, in Paul R. Sweet, *Wilhelm von Humboldt: A Biography* (Columbus, 1980), 2:257.

6. Cited in Kraehe, 281.

dependence on Russia."[7] During the rush to find widespread support for the Confederation during the Spring of 1815, however, all specific mention of parliamentary tax rights was struck in favor of the vague reference to "estatist constitutions." With Napoleon on the march again, here, too, the operative details were too divisive to permit agreement.

The coming of peace in the summer of 1815 soon provided more disappointments on the constitutional front. For traditional elites in many states employed the word *landständisch* to justify a return to historical arrangements which had allowed noblemen, clergymen, and guildsmen to monopolize politics. These *altständische* institutions reappeared, for example, in the urban republics of Hamburg, Bremen, Lübeck, and Frankfurt where merchant and artisan interests had ruled in the time of the Holy Roman Empire. Corporate bodies were also restored or reconstituted in Hesse-Kassel, Brunswick, Hanover, the two Mecklenburgs, the three Anhalts, and the four Reuss states. In the Kingdom of Saxony, moreover, the old nobility and upper clergy were returned to their ensconced position in the first chamber, while delegates from the towns and landholders of common birth were relegated to a less influential lower house. It is important to distinguish between restorative developments like these (which set the clock back to an earlier time) and the altogether new assembly created in Nassau. Indeed Duke Frederick William was trying to *prevent* the old nobility from recapturing its former influence by coopting broader middle class elements into the state. Almost unnoticed by contemporaries, representative bodies like Nassau's were promulgated in Waldeck, Schwarzburg-Rudolstadt, Schaumburg-Lippe, and the much more prominent Saxe-Weimar.

Postwar trends in Württemberg are a good illustration of these social and political dynamics. King Frederick was easily one of the greatest beneficiaries of the turbulent revolutionary period. His new kingdom had not only extended the territory of the old Duchy, but he had also exploited the situation to break the back of the estates – in this case, town magistrates and clergymen who had effectively shared power with the Dukes of Württemberg. In

7. Ibid. 281.

early 1815, however, Frederick faced a new challenge from the imperial nobility of Württemberg: petty princes who sought to replace their former rights under the defunct Holy Roman Empire with political control in Württemberg. To forestall this threat, Frederick decided to establish a unicameral legislature with wide-ranging powers. The imperial knights would be outnumbered by elected representatives loyal to the king. He hoped to prevent the towns from wielding their "good old rights" by denying magistrates the vote. But the scheme quickly went awry. The elections of March 1815, produced a divided yet hostile majority composed of noblemen, lawyers (who spoke for the disenfranchised magistrates), and radicals who felt Frederick had not gone far enough in the direction of parliamentarism. Until his death in October 1816, the beleaguered monarch sought vainly for a way out of the embarrassing impasse.

Meanwhile, as 1816 gave way to 1817, no news was heard of constitutions in the other large states. In Baden and Bavaria, officials were secretly at work on modern-style constitutions, but felt no special need to hurry their deliberations. Austria reconstituted older estatist diets in the provinces of Tyrol, Bohemia, and Galicia, but neither Emperor Francis nor Metternich wanted to restore real powers to the local nobility, hence these bodies were granted purely consultative rights. It was only a slight exaggeration, therefore, when Heinrich Hermann Riemann protested on the Wartburg that Duke Karl August of Saxe-Weimar was the only German prince who had kept his word. For, with the exception of the tiny duchies mentioned above, this was the only state of even moderate significance which had established a representative assembly.

Developments in Prussia, where Riemann had earned the Iron Cross, are of particular significance to our story. Hardenberg had proceeded in his constitutional direction for years with the confidence that he had the ear of the king. As early as 1810, the struggling people of Prussia were promised a constitution. The pledge was repeated months before the Battle of the Nations, then distributed for public scrutiny in July 1815. Even before the final defeat of Napoleon, however, King Frederick William III had slowly begun to assert himself against the forward-looking designs of his chancellor. The draft of Hardenberg's aide, Frederich Stägemann, was altered in its published version to avoid the notion of Prussian-wide elections and permit an opening toward *altständische* institutions. Reflecting the monarch's determined bid to preserve sovereignty, however, the Prussian estates would have merely consultative influence. With Napoleon in seemingly permanent captivity on St. Helena, even these backsliding concessions appeared doubtful. Reactionary advisers around the king who were in contact with Metternich urged caution, while the monarch himself, disturbed by his counterpart's ongoing debacle in Württemberg, opted for a fact-finding survey of the provinces rather than the potentially embarrassing convening of a constitutional assembly in Berlin. The cumbersome process did not begin until the autumn of 1817. Impatient petitioners from the Rhineland, meanwhile, submitted a petition to Berlin. Its author, Joseph Görres, who had once welcomed the French Revolution, noted that the fires of liberty could not be extinguished. Rather, "those who are supposed to put them out will themselves go up in flames."[8]

It is against the backdrop of these escalating political events in Prussia and Germany that the culminating demonstration on the Wartburg must be understood. Its deepest roots extended back to the time of Napoleonic victories in Germany when courageous, nationalistic words began to sound from the pulpits and lecterns of Friedrich Schleiermacher and Ernst Moritz Arndt in Berlin, Heinrich Luden in Jena, and the brothers Friedrich Gottlieb and Karl Theodor Welcker in Giessen. By 1815 their first students and followers were young lawyers, pastors, civil servants, and professors whose places at the feet of the fiery orators were taken by a new generation of students. Many of these professionals and students were veterans eager to translate ideals into action. Emanating particularly from Giessen and spreading throughout the Southwest, German Societies came into being to discuss political strategy and circulate petitions to the princes.

Friedrich Ludwig Jahn's nationalistic gymnastic movement was a second important source of unrest after its founding in 1811. The gymnasts who returned from the last campaigns spread the

8. Cited in Walter M. Simon, *The Failure of the Prussian Reform Movement, 1807-1819* (New York, 1971), 131.

popularity of the movement among university students in Prussia, and, at Jahn's urging, to nearby Jena, which enjoyed the civic freedoms of Saxe-Weimar's new constitution. It was also in Jena where the new, politically minded fraternity movement got its start in 1815. Inextricably bound together with the petition and gymnastic movements, the *Burschenschaften* quickly spread to Halle, Göttingen, Giessen, Marburg, Berlin, and other university towns in the Germanic Confederation.

All three movements were insistent that the princes introduce freedom of press, speech, assembly, and religion; guarantee the sanctity of property; establish equality before the law; and anchor these liberties minimally in state constitutions – but preferably in a constitution for one, united Germany. It was this lofty purpose which drew over 450 demonstrators to Eisenach in October 1817.

It is almost impossible to exaggerate the controversy stirred up by the Wartburg Festival, as it was called. Riemann's curse of damnation to the princes was a clear enough message, but that night when the students marched back to the summit in traditional torchlight procession even more disturbing events occurred. Before a blazing bonfire, Ludwig Rödiger of Jena proclaimed that "those who are allowed to bleed for the Fatherland also have the right to speak about how they can best serve the Fatherland in peacetime ... For, thank goodness, the time has come when Germans need no longer fear the poison pen of spies and the executioner's axe of tyrants."[9] Then his friends threw numerous reactionary publications into the flames after reading a few well-chosen lines from each one. The chants of "into the fire" grew louder as Rödiger's classmates worked themselves up into a nationalistic frenzy. Finally, three additional items selected carefully for their symbolic political importance were tossed into the inferno: an Austrian corporal's cane and a uniform from the Prussian Ulanen cavalry, to thumb noses at the two great German Powers, and the braided, pigtail queue from a Hessian official's wig, to warn the small states to break from their outmoded practices and keep their political promises. Afterwards a messenger with another petition was dispatched to the Federal Diet in Frankfurt to compel action before the spirit of the times (Zeitgeist) took a more violent turn.

9. Rüdiger's speech is in Kieser, *Das Wartburgfest* , 114-27.

Frederick William III was irate: "It is an urgent duty," he notified one of his ministers, "to counteract vigorously the highly dangerous and criminal state of mind which has gained ascendancy among the inexperienced youth of the German universities." Even the free-thinking General Gneisenau, whom no one could accuse of reactionary tendencies, was taken aback: "The demand for a constitution is getting dangerously out of hand, and some Jacobin yeast is mixing in with it."[10]

Austrian representatives in Frankfurt were soon surprised to learn that the students' emissary, Karl Theodor von Beck, was making headway among the delegations with his demands for constitutional action. This was especially true of Bavaria and Baden. The head of the Bavarian team warned Munich that it was "high time" to pay heed to "the loud and general call of the German peoples." Moreover, it could be "dangerous" to oppose "the public voice"[11] with force. Metternich sought to sooth the Bavarians, while scheming simultaneously for federal resolutions which would prepare the ground for old-style – yet powerless – provincial diets that would not threaten his bid to buttress the power of the crown. This Bavaria could not tolerate, for a truly representative assembly was necessary to integrate new territories into the kingdom and provide incentives to holders of wealth to support their state financially. With the exact same needs, Baden also viewed with alarm the possibility of a reactionary decision in Frankfurt.

Preemptive steps were the logical result. Bavaria hurried forward with a constitution in May 1818, while Baden followed suit in August. Both documents provided for upper chambers to assuage the fears of the nobility and soften the blow in Vienna. More importantly, however, the lower houses were charged with representing the whole country, not one class, special interest, region, or town. Suffrage was based on a variety of limited property qualifications, and both assemblies received power of the purse and the right to participate in domestic legislation. Grand Duke Karl of Baden and King Max Joseph of Bavaria retained impressive exec-

10. Both citations are from Simon, 134-35.

11. Johann Adam Aretin's report of 21 November 1817, is in Karl Otmar von Aretin, *Bayerns Weg zum souveränen Staat: Landstände und konstitutionelle Monarchie 1714-1818* (Munich, 1976), 243.

utive powers, but with these constitutions, two of the bigger German states had stepped into the parliamentary era.

Austria was not pleased. The demonstrative effect of South German constitutionalism was obviously something which neither Francis nor Metternich could take lightly. Would their noblemen and bourgeoisie demand similar institutions? Worse still was the possibility that Prussia's monarch might succumb to the Zeitgeist, thereby prompting other German states to yield to their people – with the result that Austria would be politically isolated in the Confederation. The key to control of Germany, it appeared, lay in Prussia. Hence the Austrian chancellor worked diligently throughout 1818 to shore up the Hohenzollern king. Contacts at the Prussian court, written memoranda to Hardenberg, and personal appeals to Frederick William at international congresses were all employed.

Burning of the books at the Wartburg, 1817.

It was as difficult in Vienna – as it remains now – to assess the effectiveness of these intrigues. Thus Hardenberg was severly reprimanded by his king for reporting to the federal diet that Prussia was progressing toward a country-wide legislature. The beleaguered head of state could not permit "this extremely difficult and involved matter to be hurried, just because it appears to have been delayed." Frederick William also found time to answer the Rhenish petition of the previous autumn: "I [alone] will determine when the promise of a constitution shall be fulfilled, and I will not be swayed by untimely remonstrances from steadily progressing towards this goal."[12] Metternich obviously had no definite assurances one way or the other. What was disconcerting, however, was Frederick William's seeming determination someday to keep his parliamentary promise. The granting of ministerial portfolio to Wilhelm von Humboldt in January 1819, along with the new minister's immediate submission of a pro-constitutional memorandum, lengthened the pessimistic shadow in Vienna.

A truly shocking event in March 1819 brightened prospects for Metternich. Karl Sand, a radical theology student from Giessen who had accompanied the black, red, and gold colors into the Wartburg, brutally assassinated August von Kotzebue, a conservative publicist and playwright. Having thrust his dagger in the cause of freedom, Sand stabbed himself, proclaiming: "Thank you, God, for the victory."[13] The manipulator of events in Vienna knew, like all Germany, that it was an "evil" deed. Nevertheless, he calmly stated to an aide that "[it is] my concern to turn the affair to good account."[14]

For the most part, he succeeded. Meeting with Frederick William at Teplitz in June, Metternich easily obtained a commitment from the angry, frightened monarch that estatist institutions in Prussia would not proceed beyond the largely meaningless provincial diets favored in Vienna. Hardenberg was forced to scuttle all other plans, and in succeeding months, Humboldt and other progressive ministers were dismissed. All that remained of earlier promises was another pledge to convene a representative assembly should the kingdom need to borrow money from its people – an eventuality which budget cuts, it was hoped, would postpone indefinitely.

In Württemberg, however, Metternich was rebuffed. Parliamentary developments there had advanced from the political chaos of 1816 to a workable compromise in the summer of 1819: the nobility would be entrenched in a meaningful upper chamber; town magistrates and others who owned enough property would have budget rights in a lower house that represented the entire king-

12. Citations from Simon, 131, 133.

13. Cited in Sheehan , 407.

14. Cited in Simon , 139.

dom. Before the final vote in September, Metternich attempted to intimidate the constitutional convention by announcing that "the outcome of the Württembergian Assembly will perhaps determine the fate of Germany."[15] In a demonstration of courageous defiance, however, the delegates unanimously approved Germany's next modern constitution.

Unanimity was required in September 1819, for that same month Metternich was proceeding to the next stage of his campaign to gain control of the German Confederation. Hoping to capitalize on the widespread fear resulting from Sand's crazed act, he found approval at the Federal Diet for oppressive decrees which a caucus of ministers from ten states had drafted at Carlsbad the previous month. Each government in the Confederation had to ensure that its professorate would not disseminate "harmful ideas which would subvert public peace and order and undermine the foundations of the existing states." Guilty teachers could not be rehired in another German state. Censorship of the press would be tightened, moreover, by a new federal coordinating commission. The final agreement of the infamous "Carlsbad Decrees" called for a central investigating committee based in Mainz whose charge was to trail and uproot "revolutionary agitation discovered in the several states."[16]

But Metternich's revenge was not yet complete. That November he convened another series of ministerial sessions which resulted in the so-called Final Acts of Vienna. These agreements, accepted by the Frankfurt diet in July 1820, put a definitive, Draconian stamp on the loosely-worded federal documents of 1815. Unanimity was still required for important decisions, but the diet could only vote on, not debate, resolutions presented to it. The confederate governments had the right to intervene militarily in a separate state's affairs, moreover, if that state was paralyzed by disorder. Finally, all princes were prohibited from accepting a constitution "that would limit or hinder them in the fulfilment of their duties to the Confederation."[17] This final provision was too much

15. Cited in Hartwig Brandt, *Parlamentarismus in Württemberg 1819-1870* (Düsseldorf, 1987), 31.

16. Cited in Sheehan, 408.

17. Ibid., 408-09.

for King William of Württemberg, who tried to move his cousin, Tsar Alexander, to intervene. But Metternich had Prussia at his side, and Alexander decided not to meddle. "A word spoken by Austria," gloated the Austrian chancellor, "is an unbreakable law for Germany."[18] As James Sheehan aptly concludes, "the Confederation ... became a kind of counter-revolutionary holding company through which Metternich could co-ordinate governmental action against his political enemies."[19]

Everything had turned out differently than the German Societies and dissident movements had expected. Riemann said in 1817 that student plans for a liberal and united fatherland – dreams which they assumed would inevitably be fulfilled – had stalled. His remarks on the Wartburg indicate that this young man had already come to appreciate the rhythm of history and politics. Nothing is inevitable or given or automatic. Developments are always negotiated with the outcome dependent on the skill of the negotiators and the *power* at their disposal. In this struggle, the Riemanns, Rüdigers, and Becks of the nationalist movement were sorely outmatched. History has rarely produced a politician as skillful and deceptive as Clemens von Metternich. The stubbornness and pride of Frederick William III is also too easily overlooked by historians drawn to his admittedly more illustrious ministers. In Germany, moreover, *power* resided primarily in Vienna and Berlin. Metternich was nevertheless right in assuming throughout this turbulent period that the political destiny of Germany hung in the balance. The outcome, as described above, allowed the clouds of a reactionary and oppressive regime to settle over the German Confederation – clouds which did not really begin to lift until 1848.

18. Cited in Robert D. Billinger, Jr., *Mettnich and the German Question : States' Rights and Federal Duties, 1820-1834* (Newark, 1991), 24.

19. Cited in Sheehan, 409.

Chapter 6

POLITICAL LIFE IN THE ERA OF CARLSBAD

The most prominent characteristic of politics in the decades after Metternich's triumph was repression. For this was indeed an authoritarian era accompanied by much of the ugliness which we know from our own imperfect world. To the fraternity brothers, inspired professors, and agitators pressing for freedom and German unity, life became a difficult and dreary descent into political oblivion. Sand, the unstable assassin, was unable to kill himself. He was nursed to health, tried, and hanged. Sand's mentor, Karl Follen, eventually made his way into exile in the United States. Jahn, the father of the gymnasts, was arrested and locked away in the Fortress of Kolberg for six years. Arndt buried his correspondence under the floorboards, but could not outsmart the police. His professorial career was cut short when Prussia summarily rejected his appointment to the University of Bonn. In Giessen, the brothers Welcker were released from their teaching positions. A similar fate awaited professors throughout the Confederation. Riemann's mentor from Jena, Heinrich Luden, was one of the few notable personalities from the Wartburg to escape this vindictive crusade. Prussian efforts to unseat the demagogic professor failed to impress Weimar authorties, even though two of his colleagues were actually dismissed.

The *Burschenschaften* and gymnastic clubs were everywhere disbanded. They proved, however, more difficult to repress. Jahn's movement seems to have grown in numbers, thriving under the stigma of illegality which is so often attractive to young people. During this decade of political reaction and police surveillance, the fraternities, too, quickly regrouped, even daring occasionally to march in the streets carrying the forbidden black, red, and gold. Students were soon joined by townspeople and craftsmen, thus giving the sects a broader socio-economic base. As police spies were able – all too soon – to report, the movement also grew more single-mindedly nationalistic. The more religiously oriented types like Riemann abandoned politics to those like Arnold Ruge of Jena who created a new secular religion around the old symbols and traditions. In secret gatherings in Halle, Dresden, and on the Kyffhäusser Mountain, where legend said that Emperor Frederick Barbarossa slept, the young radicals unfurled the colors, lit the holy flame, and sang patriotic songs before the sacred German oak tree. "The symbols employed were appeals to the Germanic past," writes George Mosse, "and to historic memories supposedly embedded in the Volkish soul."[1] As is often the case, history was pressed into the service of a future which, it was hoped, would overshadow the miserable present. Although the movement survived the reactionary twenties and bequeathed a new nationalistic tradition to later generations, many of its leaders fell victim to police vigilance. Thus Ruge was soon cooling his heels next to Jahn in Kolberg.

Censorship was another dark side of the Metternichian epoch. The Carlsbad Decrees stipulated that brochures, newspapers, journals, plays, operas, and short books be censored before publication or performance, while longer works (of more than 320 pages) be subjected to post-censorship. Austria set the example in implementing these ordinances which other states were to follow. Indeed, any idea which even obliquely questioned the principle of absolute monarchy or hinted at revolution was suppressed in the Danubian monarchy. Julius Schneller's history of Austria was condemned as Jacobin, for instance, because it did not sufficiently praise the monarchy or the church, while Schiller's "William Tell"

1. George L. Mosse, *The Nationalization of the Masses: Political Symbolism and Mass Movements in Germany from the Napoleonic Wars through the Third Reich* (Ithaca, 1975), 81-82.

was so drastically reworked by the censors that audiences could not recognize it as the piece which had excited Berlin in 1804. Similarly, Franz Grillparzer's play, "King Ottokar's Happiness and End," was held up for two years because police worried that Ottokar's divorce from Margarette might somehow remind Austrians of Napoleon and Josephine.

Newspapers were sometimes allowed more license if they were moderate or conservative and offered advantages to the establishment in the battle of ideologies. Vienna granted the greatest freedom of expression to Johann Cotta's *Allgemeine Zeitung*, which claimed to speak for many different parties, boasted a large circulation throughout the Confederation, and was therefore useful to conservatives as an organ and a source of information. There were definite limits, however, to the censors' tolerance. "If [the *Allgemeine Zeitung*] should proceed, even by ill-tempered insinuation," the Württembergian publisher was told in 1821, "to mishandle the state system, the statesmen, or the state credit of Austria, then our honor – if not our interest – will force us to deny this newspaper entry to our lands."[2] Metternich's close associate, Friedrich Gentz, who penned this warning, complained to his chief that Austrian censorship was "too lowly," to which Metternich replied: "unfortunately." That suppression of ideas could sometimes proceed to counterproductive lengths was something that both appreciated. But Kaiser Francis – who once remarked himself that Austrian censorship was "stupid" – basically wanted no change in the system.

Censorship in southern Germany contributed to the bleak reality of the 1820s. Baden was in many ways the freest German state. But the Carlsbad Decrees represented a sword of Damocles which could fall at any time on the Grand Duchy. For this reason censorship was strict and freedom of the press non-existent. The example made of Württemberg served as a constant reminder. King William had largely ignored the universal censorship decreed at Carlsbad, primarily to allow journalists to promote the cause of constitutionalism in the South. Indeed William hoped to forge a coalition of "Third Germany" between Baden, Württemberg, and

2. Cited in Daniel Moran, *Toward the Century of Words: Johann Cotta and the Politics of the Public Realm in Germany, 1795-1832* (Berkeley, 1990), 214.

Bavaria that would possess the backbone to resist Vienna and Berlin. In 1823, however, Metternich succeeded in uniting the Federal Diet behind an order of execution banning one of Stuttgart's most outspoken organs, the *Teutsche Beobachter*. Faced with the opposition of his fellow princes, William had to abandon his campaign. Indeed Baden had supported the order, as had Bavaria, whose constitution supposedly guaranteed freedom of the press. But the Bavarian king Max Joseph also had to contend with Vienna's criticism of his kingdom's "miserable newspapers"[3] and was therefore in no position to oppose Metternich in Frankfurt.

That Prussia allowed little freedom of expression should come as no surprise. Frederick William ordered his censors in 1819 to permit "freedom of the press," but to guard against "abuses." His conservative officials then stretched the meaning of the final word to ridiculous lengths. Thus General Minutoli's remark that there was little trace of intelligence in the *Berliner Intelligenzblatt* was disallowed because the independent paper was nevertheless published with the king's permission. Schleiermacher's sermons had to be approved by the police in advance and officers were present to ensure that the text was delivered as approved. And when Georg Andreas Reimer's firm sought to publish a new edition of Fichte's *Addresses to the German Nation*, a collection of patriotic speeches from the Napoleonic Wars, it was halted because they were deemed "inappropriate for contemporary times." That the *Addresses* were already widely in circulation made no difference in the witch-hunt atmosphere of the *Demagogenjagd*.[4]

While censorship was undoubtedly taken to extremes by the Confederation's dominant powers, we should nevertheless be careful not to condemn the effort itself as absurd. Indeed it made a great deal of sense for these regimes to err on the side of caution. For, as important as underlying material conditions can be in determining action or inaction, what one reads, sees on the stage, or is told by others about truth, goodness, and political virtue is also a weighty factor. This is particularly true of the young, the naive, or

3. Ibid., 208.

4. Literally, the "hunt for the demagogues." This term, and the other citations, are from Heinrich von Treitschke, *Deutsche Geschichte im Neunzehnten Jahrhundert* (Leipzig, 1903), 3:433, 450.

the politically uninitiated. But even seasoned veterans of the political world can be influenced by the definitions of reality that others formulate. We should not forget William Shirer's observation in *The Berlin Diaries* of how twisted and warped his own views seemed when he periodically left the propaganda world of Hitler's Germany for the freer West. Or consider the poet Heinrich Heine's more contemporary advice to Cotta's editor, Gustav Kolb, himself an ex-*Burschenschaftler*. The *Allgemeine Zeitung* had to be sustained "in the liberal spirit, which has so few dedicated organs in Germany." In a time "of intellectual struggle," he continued, "journals are our bastions." Thus the new motto should be, "There are no longer any nations in Europe, only parties."[5] This was essentially the view from Vienna. In supping with Cotta's devil, therefore, Metternich and Gentz wanted to be sure to use long spoons.

* * * *

Frederick William III of Prussia appreciated these realities. For five years after passage of the Carlsbad Decrees, he gave Heinrich von Kamptz, the feared "persecutor of the demagogues," free rein. His police opened mail, searched homes for evidence of plots and intrigues, and made arrests. As in Vienna, the goal of these reactionary policies was to uphold the power of the crown. Frederick William was not a domineering personality, but during his third decade on the throne he grew increasingly adept at preserving his position, not only from those, like Sand and Follen, who strove for truly revolutionary change, but also from those close to the top who sought in more acceptable ways to influence him. Indeed Heine's reference to parties is not as odd as it may seem. While we are accustomed to think of party politics in the modern sense of organized structures, public campaigning, and parliamentary maneuvering, parties also existed in authoritarian monarchies like Prussia. They were usually small circles of like-minded friends who pursued their goals, often in alliance with discussion groups, salons, and sometimes Masonic lodges, which had the same basic objectives, all operating through the private, personal channels available to them. Put more simply, one sought directly or indirectly to influence the king.

5. Heine to Kolb, 11 November 1828, in Moran, *Toward the Century of Words*, 245.

Party politics in Prussia encompassed everything from attempts to procure appointments to influential positions around the monarch to business lobbying from faraway towns like Cologne, Crefeld, and Aachen to change tariff or monetary policy. But there were also more concerted efforts designed to affect the overall direction of the political system itself. These more permanent, ongoing campaigns were waged by two opposing party groupings seeking similar but very distinct goals. One liberal party bloc strove to regain the lost momentum toward modern, parliamentary institutions, while another conservative bloc wanted to weaken the absolute powers of the king by reestablishing the traditional rights of the nobility. Both objects clearly ran counter to the interests of Frederick William. While outright suppression was always an alternative, the Prussian king, as we shall see, opted more often for a clever playing of one party bloc off against the other.

Until his death in 1822, Karl August von Hardenberg was the undisputed leader of the liberal movement. Although it became increasingly difficult for him after Carlsbad to broach such topics to Frederick William, there can be little doubt that he continued to hope for a Prussian parliament. Around him were numerous cliques based on friendship which fanned out into a bureaucracy that he had largely created. Wilhelm von Humboldt was another leading liberal personality. From his villa in Charlottenburg, the ex-minister pursued his studies, entertained politically sympathetic friends, and waited for an opportunity to shape Prussian politics to his liking. Undoubtedly the best connected of Humboldt's associates was Job von Witzleben, one of the king's closest advisers. Alexander von Humboldt recalled that his brother was "Witzleben's truest political and also intimate friend."[6] There were also a number of liberal parties in the army. The most prestigious of these was headed by Neidhardt von Gneisenau, whose personal ties extended throughout the military and into the civilian bureaucracy.

The most influential man in the conservative movement was Friedrich Karl zu Sayn-Wittgenstein-Hohenstein, Minister of the Royal House. Another was Duke Karl of Mecklenburg, comman-

6. Cited in Eric Dorn Brose, *The Politics of Technological Change in Prussia: Out of the Shadow of Antiquity, 1809-1848* (Princeton, 1993), 74.

der of the elite Guard Corps and the king's brother-in-law. A third noteworthy faction among so many was led by Gustav and Caroline von Rochow, scions of an old noble family. In their Berlin mansion, the "party" of the aristocratic "opposition," as Caroline von Rochow described it, discussed "old conservative views"[7] and plotted political strategy. As mentioned above, these highly placed people wanted to strengthen the power of the estates and turn back the clock to a day when Junkers could claim sarcastically that "we want an absolute king – as long as he does our bidding."

The immediate aftermath of Hardenberg's death provides us with an excellent opportunity to peer inside the world of Prussian party politics. Conservatives intrigued at first quite successfully to place one of theirs, Otto von Voss-Buch, in the vacated chancellery. His untimely passing gave the liberals a chance for counter-intrigue. In early 1823, Witzleben exerted all of his influence to convince the king to appoint Wilhelm von Humboldt as chancellor. Now, however, Frederick William groped his way to tactical victory by deciding to appoint no one, allow the office to expire, and thereby enhance his power. The pattern was set in the 1820s for the manipulative strategy mentioned earlier.

The Hohenzollern monarch employed a similar technique in upcoming years to frustrate the parties scheming against him. The conservatives had tried for years to establish estatist diets similar to those which had wielded power over Prussian kings in earlier centuries. In a compromise decision, Frederick William consented to eight provincial diets in 1823, but was careful to insist that they be chaired by royal marshalls, that they never meet simultaneously, and most importantly, that they have merely advisory rights. Liberals like General Ernst von Pfuel greeted the diets as at least a start toward "the organic structuring of the nation,"[8] while conservatives grumbled about a carefully laid plot gone awry. Another conservative effort in 1824 to rescind Hardenberg's anti-guild legislation of 1811, thereby weakening the bourgeoisie, was refused by Frederick William on the grounds that such a move would "only lead to new disturbances"[9] and also because these freedom of

7. Ibid., 53.
8. Cited in Treitschke, 3:365.
9. Cited in Brose, 59.

enterprise laws were beginning to yield significant revenues. In the late 1820s the evermore wily monarch also denied "the better party,"[10] as one conservative labeled his faction, a controlling number of seats on the Council of State, an advisory body of bureaucrats and princes of the royal family which the king allowed rather consistently to influence his decisions. Meanwhile, liberals watched with approval as Kamptz, the pursuer of the "demagogues," was finally restrained, and leaders like Gneisenau promoted to Field Marshall. These examples indicate clearly that Frederick William considered the conservative parties a greater threat to his prerogatives – powers which he refused to yield to either side. It was, noted Karl August Varnhagen von Ense, member of one of the liberal salon cliques, as if "an invisible force reigned in all things," blocking "extremism of all kinds" and constantly "turning everything back to the middle."[11]

The Prussian king had only to look at neighboring states to find reinforcement for the correctness of his own policies. The duchies of Mecklenburg were so thoroughly controlled by their Junkers that legal experts debated whether it was possible to call them centralized states. In Hanover, aristocrats had a confusing array of local, provincial, and central offices in their hands. "The infernal muddle of these relationships showed clearly," wrote Heinrich von Treitschke, "what would have become of Prussia if the feudal party there had succeeded in reestablishing the old diets."[12] And in Saxony King Frederick August wielded a mere fraction of the power that had been at the disposal of his medieval forbearers. The state machinery was dominated by a handful of noble families who doled out important offices and privileges to one another. The church also enjoyed an autonomous position – as did the cities. "Who can oppose God and the City Council of Leipzig,"[13] ran the saying.

Across the border in Austria there was also no question of allowing power to slip away from the monarch. As we have seen, the importance of suppressing dissent and controlling ideas was completely understood in Vienna. There were significant differences,

10. Ibid., 64.
11. Ibid., 62.
12. Cited in Treitschke, 3:547.
13. Ibid., 509.

however, between the political cultures of Germany's two major authoritarian states. One measure of these differences was Francis's preoccupation with the threat of the liberal, not the conservative party groups as in Prussia. The aristocratic opposition was so thoroughly defeated by nearly three centuries of absolutism that – with notable exceptions like the Czech nobility and, above all, the Hungarian Magyars – noblemen rarely questioned the monarch's right to do as he pleased. The king was much more concerned with the political network of Bernard Bolzano, a highly influential professor of theology and Dean of the College of Philosophy at the University of Prague. Bolzano had drunk deeply of the Catholic Enlightment, teaching that progress was inevitable, that a better social order was necessary, and that true Christians could brook no tyranny. His Sunday lectures were a political phenomenon in Prague, attended not just by students but also many colleagues and lay professionals. Disciples of his like Michael Joseph Fesl of Leitmeritz were numerous and well ensconced in the academic establishment. He also had party friends in Vienna like Count Franz von Saurau, Chief Chancellor of the Kaiser. "The Bolzano-Fesl Sect will now conquer the old world," worried one conservative in 1819, "and [the old world] will suffer because of it."[14]

Francis responded to the challenge shortly after Carlsbad. Bolzano was dismissed from his position, Fesl brought in chains to Vienna, and forced, despite the best efforts of Saurau, to renounce his mentor. When Bolzano continued to criticize the regime, Francis warned the Archbishop of Prague about "the bad seeds whose fruits must lead simultaneously to the toppling of our holy religion and the existing state order."[15] Bolzano was brought to trial in 1825 and told to recant – which he refused to do. Realizing that persecution was merely adding to the martyr's following, the king finally agreed to leave Bolzano alone.

The major conservative cause in Austria was restoration of church autonomy. The eighteenth-century reforms of Maria Theresa and Joseph II had reduced the Catholic Church to a posi-

14. Cited in Eduard Winter, *Romantismus, Restauration und Frühliberalismus im österreichischen Vormärz* (Vienna, 1968), 112.

15. Ibid., 153.

tion of dependence on the state: fiscal privileges had been revoked, parishes and dioceses reorganized, monastic orders expelled or disbanded, and education of the clergy and appointment of bishops brought under state control. In the era of Carlsbad, however, conservative spokesmen renewed their argument that a freer church would be more valuable to the state in its struggle against revolutionary ideas and movements. The *spiritus rector* of the conservatives was Clemens Maria Hofbauer, a Redemptorist priest. Most of the court chaplains and Empress Caroline Auguste were under his sway. After Hofbauer's death in 1820, Anton Günther stepped to the fore.

Fairly closely allied with the Hofbauer circle were publicists like Adam Heinrich Müller and Friedrich Schlegel. Here, however, we find arguments similar to those of Prussian conservatives. Both included church emancipation from state tutelage in a broader program to restore the nobility and the guilds to their former autonomy. Francis was clearly impressed with these highly placed conservatives, but, no stranger to party politics, he could be moved to make only a few concessions. The Redemptorists and Jesuits were readmitted to Austria and the church regained the right to appoint its own bishops. The rather one-sided political alliance between church and state was on public display when the emperor visited the pope in 1819. Angry that his allies had settled for less, Schlegel complained bitterly that this joining of two restorationist forces "is meant and pursued as merely a party affair." Even though Hofbauer was "at the head of this party," moreover, Schlegel blurted that he would "certainly not belong to it, even though it will hurt me."[16]

Any discussion of party politics in Austria, of course, must certainly include Metternich. Although he had to share the emperor's ear with other chancellors like Saurau, Metternich was without a doubt the most important personality in Francis's entourage. In fact, most party intrigues, whether spun by "friends, fellow travelers *(gleichgesinnten)*, or opponents,"[17] had to come through or around

16. Ibid., 126.

17. Heinrich Ritter von Srbik, *Metternich: Der Staatsmann und der Mensch* (Munich, 1925), 544.

him. Metternich's party was obviously an international one, extending to agents and contacts in every German capital and to close compatriots like Wittgenstein in Berlin. Indeed, while the influential Austrian chancellor strove above all else to protect the throne from enervation, he thought it would be wise to grant the estates more comprehensive consultative status in Vienna. But a joint proposal in 1818 with Saurau – who, like Prussian liberals, saw this as a bridge to grander institutions – failed to move Francis to action.

After 1826, moreover, the emperor found in Count Franz Anton Kolowrat, the interior minister, a useful tool against a chancellor whom he personally liked, but intuitively knew was growing too powerful. Kolowrat, a Czech nobleman, was the great hope of the liberal parties and the businessmen's lobbies at the end of the decade. Kolowrat himself was a friend of the Czech nobility, but was not above playing this party off against the liberals – and also against Metternich. It is interesting, however, that Kaiser Francis cleverly trumped both Metternich and Kolowrat by exploiting their jealousy of one another. For he preferred "to place two rivals at the head of the government so that he could balance their claims," observed one insider. "In the summer Metternich's plate is full, in the winter, Kolowrat's."[18]

The states of southern Germany offer an interesting basis for comparison with Prussia and Austria. The parliamentary epoch had begun there with all of the confusion and seeming chaos that usually accompanies the early transition from authoritarian to somewhat freer institutions. There is probably a general rule of politics at work in such situations. Authoritarian systems force dissent underground and lend, as we have seen, a private and fragmented structure to party politics. Barring outside interference like that of Metternich, the new liberal order affords these parties and some of the oppositional sects an opportunity to surface and pursue a more open and public brand of politics. But the old party structures persist, cemented by dominant personalities, tight bonds of friendship, suspicion of outsiders, and the continuing need to operate close to the throne. Very gradually, party groupings that had sometimes cooperated before learn to work together under

18. Ibid., 541.

the new rules, and eventually, modern, broad-based parties evolve. In the meantime, parliamentary life is stamped by a fragmentation which hinders and hampers legislative work and a desire for quick change which alarms the established powers. These divisions were exacerbated in South Germany by local particularism and religious splits – the very lack of state-wide integration which their parliaments were designed to overcome in the first place. For these reasons the task of forging efficient, integrated state structures proved much more difficult than any of the southern monarchs and progressive bureaucrats expected.

We have already described the gridlock which characterized politics in Württemberg after 1815. The impasse was finally broken in 1818/1819 when the government made concessions to the nobility and the smalltownsmen, then coopted leaders of the moderate liberal parties like Jakob Friedrich Weishaar, who became president of the lower house in the 1820s. During this decade, in fact, King William and his advisers managed the political scene with great finesse and success. District officials and judges skillfully manipulated elections by arranging candidacies for untroublesome types who would avoid "quarrelsomeness and selfish pretension" and "advance the welfare of the country in union with the government."[19] Later, successful candidates were awarded local offices of the central government, thereby making these politicians even more dependent on Stuttgart. During the elections of 1826, over 48 percent of the seats were captured by officials beholden to the government. The next largest bloc that year were the "political wrens,"[20] local notables and town officials whose party base lay in the hometown. Their parliamentary agendas were their local interests, and they rarely opposed a government which could easily circumvent trouble by promoting some of these interests. William's budgets passed with large majorities in the 1820s, creating the impression of a diet that was more a "subordinate branch of the bureaucracy" than "a legislative power."[21]

19. These instructions of the Ministry of the Interior to district officials of 1819 are cited in Brandt, *Parlamentarismus in Württemberg* , 91.

20. Ibid., 80.

21. Helmut Kramer, *Fraktionsbindungen in den deutschen Volksvertretungen 1819-1849* (Berlin, 1968), 30.

The art of controlling parliament was also practiced with great skill in Bavaria. Max Joseph I and his officials knew how to manipulate bureaucrats elected to the diet by reserving a very political judgement on promotions, favorable assignments, or even leave from work to attend parliament. Regional differences between the Palatinate, the Frankish highlands, and the heartland of southern Bavaria also kept the country's many parties from uniting, as did confessional gaps between Catholics and the Protestant minority (largely from the Palatinate). But Max Joseph did not have his deputies as firmly in hand as William in neighboring Württemberg. Thus the diet's obstinancy and refusal to accept passively all royal initiatives contributed to the king's willingness to undercut Württemberg's plans for a "Third Germany" and join Baden in renewing the Carlsbad Decrees in 1824.

We have wider knowledge of party politics during the early reign of Max Joseph's successor, Ludwig I. Soon after ascending the throne in 1825, Ludwig elevated one of the spokesmen of the liberal parties, Count Joseph Ludwig Armansperg, to the Ministry of the Interior. Like liberals in other German states, Armansperg had an "enlightened" agenda that included working with the diet to eliminate the last vestiges of church autonomy and noble privilege. In a clever attempt to strike a balance, however, Ludwig also appointed Eduard von Schenk to that ministry's Council of Churches and Schools. Like conservatives in Austria, Schenk believed in a restoration of the church's former freedoms. As a believer in church reform, he had ties to "the many-layered political entity"[22] of Bavaria's confessional parties: to the so-called "confederates" around Georg Zirbel in Würzburg; to the zealous "Eos" circle in Munich; and, not surprisingly, to the Hofbauer-Günther and Müller-Schlegel sects in Vienna. In close alliance with the religious reformers was the dominant feudal party in the upper house, also possessing close connections with Vienna through the Austrian embassy in Munich.

Like Frederick William III in Berlin, Ludwig was more wary of the feudal party, while genuinely desiring an accommodation with

22. Heinz Gollwitzer, *Ludwig I. von Bayern: Königtum im Vormärz: Eine Politische Biographie* (Munich, 1986), 368.

those around Schenk. Thus his relations with the upper house were tense – he created new peers in 1828, Armansperg among them, in an unsuccessful attempt to discipline the fractious noblemen. Meanwhile, the minister bombarded the diet session of 1827/28 with legislative proposals on industry, tariffs, taxes, property rights, and military justice designed to further the liberal cause. The lower house reacted instinctively against accepting all that was laid before it, however, and soon a loose grouping of liberal factions began to work for the fall of Armansperg, whom they felt was too ambitious. As liberal infighting worsened, Ludwig began to tire of his minister, complaining in 1829 that "he would really like to rule, not serve."[23] Finally the king shifted the liberal Armansperg to the Foreign Ministry where he could be a useful lever against Metternich. Schenk, who was also scheming against Armansperg, became the new interior minister. "Ludwig saw the need to play the opposing forces off against one another," writes his biographer, "and to assert himself between the 'ultras' of the left and the right."[24] Indeed he played this hegemonic game as successfully as any of his fellow monarchs.

Grand Duke Ludwig of Baden certainly appreciated such artful political maneuvering. Here, as in the other South German states, constitutionalism began as a grand attempt to integrate dispersed territories with no allegiance to the center. As one of his conservative advisers put it, "we have gone out of political childhood into the agitating, highly experimenting years of youth."[25] All too soon, however, the experiment went badly awry. A flurry of reform legislation presented to the first diet in 1819 met determined opposition from elected civil servants like Ludwig von Liebenstein and Ludwig Winter, who felt the proposals were too mild, and other bureaucrats in the diet like Johann von Itzstein, who spoke for small townspeople fearing loss of local autonomy. The Grand Duke saw himself compelled to prorogue the diet that July in hopes of more support when the delegates were reconvened the next year. But matters continued to deteriorate until early 1823 when, in a

23. Ibid., 388.

24. Ibid., 370.

25. Cited in Loyd E. Lee, *The Politics of Harmony: Civil Service, Liberalism, and Social Reform in Baden, 1800-1850* (Newark, 1980), 100.

dramatic 31-30 vote, the diet rejected the budget. Winter, afraid by now that the parliamentary experiment itself was in jeopardy, urged his backers to cooperate. Liebenstein, too, recommended compromise. But Itzstein stood firm, and, on the eve of the final vote, Karl von Rotteck, a liberal professor at the University of Freiburg, instructed his followers to "vote with Itzstein."[26]

While conservatives close to the Grand Duke wrote to Metternich about the "lamentable situation" in Baden, moderates like Winter lambasted fellow civil servants who "have misused the predominance which their knowledge and administrative experience have given them, they have created a party, or at least served to support one, and have placed themselves publicly at its head or led it secretly."[27] The Grand Duke, however, knew quite well how to deal with the situation. Itzstein was fired, the diet dismissed, and the following elections manipulated to such an extent that only a few opponents of the government returned to Karlsruhe. As noted above, Ludwig was easily converted by Metternich into approving the renewal of the Carlsbad Decrees in 1824. Not until news of revolution in France reached Baden six years later would parliament again try to assert itself.

26. Cited in Kramer, 42.
27. Both citations from Lee, 117, 121.

Chapter 7

Society and Economy on the Eve of Early Industrialization

The class contours of German Europe are the first part of our socio-economic analysis. At the apex of society stood thirty-four ruling families like the Habsburgs, Hohenzollerns, and Wittelsbachs, whose heads wielded sovereign power. One rung lower were scores of grand seigneurs like the Schwarzenbergs and Liechtensteins who owned huge *latifundia* , supported bloated household establishments fit for royalty, and often possessed great influence at court. In addition there were eighty former ruling families *(Standesherren)* like the Hohenlohes and Sayn-Wittgensteins, whose principalities had been expropriated after 1789, but who had received extensive rights and privileges at the Congress of Vienna and still owned vast family estates. Representing a tiny fraction of the population, these powerful, prestigious aristocrats were so solidly entrenched that they were invulnerable to property values, price trends, and market cycles. Only wars and revolutions could threaten to topple these dominant clans.

The same could not be said for the lesser nobility. Comprising a few hundred thousand owners of landed properties – sometimes small, sometimes quite extensive – Germany's first estate was forced to compete and survive after 1815 in the freer economic environment shaped by reforming bureaucrats in Prussia and the former Rhenish Confederation. The goal of this legislation, stretching into the 1820s and beyond, was to create strata of peasant and noble farmers who would be free to expand production without the hindrances of serfdom, noble privilege, and common property. In its struggle to preserve rights now challenged, the nobility of German Europe was rarely able to achieve more than a stalemate. In Baden, Württemberg, and Bavaria, bluebloods blocked the distribution of land to their peasants, creating an explosive situation as reformers eventually freed peasants on neighboring state lands. Determined bureaucrats fought back, however, abolishing the nobles' tax exemption and control of local courts in Baden and Württemberg and forcing Bavarian estate owners to accept state sanctioning of their traditional monopoly of local justice. The Prussian Junkers were more successful in guarding their tax and police privileges, but were unable to throttle all land reforms. In 1816 peasants with either secure tenure or with horse or oxen – about 10 percent of all families – received title to a half or two-thirds of the land they had formerly worked with the rest falling to former lords as compensation. Another decree of 1821 initiated the division of the commons, thus removing another pillar of the feudal regime which had provided considerable security for the small man. Some peasants benefited, but this act worked mainly to the Junkers' advantage, for about 80 percent of the common land in East Elbian Prussia was parceled out to nobles who were more adept at manipulating the process. In other parts of the Confederation, noblemen fared variously, ranging from the provinces of Mecklenburg, where fully half of peasant property was taken by voracious nobles, to Saxony, where laws prevented aristocrats from making any substantial gains.

On balance, the noble class probably fared worse by the 1820s and 1830s. Two decades of French rule in the Rhineland, for instance, had decimated the nobility, freed the peasants, and left commoners in control of 96 percent of the land. In many states, moreover, aristocrats experienced considerable difficulty making the transition to a capitalistic economy. Thus the percentage of Bavarian nobleman without landed property grew from a third in 1822 to nearly two-thirds in 1832. The situation was even more desperate in Prussia, where two-thirds of the Junkers had already lost their holdings before the Napoleonic Wars. "Have we not almost become comical title-holders who lack the means?"[1] asked one noblewoman. In one respect, this loss of land was not a net loss to Prussia's traditional upper class, for many properties simply shifted to the deeply entrenched clans of the grand nobility. By 1800, however, between 10 and 15 percent of aristocratic estates in East Elbian Prussia had fallen into bourgeois hands. And the figure continued to move upward: exceeding 20 percent in the 1820s; and passing 40 percent by mid-century. Junkers angrily and sarcastically resigned themselves to the fact, as one of them complained, that they had to mingle on the land with "freshly enobled bureaucrats, enobled or non-enobled plutocrats, converted or unconverted sweat-shop Jews, even for the time being with combed and uncombed scholars."[2]

The economic collapse of broad strata of the German nobility helps to explain the entry of many young noblemen into government service. For there was simply no other way to maintain the status of many families. Over 80 percent of Austria's generals were aristocrats, for example, and about 70 percent of her top administrators. In Bavaria, 60 percent of the ministerial appointments went to blue-bloods, while in Prussia, 54 percent of the officers, 50 percent of the leading diplomats, and 24 percent of the top provincial administrators were titled. It would be a mistake, however, to conclude that German states of the early nineteenth century were controlled by the aristocracy. For one thing, these figures indicate that the cultivated bourgeoisie *(Bildungsbürgertum)* also had a significant presence in the halls of power, even in conservative Austria. More importantly, noble as well as educated middle-class bureaucrats and officers did not simply represent the interests of their social class when they entered government or the army. While class background was never unimportant, one also became part of an institution with all of its departmental and party-political divisions, agendas, and loyalties. As we have argued above, these factional or party fault lines are a better map of the state than the outlines of aristocratic or cultivated bourgeois classes which, although significant, did not dominate. As we have also seen, par-

1. Cited in Brose, *The Politics of Technological Change in Prussia,* 62.
2. Hans-Ulrich Wehler, *Deutsche Gesellschaftsgeschichte* (Munich, 1989), 2:153.

ties were themselves subject to manipulation by monarchs clever about playing one end off against the other.

The urban patriciate also stood close to the apex of society. The well-to-do bankers, merchants, and the most prosperous guild manufacturers of Germany's cities and towns numbered no more than a few hundred thousand and usually represented between 1 and 6 percent of the urban population. The senates and town councils of urban Germany were usually the political preserve of these upper-middle strata. Strategic business marriages between the families of a town were common, as were marital links between bourgeois clans of different towns or nuptial ties to wealthy bureaucratic and academic families. Like those noblemen who survived, moreover, this tiny, exclusive oligarchy used its political and social influence to damn up forces of change – or, barring that, to exploit them.

Throughout the early 1800s, the patriciate fought to maintain itself against central bureaucracies which desired more integration and regulation; industrial entrepreneurs who wanted to transform the means of production; and masses of poor people who pressed before the gates longing to make a new start. As in our times, there is ultimately little authorities can do when people are on the move, but town honoraries achieved some success by erecting barriers to marriage, employment, and residence, and barring most newcomers from welfare privileges and political rights. Similarly, the struggle against the bureaucracy for home rule sometimes registered great success, as in Baden and Saxony, but more typically resulted in concessions to the state. Town ordinances in Prussia, for example, curtailed municipal judicial autonomy and transferred police power to Berlin, while in Austria, cities and towns lost all semblance of independence. The urban patriciate also looked askance at the coming of modern industry. It was an "alien phenomenon," writes Hans-Ulrich Wehler, which threatened to aggravate the social crisis and lead to new political challenges. "Every in-depth socio-historical investigation of the upper and 'Mittelständisch' bourgeoisie of commercial centers like Frankfurt and Magdeburg; port cities like Hamburg, Königsberg, and Wismar; middle-sized provincial cities like Bonn, Göttingen, and Konstanz; but also Rhenish cities like Crefeld and Cologne confirms what widespread, tradition-blessed obstinacy there was in the effort to keep economic activity within customary bounds."[3] It was certainly no coincidence, therefore, that the independent city-republics of Lübeck, Bremen, Hamburg, and Frankfurt/Main opted to continue or reinstate guild privileges from the old regime, for there was no greater or more persistent opponent of modern industrialism than the old handicraft corporations.

The *Mittelstand* of artisans, craftsmen, and small shopkeepers was indeed a conservative social and economic force. Comprising about 13 percent of the German labor force – and anywhere from 9 percent (Barmen) to 48 percent (Göttingen) of the urban population – Germany's petty bourgeoisie strove to stay afloat in a sea of change. With a robust population growth, especially in the cities, demand for most products rose, but the general prosperity of the urban *Mittelstand* fell. It became harder for apprentices and journeymen to progress to master, and most mastercraftsmen, as John Clapham notes, "were simply jobbing workmen, and ill paid at that."[4] Around 75 percent of Berlin's masters did not earn enough to pay taxes, for instance, while in Cologne the figure soared higher to 78 percent.

The cause seems to lie in the rapid influx of newcomers to the handicraft trades: while German population rose 60 percent in the early 1800s (see below), the number of craftsmen increased by 63 percent. The artisans' common lament, understandably, was that legislation had destroyed the ability of the guilds to restrict entry to trades. The French had swept away Rhenish guilds in the 1790s, and many German states followed with laws establishing at least some form of freer enterprise: Austria (1809), Prussia (1811), Nassau (1814), Bavaria (1825), Hesse-Darmstadt (1827), Württemberg (1828), Saxony (1840), and Hanover (1846). The anti-guild legislation of the capital cities penetrated to the German hometowns, undermining about three centuries of corporate efforts to restrict output to the privileged neighborhood shops of the controlling "uncles" and "communarchs."[5] As we shall see in Part III,

3. Wehler, 2:183.

4. H. Clapham, *Economic Development of France and Germany 1815-1914* (Cambridge, 1966), 85.

5. Mack Walker, *German Home Towns: Community, State, and General Estate 1648-1871* (Ithaca, 1971), 106.

these controversial laws were just part of a greater political struggle in Germany over whether to block or to promote industrialization.

State policies also had a significant impact on the peasantry, the main component of Germany's *Mittelstand*. Austrian peasants were generally the least secure in the Confederation. Although legal aspects of serfdom were abolished under Joseph II in the 1780s, the economic bondage that characterized serfdom remained in effect. On the average, Austrian peasants paid approximately one-third of their income to lords or to the state. The peasants of the Rhineland (including the Bavarian Palatinate) were generally the most secure in Germany, having won their freedom and land after France conquered the region. Other parts of Germany fell somewhere in-between. In Hanover, reforms dating from 1802 had established about 40 percent of the peasants as independent farmers by the 1830s, while the Prussian laws of 1816 and 1821 eventually created a class of small to middle-sized landowners and share-croppers comprising about 60 percent of the former serfs. Bavaria was fairly representative of southern Germany. About 24 percent of the peasantry were economically dependent upon noblemen or former ruling families (*Standesherren*) who succeeded in stifling emancipatory legislation, but the remaining 76 percent became free farmers.

Although reforming bureaucrats had accomplished very much, there were nevertheless two explosive aspects to these varying conditions. For one thing, peasants who still lived in serf-like conditions grew angrier by the decade, especially in Baden, Württemberg, and Bavaria where neighboring former state serfs, now freed, provided a constant reminder of lowly status. Even more incendiary was the fact that millions of Germans in the countryside neither owned nor rented any land at all, surviving as day laborers and country outworkers if there was work, drifting to other regions and to the towns if there was none. Many of the smallholders scratching out a living from farms of a few acres were also dependent on odd jobs and cottage industry for their survival – in Bavaria, for example, between a third and a half of all peasants with land. Worse still, dependence on supplemental incomes left most country families vulnerable to cyclic and structural economic changes. Recessions undermined cottage industry as merchant manufacturers cut back on the materials they put out, while farm jobs planting hedges or building fences disappeared after the movement to consolidate former common land had run its course. Too many parents who had children in a prosperous period learned the error of their ways during leaner years. Small wonder that reformers in some German states fostered rural industries in the illusory hope that factory work would absorb Germany's surplus country population. We shall return to this theme in Part III.

* * * *

German society and economy in the 1810s appeared to have changed very little from the days of Martin Luther. The overwhelming majority of Germans lived in farm houses or country villages near the fields where they worked. Transportation throughout the Confederation remained difficult, even for farmers and villagers who rarely ventured far off. There was little sense of time as an entity: it was still marked by the changing seasons, by the rising and setting of the sun, and occasionally by the ringing of church bells. Most towns were small and still easily contained within ramparts and fortifications built in earlier centuries. Homes were constructed in the old ways by craftsmen and artisans proud of their traditional techniques. Candles and wood were the main sources of light and energy, while animals or humans provided most of the power. Mechanized production was still a novelty, confined mostly to a few towns in Austria, Saxony, and Prussia. "A time-traveller, suddenly transported from the sixteenth century," remarks James Sheehan, "would have been amazed at German politics and culture, but would have found the social and economic order quite familiar."[6]

Agriculture was still the main source of livelihood throughout Germany. Saxony was the most industrialized and urbanized state in the German Confederation in the 1820s, yet about 72 percent of the population lived and worked on the land. Agriculture and non-industrial pursuits were even more predominant in Prussia, claiming around 75 percent of the labor force, while in Austria and Bavaria the figure was higher still, rising, respectively, to 84 percent and 88 percent of all workers. Decades of very early industrialization had

6. Cited in Sheehan, *German History*, 470.

little effect on these numbers. Thus Saxony had 66 percent, Prussia 71 percent, and Austria 81 percent at mid-century. Despite considerable investments in public buildings, roads, and railways, moreover, agriculture's share of net investment, which had stood at 70 percent in the 1700s, declined very gradually to 60 percent in 1840.

The inverse, of course, was true of German cities and towns. There were only three cities in the Confederation of 1815 that would qualify as big by today's standards: Vienna (250,000), Berlin (190,000), and Hamburg (135,000). There were another twenty large towns like Breslau (76,000), Dresden (60,000), Frankfurt/Main (50,000), Bremen (36,000), Munich (35,000), and Leipzig (34,000), which, together with Germany's big cities, comprised perhaps 5 percent of the population. Another 15 percent lived in small towns (between 2,000 and 20,000) like Barmen (17,000) and Remscheid (9,000). Our time traveler would have been quite at home in these urban settings. "Very many of them," writes John Clapham, "were still the quiet little places of the fairy books, with huddled roofs and spires, from which the view over the ploughlands and the orchards was so easy."[7] The overwhelming majority of Germans, around 80 percent, lived among "the ploughlands and the orchards" in villages or settlements of less than 2,000 inhabitants.

Our visitor would also have noticed little change in the physical appearance of the countryside in 1815. In the northwestern parts of Germany near Cleves and Gelders, scattered homesteads characteristic of Holland could be seen, while south and east of Düsseldorf village settlements predominated. The typical older village west of the Rhine tended to be "a jumble of houses, lanes, and courtyards about a church – primitive in its disorder,"[8] observes Clapham. East of the Rhine village layouts often reflected the planned colonization of the late Middle Ages. In the marshes between the Weser and the Elbe, and along the coast in Mecklenburg and Pomerania, houses were constructed in long rows along a dyke which kept out the water. Similarly, in the Odenwald, Thuringia, Saxony, Silesia, and Bohemia, "street villages" stretched out linearly along the valley stream which provided water.

7. Clapham, 82.
8. Ibid., 33.

Whether orderly or not, however, the village was usually central to the farming areas, or fields, all around. The large, enclosed fields typical of England and Holland were rare in Germany, largely limited to the extreme Northwest, Schleswig-Holstein, and Mecklenburg – a situation which agrarian reforms would alter very little. Most German holdings were scattered about the surrounding fields in numerous strips. Dating from earlier centuries, the rationale was one of survival: if war, fire, or disease ruined crops on one strip, a farmer could still work the remaining, unaffected strips in another field and have something to eat. Throughout Germany in the 1810s, most villages employed a three-field rotation where strips in two fields were planted annually and one field lay fallow to replenish the soil. Isolated parts of the Eifel, Hunsrück, Palatinate, and Saar held onto an ancient two-field rotation dating from the pre-colonization era.

Most manufacturing at this time was also based in the countryside. Textiles, as we know, were one such branch of production. Although about a thousand enterprising urban merchants throughout Germany were consolidating output in the first simple factories, most distributed silk, wool, and flax to spinners and weavers in town and country who spun and wove thread and cloth. Metalworking is another good example. Merchant manufacturers in Solingen and Remscheid, the two most important centers, purchased raw iron and steel from rural furnaces, then put it out to thousands of small country shops where skilled smiths and grinders hammered and polished their material into knives, files, scissors, and cutlery. Ironmaking establishments were also usually located outside city walls near the hillside mines that provided ore and the forests that supplied charcoal. This vegetable fuel played an important role in the rural economy of the Mosel, Siegerland, Harz, Silesia, and Austria, for the absence of impurities like sulfur and phosphorous created a pure wrought iron which blacksmiths could more easily shape into shovels, hammers, and other implements required on farms. The rural nature of ironmaking comes even more clearly into focus if one remembers that the mines, furnaces, and forges were often worked on a collective basis by poor farmers who needed extra income. Only state operations like those in Freiberg (Saxony), Silesia, or the Saar were run on a larger scale.

While manufacturing expanded gradually along familiar lines, economic and technological changes slowly began to transform German agriculture. As we know, the land reforms of the early 1800s swept away many institutions like the commons which had constrained the workings of the market. In the process, it gradually became easier for owners of land to exploit their property for profit. The free trade treaties of these decades had a similar effect by facilitating exchange on a regional, and eventually, a national level. Prussia was in the vanguard, eliminating all toll barriers within its borders in 1818; extending the tariff free zone to Hesse-Darmstadt, Württemberg, and Bavaria in 1828/29; and finally forging a German customs union of eighteen states in 1834 (see Part III). Transportation improvements also helped to unleash market forces. Prussia was again central to this development, constructing about 13,000 kilometers of new roads between 1816 and 1850. Throughout the Confederation, the road network expanded from approximately 15,000 kilometers in 1820 to nearly 53,000 in 1850. The length of canals and navigable rivers and lakes also grew from around 1,150 kilometers in 1815 to about 2,400 in 1850. By connecting otherwise isolated and unconnected localities and regions, the new roads and waterways enabled these areas to trade goods with one another and conduct business for the first time. The nationalist idea so dear to the students who ascended the Wartburg was nudged closer to reality by these economic developments. The aforementioned trade treaties, as well as the railroad boom of the 1840s (see Part III), greatly accelerated this process.

The new market incentives induced a 40 percent increase in arable land between 1815 and 1850. German farmers divided the commons and reclaimed and planted marshes, swamps, meadows, and wastelands. Reflecting the role of science and technology, however, overall agricultural production grew by nearly 100 percent during the same decades. The freer exchange of ideas was central to this process. The proliferation of agricultural societies which had begun during the Enlightenment continued after Napoleon's defeat, resulting in hundreds of new associations which disseminated information and recruited members from all classes. Governments also founded farming institutes with model farms – Prussia in 1806, Württemberg in 1818, Bavaria in 1822, and Saxony in 1826. These stimuli led to improved livestock techniques and the enhanced utilization of fallow land, which declined from 33 percent of the arable surface in 1815 to only 15 percent in 1850. Fallow fields were now planted with fodder crops for livestock or else with fruits and vegetables that replenished nitrogen in the soil. In general, these improvements were pursued most enthusiastically in Saxony, East Elbian Prussia, Hanover, and the Rhineland. Thus fallow land shrunk to three percent in Rhenish Prussia and a mere one percent in Saxony, while it still hovered around 19 percent in Bavaria. Typically it was the larger estate owner or the more prosperous peasant who forged ahead with these crop rotation methods. But the small, marginal peasant was not left completely behind – witness the rapid expansion of the potato crop planted mainly by smallholders on the fallows.

Population growth accompanied these developments on the land. We have seen that peace, marginal increases in nutrition, and the disappearance of the plague accounted for a 30-50 percent rise in population during the late eighteenth century. The number of people in German Europe expanded another 60 percent in the half-century after 1815, growing from about 33 to 52 million. As before, declining adult mortality rates seem to have caused this natural increase, for, nationally, marriage age and fertility remained fairly constant, while infant mortality actually increased. Again, demographers struggle to explain these trends, but it appears that cottage industry, agricultural trends, and marriage laws were indirectly related, especially when regional trends are considered.

The population of those states we have identified as centers of economic and technological change grew quicker than the average: 88% in Prussia and 97 percent in Saxony. Migrants flocked to the busiest regions of these states and found work: a surplus (over-immigration) of nearly 70,000 in West Prussia between 1816 and 1834; 74,000 in East Prussia; and 112,000 in Silesia. There were also high rates of *natural* increase in these areas, especially among the poorest rural classes where rural manufacturing prospered, like Chemnitz/Zwickau (Saxony), or sites of intensive agricultural innovation, like the province of West Prussia. The latter province had a surplus of births over deaths of twenty-three per thousand between 1821 and 1825 – the highest in Prussia. It was not that the small peasant was prospering from innovations, which, with the exception of nutritious potatoes, did not occur. Rather, he preferred to earn additional income through spinning, weaving, and other cottage industries. Similarly, the landless peasant or wage earner found plenty of work on the large estates that were expanding agricultural production. Economic opportunities as farm hands and rural laborers resulted in higher incomes, a little more food on the table, more children, and slightly better chances of survival. The fact that marriage restrictions were lifted in Prussia during the reform era reinforced these upward demographic trends in the North.

The reverse was true in southern Germany. Marriage restrictions characteristic of earlier centuries remained in place throughout the south. While illegitimate births increased as a result, overall fertility was still reduced by delaying or preventing wedlock. Farmers also tended to resist technological innovation, thus creating little of the extra income for idle laborers and smallholders. Because the land was crowded from the practice of dividing inheritances among all sons, moreover, emigration overseas (or to other German states) was far heavier than any influx. Accordingly, population in southern Germany grew slower than the 60 percent national average: only 24 percent in Württemberg, 35 percent in Bavaria, and 42 percent in Baden.

Most smallholders and rural laborers, therefore, did not fare well after 1815. Even in Saxony and Prussia it is necessary to emphasize the marginal nature of the improvement, for the little man had not advanced far beyond subsistence levels. Public health improved as the number of doctors and hospitals increased, scientific practices like innoculation became more widespread, and medicine grew more professional. Charlatans still abounded, however, and hospitals could be very unsanitary and full of infection. Smallpox, cholera, and typhus fever were not as deadly as they had been in previous centuries, yet epidemics still occurred. Thus cholera ravaged central Europe in 1816 and again in 1831, killing about 1 percent of the population in the latter year. Infant mortality also remained terribly high, totaling 183 deaths per thousand births in Prussia during the 1830s, 266 in Saxony, and 296 in Bavaria. Despite the farming advances of the early 1800s, moreover, crop failures like those of 1816 and 1817 imperiled poor families living too close to the edge of survival. As we shall see, such problems reoccurred, adding an angry social dimension to the revolutions of 1830 and 1848/49.

Cities and towns confronted a similar set of social problems. Some, like Königsberg and Augsburg, declined as trade routes and market advantages passed to others. Prospering cities like Hamburg and Berlin or industrial boom towns like Elberfeld and Barmen, on the other hand, could be very attractive sites for migrants in search of livelihood. Because strangers were no more welcome in those days, however, than they are in today's world, magistrates erected a number of barriers to unwanted aliens. Citizenship usually required ownership of property, while residence permits were impossible to acquire without certificates proving legitimate birth, testimonials to good character, proof of income, or guild contacts. And a high fee was often charged for moving into town.

Expansion occurred most rapidly in big cities with less autonomy, especially in states like Prussia. Berlin expanded from 190,000 in 1815 to 283,000 in 1837, largely on the basis of 68,000 newcomers. Cologne kept an even faster pace, growing from 53,000 in 1816 to 97,000 in 1850, attracting about 25,000 immigrants in the process. These numbers reflect the slower rate of natural increase common in most cities, probably due to horrendous infant mortality figures which could rise as high as 500 per thousand, as they did in Berlin. Exacerbating this social problem was the growing threat of the underworld: thieves, thugs, pimps, and prostitutes whose numbers swelled when economic downturns, personal mishaps, and job-related accidents undercut the urban working class, or when hard times hit the countryside. These, too, were revolutionary ingredients.

* * * *

In turning now to the relations between men and women, we find that questions of work and economic survival were determining factors. Gender relations in the Early Modern countryside were characterized by a reciprocity of duties designed to ensure that there would be adequate money, food, and clothing. Men cleared fields, did the plowing, planting, and harvesting, chopped wood, and constructed houses, barns, fences, and roadways. Part-time work in the hillside mines, charcoal gangs, and smelting furnaces was also performed mainly by men. Women cooked and prepared food, made and mended clothes, crafted household items like soap and candles, fed and grazed livestock on the fallows, tended the family garden, sometimes helped in the fields, and, of course, gave birth to the next generation. Able-bodied sons helped their fathers, while daughters assisted mothers or were sometimes sent to neighboring farms or estates as servants to earn extra income. It was this "sexually based division of labor in which the halves were joined in an interlocking way," observes Bonnie Smith, "which characterized rural life most of all." Only the "full activity of each part united with that of the other ensured the family's survival."[9]

Gender relations began to worsen in the eighteenth and early nineteenth centuries. As we know, many peasant families found it impossible to make ends meet in the traditional ways as peasant land was sacrificed to compensate noblemen, holdings were fragmented through inheritance, and common land unfairly divided. Men were forced to seek work as construction laborers or hired hands and were sometimes absent for months at a time. In the meantime, women had to assume a variety of additional duties. Cottage industry absorbed more of their time, for example, as did washing necessitated by the trend toward linen and cotton. The disappearance of common grazing land compelled peasant families to haul fodder from the fields to feed their animals in stalls, moreover, while the adoption of turnips, sugar beets, and potatoes on fallow fields required more weeding than traditional cereal crops. Putting-out work, cleaning, stall feeding, and weeding were all jobs that fell to women, placing tremendous strain on marital relationships in poor as well as prosperous rural families. David Warren Sabean's study of Neckarhausen found a twelve-fold increase in demands for divorce or separation from the late 1700s (1770-1800) to the early 1800s (1800-1830). The frequency of wives' complaints about husbands' drinking also doubled during these decades. "When we find women calling on the devil … or calling

9. Bonnie G. Smith, *Changing Lives: Women in European History Since 1700* (Lexington, MA, 1989), 11.

on lightening to act in their service," he writes, "we encounter … a fundamental challenge to hierarchically modeled relations and … a strong claim on the part of women for an altered understanding of reciprocities."[10]

One alternative, especially for single men and women, was to leave the country altogether for towns and cities. As we already know, many were lured away by the prospect of steady work and higher incomes. Young women tended to use those skills they had employed in the countryside. Because needlewomen were in great demand as the textile trades became more industrial, women who had made clothes on the farm often found out-work or perhaps a shop position finishing garments and apparel. Others found part-time employment cooking, cleaning, and ironing. But these jobs rarely fulfilled the dreams of economic security that had drawn young people into the cities. Prostitution was frequently the logical but dangerous consequence, for a woman could sometimes earn as much in one evening as in a week of sewing or cleaning. Thus seemingly idyllic Schwäbisch-Hall was rocked in 1824 by the exposure of a well-run ring of prostitutes – even featuring a brothel – staffed by desperate country girls for the pleasure of townsmen. This, too, was a carryover from rural Germany. In Württemberg in 1831, for instance, village girls were reported selling themselves near local inns and military camps.

The most attractive position for country girls was domestic service in the home of a weathy urban merchant, banker, magistrate, or lawyer. The wives of these bourgeois magnates had withdrawn into the separate sphere of domesticity, managing the household and overseeing the raising of children. The servant was a symbol of status for such women, a kind of reverse image which emphasized her "removal from productive activity, her separation from the economic sphere, and her sole function of bearing children."[11] The servants themselves enjoyed an elevated standard of living in such surroundings. They were fed, clothed, and usually cared for when ill. Hours were long, but work had a country rhythm to it: one toiled in a familial setting and there were no factory bells or hazardous

10. David Warren Sabean, *Property, Production, and Family in Neckarhausen, 1700-1870* (Cambridge, 1990), 145.

11. Smith, 149.

machines. Domestics also acquired a higher rate of literacy and other useful skills while living with the upper middle class. This, together with the savings that could be accumulated for a dowry, help to explain the high percentage of servant girls who married above their station into the shopkeeping or handicraft class.

Marriage to a baker, butcher, cobbler, or weaver was more of an economic partnership than a love match. In the earlier period of the seventeenth and eighteenth centuries, mastercraftsmen controlled an extended household which included the nuclear family as well as servants, apprentices, and journeymen, the number (if any) depending on the extent of a man's business. A woman was both legally and physically subordinate to her husband, but was also his partner because she ran the family, managed the food, supervised the female servants, often assisted in running the business, and sometimes ran the shop after her husband died. We have observed the same complementarity between women's and men's roles on the farm. While a certain emotional security and happiness undoubtedly resulted from the close bonds formed in such a "patriarchal household,"[12] we should do well to remember James Sheehan's qualification: "if times were good and the people decent, the traditional household was probably a bearable place, but when things went wrong, when the crops failed or the soldiers came, when people broke under the burdens of overwork and undernourishment, when disease or disappointments became unbearable, then the close spaces of the household could become the scene of endless torment."[13]

Such scenes of torment were undoubtedly on the rise in Germany by the 1820s and 1830s as certain handicraft trades like textiles succumbed to factory competition or non-guild manufacturing permissible under the reform legislation which some states had introduced. In these altered circumstances, men sought work in factories, construction, or transportation, wives fell back on skills like sewing, cooking, cleaning – or prostitution – and marriages bent and often broke under the strains. The social crises of the countryside were thus compounded by stressful and potentially

12. Peter Laslett, *The World We Have Lost: England Before the Industrial Age* (New York, 1973),1.

13. Sheehan, 86.

revolutionary situations in many cities and towns throughout the German Confederation.

* * * *

Relations between Catholics and Protestants were another source of trouble in German Europe. As we observed in Part I, the Holy Roman Empire had fashioned a workable peace between the confessions. Accommodations in the Imperial Diet gave representatives of both religions caucuses from which to negotiate, while successive peace treaties had confirmed the right of princes to determine official religions in their lands. The latter arrangement triggered voluntary and involuntary migrations and exoduses as Catholics and Protestants either sought havens from persecution or were forced to do so. Austria and Bavaria were the major Catholic states in the Empire, while Prussia and Hanover were the main Protestant powers. Throughout the southwest, the Rhineland, and Westphalia scores of petty states existed where one could find refuge from the intolerance of the other side. The process of state building which culminated at Vienna in 1815, however, undermined the religious peace. Although Catholics held a slight majority in the Confederation, there were only three states – Austria, Bavaria, and Baden – which had Catholic majorities. And in Baden, the family of the Grand Dukes was Protestant. In Württemberg, Nassau, Hesse-Darmstadt, Hesse-Kassel, Saxe-Weimar, Hanover, and Prussia, Catholics belonged to significant religious minorities in Protestant states.

Under these circumstances Protestants had relatively few complaints. Ludwig of Bavaria forced Protestant soldiers to kneel during the Corpus Christi processions, for example, and devout Saxons found it difficult to tolerate their Catholic royal family. But the real consequence of the Confederation's religious division was a persecution of Catholics that drove them into the ghetto of second-class citizenship. While not as bloody as earlier periods in German history, this persecution nevertheless stirred considerable controversy. Thus Catholics were irritated that academic and bureaucratic positions were awarded disproportionately to Protestants, even in predominantly Catholic areas like Baden and Rhenish Prussia. Protestant states also supervised Catholic education and interfered with the appointment of bishops. Sometimes the slights and indignities were petty, witness the Prussian practice of compelling Catholic recruits to attend Protestant church services or the banning of religious pilgrimages on the grounds that they undercut economic productivity. On other occasions, however, persecution could provoke crises. When Prussia arrested the Archbishop of Cologne for refusing to allow priests to participate in mixed marriage ceremonies unless the children were to be raised as Catholics, for instance, angry Catholics demonstrated and rioted. The so-called Cologne Troubles of 1837 became a national sensation. In faraway Munich, Joseph Görres championed the Catholic cause with a denunciatory pamphlet entitled *Athanasius*. Prussia should allow the church a lawful freedom and create true parity between the denominations. The present policy, he charged, would lead to revolution and the total disintegration of society. Although Berlin eventually compromised, the mood remained tense for years. Thus Catholics in Essen rioted during the Corpus Christi procession of 1845 when rumors spread that Protestants were plotting to abscond with a sacred flag.

Religious controversy also sprang up from within the Protestant and Catholic communities. Both camps were torn by feuds between pious, zealous factions and adherents of modernist or rationalist theology. On the Protestant side, rationalism was associated with freedom of conscience, rejection of predestination, and even a questioning of the divinity of Jesus, all of which provoked the wrath of pious Protestants, who offered biblical fundamentalism and revival meetings as a cure. On the Catholic side, the reformers favored a German-language mass, freedom from papal control, and opposed allegedly superstitious practices like the rosary, clerical celibacy, pilgrimages, and intolerance toward mixed marriages and Protestantism. More orthodox priests, theologians, and parishioners vehemently condemned the reformers and called on the hierarchy for support.

Intraconfessional violence was sometimes the result. Thus one rationalist priest in the Eifel was assaulted by devout women when he appeared before his congregation in a frock coat, the symbol of reform Catholicism, rather than a traditional cassock. Protestant metalworkers of the right-bank Rhineland were also known to take sides in parish politics. "On polling day," writes Jonathan Sperber, "they crowded the church, cheering for their favorite [pastor], physically attacking his opponents if he lost, marching in riotous fashion to his home if he won, and demanding payment for their support."[14] Frederick William III of Prussia added another raucous dimension to Protestant politics in the 1820s when he imposed a union of the Protestant churches accompanied by a new liturgy similar to the High Anglican. The new ceremonial forms were widely condemned as papist, especially in the Wupperthal, a Rhenish bastion of fundamentalism, and Silesia, where resistance was so fierce that troops had to restore order.

Religious fundamentalism and orthodoxy were also gaining momentum in the Catholic church. Rocked and weakened by decades of war and revolution, the authority of the hierarchy had reached its nadir in 1815. Rationalist priests, theologians, and seminarians who had struggled for decades to reform Catholic practices now saw an opportunity to implement their views. During the 1830s, however, papal and diocesan officials appalled mainly by proposals for permitting mixed marriages and ending clerical celibacy struck back, removing most of the liberals from their posts and, in some cases, excommunicating them. The popular reaction to the arrest of the Archbishop of Cologne in 1837 was one indication that these countermoves had considerable backing in the parishes. The great pilgrimage to the Holy Tunic of Trier in 1844 was another sign of mass piety, as a half million faithful Catholics flocked to see a garment supposedly worn by Jesus.

This phenomenal occurrence, however, was a catalyst for the secessionist German Catholic movement. Zealous, but disgusted by the neoorthodoxy sweeping his church, Joseph Ronge, a charismatic former priest from Silesia, protested openly to the Archbishop of Trier that church officials were lying about the authenticity of Christ's robe. He then led between 100,000 and 150,000 dissenters into a radical new church which abolished celibacy, promoted equality between clergy and laity, encouraged mixed marriages of all sorts, and trumpeted its national mission as being to overcome,

14. Jonathan Sperber, *Rhineland Radicals: The Democratic Movement and the Revolutioin of 1848-1849* (Princeton, 1991), 80-81.

through love and marriage, a religious division which had weakened Germany for centuries.

Recent research indicates that there were distinct class and gender dimensions to these intraconfessional tendencies. Rational, reformist Catholicism, for instance, was largely confined to an upper-middle class characterized, as one priest observed, by "religious indifference and a certain smugness."[15] Only in Aachen did one find a widespread piety among wealthier Catholics. German Catholicism, an interesting mixture of reformism as well as piety, attracted many bankers, manufacturers, and notables, but was predominantly a movement of men and women from the handicraft and working classes repelled by the wealth of both established churches. Sperber's data on the composition of several Catholic pilgrimages in the Rhineland between 1816 and 1824 suggests, similarly, that religious zealotry, while certainly a complicated mix of motives, was mainly a class phenomenon of the lower orders of society associated with the marginal existence of these strata during a stressful period of economic transition. Of the men, almost 70 percent were farmers, rural weavers, artisans, and workers, while a mere 2 or 3 percent were well-to-do. On the Protestant side, the above-cited episode of unruly metalworkers lends support to the interpretation that piety was a manifestation of economic distress, as does evidence from other parts of Germany. The leaders of the Pietist awakening of the 1810s and 1820s were Silesian and Pomeranian noblemen, but their regional followers came largely from the struggling rural population and the lower middle classes of the towns. Impoverished Württemberg, from which so many German Americans hailed, was another center of the Pietist revival. It should come as no surprise, therefore, that Sabean's case study of Neckarhausen uncovered a thriving Pietist prayer circle.

Interestingly enough, Sabean inclines to the view that Pietism was to some extent a "religion of self-exploited farm women." It "organized their energies and provided an escape from what was otherwise an intolerable work situation."[16] Sperber's research provides some confirmation. Roughly two-thirds of the predominantly

15. Jonathan Sperber, *Popular Catholicism in Nineteenth-Century Germany* (Princeton, 1984), 36.

16. Sabean, 428.

lower class Rhenish pilgrims were women, lending credence to the view that they were escaping familial or marital tensions like those we have observed in Neckarhausen. Protestant women were drawn to German Catholicism in large numbers, similarly, out of opposition to the male patriarchalism found in the established church – and at home: 34 percent and 21 percent, respectively, of married female members in Leipzig and Dresden joined without their husbands. Of the middle class Rhenish pilgrims studied by Sperber, most were also women. Like their Protestant and Jewish counterparts in the salons of Berlin and the Pietist prayer circles of rural Prussia, the bourgeois female pilgrims turned to religion, among other spiritual reasons, as the only independent intellectual pursuit available to them. Bertha Traun, a German Catholic from Hamburg, expressed this longing for cerebral engagement when she defined God simply as "the process of the striving after truth." The Women's Club of 1847, also from Hamburg, elaborated on these sentiments: "The more clearly and self-consciously we came to an appreciation of the significance of our own spiritual lives, the more we felt called upon … to work for the intellectual and material well-being of our own sex."[17] A similar phenomenon was at work in Amalie Sieveking's benevolent prayer society. Along with seventy women from Hamburg's patrician class who, according to Catherine Prelinger, "were frustrated by their own leisure,"[18] Sieveking took the good word into the homes of the city's destitute and poverty-stricken.

Jewish-gentile relations were another source of friction in German society. The infamous "Hep-Hep" disturbances of 1819 are a good example. Inflamed by the miserable harvests of 1816 and 1817, growing competition from factories, and the current discussion of Jewish emancipation, poor farmers and craftsmen unleashed their fears and anxieties on the Jews. Farm houses and shops throughout the Confederation were destroyed in the worst pogroms in Germany since the early 1600s. The distress among Jews was compounded by the fact that legislation, contrary to irrational

17. Citations in Catherine M. Prelinger, *Charity, Challenge, and Change: Religious Dimensions of the Mid-Nineteenth-Century Women's Movement in Germany* (New York, 1987), 64, 80.

18. Ibid., 39.

popular fears, no longer favored them. States like Hanover and Saxony, which had not stopped discriminating against Jews during the Napoleonic period, continued to do so after 1815, while cities like Hamburg, Bremen, Lübeck, and Frankfurt/Main, which had granted full rights under the French, rescinded them and returned their Jews to the ghetto. Similarly, earlier emancipatory legislation in Baden, Bavaria, and Prussia was amended after 1815 with new restrictions and indignities for Jews. Nearly everywhere they were treated as untrustworthy aliens whose participation in state and economy was regarded as threatening to the majority and therefore either forbidden or closely monitored. The tiny duchies of Anhalt-Bernburg and Anhalt-Köthen were the only German states where Jews and gentiles were equal under the law.

Dagmar Herzog's study of Baden before 1848 demonstrates how inextricably related class, gender, religious, racial, and political issues could be in this era of change and uncertainty. Her point of departure is the resurgence of Catholic neoorthodoxy mentioned above – a reactionary backlash against reform-minded priests and theologians that was strikingly successful in a Grand Duchy where state officials perceived the church as a useful ally against socially disruptive forces. The offensive of Catholic conservatives was a demagogic affair, however, replete with misogynous and anti-Semitic outbursts. Opponents of clerical celibacy were lambasted as "woman-craving whimperers" who overlooked "the weaker, more negative nature of this sex," for once females lost their morality their "savage, hideous and unnatural" nature surfaced. Another conservative accused critics of celibacy of "the most vulgar Jewish and pagan weakness."[19]

Protestant and Catholic liberals in the diet were revolted by the church's counteroffensive for a variety of reasons. Since the Reformation and Thirty Years War it had been an article of faith among Protestants that any intervention by Rome in German affairs was thoroughly negative. Liberals were also alarmed by conservative success in mobilizing popular support for this virulent campaign, especially in rural districts. At the core of their disgust, however,

19. Citations from Dagmar Herzog, *Intimacy and Exclusion:Religious Politics in Pre-Revolutionary Baden* (Princeton, New Jersey, 1996), 30-31.

was the knowledge that clerical celibacy and restrictions against mixed marriage were an affront to the man's right to enjoy the untrammeled marital bliss that resulted from sexual intercourse. Liberal ire increased after the church succeeded in moving Baden to persecute the German Catholics, for here was a movement that openly espoused these reformist causes dear to men, and did so in the name of gender, interfaith, and national harmony. Concerns like these led to parliamentary motions in 1845/46 guaranteeing religious freedom not only to German Catholics, but also, oddly enough, to Jews. This was bizarre, for Badenese liberals, like their counterparts throughout Germany, harbored deep-seated prejudices against Jews, rejecting the argument of a minority of liberal politicians that emancipation would overcome "Jewish difference" and integrate them into German society. "The Jew is completely incapable of amalgamating himself with the peoples among whom he lives, so that a homogeneous whole can emerge," wrote one liberal member of the diet. "He remains a Jew in all situations."[20] Threatened by the church's counteroffensive against religious freedom and male sexual prerogatives, however, a majority of diet liberals placed their prejudices aside and voted for Jewish emancipation in August 1846. But nothing changed, for the grand duke guarded his own prerogatives and ignored the 36 to 18 vote.

20. Ibid., 78.

Chapter 8

ART AND THE SPIRIT OF THE TIMES

The decades after the Congress of Vienna were a time of turbulence and transition in central Europe. After 1819, years of radical demonstrations, petitions, and unsettling political strife led to repression, censorship, and manipulation by triumphant conservatives. Simultaneously, land reforms, free enterprise laws, trade treaties, transportation improvements, and unchecked population growth slowly unraveled the social and economic fabric of the old regime. We would expect to find the world of art strongly influenced by these developments, for culture serves minimally to facilitate a people's understanding of controversy and change. Sometimes, however, culture becomes part of that controversy and an agent of that change. It was art's political role that prompted rulers to promote official culture with operas, public monuments, and palaces. As we know, rulers were also on guard against cultural attacks, especially from the print medium. Artists wishing to criticize can counter by interpreting reality and conveying overtly political messages at a level beyond the censors' reach. It is this indirect, sheltered politics of art that makes the cultural arena at times the sole outlet for the criticism of oppressive regimes. Yet art can also become embroiled in political struggles beyond the intent and control of its creators. In turning first to music, we find culture an unwitting party to politics.

* * * *

Gasparo Spontini liked to think of himself as the Napoleon of music. The tall, handsome Italian composer had gravitated to Paris in 1803. Gradually over the next decade he strengthened the light, southern style of his operas to please the imperial French. The debut of "La Vestale" in 1807 raised the curtain on a new type of opera with more singers, more dancers, more orchestration – and more sound. A joke was soon circulating among startled Parisian audiences about a physician who had advised a deaf friend to accompany him to "La Vestale" as a cure. After one of the orchestra's loudest bursts, the friend cried out that he now could hear, but unfortunately the doctor did not reply, for the blaring had deafened him. Spontini labored assiduously to perfect his grand operas, bringing "Ferdinand Cortez" to the stage in 1809, where it remained for many years. Frederick William III saw one performance in 1814 and was deeply moved by the music – and by the conductor. "His appearance at the head of his musicians was almost that of a general leading an army to victory," notes one historian. Spontini's baton was a thick ebony stick which he held with his fist in the middle, waving it "like a marshall's staff."[1] Frederick William, a more confident king after the wars, was desirous of improving the state of opera to reflect the enhanced status of his kingdom. The Napoleon of music seemed the perfect man to fill the bill.

Count Karl von Brühl, Intendent of the Royal Theater in Berlin, was more impressed with Carl Maria von Weber. The young director of the Prague Opera had met and befriended Brühl in 1812 while touring Germany. During the following years Weber completed a three-book collection of nationalistic songs *(Lyre and Sword)* and a cantata to celebrate Waterloo *(Struggle and Victory)*. Both works portrayed the events of battle with strains of authentic bugle calls and marches, while not ignoring the emotions of battle, which he depicted with quavering flute accompaniment (to represent prayer) and dotted rhythms (to signify strength and resolve). Understandably, these compositions cemented his reputation with veterans and patriots like General Nostitz, a veteran of Leipzig, who told the composer that he could hear "the voice of the

1. *Grove's Dictionary of Music and Musicians*, ed. by Eric Blom, {London, 1954), 8:22.

nations."[2] But unfortunately for Weber, some of the *Lyre and Sword* songs had spread among Prussian militiamen. This angered Frederick William because he felt that melodies like "Lützow's Wild Ride" undermined the dignity of line regiments. Brühl's bid to engage Weber as conductor in Berlin failed as a result. Despite the Count's obstructive maneuvers, the post finally went to Spontini in September, 1819.

The Italian who had served Napoleon was not a popular appointment in Berlin, the city Napoleon had taken. Spontini added to the controversy with an arrogance and bad temper which quickly alienated Brühl. In May 1821, after forty-two rehearsals, the newcomer was ready to conduct his first opera in the capital. "Olympia," based on a tragedy by Voltaire, highlighted Spontini's penchant for the grandiose and awe-inspiring, his emphasis on dynamic contrasts, and the fusion of choral and instrumental music as an articulation of drama. Brilliantly and flawlessly performed at the private court opera, "Olympia" was a huge success for Spontini. But victory was also claimed by conservatives at court who gloated over the anger and embarrassment the opera had caused in nationalist circles.

Count Brühl served up a dish of revenge in June 1821 when Weber was allowed to perform for the opening of the new public theater designed by Schinkel (see below). Brühl knew that Weber had been working for years on "Freischütz," an opera based on an old legend. Max, a marksmen, is convinced by Caspar, a forest ranger, to call on the demonic Samiel to acquire "free bullets" that always hit the mark. At stake is victory in a shooting contest and the hand of beautiful Agathe. Frustrated in the aftermath of Carlsbad, the nationalistic parties in Berlin seized on the occasion as a demonstration of their resolve for German unity. The opera was heavily attended by middle-class patriots, veterans wearing their Iron Crosses, and students from the university. The applause and cheering in the second and third acts brought down the house. "Freischütz" went on to enjoy long runs in other cities in Germany and Europe, while "Olympia" was never seen outside of Berlin. The court had suffered a major defeat in the cultural-political arena.

2. Cited in John Warrack, *Carl Maria von Weber* (London, 1968), 170.

The composition of "Freischütz" enhanced the highly political theme of the opera. For, like Beethoven two decades earlier, Weber had offered Germans *different* music. The Berlin audience was mostly quiet and pensive during the first act, seeming to study the new role given to flutes, clarinets, bassoons, trumpets, and horns. Weber employed this new sound to highlight the leitmotif of good struggling against evil. The sinister element was a special challenge. "I gave a great deal of thought to [this] question ... Naturally it had to be a dark, gloomy color – the lowest register of the violins, violas and basses, particularly the lowest register of the clarinet, which seemed especially suitable for depicting the sinister, then the mournful sound of the bassoon, the lowest notes of the horns, the hollow roll of the drums or single hollow strokes on them."[3] Weber reinforced the effect by his use of major and minor chords to depict good and evil, each accentuated by light and dark on stage at the appropriate moment. The minor to major chord progressions of the final daylight scene where Max and Agathe escape destruction, Caspar is shot, and Samiel foiled provided an ecstatic release for liberals and patriots who shortly had to exit into the night of Berlin's political conservatism.

* * * *

The Brotherhood of Saint Luke was politicized culture of a different sort. Founded in 1809 by Franz Pforr and Friedrich Overbeck, two disaffected students at the Academy of Art in Vienna, this zealous fraternity was disturbed by the corruption of present times. Further disillusioned by the defeat of the Austrians at Wagram, they decided to withdraw spiritually from the present into the Middle Ages, an allegedly more chaste time when the German people had suffered fewer misfortunes. As if to emphasize their desire to escape, the brothers moved to Rome in 1810, where they lived simply, wearing medieval clothing, and painting religious and allegorical frescoes. The monastic lifestyle of the brothers soon earned them the nickname "Nazarenes." Their newfound purpose in life was to chasten the present by reviving religion through art.

3. Ibid., 221.

In 1816 the Nazarenes admitted Ferdinand Olivier to their brotherhood. A native of Dessau, Olivier had studied with Caspar David Friedrich in Dresden before going to Vienna in 1810. There he befriended two Nazarenes who had returned from Rome, Joseph Anton Koch and Philipp Veit, as well as Veit's father-in-law, Friedrich Schlegel, and Schlegel's influential confessor, Clemens Maria Hofbauer. Olivier drank deeply of the revivalist spirit moving his new friends – and this spirit soon appeared on canvas. His rendering of the Parish Church of Matzleindorf (1815) epitomized the Nazarenes' rejection of the bold washes and dramatic shaded contrasts taught at the Viennese Academy. Their preference for a linear outline style with shading executed simply as crosshatching imparted a static medieval serenity and placidity to such paintings – the deep calm of the faithful.

Olivier poured a different emotion into a painting of the graveyard of St. Peter's in Salzburg (1817). Entitled *Saturday*, the day of Christ's death, it featured a disorienting foreground of crosses and gravestones with outbuildings more sharply defined in the background, nestled under Salzburg's rocky mountain wall. "As though heightened by grief, everything is seen more clearly than before, emphatically outlined and described," writes William Vaughan, "and as we gradually explore the graves and grasses we find in the background a funeral procession that reflects the mood of the whole."[4]

The career of Peter Cornelius illustrates more explicitly the political uses that were often found for Nazarene art. A native of Düsseldorf who lived and worked for a decade with the brothers in Rome, Cornelius took up duties as Director of the Royal Academy of Art in his hometown in 1821. The appointment of a Rhenish artist was part of Berlin's campaign to coopt its new western provinces. A Nazarene would be religiously correct for devout Rhinelanders, but this genre of painting also served the state's restorative interests. As Cornelius argued shortly before his arrival, art should be directed "to the serious, the elevated, and the patrotic."[5] Accordingly, the master and his students set about

4. William Vaughan, *German Romantic Painting* (New Haven, 1994), 186.

5. Cited in Wolfgang Hütt, *Die Düsseldorfer Malerschule 1819-1869* (Leipzig, 1964), 12.

adorning the aulas and hallways of the region's universities, museums, and castles with frescoes that recalled the glory of the crusades and the grandeur of the medieval church. The panels in Schloss Heltorf dedicated to episodes in the life of Frederick Barbarossa, although not finished by Cornelius, were a typical theme. Wolfgang Hütt is probably right in interpreting these paintings as a reflection of bourgeois sadness and resignation over the irretrievable nature of Germany's lost Reich. As a form of passive acceptance of the status quo, however, this was certainly acceptable in Berlin.

Cornelius's work was also highly regarded in Munich. Crown Prince Ludwig managed to lure him there in 1825 to adorn the interior halls of the Glyptothek, a gallery for antique sculptures erected in neoclassical style by Leo von Klenze, a champion of the competing Greek revival (see below). This commission challenged the master painter, for the conservative Gothic messages conveyed by his style would perhaps be lost amidst the progressive impulses emanating from such massive neoclassical structures. Undaunted, Cornelius tried to solve the problem by depicting ancient times as a historical stage leading upwards to the Christian era. The physical greatness of the Greeks and Romans so evident in the sculptures of the Glyptothek had yielded to the spiritual perfection of the Middle Ages reflected in the paintings on the panels high above. As we shall explain in Part III, these artistic confrontations escalated into a full-fledged "struggle of the styles" as the years drew on to mid-century. For the moment, however, Ludwig was not pleased. Although eclectic in his tastes, the monarch leaned toward Klenze, with the result that Cornelius received few new commissions.

In 1826 Prussia gave Cornelius's vacant position in Düsseldorf to Wilhelm von Schadow, son of the accomplished classical sculptor, Gottfried Schadow. The young man had puzzled and irritated his father in 1810 by joining the Nazarene's "Gothic band"[6] in Rome. After nine years there, Schadow returned to Berlin, where relations with neoclassicists like Karl Friedrich Schinkel, the king's

6. Cited in Helmut Börsch-Supan, "Das Frühwerk Wilhelm von Schadows und die berlinischen Voraussetzungen der Düsseldorfer Schule," in Wend von Kalnein (ed.), *Die Düsseldorfer Malerschule* (Düsseldorf, 1979), 63.

great architect and builder (see below), were strained. The directorship in Düsseldorf was thus a compromise solution typical of Frederick William III: an exiled Schadow would leave the redesigning of Berlin to Schinkel – but receive an important cultural-political assignment in the Rhineland.

Because Schadow possessed neither the originality nor the ability of Cornelius, he sought to compensate by employing more color and giving his historical and religious subjects a more natural and realistic appearance. He wanted to create "poetry in form and color."[7] The panels in Schloss Heltorf completed by Schadow's team have a more lively appearance, therefore, than the static, other-worldly figures painted by his predecessor's students. Despite the differences, however, there was still what one contemporary called an "idyllic detachment" to the Düsseldorf School that served to dull the political senses. Another critic, playwright and novelist Karl Immermann, quipped that only "the thunder of cannon fire on the Rhine"[8] would shake them out of it. Until that moment Berlin could rest content.

One of Schadow's disciples, however, was already adopting a more critical stance. Karl Friedrich Lessing was probably the most talented young artist to migrate with the master to Düsseldorf. In 1829 he painted the controversial *Royal Couple in Mourning*. Lessing's inspiration was a recent poem by Ludwig Uhland which portrayed the end of a royal blood line caused by the death of a princess. Uhland's political message about the inevitable dying out of monarchy was picked up by Lessing in dramatic fashion. Monumental figures of the king and queen sit morosely before the draped casket. While the the power and splendor of the royal house are evident, the monarch's depressed stare and his partner's downcast, forlorn countenance cast doubt on their longevity as rulers. "The oversized royal figures," wrote one critic who saw the exhibit in Berlin, "project themselves like ghosts of the departed into a present day which is inherently republican."[9]

7. Cited in Hütt, 15.

8. Ekkehard Mai,"Die Düsseldorfer Malerschule und die Malerei des 19. Jahrhunderts," in Kalnein, 27.

9. Cited in Hanna Gagel, "Die Düsseldorfer Malerschule in der politischen Situation des Vormärz und 1848," in Kalnein, 68.

Unlike Schadow and the Nazarenes, Caspar David Friedrich sought no escape from the political realities of the present. During the wars of liberation, works like *The Grave of Arminius* and *Cuirassier in the Forest* were deeply imbued with the patriotic spirit of the day. Friedrich also sympathized with the nationalistic goal of a liberal and united Germany which lured so many young men to the Wartburg Festival in 1817. His circle of immediate friends in Dresden was linked with Arndt, Schleiermacher, and Reimer in Berlin, and the suppression of their political dreams depressed him as it did them. Reflecting on Prussia's military hero, Gerhard Scharnhorst, Friedrich lamented that "so long as we remain the menials of princes, nothing great of this kind will be seen."[10] As the dark years of Carlsbad descended over Germany, he found ways to keep Germanic goals alive on canvas. Many of his male figures appear in the old German blackcoats that Arndt had designed for true patriots. In many of Friedrich's sea and harbor paintings, ships fly the flag of liberal Sweden. His many Swiss landscapes, moreover, were a reminder of the asylum that so many of the politically persecuted had found in the land of the Alps.

Friedrich's paintings also addressed political issues at a symbolic level. *Sea of Ice*, finished in 1823 or 1824, expressed gloom over the victory of conservatism, as did *Dashed Hope*, a variation from the early 1820s depicting a shipwreck in an icy sea. Very often, he juxtaposed the dark, the ruined, or the icy cold, symbols of the barren, doomed present, with signs of life or a distant light to symbolize political hope for the future. *Oak in the Snow* (1827/28) is one such work. The thick-trunked oak, a special tree to the nationalists, stands upright and alive amidst a motionless, frozen wasteland. Similarly, *Two Men Looking at the Moon* (1819) presents a rugged, nearly lifeless hillside where two men dressed in old German coats stand affectionately close to one another. With backs to the viewer, they peer at rays of moonlight which cut through a foggy night. In *Wanderer above a Foggy Moor* (1818), Friedrich positions a stolid figure on a rock looking over the depressing moor at a mountain rising into the bright sky. In both paintings the viewer is invited to turn *his* back on an unacceptable present, step into the faceless fig-

10. Cited in Sheehan, *German History*, 405.

ure, and hope, perhaps struggle, for change. "For ... only through struggle and conflict," wrote the painter, "can 'the New' make a place for itself and prevail."[11]

Like many Germans who longed for political reforms, however, Friedrich had little sympathy for the economic transition then underway. This rejection of so many aspects of the modern world caused him no small amount of anguish because, as a deeply religious man, he assumed they were part of a divine plan. "No human power can stop our great and fateful era, a time of upsurgance and transformation which seizes all branches of the economy, the arts, and the sciences, for God has brought about these times – and will see them through." Despite such conclusions, he clung desperately to the notion that it would be possible to ward off the seemingly inevitable. He had no desire "to work against the demands of the times ... rather I cherish the hope that the times themselves will destroy that to which they have given birth – and that they will do it soon."[12]

In the meantime, Friedrich's art could keep this hope alive. Some of his first canvases from the early years in Dresden took a direct approach to social criticism, depicting nearby flour mills, glass works, and the resulting environmental damage. After 1800, however, Friedrich's landscapes show none of this sad scene. Years later, he criticized a realist who had been "painfully true to the beautiful as well as the ugly forms of nature, like people, driven by hunger and need, spoiled inside and out by the construction of houses, disgusting criss-crossing fields and the chopping away of forests." It was better "to imagine our way back to a pure nature in its original or primeval state."[13] This was not romantic escapism, but rather, a more poignant political statement.

Friedrich's *Bohemian Landscape*, completed around 1810, conveys this impression. Although the background is the Milleschauer, a mountain in Bohemia, the painting is not simply a portrait of the area. The trees, bushes, and rolling hills were taken from separate generic sketches dating back to 1799 and placed in dark green, light green, dark brown, and gray-green layers that advance toward

11. Cited in Getrud Fiege, *Caspar David Friedrich in Selbstzeugnisse und Bilddokumenten* (Hamburg, 1977), 109.

12. Ibid., 72.

13. Ibid., 68-69.

the mountain. The effect of these colored zones is a certain tension or turbulence created by an immediate foreground rising from the middle and a farther ground descending from the middle, separated from one another by a forest barrier. In the distant, seemingly inaccessible background, the Milleschauer rises into the yellow and blue of an evening sky. "It is not clear," writes Gertrud Fiege, "whether [the mountain] represents things past, things present, or some kind of religious, socio-political, or indefinite yearning, a dream of a better world."[14]

There are thus two levels of meaning in many of his paintings. On one plane the viewer finds a symbolic critique of political conservatism, while on another he sees a superior primeval state of hills, valleys, forests, and seas. Like the patriotic figures in *Two Men Looking at the Moon*, Friedrich simply turned his back on the emerging world of machines, industry, and cities.

* * * *

The earliest rumblings of industrialization were heard differently by Peter Wilhelm Beuth, head of Prussia's Business Department, and Karl Friedrich Schinkel, the state's chief architect and builder. The two close friends had visited England in the 1820s and were thus well aware of the ugly, unaesthetic potential of the industrial revolution. Writing to Schinkel in 1823, for instance, Beuth labeled English cities "chamber pots." They were, however, confident that German industrialization would take a different trajectory. Even England offered glimpses of that altered, superior future that Beuth and Schinkel envisioned for their home-

Karl Friedrich Lessing's *Royal Couple in Mourning*, 1829, symbolizing the dying out of monarchy.

14. Ibid., 72.

land. Near Leeds Beuth had been impressed by one woolen manufacturer whose villa contained "beautiful paintings" and "beautiful things from Athens" and sported a view "onto two lovely water-blessed valleys."[15] Beuth and Schinkel dreamed of a refined industrialization which would move Germany out of the shadow of ancient Greece and Rome – beyond memories of former times and glorious accomplishments which had inspired awe for over a millennium.

They wanted the new industries to grow up in the countryside where both homes and factory buildings could be placed in quaint settings pleasing to the eye. An aesthetic dimension, in other words, would be added to the economic advantages of cheap surplus labor, water wheels, and proximity to flax, wool, dye crops, and other raw materials. The textile products – even the factory buildings themselves – would also have a cultivated touch. To effect this "refining influence on manufacturers," Beuth and Schinkel coauthored a factory manual containing copper engravings and lithographic prints of buildings, fabrics, rugs, tapestries, and curtains, all with artistic motifs from antiquity. Industrialists were encouraged "not to be misled into composing on your own, but rather to duplicate [the manual's designs] faithfully with industriousness and good taste." In the cities and towns, moreover, the practitioners of industrial arts like ceramics, enameling, gilding, and casting could fill up the homes of the wealthy with their artistry.

Caspar David Friedrich's *Wanderer above a Foggy Moor*, 1818. Friedrich turned his back on contemporary state and society.

15. The quotations here are cited in Brose, *Politics of Technological Change*, 99, 113.

While aesthetic industrialization was destined, for the most part, to remain in the realm of dreams, Schinkel and Beuth did effect a revolution in taste among upper class consumers. "The smallest and the largest [objects] took on more refined forms," remembered the poet and novelist, Theodor Fontane. Ovens and stoves which previously stood out like "monsters" turned into enameled "ornaments," while iron grilles and gates "ceased to be a mere collection of rods and bars." But the two friends wanted their revolution to go farther. "We lack neither the means nor the opportunity," wrote Beuth in 1824, "to reproduce the artistic treasures of antiquity in plasters, prints, and castings, then use them in a practical way as decorations." By the late 1830s, however, he bemoaned his country's turn away from "the clear forms of antiquity"[16] toward baroque and rococo decorations with their conservative, absolutist overtones of official culture. The intervening revolutions of 1830 (see below) had created a somber mood in liberal circles.

Indeed there was a distinct political dimension to this preference for ancient motifs. By exposing manufacturers to classical aesthetics, Beuth and Schinkel were attempting to impart a social status or pedigree which would elevate the bourgeoisie in its quest for power and influence. Classical designs and art forms were also highly charged political symbols which expressed a clear choice for political change: Prussia and Germany, like Athens, would rise to greatness under just institutions, not tyranny. "Knowledge of the Greeks is not merely pleasant, useful, or necessary to us!" exclaimed Wilhelm von Humboldt, a good friend and party associate of Beuth and Schinkel. "No, in the Greeks alone we find the ideal of that which we should like to be."[17] It should come as no surprise, therefore, that the conservative parties were highly suspicious of all forms of neoclassicism, especially liberal schoolmasters who used the study of Greek mythology and the reading of Polibius and Livy to preach about the inevitable death which came to tyrants.

Schinkel is best known, of course, for his great architectural achievements. Anyone visiting Berlin today, in fact, can view many of the private dwellings and public buildings that gradually

16. Ibid., 114-17.
17. Ibid., 112.

transformed the city from its pre-war drabness. The first structure erected under his talented gaze was the New Guard House in 1816. Scores of commissions followed, including the Theater (1821), the Glienicke Palace outside Potsdam (1824), the New Pavilion in Charlottenburg (1825), the Royal Museum (1830), and the Academy of Architecture(1836).

The Royal Museum – commonly known as the Old Museum – is perhaps the most famous. The exquisite grandeur of its eighteen Ionic columns mounted proudly on a vaulted base, all rising high above a park in central Berlin, elegantly complemented the nearby royal palace, armory, and cathedral. To these other symbolic pillars of the state – throne, army, and altar – he wanted to add cultivation *(Bildung)*. Indeed science and education were the great bourgeois contributions of the new age. It was no coincidence, therefore, that the Old Museum, like most Schinkel buildings, was neoclassical in style. While it is certainly true that he was not wedded to neoclassicism and often experimented with other styles, there can be no doubt about Schinkel's love of antiquity or the political agenda behind this stylistic choice. Schinkel wanted his Greek edifices to remind adjacent official Berlin of the political ideals of Periclean Athens. His columniation was an architectural inspiration "which helps us to persevere through the injustices of time."[18] Schinkel inscribed the name of Frederick William III above the Old Museum's columnade, and, significantly enough, the aging monarch supported his architect's neoclassical preferences. There was no confusion or contradiction here. The king opposed parliamentarism, but he had also opened his government to the bourgeoisie and promoted some of the liberals' programs as a foil against overreaching conservative ambitions. Architecturally, central Berlin symbolized the nature of the state in Prussia during the 1820s.

The Greek revival in architecture was not limited to Berlin and Prussia. One need only view the Capitol in Washington, D. C., the Philadelphia Art Museum, or Jefferson's Monticello in Virginia to appreciate neoclassicism's transatlantic popularity. In the United States, this centuries-old style was preferred by an exclusive, tal-

18. Ibid., 112.

ented elite dedicated to the challenge of creating a successful republic for the first time since antiquity. Architecture was less a weapon in the struggle for change, in other words, than a celebration of victory in the early stages. Is it possible that public edifices played a similar inspirational role in liberal South Germany? Friedrich Weinbrenner's work in Karlsruhe and Leo von Klenze's commissions in Munich were certainly devoted to the belief that the Greek past should grace the German present.

There was probably a good parallel with American trends in the Bavarian case, for Klenze was backed – prodded is perhaps a better word – by his sovereign. Although he financed Gothic and Romanesque construction too, Ludwig I was essentially committed to Greek revivalism, particularly before the revolutionary outbursts of 1830. This philhellenic enthusiast wanted to transform Munich into a new Athens as part of a crusade to preserve the progressive cause in Bavaria and Germany. Klenze's Glyptothek, finished in 1831, was central to this effort – Cornelius's frescoes notwithstanding. Erected as a Greek temple for the arts, its Ionic facades symbolized the elegant harmony of Bavaria's political order and glorified the monarch who strove to keep freedom and authority in balance.

Not surprisingly, travelers to Vienna in the 1820s saw no such transformation underway. The inner reaches of the imperial capital were still surrounded by an Early Modern glacis, a "cincture of stone which for many centuries kept Vienna's noble limbs imprisoned in an evil spell,"[19] wrote a liberal journalist years later. Inside this imposing ring of fortifications, the inner city "was dominated architecturally by the symbols of the first and second estates,"[20] observes Carl Schorske. The Baroque Hofburg of Emperor Francis, the ornate Palais of the Aristocracy, and the Gothic Cathedral of St. Stephen expressed Austria's reactionary political reality and official culture as well as any liberal newspaper criticism that may have slipped into print. The Greek revival that was sweeping the east coast of America, Berlin, and Munich stopped at the frontiers of Austria.

* * * *

19. Cited in Carl E. Schorske, *Fin-De-Siècle Vienna: Politics and Culture* (New York, 1981), 29.

20. Ibid., 31.

Georg Wilhelm Friedrich Hegel was twenty-three when revolution claimed Louis XVI and Marie Antoinette. The young Swabian student of theology soon had more earthshaking events to interpret and explain, for, as if aided by some invisible hand of genius, French armies marched east, conquered German kingdoms, and swept away institutions that had survived for centuries. Serfdom, the guilds, ecclesiastical states, even the Holy Roman Empire itself were destroyed. Yet, inspired by western ideas, the eastern states rose up with a new spirit to conquer the conquerors. The French were gone by 1815, but so was the Germany of 1789. Hegel knew that he had lived through a remarkable period in world history, but he also realized that existing philosophical systems were unable to explain the dynamic process of change that had stamped an entire era. As professor of philosophy at the University of Berlin after 1817, he published his own explanations. The world received a new philosophy of history with the appearance of works like the *Encyclopedia of the Philosophical Sciences* (1817, 1827, 1830) and *Philosophy of Right* (1821).

The motive force in history, according to Hegel, was the gradual unfolding of the absolute idea or divine spirit in human consciousness. It advanced ineluctably and inevitably through time, but its progress was uneven and unpredictable, characterized by division against itself, a spiritual struggle between the parts, restoration of unity on a higher plane closer to the ultimate goal of human perfection, then division and renewed struggle toward that noble end. States were the vehicles of this usually cruel and violent process of change and progress. The divided spirit revealed itself to those whose reason was cultivated to the point where they could fathom it: theologians, philosophers, artists, and gifted statesmen. Art and education therefore required autonomy from state controls. State leaders were wise if they understood and facilitated the workings of the spirit, avoiding all futile opposition as the absolute idea struggled from one historical stage to the next. "It is a dialectical movement proceeding from thesis through antithesis to synthesis," writes Hajo Holborn, "or, concretely, from the Oriental, who knew that one man was free, to the Greeks, who knew that some men were free, to the Christian-German nations which knew that man, as man, is free."[21]

21. Hajo Holborn, *A History of Modern Germany 1648-1840* (New York, 1964), 512.

Hegel believed that the wars of the French Revolution had resulted in the restored unity of the divine spirit and that it was lodged – or actualized – in Prussia, a state destined to become the agent of progress.

The Hegelian dialectic became immensely popular in German universities during the 1820s. "Academic studies were entirely transformed," observes Isaiah Berlin. "Hegelian logic, Hegelian jurisprudence, Hegelian ethics and aesthetics, Hegelian theology, Hegelian philology, Hegelian historiography, surrounded the student of humanities wherever he turned."[22] This was so in part because the philosophy of the spirit offered disappointed intellectuals a means to rationalize defeat. If the spirit had reunited itself in Prussia, authoritarian monarchy must somehow fit into the divine scheme. One had to trust that freedom's road could in fact lead through Berlin and search, in the meantime, for signs of present and future greatness. Wasn't Prussia the first German state to turn against Napoleon in 1813? And weren't her bureaucrats champions of enlightened causes like peasant emancipation, customs unification, and industrial development? Such reasoning led Hegel to the famous dictum that "what is real is rational, what is rational is real." The reality of Prussia was rational, in other words, because its institutions were in conformity with the current progress of the spirit.

Despite the obvious reactionary uses of Hegelianism, the conservative parties in Germany were correct in counting Hegel among their political enemies. They objected to the use of reason to question the established order, concluding rightly that some might view the state as irrational and thus in opposition to the divine spirit. Here was an argument for revolution not unlike that employed by the eighteenth-century French philosophers. Conservatives also disliked the pantheistic nature of Hegel's philosophies as well as his relegation of religion to a mere stage in the development of human consciousness. As explained in Part III, their fears that Hegelianism contained "the principle of revolution" would prove warranted.

These trends from the world of academic philosophy – as well as music, painting, and architecture – reflected a new historical con-

22. Isaiah Berlin, *Karl Marx: His Life and Environment* (New York, 1959), 56.

sciousness in Germany. A more pronounced preoccupation with the past had first become evident during the Enlightenment as Germans sought to cope with indications that the long history of the Holy Roman Empire might be nearing an end. In the late 1700s, moreover, progressives had begun to employ Greek or Roman antiquity as a beacon for present and future reformers. As we have already observed with Hegel, however, it was undoubtedly the searing experience of the French Revolution and the conquests of Napoleon that heightened this awareness for things past. "Anyone who has lived through the revolution feels impelled towards history," wrote Goethe. As Barthold Georg Niebuhr, a historian of Ancient Rome at the University of Bonn, explained: "We could do little more than ardently hope for better days and prepare for them. I went back to a great nation to strengthen my mind and that of my hearers."[23] Historical thinking became an even more prominent part of the German mentality after 1815 as social and economic change increased appreciation for values and institutions that threatened to pass from the scene.

Niebuhr's method of historical inquiry was obviously influenced by his position in the present. "True historical writing is only possible on the basis of what we have ourselves experienced," he wrote, "for in the past we can at best perceive what we have a certain impression of in the present." His history was not distorted by his politics, however, for he strove to create a certain distance between himself and the object of study. Influenced by the theories of Johann Gottfried Herder, Niebuhr believed he could achieve this objectivity by probing the origins and usage of language. His contemporary at the University of Berlin, August Boeckh, also followed Herder in believing that the discipline of history was basically a branch of philology. Boeckh's works on Greek history and literature sought to recapture the essence of a people, its "entire mental development," by analyzing and interpreting language in its historical context. It was only with Leopold Ranke's *History of the Latin and Teutonic Nations from 1794 to 1514* (1824) that German historians began to break from this type of linguistic historical inquiry (see Part IV). Ranke wanted "to show how things really

23. Citations in Sheehan, 544-45.

happened" by amassing and analyzing documentary evidence. He joined Niebuhr and Boeckh, however, in rejecting Hegelian philosophical methods of ascertaining historical truth. All three found the Master's generalizations not sufficiently grounded in factual research, arguing that answers to historical questions flowed from the details of each particular situation. Only after hard empirical research would it be possible to discover a divine pattern to events. As Ranke put it, one had to search for these "coded messages scattered by God through time."[24]

Karl Friedrich Eichhorn and Friedrich Karl von Savigny, professors of jurisprudence at the University of Berlin, were also important contributors to the new empirical historicism. Like their colleagues pioneering academic history, Eichhorn and Savigny were deeply affected by the destruction and disruption of the revolutionary era. Angered by the arrogance of French philosophy's claim to universality, and resentful of changes imposed on Germany in the name of these alien principles, both felt compelled to study the uniqueness and peculiarity of the law in Germany through analysis of the language in which it was written. "It was more important than ever," wrote Eichhorn, "to turn our gaze to the past and become acquainted with the spirit of our former condition." The ultimate goal for both men was to discover through their research what Savigny called the "fundamental and necessary individuality"[25] of the German people. Rejecting the "sterile reasoning" and "diffuse and superficial philosophizing"[26] of the Enlightenment, they prepared to embark on a winding and complicated empirical journey backwards to the source of the folk's unique nature. Eichhorn and Savigny established the *Journal of Legal History* in 1815 as a vehicle for this scholarly and political mission.

The German Question already swirled turbulently around the work of both jurists. One year earlier a South German legal scholar, Anton Friedrich Justus Thibaut of the University of Heidelberg, published an appeal for a codification of German law. Thibaut bemoaned the vast regional and local variations of the law in Ger-

24. Ibid., 545, 547, 552.

25. Ibid., 548-49.

26. Savigny is cited in James Q. Whitman, *The Legacy of Roman Law in the German Romantic Era: Historical Vision and Legal Change* (Princeton, 1990), 88, 108.

many, reciting mockingly the popular saying that each town and village preserved its law "in an old tale and in a grimy community chest." He also opposed the Roman legal practices that had spread throughout the Holy Roman Empire after the creation of an autonomous Imperial Cameral Tribunal in 1495. Thibaut preferred the native Germanic rituals that had prevailed before this time. The South German struck a resounding chord with many educated Germans who welcomed an ally to the cause of restoring German unity. Both Savigny and Eichhorn rejected Thibaut's views, however, feeling that they smacked of the centralizing, universalizing, and "philosophizing" tendencies of the French. For legal codes meant new laws by legislative fiat that could "dispense with all actual reality," that is, with existing German laws.[27] Moderate conservatives at heart, they preferred a form of legal unity that preserved Germany's rich diversity. Codification would eventually occur, but it had to be preceded by decades of philological research into the details of local legal peculiarities.

Eichhorn and Savigny differed on the Roman legacy. While the former preferred native hometown law, the latter saw in Roman forms a bridge to the public peace of the Holy Roman Empire, and, farther back in time, to that glorious ancient epoch, the Pax Romana, so temptingly impressive after Europe's generation of violence. Savigny and his followers believed that legal practices of the Roman Republic had persisted into Rome's imperial period, imparting a legacy of freedom and fairness to the reigns of Hadrian and the Antonines. In much the same way, Roman legal traditions which had guaranteed a German sort of freedom from the abuse of princes in the Holy Roman Empire could ensure justice in the confusing, uncertain world of the 1820s. Savigny wanted to free judges from political pressures by having them base decisions on the learned treatises of university scholars versed in German local laws as well as the Roman principles which he believed had permeated these laws after the late medieval period. Litigants should also enjoy the old sixteenth century practice of dispatching the record *(Aktenversendung)*. When the new German Confederation revived

27. Ibid., 102; and Michael John, *Politics and the Law in Late Nineteenth-Century Germany: The Origins of the Civil Code* (Oxford, 1989), 19.

this right to transfer jurisdiction of a case to an impartial law faculty in 1815, Savigny waxed optimistic about the future of freedom from tyranny. "We have uncovered, in the estate of the jurists, a subject for living customary law, and so for true progress."[28]

One of Savigny's most talented and sensitive students was Jacob Grimm. The dissatisfied young law student had studied with Savigny at Marburg before the professor received his call to Berlin in 1810. In turning to German literature and philology, Jacob and his illustrious brother, Wilhelm, would find infinitely more gratifying careers. The critical historicism imparted by Savigny, however, colored all of their remarkable labors. Indeed as the decade of the 1810s drew to a close, the fame of the Brothers Grimm had spread well beyond the borders of their native Hesse-Kassel. The first volume of *The Children's and Household Tales* appeared in 1812. A second volume followed in 1815. German readers were now familiar with "Little Red Riding Hood," "Hansel and Gretel," "Snow White and the Seven Dwarfs," and other fairy tales meticulously gathered by the brothers from storytellers in the Hessian countryside. *German Folk Tales* appeared in 1816 and was quickly succeeded by a second volume in 1818. Drawing on oral as well as written sources, Wilhelm and Jabob entered the world of popular history and local legend by recapturing stories like Lohengrin the Knight of the Swan, William Tell, Tannhäuser at the Wartburg, and Emperor Barbarossa Sleeping at Kyffhäuser. Recognition followed fame in the form of honorary doctorates and special tributes.

The Grimms were convinced that their tales and legends could lead readers backward into the nation's past. The simple language of the stories was central to this journey. Like a grand old tree whose concentric rings descended into some original time, the rough peasant dialect of the fairy and folk tales was supposedly rooted in some primeval epoch. They were "wonderful last echoes of ancient myths" from the "childhood of the race."[29] The brothers attributed almost animate qualities to language, believing that its spirit embodied the consciousness of early Germans and transmitted the growing, evolving truth and essence of a people across

28. Cited in Whitman, 109.

29. Cited in Murray B. Peppard, *Paths Through the Forest: A Biography of the Brothers Grimm* (New York, 1971), 48, 49.

the ages to modern times. The spirit of the language communicated with sensitive artists, made them its servants, and thus ensured that the folk's glories and greatness were preserved for posterity. While there were certainly pedagogical and educational reasons for the brothers' research, "their motive in discovering the old language and reediting old manuscripts was not primarily academic," writes Murray Peppard, "but rather patriotic: it was a means of discovering the spirit of the past."[30]

Growing to manhood in Hesse-Kassel during the chaos of the Napoleonic Wars, the Brothers Grimm sought escape in "the peacefulness of scholarship." Not surprisingly, the bleak years before Napoleon's demise in Russia saw the most intense work on the *Fairy Tales*. "But we did not only seek consolation in the past," wrote Wilhelm. "We hoped naturally that this course of ours would contribute to the return of a better day." Somehow the tales would strengthen love of Fatherland and contribute to the liberation of Germany. Once this task was accomplished, however, the need for patriotic motivation gradually shifted from the military arena to politics on the homefront. For, like many intellectuals, the brothers were disappointed that Germany's "recent time of greatness" had lead to nothing better than the German Confederation. "We Germans are one body," exclaimed Wilhelm, "and all the limbs demand and need only one head." While not opponents of monarchy in theory, they grew tired of "perfumed monarchism," as Jacob described it, "which won't permit the slightest or most honest objections and which scoffs at the nature of human feelings and rights."[31] As the 1810s drew on to the 1820s, the Brothers Grimm viewed their scholarship as a means to revive moral forces which could regenerate state and society.

Jacob's monumental *German Grammar* was published in 1819. An extended and revised second edition appeared in 1822 and a second volume in 1826. In nearly 4,000 pages, he documented the growth of the Germanic dialects from the fourth century to the early nineteenth century. His purpose was "to follow modestly the profound spirit of the language" and thus to bolster modern Ger-

30. Ibid., 29.
31. Ibid., 40, 90, 124-25, 126.

mans in an uncertain, unhappy age. Contact with "the old language, simple and rich within its own resources" was important to the cure, for modern language had "lost its innocence."[32] Wilhelm's great contribution of the decade was his *German Heroic Tales* of 1829. The book documented the growth of epic poetry like the famous "Song of the Niebelungs" from the sixth to the sixteenth century. Like all of their previous works, the *Heroic Tales* were designed to reacquaint Germans with their ancestry. Further recognition followed in 1829 when the Brothers Grimm received a call to the prestigeous University of Göttingen. Revolutionary developments awaited them there.

32. Ibid., 130.

Chapter 9

The Revolutions of 1830

It was nearly midnight in the early spring of 1830. The new gas lamps on Berlin's Mauerstrasse cast a cold, incongruous glow on a candelabra-lit bust of Prince Louis Ferdinand displayed lovingly in the front room of Rahel and Karl August Varnhagen von Ense. Most of their guests had already departed – the singers, the *après* theater visitors, the usual smattering of foreign personalities and out-of-town liberals, even Alexander von Humboldt, who was usually the last to leave. Rahel's brother, Ludwig Robert, suppressed a yawn as the typically more lively and intimate portion of the evening began.[1]

"So tell us, Eduard," Rahel said seriously, "will Prussia travel the French road toward constitutionalism – or, if you will humor me, republicanism?" The perfect hostess even at the most challenging intellectual moments, Rahel knew how Hegel's good friend Eduard Gans loved to debate politics. It was much more a part of him than the mundane legal studies he pursued at the university. The veteran dialectician responded somewhat evasively, however, for he preferred to enter the fray at a later stage, countering and dissect-

1. This scene is based mainly on a detailed, anonymous description of an evening at the Varnhagens in March 1830. See "Der Salon Frau von Varnhagen," in Karl August Varnhagen von Ense, *Vermischte Schriften von Karl August Varnhagen von Ense* (Leipzig, 1876}, 19:183-210. I have also drawn on Varnhagen's diary [printed in Ludmilla Assing (ed.), *Blätter aus der preussischen Geschichte* (Leipzig, 1868-69), 3:244-45] and on the entry for Eduard Gans in the *Allgemeine Deutsche Biographie*, 8:361-62.

ing opposing arguments advanced by others. "It could come to either one, but if the transition is to be peaceful, only the bureaucracy can ensure this. It must be the organism which holds state and society together." Rahel acknowledged the point with a quick, polite nod, but did not respond. Her strength was her ability to elevate a mature discussion above the narrow and obvious. She too would wait for a later word.

Varnhagen obliged them both. "Ah yes, the bureaucracy," he began in a sarcastic vein. "The various officials which make up the bureaucracy remind me of the many petty states, imperial knights, and corporate entities of the Holy Roman Empire. It is a war of all against all – a feud between the parts. Each ministry is a castle which concerns itself primarily with defense. Some of these fortresses are controlled by robber barons who steal from the commonweal. Most of the best and noblest forces in the state are consumed by this internal struggle. Sometimes the king stands above these battles and at other times he takes part in them – again, somewhat like the Emperor of the medieval Reich. Often he makes decisions, occasionally with no success. But mostly he allows events to take their own course. So I am not as sanguine as you, Eduard. I fear a disintegration of the whole."

Throughout this lengthy statement, Gans studied his opponent carefully, listening for weak or exaggerated points in Varnhagen's oratory, not wishing to speak until his friend's eloquent comparison was complete. Then he tried to demolish it. "What you say has some merit, of course. All states have internal divisions and this is as natural as disagreements among friends. But I would rather emphasize the common ties which bind together the bureaucratic estate. Foremost among these is the patriotic bond. Grasping enemies without, greedy, self-interested classes within – all antithetical demands must be synthesized in the great courtroom of power. Take, for instance, the decadent truculence of our Junkers."

Rahel's gaze shifted from her husband to Gans as the professor of law presented his counter-arguments in a flowing crescendo of impeccable French. Unless Ludwig joined the discussion, it would soon be her turn to lift the dialogue to a higher plane.

* * * *

Rahel was fond of citing Goethe's words: "Come in friends and kindred spirits." The citation was very appropriate in the Berlin of early 1830, for salon life during the 1820s had grown increasingly polarized between advocates and enemies of constitutionalism. More and more one tended to seek out "those with a like mind," as Varnhagen himself put it. In the company of friends, one could relax, talk about trivial matters, or engage in serious political discussion. Horizontally across the political spectrum and vertically from state into society, there were myriad small parties such as that depicted in our scene. In provincial town councils and chambers of commerce these factions were fortunate if they could count a general or highly-placed bureaucrat as a friendly contact. The Varnhagens' "dear circle of like-minded friends" was more influential, including, as it did, renowned scholars like Hegel, Gans, and Alexander von Humboldt, the king's frequent guest. As we shall see, however, there were similar – and related – cliques in the army, civilian bureaucracy, and at court which rose much higher into the citadel of power. In normal times, these liberal factions were little threat to the establishment. But in times of crisis this fragmented political opposition could coalesce and pursue loosely coordinated action.

The summer of 1830 was such a time. Anxious conservatives had studied France in recent years, afraid that revolution would erupt again and sweep eastward. "I am not concerned about the [Middle East]," declared Emperor Francis. "One should look to Paris – there lies the danger."[2] This fear seemed justified after Charles X appointed Jules de Polignac premier. For how could domestic peace endure in a country where the monarch believed in his divine rights, the premier thought he could converse with the Virgin Mary, and the Chamber of Deputies was packed with liberal anticlerics? Poor harvests and a harsh winter across Europe (with the resulting rise in rural and urban unemployment) added to escalating worries. The volatile mix of circumstances exploded during the bloody July Days of 1830. Within hours, Charles X was deposed.

The news of Bourbon demise shocked conservatives and emboldened Hotspurs throughout Europe. "My entire life's work is

2. Cited in Bibl, *Kaiser Franz*, 328.

destroyed,"[3] lamented Metternich as revolution spread to Belgium, Italy, and Poland. Nor was his native Germany spared. Threatened craftsmen vented their ire on factory machinery in Aachen, Berlin, and Leipzig, while in Hesse-Kassel, peasants destroyed manorial records and bread riots rocked the capital city. The mob also struck in Brunswick after an officer guarding the ducal palace spoke condescendingly to the throng he confronted. "Now children, what do you want anyway?" "Bread and jobs!"[4] was the angry reply, as they proceeded to torch the baroque residence. Not present for the humiliation, Duke Karl of Brunswick had already joined Charles X in exile. Similar disturbances occurred in Göttingen, Cologne, Elberfeld, Frankfurt am Main, Chemnitz, Freiberg, Dresden, and Munich.

Mob violence in numerous Saxon cities – plus a desperate royal promise there of parliamentary reform – worried Count Karl Chotek, Provincial Governor of neighboring Bohemia. The prospect of Czech peasants following the Saxon lead moved him to propose the easing of manorial labor burdens, but the kaiser was only annoyed by the suggestion. "It seems to me that Count Chotek has also become infected with liberal ideas," Francis said to Interior Minister Kolowrat. "What has happened to him anyway?" When Kolowrat dared to agree with Chotek, however, the emperor grew even more adamantly opposed to the idea of reforms: "No, no, we shall leave well enough alone!" Like the liberal cliques which placed their hopes in him, Kolowrat was convinced that grave times necessitated timely reforms. So did Baron Franz Xaver von Pillersdorf, Saurau's successor as chief chancellor. Yet his entreaties met the same stone wall of imperial obstinacy: "Just apply the laws fairly; our laws are good and adequate." Now was no time for reforms, he felt, because the people were like the severely wounded, and common sense taught that "touching and straining a wound should be avoided lest it reopen." There were also voices in the military favoring change. General Joseph Radetzky trumpeted the "great and wise" principle of constitutionalism in order to turn Austria's wooden warriors into "citizen soldiers." But the only military action on the Emperor's mind in the autumn of 1830

3. Ibid., 330.
4. Cited in Treitschke, *Deutsche Geschichte*, 4:101.

was a sanitizing expedition against France. Not even Kolowrat's warning about the dismal state of Austrian finances deterred Francis from these plans. "What does it matter?" he told his minister. "Bankruptcy is a tax like any other; one only has to proceed in such a way that everyone loses equally."[5] While Hanover, Brunswick, Hesse-Kassel, and Saxony turned the constitutional corner, Kaiser Francis and Metternich held fast, plotted counterrevolution, and anxiously studied political developments in Berlin.

Like his fellow monarch in Vienna, Frederick William was besieged by liberal cliques whose leaders were no longer content to dream about politics with friends over a quiet dinner. Bourgeois dignitaries in the Westphalian Diet united behind the resolution of businessman Friedrich Harkort that their sovereign be officially reminded of his parliamentary promises, while in Aachen, a young entrepreneur named David Hansemann sent a long memorandum to the king expressing his colleagues' desire for representative institutions. Prince William, Frederick William's brother, argued for parliamentary action before war came, as did ex-Minister of War, Hermann von Boyen. In Berlin, Job von Witzleben, the king's closest adviser, was the target of numerous liberal party plots to move the monarch to establish a diet. Not without success, it would seem, for Witzleben and his good friend, Wilhelm von Humboldt, were widely rumored to be working on a constitution in the hopes that one would soon be ordered from above. Humboldt's appointment to the Council of State was interpreted by crestfallen conservatives as proof that Frederick William was "entirely in the hands of the liberals." But Count Wittgenstein, Duke Karl of Mecklenburg, and other reactionaries were wrong. "No representative constitution will help in the least," the king answered his brother William, against "the crazy drive to topple everything which exists." The "most complete proof of this" was the record of parliamentary countries where "things were really the worst." Thus "[even] if one could come to say heartfelt things about [adopting] the same [institutions] for here, that which really happens [in the world] fully suffices to bring one back away from this."[6] The will of

5. The citations here are from Bibl, 343, 346-47, 350.
6. The quotes in this paragraph are from Brose, *Politics of Technological Change*, 94.

two men in Vienna and Berlin sufficed, for the time being, to keep Germany's political fulcrum monarchical and authoritarian.

But there were critical differences. Austrian liberalism had been suppressed in Draconian fashion by an emperor who perceived liberal plots as the worst threat to his power. Accordingly, policy was set almost entirely by Francis and the conservatives. Kolowrat was not a genuine liberal, functioning more as a convenient counterweight to the ambitions of Metternich. Prussian liberalism, on the other hand, was not as seriously threatened by a monarch who guarded against conservative intrigues and "was ruled," according to one conservative spokesman, "by the humanitarian concepts of the Enlightenment."[7] Hence liberal factions were entrenched in every ministry, throughout the army, and at court. While Frederick William was interested in *balancing* the parties, not championing one over the other, Prussian policy was nevertheless more affected by liberal ideas than could ever be the case in Vienna. Tension between the two powers mounted, therefore, as 1830 yielded to 1831.

Prussian Foreign Minister Christian von Bernsdorff and his undersecretary, Johann Eichhorn, were at the center of this growing quarrel. They represented the ministerial tip of a party coalition which was dissatisfied with Prussian acquiescence to Austria's dominant position in Germany. Extending to Georg Maassen and Ludwig Kühne in Finance, Peter Beuth in Interior, Otto August Rühle von Lilienstern in the military schools, Johann Krauseneck in the General Staff, Prince August in the artillery, and Witzleben at court, these political compatriots wanted their kingdom to advance the liberal cause at home and draw the constitutional states in the Confederation away from Vienna and into Berlin's orbit. The European crisis that followed the revolts in Paris and Brussels seemed to create an opportune moment. If France attacked Germany, only Prussia could provide a firm defense, for Russia and Austria were suppressing revolutions in Poland and Italy. And if Prussia went to war, Frederick William would probably be forced to raise loans and fulfill his last parliamentary promise of 1820. Against the backdrop of these realities, Rühle von Lilien-

7. Ibid., 264 n.51.

stern was dispatched in February 1831 to the South German courts to negotiate Germany's defense. "So much remains certain," wrote Metternich, "something must happen or Germany will go to ruin." But he warned that the "Eichhorn-Bernsdorff party" and the political "clubs" in the ministries of Prussia and South Germany were wrong to underestimate Austria. "These good people have forgotten a few things."[8]

Four new parliamentary states in the Confederation were cause enough for concern in Vienna. Compounding these worries, however, was the escalating situation in the older constitutional states of the south. Shortly before the revolutions, Grand Duke Leopold, the so-called citizen's friend, had come to the throne in Baden. The reform-minded ruler soon had an opportunity to prove himself, for under the impact of the dramatic news from Paris, liberal deputies were returned to the diet in overwhelming numbers during the autumn of 1830. A flurry of liberal legislation followed, including a progressive reform of Baden's press laws. An interesting transition was also underway in the diet itself. The Duchy's numerous small parties, formerly grouped around many key personalities from different regions and towns, began to coalesce into two loose blocs which coordinated their strategies: one, the moderates, under Ludwig Winter; another, the radicals, under Johann von Itzstein.

A similar process was unfolding in Württemberg. Elections gave liberal candidates a strong plurality in 1831, but, anticipating progressive initiatives, King William refused to convene parliament. The monarch's stubbornness galvanized the factionalized liberals into closer union. Assembling in Bad Boll, they agreed upon a petition urging William to listen to the voice of the people. Later in Stuttgart, a series of luncheons and evening meals brought deputies from all over the kingdom together to discuss political tactics. The small circles of political associates with their local allegiances appeared to be evolving into a united parliamentary opposition.

In Bavaria, deputies from the diet had mingled at social gatherings since the 1820s. After the revolutions and new elections,

8. Citations in this paragraph are from Billinger, *Metternich and the German Question*, 71, 88, 102.

however, these social evenings grew more polarized and overtly political as opposition-minded politicians plotted the liberalization of Bavaria. The so-called stormy diet finally eroded the last of the king's patience in December 1831. Ludwig appointed the reactionary General Wrede his first minister and dissolved parliament. In Bavaria and Württemberg, monarchs began to listen more intently to Metternich's complaints about "the democratic spirit that masked itself in the constitutional garb of the parliamentary opposition."[9]

While South Germany was important, the wily Austrian realized that his counterattack against the "destructive party spirit"[10] had to succeed in Prussia if it were to carry the day. Duke Karl of Mecklenburg had warned Frederick William repeatedly throughout 1831 that something had to be done about the liberals, but was largely ignored by an experienced monarch who knew on which side his bread was buttered. In August, moreover, he raised no objections to a note which Bernsdorff sent to the South German courts. Indirectly criticizing Austria's intervention in Italy, the foreign minister warned of French retaliation in Germany, invited the South Germans to cooperate in the formulation of a common military defense, and declared that it was the duty of German princes to create institutions that would foster the common German patriotism of their subjects.

A radically nationalistic and provocatively anti-Austrian policy was something that Frederick William did not intend, however, and could not afford. Yet Metternich accused Bernsdorff and Eichhorn of just this in a letter to Wittgenstein which was quickly presented to the king. Bernsdorff was censured by his sovereign, then compromised further in early 1832 when Frederick William learned from Metternich of a worse indiscretion. An internal and confidential Prussian memorandum drafted by Eichhorn advocating liberal press laws, economic unity in Germany, and north-south military cooperation had been leaked and allowed to circulate for liberal effect in the southern capitals at the time of Rühle von Lilienstern's mission. The liberals had gone too far – and now paid

9. Ibid., 116.
10. Ibid., 116.

the price. Eichhorn and Rühle lost influence, Bernsdorff was forced to resign, and Witzleben exiled to a ministerial post. Just as disappointing from the liberal perspective, the peace held as monarchs in Paris, Berlin, Vienna, and St. Petersburg restrained themselves from provoking a European war. Without it, liberal bargaining power was greatly diminished.

The stage was set in April 1832, for the so-called Six Articles. Approved initially by Austria, Prussia, and Württemberg, the articles were designed to reinforce the authority of the princes and the German Confederation. Wary of great power meddling – but weary of parliamentary initiatives – Grand Duke Leopold of Baden and King Ludwig of Bavaria also gave their assent. The draft articles compelled princes to reject parliamentary resolutions which undermined their authority; denied parliamentary power of the purse; nullified state laws which conflicted with those of the Confederation; established a federal commission to monitor state laws in this respect; obligated the princes to take measures to oppose and prevent such anti-confederate laws; and stipulated, finally, that only the diet of the Confederation could interpret federal laws. The articles were laid before the Diet for consideration in June.

Luck intervened in 1832 – just as it had in 1819 – to make Metternich's victory much more complete. For, on the morning of 22 May, the real radical nationalists in Germany unfurled the black, red, and gold colors and marched, over 25,000 strong, to the ruins of the Hambach Castle near Neustadt in the Palatinate. Like the Wartburg Festival, students and academically-trained professionals were well represented: about 46 percent according to one sampling of the demonstrators. Reflecting the social broadening and deepening of the nationalist movement, however, around 37 percent were businessmen, merchants, printers, and booksellers, while another 25 percent were craftsmen and laborers of various sorts. There was also a strong contingent of women at the Hambach Festival. The speakers at the castle were representative of the new social mix – and the rhetoric was no less frightening to embattled rulers than that of fifteen years earlier. Jakob Siebenpfeiffer, a tailor's son who became a civil servant, saw the day coming when "the princes will exchange the ermine fur of feudal divine rights for the manly toga of German national honor," while August Wirth, a journalist from the region, predicted that "the forces of treason [will] sink into the dust before the power of patriotic love and the omnipotence of public opinion."[11] With prodigious quantities of wine loosening tongues, others spoke of princes as leeches, born traitors, and dragons ready for the slaughter.

These speeches were so alarming that Grand Duke Leopold moved units of his army from Freiburg to Karlsruhe and King Ludwig dispatched Wrede and 8,500 soldiers to the Palatinate. In reality, the ringleaders of the Hambach Festival were no immediate threat, consisting of a handful of personal political groupings and circles which were just beginning to coalesce into loose union. "An alliance of patriots" was sorely needed, said Wirth, to overcome confusion and division. "If only the purest, most able, and courageous patriots could agree ... if only twenty such men, bound together by a common cause and led by a man they trusted ... tirelessly pursued their mission ... then the great work must succeed – ".[12] The appeals were in vain. Soon in jail or exile, the leaders of the demonstration had ample time to ponder their organizational weaknesses.

The radicalism of the rhetoric speeded up passage of the Six Articles in late June 1832. The Hambach Festival also made it easier for Metternich to gain acceptance of additional reactionary measures. Passed ten days later, the so-called Ten Acts reinforced many provisions of the Carlsbad Decrees such as university surveillance, strict censorship, and mutual military assistance to quell disturbances. The acts also banned all political clubs and assemblies, forbade the display of illegal insignia and flags, and obligated states to exchange police information on subversive activities. For the most part, the Six Articles and Ten Acts had the desired effect. In Saxony, the new diet became "a spectacle of decorum and pliability."[13] In Baden, reactionaries revoked Karl Rotteck's election as mayor of Freiburg and curbed the activity of liberals in the bureaucracy. In Württemberg, King William waited until 1833 before finally convening the diet, then outlawed associations among the

11. The citations are from Treitschke, 4:263-64; and Sheehan, *German History*, 610-11.

12. Cited in Sheehan, 611.

13. Ibid., 614.

deputies. The diet in Hesse-Kassel had to suffer a campaign of abuse which included the arrest of the leading liberal parliamentarian. When scores of dissidents persecuted under these discriminatory federal laws attempted to "dispatch the record" to impartial university jurists, moreover, additional decrees were adopted in Frankfurt which abolished this old right of appeal. Only in Brunswick and Hanover were liberal constitutional forces still alive. Both states completed constitutions and elected representatives in 1832 and 1833. On balance, therefore, Vienna was content as mid-decade aproached. The amount of damage to the monarchical principle had been rather successfully controlled.

The sad case of Hanover is an appropriate epilogue to the history of the Revolutions of 1830 in Germany. For several years after Metternich's crackdown, this northern state grew politically in the direction of England, the parliamentary land whose king was Hanover's head of state. In 1837, however, the ascension of Queen Victoria forced a separation of the union under laws which forbade a woman on the throne. Ernst August, the Duke of Cumberland, became king instead. One of the conservative political dandies in Berlin where he had spent the last two decades, Duke Ernst August promptly revoked the constitution of 1833 and forced all state employees to take a new oath of allegiance. Seven professors from the University of Göttingen, including Wilhelm and Jacob Grimm, refused to sacrifice their principles. But the ending to this protest was as unhappy as most of the brothers' tales. All were removed from their chairs and three, including Jacob, were forced to leave Hanover. Successful appeals to the indignant law faculties of Heidelberg, Jena, and Tübingen were simply ignored. The Göttingen Seven became martyrs to the liberal cause. But they were also symbols of the near total defeat of that cause. Viewed from Vienna, all was well in Germany. Or nearly so.

Part III

OPENING PANDORA'S BOX

The town of Lindau was connected to the shore of Lake Constance by an old wooden bridge. For two wandering journeymen tanners in early March 1837, it was the gateway from Württemberg to Bavaria. The first proud handicraftsman, Johann Dewald, approached the guardhouse.[1] "Your papers!" barked the officer on watch. Lindau, like all towns in Germany, was wary of newcomers without means. Dewald and his companion promptly obeyed, only to be marched off to the town hall, stripped, searched, and forced to show their travel money. When his mate failed to produce the minimum ten gulden required to avoid doing hard labor for the town, Dewald lied, claiming that some of his money actually belonged to the poor tanner. Foiled, but determined to maintain his authority, the magistrate reminded them to behave themselves. "Remember, you are in Bavaria now, not just anywhere in the world!" "Yes, of course," replied Dewald disingenuously, "we knew this right away by the pretty uniforms." The gullible magistrate took this seriously and let them go.

High on a hill outside of town, the two wayfarers paused. The lake was beautiful that day, its clear, shiny surface mirroring the

1. The following scene is based entirely on the traveling diary of Johann Eberhard Dewald, a journeyman tanner from Königsfeld in the Black Forest, printed in Wolfram Fischer (ed.), *Quellen zur Geschichte des deutschen Handwerks* (Göttingen, 1957), 123-35. The diary is also translated in Eugene N. Anderson, *Europe in the Nineteenth Century: A Documentary Analysis of Change and Conflict* (Los Angeles, 1961), 107-20.

snowy peaks of the Alps. As he took in the view, Dewald's thoughts turned back to Lindau and the many towns like it they had seen. The prying into passports by constables and soldiers, the insulting strip-searches, and the seemingly endless passage of road controls were a spider's web which captured the best of Germany's working youth. But Dewald also remembered the merry university students from Freiburg, not far from his *Heimat*, who had raised their glasses of Kaiserstühler and sung rousing songs of German unity. Could they have been right, after all, that all Germans are brothers? Probably not. "Idle talk alone changes nothing," he concluded, "and the nine-times wise have not advanced the world a yard."

Soon they turned inland on the road to Nellenbrück and the great Seltmann tanning factory. Stories they had heard had made them curious about working in such a large place. In the tavern near Seltmann's plant, however, Dewald and his companion were shocked to see that the workers did not greet them in the manner of guild custom and ask them about their journeys. Instead they rudely stared, laughed, and walked away. Weeks later in Munich, this negative impression of the new world of factories was reinforced. Most tasks in these large establishments were divided and sub-divided. "I do not like this work," wrote Dewald in his diary. "All day long one has to do the same thing and so loses all sense for the whole." Guilds were dying out in Munich, moreover, and there was no unity among the journeymen. Now the students' arguments and songs seemed to make more sense. "If they were to go to school for a while with the students of Freiburg," mused Dewald, "the [factory workers] would soon learn how to respect worthy people and how the heart stirs when anyone calls another brother, as it should be everywhere in Germany." So they left Munich, as they had Nellenbrück, without working in a guild shop.

In early April 1837, they crossed into Austria near Salzburg and made their way to Wels. There, it was said, one could take a horse-drawn railroad at great speed to Linz, covering a day's walk in minutes. This they were eager to experience, but a coachmen along the way warned them that the new-fangled device was designed by the devil to deprive honest carriers of their small wage and drive their families into destitution. "What in the name of heaven will develop out of this?" he asked. "The world is becoming a madhouse and everyone is crazy for novelty and for machines. What once was proper and what passed for generations as honorable is now nothing and just to be laughed at. Nothing will come of all this cleverness except that there is no longer enough to eat."

Later, aboard a raft on the Danube, Dewald thought about the angry coachman. The young craftsman knew from his own experiences and feelings that novelties were usually cursed by those who mourned the passing of all to which they were accustomed. Perhaps because he was young and less entrenched in his ways, Dewald had taken the train to Linz. He arrived at mid-morning, finished his business, boarded the raft, and was a full day ahead of schedule. "The new always seems bad," he thought, "even though it has brought much gain for us."

Factories, railways, political unification – change was sweeping across the land. Whether one liked it or not, these things would happen. Or so it seemed to one young man.

Chapter 10

The Politics of Industrialization

There were indeed powerful forces driving the changes Dewald observed on his journeys through Europe. The wheels of this new technological order began to revolve in England during the late eighteenth century as fossil fuels, reciprocating steam engines, coke blast furnaces, puddled bar iron, spinning mules, and lead chambers for mass-producing sulfuric acid revolutionized the means of production. Economies of scale pushed unit costs progressively lower in the 1810s and 1820s as the novel machines and materials spread to every sector of the British economy. After the Napoleonic Wars, cheap British iron, textiles, and chemical products spilled into European markets. Unless quality differentials insulated them, craftsmen found it much harder to survive. Prohibitive import tariffs were one answer, but smuggling was all too often the English rejoinder. The most enterprising continental merchants and businessmen therefore realized the wisdom of emulating British productive techniques. And they asked governments to help them.

Yet this course of action proved to be even more controversial than English dumping. It was wrong, argued the guilds, for the state to abandon corporations whose rights and customs were centuries-old and provided stability during turbulent times. Others who were threatened, like Dewald's coachman, spoke of a devilish plot to ruin families and spread starvation. Social observers in both the liberal and conservative camps tended to agree with many of the artisans' arguments. Visitors to England reported the growth of an impoverished factory proletariat congregated in ugly, filthy, riot-prone towns. Did it not make more sense to shore up the old social order than to sacrifice it for such unfortunate and precarious circumstances? Soldiers also cast a wary eye at the industrial future. Long hours in unsafe factory conditions weakened the mind and body, thus limiting these wretched souls' potential as fighting men. To Germans who saw little or nothing positive in the industrial revolution, government's role should be to stop the wheel from turning by raising tariffs, catching smugglers, enforcing guild regulations, and banning factories.

On the other side were those who argued that economic disaster and attendant national decline awaited the country which ignored England's challenge. Success in this new form of economic warfare could guarantee the tax base and line government coffers. The state should therefore teach modern subjects in school, improve transportation, provide tax breaks to aspiring entrepreneurs, throttle the guilds, and help businessmen access the new technologies. Industrialization may have appeared inevitable to Dewald, but this was a false impression. Industrialization had always been a matter of political choice.

The unpredictable politics of uncertain industrialization are clearly evident in the southern German states that our wandering tanners traversed. In Bavaria, for instance, we know that Maximilian von Montgelas retreated from earlier efforts to undermine the guild system. The reform-minded chief minister had tried to weaken the old corporations by inhibiting the sale or inheritance of the right to open a shop *(Realrechte)* and by putting the licensing of new businesses in state hands. Both steps provoked heated objections from the guilds because they promoted unwanted competition and reduced the market for real rights. Bending to this pressure in October 1811, Montgelas restricted new businesses to those that met the "general public need"[1] and granted guild leaders and sympathetic town officials a major role in implementing policy. The result was tantamount to a ban on new shops and

1. Cited in Dirk Götschmann, *Das Bayerische Innenministerium 1825-1864* (Göttingen, 1993), 503.

industrial ventures that remained in effect for well over a decade. New handicraft establishments grew only 3 percent between 1812 and 1825, well below the urban population rate of 12 percent. Factories were even harder to found.

By the mid-1820s, however, different winds were blowing in the Bavarian Ministry of the Interior. Count Friedrich von Thürheim and a staff of economic liberals were convinced that the kingdom's restrictive ordinances had condemned the nation to technological backwardness, economic stagnation, and social misery. New laws that opened business to venture capital and afforded patent and tariff protection to inventors were vitally necessary. But how could this breakthrough occur without provoking opposition in the diet from deputies who were liberal in a *political* sense – that is, who favored parliamentarism – but were wedded socially to the guilds, handicraft production, and other non-industrial traditions? Thürheim opted to limit the letter of the law to innocuous general paragraphs that were capable of *laissez faire* interpretation, then implement the necessary measures "through administrative channels." The bureaucratic route might be a halfway solution, "but this was better than doing nothing at all."[2] The diet passed the new business code in September 1825.

Opening of the Munich-Augsburg line, 1839.

2. Ibid., 512.

paramount and most valuable branch of production. They also idealized the rural cottage industries and small-town handicrafts that serviced the countryside. Modern industry was viewed askance as an unreliable source of livelihood that was far too dependent on foreign tariffs, foreign investment decisions, or just "the luck or whim of a single factory baron."[8] It appears, moreover, that officialdom in Stuttgart regarded factory developments in the west as ugly, unaesthetic, and unpleasing to the eye. These prejudices probably explain the series of exhibitions that began in the capital during the early 1820s. Every three years objects of "high art" were displayed with hundreds of works that were "not actually art in a higher sense."[9] These included mechanical devices and products of industry and agriculture. We have encountered the same goal of aesthetic industrialization with Peter Beuth and Friedrich Schinkel in Prussia. Elites in both countries wanted to add cultural refinement to the process of economic advance.

The comparison with Prussia is instructive in another sense. While William's officials may have preferred agriculture and cottage industry, they did remarkably little to hinder newer forms of production. Guild laws remained formally in effect, but increasingly, bureaucrats who were conscious of the need to raise tax revenues looked the other way and approved factory concessions. The kingdom's 100 small industrial plants of 1816 grew to 158 by 1825.

A turning point of sorts was reached in 1828. Prolonged agricultural depression had weakened the position of the pastoral idealists, providing industrial enthusiasts like Robert Mohl, a young professor at Tübingen, an opportunity to propagandize factories and freedom of enterprise as remedies for poverty and misery, especially in the countryside. Accordingly, Württemberg made a beginning that year with the dismantling of guild controls. Equally important, the practice of concessioning factories was formalized in law, sending their number to over 230 by 1831. Other estimates place more than 300 factories in Württemberg by the early 1830s. While many were small operations (averaging seventeen workers),

8. Ibid., 414.

9. Cited in Paul Gehring, "Das Wirtschaftsleben in Württemberg unter König Wilhelm I (1816-1864), *Zeitschrift für Württembergische Landesgeschichte* 9 (1949-1950), 215.

an increasing number were larger-scale plants of fifty or more. Conservatively figured, Württemberg's factories were growing over five times faster than population. The kingdom's top bureaucrats continued to prefer – and to promote – economic projects connected with the land. Nor was the aesthetic industrial agenda abandoned, witness the continuing art and industry fairs and the opening of a new school for aspiring businessmen that incorporated art education with vocational training. Nevertheless, industry was clearly more entrenched – and more acceptable politically – as the new decade began.

Industrial policy in the Grand Duchy of Baden – where Dewald's Blackforest hometown of Königsfeld was located – provides us with yet another contrasting pattern. Throughout the 1810s and 1820s, Baden's leading civil servants were ambivalent about the embryonic industrial revolution. They listened patiently and hopefully to *laissez faire* arguments about alleviating rural and urban poverty by emancipating forces of production from guild restrictions. They balked at full-fledged freedom of enterprise, however, worried that the good works of the old corporations would yield to social and moral depravity in the brave new world of factories. Rather, like Bavaria and Württemberg, Baden combined guild controls with factory licenses considered on an *ad hoc* basis.

A number of factors combined, however, to limit the number of licenses granted. For one thing, approved businesses were left to fend for themselves without tariff or patent protection. While farms and small shops paid no taxes on business capital, moreover, factories paid a high rate. Already unpopular, these taxes became even more controversial in business circles when they were increased in 1825. Even more important was the fact that local officials opposed to industrialism retained a voice in licensing decisions that was rarely overruled in Karlsruhe. And all too often the aid that industrialists received from the bureaucracy was unsolicited and unwanted. Beginning in 1821, for example, the state sponsored biannual art and industry exhibits to promote domestic wares and raise the cultural level of the business world. Few entrepreneurs were interested. These policies contributed to Baden's slow industrialization. The number of factories (averaging nineteen workers apiece) rose from 146 in 1809 to 153 in

1829 as those that went under were barely outbalanced by newly established businesses.

Political objections to the unshackling of Prometheus were also heard in the Hessian states. As in southern Germany, licensing policy was usually the most critical factor. Hoping to stimulate small business and commerce, for example, Nassau eliminated guild controls in 1814. Its officials were so sure of industry's evils, however, that factories almost never received concessions. Unlike Nassau, Hesse-Kassel and Hesse-Darmstadt opted to retain guild rights. More importantly, they reinforced these privileges with restrictive industrial practices. Of the two states, licenses were somewhat easier to obtain in Hesse-Darmstadt. But even there conservative ministers like Baron du Thil gave approval only rarely and grudgingly, interpreting periodic recessions as proof that industrialization was unstable, unreliable, and unworthy of significant state aid.

The Kingdom of Saxony was equally inhospitable to factory owners in the 1820s. Ministers comfortable with non-industrial institutions stubbornly ignored entrepreneurial pleas for higher external tariffs, tax breaks, subsidies for mechanization, elimination of internal tariffs and road tolls, and abolition of the guilds. "Out of concern that certain [traditional] things might be destroyed," observed one critic, "everything, even the completely antiquated, was retained."[10] In one critical respect, however, Saxon officials were lenient. Undeterred by hostile state policies, merchants and manufacturers responded to market opportunities by flooding government offices with proposals for new factory investments – and most of them were approved for tax reasons. The number of larger-scale factories expanded meteorically from 65 in 1817 to 191 in 1830. If smaller operations are included, the total rises to 315. The greatest concentration of large factories was in cotton spinning – 78 plants averaging 97 workers apiece. There was a growing realization in Dresden by around 1828, in fact, that the bureaucracy needed to reconsider its inconsistent stance to industry and adopt more positive economic policies. Over a third of Saxony's larger

10. Cited in Hubert Kiesewetter, *Industrialisierung und Landwirtschaft: Sachsens Stellung im regionalen Industrialisierungsprozess Deutschlands im 19. Jahrhundert* (Vienna, 1988), 94.

factories, for instance, were approved and founded between 1827 and 1830.

Thus statesmen and entrepreneurs in central and southern Germany aired the advantages and disadvantages of the new industrial order. In Württemberg and Saxony, industrialization accelerated despite hostile political milieus. In Bavaria, Baden, Nassau, Hesse-Kassel, and Hesse-Darmstadt, on the other hand, politics nearly stifled industrial growth. Throughout most of the remaining small states in the Confederation, reactionary, anti-industrial patterns were also the norm – from the Mecklenbergs and old Hanseatic cities in the North to Hanover, Brunswick, and Thuringia farther south. If Germany were to avoid becoming an economic backwater, falling farther and farther behind Great Britain and France, the decision lay with Austria and Prussia. What can be said, therefore, about the politics of industrialization in Germany's most powerful kingdoms?

The Austrian Empire had struggled with the issue of mechanization and factory production during Napoleonic times. Between 1794 and 1809, decrees barred the importation or use of flax-spinning machines, forbade the opening of new factories in Vienna and other cities, and encouraged the dispersion of industry into the countryside. There, it was felt, proletarians would not threaten the state. After the defeat at Wagram (1809), however, a pro-industrial faction around Ritter von Stahl, chairman of the Royal Commerce Commission, convinced Kaiser Francis of the financial merits of lifting the decrees. Stahl's efforts were delayed by years of recession after 1811, bearing fruit only with the coming of peace in 1815. His strategy was to maintain the prohibitive external tariffs erected under Joseph II, then to extend the Great Reformer's internal free trade zone from the Austrian, Czechoslovakian, and Polish provinces to Hungary, the Tyrol, and northern Italy. This huge protected market would stimulate business investment in newly licensed factories. The government could facilitate technological innovation with subsidies, an institute that disseminated information, and policies which legalized joint-stock companies and expanded the money supply. Despite rampant smuggling, Stahl's neo-mercantilistic reforms were producing noticeable results by the early 1820s.

His policies also triggered a powerful backlash. Guildsmen throughout the provinces seethed in anger over the creation of competition that, they argued, violated their legal privileges. Entrepreneurial proposals for factory licenses were routinely challenged with provincial officials, creating delays and headaches for Stahl's Commission in Vienna, for the emperor insisted that all complaints be investigated. Unsatisfied with merely prolonging the process of factory licensing, the guilds petitioned the emperor in 1822 to put an end to Stahl's "liberal" regime. Francis paid heed, worried that factories and industrial technology would impoverish the small shopowners, undermine a still-important part of the tax base, and provoke dreaded riots. The kaiser ordered the Royal Commerce Commission to limit concessions to those factories that were "absolutely necessary," then, after repeated guild complaints, to cease licensing altogether until the matter could be thoroughly investigated.

Stahl lashed out at his enemies, mocking their pettiness and short-sightedness and warning that the fulfillment of their wishes would be a "death blow" to modern industry. For years the contending parties fought over these issues until Francis finally compromised in 1827. The emperor agreed that Austria needed more industry, not less, but warned his officials against increasing the number of businesses without good reason. When renewed guild objections provoked another inquiry in 1831, bureaucrats prevailed again by depicting "the grave of industry"[11] that would be dug if the handicraftsmen had their way.

Prussia had also faced tough economic decisions after the debacle of Jena and Auerstädt in 1806. As we know, the desperate circumstances in Frederick William III's kingdom lent a certain radicalism to the solutions that were proposed. Economic liberals around Karl August von Hardenberg broke completely with the old mercantilistic policy of supporting industrial growth with subsidies, monopolistic charters, and prohibitive tariffs. The guilds were also abandoned. Hardenberg's men were even willing to push industry out of the towns into the countryside where cheap water

11. The quotations in this paragraph are cited in Johann Slokar, *Geschichte der österreichischen Industrie und ihrer Förderung unter Kaiser Franz I.* (Vienna, 1914), 88-89, 109.

power, raw materials, and labor would allow Prussia's entrepreneurs to compete without significant state aid. The new system was largely in place by 1818. Bureaucrats in Berlin like Peter Beuth offered free advice and information on the latest technologies and the most aesthetic surroundings for the new machinery. The government also eliminated internal tolls and furthered road construction throughout the kingdom. But otherwise, businessmen had to fend for themselves. External tariffs were moderate: significantly higher than most of the smaller German states – even Bavaria – but much lower than Austria, Russia, France, and England. Moreover, patents were hard to receive; subsidies next to impossible; and guild privileges a relict of the past.

The death of Hardenberg in 1822 triggered a bitter fight over the future of industrialism in Prussia. Conservative party leaders not only wanted to turn back the clock to a day when Junkers wielded autonomous political power, but they also wished to shore up an economic system based on landed wealth and abundant agricultural labor. Thus Prussia's large landowners viewed industrial entrepreneurs warily as competitors for economic and political power. It was logical, therefore, that the conservative agenda would include support for handicraftsmen who were also threatened by unrestrained industrial expansion and longed for a restoration of the legal means to restrict all newcomers. With Hardenberg gone, Duke Karl of Mecklenburg, Prince Wittgenstein, the crown prince, and other conservatives exploited their easy access to the king to further this cause. Largely manipulated by aristocrats, six of Prussia's eight provincial diets reinforced these efforts by calling for a full restoration of the guilds.

Frederick William was known to sympathize with the old corporations and had urged Hardenberg repeatedly to modify the anti-guild laws of 1811. By the mid-1820s, however, the king had begun to doubt the wisdom of this step. In a memorandum to the crown prince in November 1824, Frederick William warned his son that "a rapid, forcible transition to a different legal order will only lead to new disturbances and destroy lawful relationships and procedures which have more or less put down roots." The tax monies which prospering industries secured for the state did not allow it, moreover, "to take back institutions on which it relies for revenue without replacing them with others which guarantee the same financial results."[12] Pragmatic reasons of state terminated the conservative bid to curb Prussia's industrial revolution.

Thus German Europe was nudged toward industrialization as these political controversies were resolved. While most states rendered negative verdicts, several crucial members of the Confederation had turned their backs on the past: Prussia by 1824; Austria by 1827; and Württemberg and Saxony by 1828. This did not mean, however, that statesmen in these countries had embraced the industrial future as *we* have come to know it. In fact, industrial reformers commonly envisaged an industrial transformation well-contained within the boundaries of the old non-industrial order. And logically so, for most factories tended to be large workshops of ten to twenty workers powered by hand- or water-driven machines rather than steam engines. Transport moved on roads, rivers, and canals at the same pace it had for centuries. Faster movement on rails was either unheard of or considered bizarre. Many civil servants wanted to integrate art and industry, moreover, in rural settings pleasing to the eye. Rural industry was also seen as a solution to peasant distress. As we shall see, the acceleration during the 1830s of larger-scale, railroad-driven, urban-based, unaesthetic industrialization led to renewed controversies that once again had to be resolved politically.

* * * *

William of Württemberg had ample reason for disillusionment in 1826. Three years earlier the Diet of the German Confederation had stifled his press campaign to promote a "Third Germany" free of Prussian and Austrian control. Two years earlier Bavaria and Baden had deserted him, throwing their support to Metternich in renewing the Carlsbad Decrees. And one year before, lengthy negotiations for an economic union of the smaller southern states had finally ended in failure. From 1819 to 1825, Württemberg, Bavaria, Baden, Hesse-Darmstadt, Nassau, and the Saxon duchies struggled to achieve some form of cooperation against Prussia,

12. Cited in Eric Dorn Brose, *The Politics of Technological Change in Prussia: Out of the Shadow of Antiquity, 1809-1848* (Princeton, 1993), 59.

whose tariffs had been raised far above theirs in 1818. The Darmstadt conferences broke up over the conflicting interests of the Rhenish states, which favored cheap importation or transit of manufactured items, and Bavaria, which advocated protective tariffs as one means to fulfill Thürheim's industrializing agenda. The final indignity to the Württembergian monarch came in 1826 when Bavaria unilaterally raised tariffs to more than twice their previous level. William's plans for a Third Germany seemed very far from realization.

In a bid to reverse his political fortunes, William made a personal appeal to Ludwig I of Bavaria. The Bavarian move jeopardized Württemberg's economic interests, he wrote in December 1826, and undermined South German solidarity at a time when it threatened to disappear. The tactic worked. Deliberations in early 1827 led to an agreement that took effect the following year. Bavaria and Württemberg formed a customs union guaranteeing free trade within and between the two states. External tariffs were set at the higher Bavarian level. An annual congress consisting of two plenipotentiary representatives from each state would monitor the union and approve any statute changes. Reflecting the Third Germany agenda in Stuttgart, provision was made for extension of the treaty's wording to six additional states. Each would be allowed one seat at the congress – a stipulation that a small state might accept, but never Prussia or Austria.

Baron Du Thil of Hesse-Darmstadt was unimpressed. His impoverished state was interested in export markets for Hessian wine and farm products, not in protection for industries that threatened the social and political order. The wily minister also had political motives for rejecting the southern overtures. The Confederation's presiding power, Austria, was highly suspicious of William's intrigues and would perhaps not object, moreover, if Hesse approached Austria's current ally in the North, Prussia, with the idea of trade talks. Secretly, Du Thil reckoned that Prussia possessed "the greatest intelligence [in Germany], after a temporary absence [since Hardenberg's death]," and that gradually "the leadership of German affairs"[13] would gravitate to Berlin. In

13. Cited in Arnold H. Price, *The Evolution of the Zollverein* (Ann Arbor, 1949), 207.

August 1827, therefore, he sent out feelers to contacts in the Hohenzollern capital.

The Hessian initiative coincided with high stakes party intrigues in Berlin. Unlike many of the South German progressives, most (although not all) of the liberal parties in the Prussian bureaucracy favored economic as well as political reform. By 1827 the new Minister of Finance, Friedrich von Motz, had adopted their economic vision of "bigger industry" and "superior fabrication" in the Prussian countryside. While the liberals who had coopted him were much less content with the political status quo, desiring a constitution and a foreign policy realignment directed against conservative Austria, Motz was enough of a Prussian patriot to express disgust with Prussia's subordinate position in the Confederation. "Only a war can help us,"[14] he declared.

Indeed war in Europe was not unlikely, for the Greek revolt against Turkey had triggered Great Power intervention. Naval units of England, France, and Russia crushed a Turkish-Egyptian fleet at Navarino in October 1827, much to the dismay of Austria, which wanted to preserve Turkey's position in the Balkans. These developments encouraged liberal Hotspurs in Berlin while simultaneously appalling conservatives who viewed confrontation with Austria as subversive and treasonous. Frederick William III had every reason to side with the conservative parties on this issue, leaving liberals with only one oblique means to further the anti-Austrian cause: commercial treaties with the South Germans that undermined allegiances to Vienna. Thus Du Thil's offer could not have been better timed for the Prussian liberal parties. Hesse-Darmstadt formed a tariff union with Prussia in February 1828, only weeks after the ink had dried on Württemberg's treaty with Bavaria.

Ludwig was angered by the new transit barrier separating the Palatinate from the Bavarian heartland. In Württemberg, William was resigned, sensing correctly that Prussia's coup had thoroughly undercut his Third German customs union. "Sooner or later we shall be forced to follow [Prussia's] example,"[15] he observed. Indeed the lure of customs-free access to the extensive, fairly well-pro-

14. The quotes here and above are cited in Brose, 68, 81.
15. Cited in W. O. Henderson, *The Zollverein* (Chicago, 1959), 53.

tected North German market was too great. A visit to Berlin that fall by the monarch's friend, Johann Friedrich Cotta, provided an unofficial opportunity to discuss a merger of the two systems. Cotta found Motz preoccupied with the escalating crisis in Greece. The Prussian minister remarked that units of the army were on alert against Saxony, which he claimed was leaning toward Austria, and suggested that Bavaria and Württemberg draw closer to Prussia. "The most suitable [means] to this [friendship] would be a closer understanding on trade policies."[16] Negotiations began during the winter, and by spring 1829, Bavaria and Württemberg had followed Hesse-Darmstadt into Prussia's expanding free trade zone.

The other states of northern and central Germany were alarmed. Hanover, Brunswick, and Oldenburg were agricultural countries that favored cheap importation of any manufactured items their stolid artisans could not produce. Transit duties on foreign (especially British) goods bound for the markets of Frankfurt, Leipzig, Switzerland, or Italy were an important source of revenue, moreover, that would be jeopardized by higher tariff walls. Hesse-Kassel and Nassau had similar interests, while Saxony and the neighboring duchies were determined to preserve access to the last open markets for their industrial exports. Negotiations begun at Kassel in August 1828 led to a quick agreement the following month. The member states of the new Middle German Commercial Union pledged not to join another commercial union, to keep existing roads in good repair, and build new ones. Transit duties could not be raised, except – they agreed secretly – on goods moving across the union from the divided parts of Prussia. The British representative to the Frankfurt diet was pleased, predicting that "besides [the] lawful commercial advantages, [the Middle German Commercial Union] will afford immense facilities for carrying on the contraband trade in the dominions of Prussia, Bavaria, Württemberg, and Hesse-Darmstadt." In Weimar, Goethe looked more presciently past the competing trade blocs into a future where "thalers and groschens may have the same value throughout the country and my luggage may pass unopened through all the thirty-six states [of the Confederation]."[17]

16. Cited in Brose, 87-88.
17. For this and the above quotation, see Henderson , 66, 69.

Metternich could envisage the same thing – but it was more nightmare than dream. The Middle German Union was a welcome development that he actively supported, but he realized that the essentially negative motives and disparate economic interests of its members would not long endure the bribes and blandishments that could be expected from Berlin. And, while the experience of the Darmstadt conferences left room for skepticism that the states to the north could bridge their economic differences, the possibility that Prussia could lure these states away from Vienna unnerved him. The plot was all the more frightening because it was reportedly the work of northern liberals – "a faction known only too well to me." Metternich therefore warned the Prussian ambassador that trade relations must remain a "purely administrative" matter. "When they are based upon a political tendency, they are opposed to the fundamental laws of the Confederation."[18] Showing no aversion to double standards, however, the veteran schemer urged Kaiser Francis in late 1829 to discard the empire's prohibitive tariff system in order to be in a position to compete with Prussia for the economic and political favor of the confederate states.

Metternich was fully aware that this was a tall order. Austria's virtual prohibition of industrial imports was regarded by the beleaguered guilds as one of the last props of their sagging edifice. The handicraftsmen of the empire could almost always count, moreover, on a sympathetic hearing from the emperor. Locked in struggle with the guilds, Austrian entrepreneurs and their sympathizers in Vienna like Baron Kolowrat and Ritter von Stahl had based their developmental strategies from the beginning on this political reality. The huge, shielded domestic market would provide the impetus to industrial take-off. And the stratagem had worked. Austria's output of pig iron exceeded Prussia's in the late 1820s and was about three-quarters as much as all of Germany's. The empire's 115 large cotton-spinning factories dwarfed those of any other German kingdom and represented a quarter more spindlage than all states to the north. Protection had also enabled Austria to advance qualitatively: its spinning mules, steam engines, and blast

18. Both citations here are from Robert D. Billinger, *Metternich and the German Question: States Rights and federal Duties, 1820-1834* (Newark, 1991), 43-44.

furnaces more than held their own with everything north of the border. Such progress certainly sheds a questionable light on what David Good describes disapprovingly as "the reigning interpretation of the Habsburg Monarchy's economic failure."[19] It is true, nevertheless, that this success had bred caution in an industrial establishment that had no reason to risk reduced domestic sales in exchange for uncertain export gains against other German states. Merger with the northern tariff systems "would be linked to such great sacrifice on the side of Austria," pleaded the factory party at court, "that it would outweigh any possible advantage."[20] Metternich was more impressed with the *diplomatic* risks of the current system, but his proposals crashed against the rocks of a gigantic vested interest in the status quo. The Kaiser, who abhorred change anyway, permitted only a few insignificant tariff reductions.

Metternich's loss was Prussia's gain. As the chancellor had feared, Motz and his successor in the Finance Ministry, Georg Maassen, cajoled one state after another into joining their system. As early as July 1829, financially-strapped Saxe-Meinigen and Saxe-Coburg allowed Prussian goods free transit in return for the construction of new roads. The Reuss principalities followed suit in December. Now the members of the Middle German Union began a scramble to acquire the most favorable terms from Prussia. Hesse-Kassel and Saxe-Weimar consented to join the Prussian trade zone in 1831; the Kingdom of Saxony and the remaining Thuringian duchies came on board in 1833. Baden, Nassau, Hanover, and the Hanseatic cities remained aloof. Nevertheless, on New Year's Day 1834, a Customs Union *(Zollverein)* of eighteen German states went into effect. Anticipating the opening of this vast, lucrative market, thousands of wagons were backed up for miles along common borders throughout the previous evening.

Metternich had continued his bid to prevent this until the very end. In 1832 and 1833, he convinced Hanover to undertake efforts in the Frankfurt diet to alleviate transit duties throughout the Confederation. In conjunction with this initiative, the master

19. David F. Good, *Der wirtschaftliche Aufstieg des Habsburgerreiches 1750-1914* (Vienna, 1986), 12.

20. Cited in Adolf Beer, *Die österreichische Handelspolitik im neunzehnten Jahrhundert* (Vienna, 1891), 61.

manipulator urged Kaiser Francis to reconsider his support for the prohibitive system. Insurmountable tariff barriers that contradicted commercial developments in the North would prove far more threatening to "the welfare and influence of the monarchy"[21] than any possible sacrifice that industry and finance might be required to make. Before Francis or the diet acted, however, the Zollverein treaties went into effect. Metternich's last hope lay with the conservative parties in Berlin. But the King of Prussia had allowed events to drift far enough to the political right since the conservative aftermath of the revolutions of 1830. Maassen was able to convince his monarch not to reverse the course of Prussian commercial policy. It was a typical balancing act for Frederick William III – but one that would have far-reaching political and economic repercussions.

* * * *

Railroads had been in the air for a long time before the opening of the Zollverein. Friedrich Harkort, a Rhenish businessman, had written futuristically in 1825 about railway lines stretching over 400 miles. The visionary entrepreneur looked forward to a day when "the triumphant car of technological progress is harnessed to smoking colossuses."[22] Harkort had also convinced Prussia's dynamic Minister of Finance, Friedrich von Motz, that western railroads would enable Prussian and middle-German exporters to circumvent Holland's high toll barriers on the lower Rhine. Accordingly, Motz commissioned studies in 1828 for railroad lines connecting the Rhine with the Weser or Ems. Mine owners and officials in the Ruhr and the Saar, moreover, were eager to link coal fields with market towns. But nothing came of these early schemes. Economic and technological experts expressed skepticism about the ability of steam engines to pull loads uphill in bad weather and doubted whether German economies were sufficiently developed to sustain such steep investments. As the decade closed, Germany possessed only a few insignificant, horse-powered colliery roads.

21. Ibid., 69.
22. Cited in Brose , 210.

In England, meanwhile, railroad technology was evolving very rapidly. The directors of the Manchester-Liverpool line conducted tests on steam locomotives in October 1829 – the famous Rainhill Trials. George Stephenson's "Rocket" hauled a twenty-ton load easily up moderate grades, achieving speeds on level ground of thirty miles per hour. The secret to his success was a multiple fire-tube-boiler which produced twice the heat relative to engine weight of the older, single-flue designs. By 1832, Stephenson had made improvements to his boilers and added a third set of wheels to distribute weight. His locomotives now possessed twice the tractive power of the Rocket that ran at Rainhill. Harkort's vision of "smoking colossuses" seemed much more realistic.

In fact, these technological changes complicated investment decisions in the transport sector. Because locomotives could ascend steeper gradients, railroads could traverse and climb hills, thus reducing initial outlays and quickening the amortization of capital by avoiding the deep cuttings and high embankments typical of level English lines. The trade-off was in higher operating costs and lower profits, however, for winding, hilly routes meant heavier, costlier locomotives, increased fuel consumption, slower speeds, added wheel and track wear, and a greater chance of accidents. Complicating investment options still more was the fact that horses could pull as much as ten times more load on rails than on roads, while river dredging schemes, canals, and toll roads all offered investors tempting improvements over the status quo.

This welter of options helps to explain some of the controversy over German railroad schemes in the early 1830s. Bureaucratic experts like Peter Beuth of Prussia continued to doubt the economic and technological feasibility of railways powered by steam locomotives. He was willing to promote a horserail line from the coalfields of the Ruhr to the nascent industrial town of Elberfeld, for instance, but mocked businessmen who wanted a 150 mile railroad connecting the Rhine and Weser. His office would always further projects which enhanced the general welfare, but these entrepreneurs possessed "neither sufficient intelligence nor sufficient capital."[23] But, intelligently or not, promoters began to pres-

23. Ibid., 217.

sure the German states to support railroads – or at least not to inhibit them – as early as 1829. Four years later, calls were mounting to a crescendo pitch throughout the Confederation. Thus Friedrich List, the indefatigable champion of industry from Leipzig, lured Prussian officials with the notion of an all-German railway network. "As if by magic," he wrote in October 1833, "Berlin will see itself elevated to the central point of 30 million people." The "moral, political, and military as well as industrial, commercial, and financial" effects of having Hamburg, Bremen, Cologne, Strassburg, and Munich only a few days away would be "immeasurable."[24]

As we shall see, Prussian officials turned a deaf ear to these entreaties. And yet, ironically, their own actions were fueling the fires of the railroad enthusiasts. For behind much of the excitement over railways was the impending opening of the Zollverein. One could easily predict – and eagerly anticipate – the economic and technological effects of this huge free-trade zone. Trade would rapidly intensify and investments in new and expanded plants would multiply as economies of scale were reached. The remunerative advantage of having the correct location, moreover, would greatly increase. Thus the day of railroads had dawned *before* New Year's Day 1834, for railroad construction, writes Hans-Ulrich Wehler, "fed on the expectation of an expanding volume of trade and a concentration of business contacts."[25] Or, as Friedrich List put it, the railroads and the Zollverein were Germany's "Siamese Twins."[26] The economic logic would not count for much, however, if Germans erected political barriers to the revolutionary new transportation technology.

We turn first to railroad policy in Saxony, the most important industrial state in the Confederation next to Prussia and Austria. While the revolutions of 1830 did not bring a genuine liberal regime to power in Saxony (see Part II), they nevertheless induced a bureaucratic shake-up which moved innovators to the top. Comprehensive reforms followed, including a more systematic promotion of agriculture and industry. These programs, together with the

24. Ibid., 219.
25. Hans-Ulrich Wehler, *Deutsche Gesellschaftsgeschichte* (Munich, 1987), 2:134.
26. Cited in Gehring, "Das Wirtschaftsleben in Württemberg," 243.

economic stimulus of membership in the Zollverein, triggered an industrial boom – 242 new factories were established in Saxony between 1834 and 1836. Saxon railroad policy was consistent with this new-found bureaucratic enthusiasm for developing industry. Officials in Dresden encouraged the promoters of the Leipzig-Dresden Railroad in December 1833, and when the company formed in early 1835, it received generous aid. The state guaranteed a 3.5 percent return to investors and pledged to buy shares itself should capitalization problems arise. The bureaucracy also facilitated the expropriation of land and placed state engineers at the disposal of the railroad company. The staggered opening of the line during 1837 and 1838 brought Germany its first railroad line of significant length (116 kilometers).

The situation was quite different in southern Germany. Pride of place in German railroad history usually goes to Bavaria, which boasted the first German railway powered by steam locomotives. Opened in December 1835, the short stretch between Nürnberg and Fürth was destined, however, to remain that state's only railroad of the 1830s. For private initiative was unable to muster the capital required for construction in Bavaria's hilly countryside – and the government, considering waterways a more sensible investment, refused to help. Thus Munich poured nearly 17 million florins into the Ludwig Canal (between the Main and Danube rivers) while the desperate owners of the Augsburg-Munich Railroad, who needed one fourth of that amount to complete construction, pleaded in vain for state support.

Railroad development also stalled in Württemberg despite the fact that industry was more welcome there than in Bavaria. King William, many of his ministers, and influential legislators like Johann Friedrich Cotta were eager to finance railways, but their plans proved too controversial. Towns far away from any of the projected routes objected to the expense, and the Minister of Finance, worried by stories of companies that had gone bankrupt in other states, urged restraint. Swabian industry was prospering in the Zollverein as the number of factories approached 400 by mid-decade, so why jeopardize such good fortune on the risky railroads? Like Württemberg, Baden also refused to enter the uncertain railway age. Private companies that were established in both states in the mid-1830s went under during the financial panic of 1837. The three and a half miles of track connecting Nürnberg and Fürth was the only operating line in all of southern Germany when the 1840s began.

Political decisions also delayed the debut of railroads in Austria. In this case, early proposals foundered on the deeply ingrained conservatism of Kaiser Francis. "[Railways]," he said, "will only bring revolution into the country."[27] Reinforcing the monarch's prejudice was the skepticism of leading technocrats "who were convinced of the fleeting nature of the whole railroad mania and were [therefore] staunchly against approving any extensive experiments in this direction."[28] At the time of his death in 1835, Austria had only the short horse-drawn line between Budweis and Linz – the railroad that would thrill Dewald in 1837. But "hardly were Francis's eyes closed,"[29] writes one historian, before banking magnate Salamon Rothschild convinced Metternich of the commercial necessity of railroads in the vast Austrian Empire. By the late 1830s, concessions had been granted for rail lines connecting Vienna with Galicia, Budapest, and Triest. The empire boasted nearly 500 kilometers of track in 1841 – more than any other continental state at that time. The network had nearly tripled to 1,350 kilometers by 1847. As we shall see, this rapid expansion greatly accelerated the birth of modern industry.

Prussia underwent a similar struggle before entering the new era of rapid transportation. As early as 1832 officials were considering proposals for railroads in Westphalia, the Ruhr, and lower Rhineland. The routes were approved, but Berlin left the financially strapped companies to fend for themselves lest government borrowing force the king to fulfill his parliamentary pledge of 1820 (see Part II). By 1835 even more ambitious projects were under government scrutiny: railroads linking Cologne and Aachen; Cologne and Minden; Magdeburg and Leipzig; Magdeburg and Berlin; Hamburg and Berlin; and Potsdam and Berlin. Official

27. Cited in C.A. Macartney, *The Habsburg Empire 1790-1918* (New York, 1969), 259.

28. Hermann Strach (ed.), *Geschichte der Eisenbahnen der Oesterreichisch-Ungarischen Monarchie* (Vienna, 1898), 1:132.

29. Macartney, *The Habsburg Empire* , 259.

counsels were bitterly divided. Civilian chiefs like Peter Beuth remained staunchly opposed, fearing financial crises as huge investments were diverted from textiles and aesthetic country factories into the questionable new transportation technology. Railroad promoters found a champion in Crown Prince Frederick, on the other hand, who pressed his father to ignore the bureaucrats. Making the king's decision more difficult, however, was the fact that the technical experts argued amongst themselves. Thus the Mining Corps was torn between those who saw railroads as a stimulus to state ironworks and others who worried that private mines would deplete the nation's coal reserves. The army, too, was split. Cautious officers "shuddered at the thought that some fine spring morning a hundred thousand Frenchmen, thirsting for war, will suddenly invade our peaceful valleys at bird-like speed, thanks to the new means of locomotion, and begin their old game over again," while bolder types were tantalized by "the military fantasy of entire [Prussian] armies flying across vast territories in a few days."[30]

For three years, in fact, Prussian railroad development was halted as factions and parties in and out of government fought and schemed. Finally, with military opinion leaning increasingly toward railroads, the king abandoned his own skepticism and allowed construction to go forward. "These cars rolling across the earth," proclaimed a jubilant crown prince in October 1838, "will be delayed no longer by the hands of man."[31] Spurred by positive railroad legislation and inducements, the Prussian network expanded quickly to 375 kilometers in 1841, then literally took off, reaching 2,325 kilometers in 1847. Not wishing to be left behind, other German states had begun to build railways too – witness the turn to state lines in Hanover, Baden, Württemberg, and Bavaria in the 1840s. But Prussia alone possessed 56 percent of all railroad line in the Confederation by 1847, while Prussia and Austria together made up nearly 89 percent.

The railroads of German Europe were constructed differently from those of England, France, and Belgium. Planners in these countries spared no expense to achieve straight, level roadbeds,

30. Cited in Brose, 212, 225.
31. Ibid., 228.

while German lines had fewer viaducts and tunnels, tending to follow the lay of the land in American fashion. As explained above, higher operating costs were exchanged for greatly reduced initial investments – averaging one-half of Belgian, one-third of English, and one-fifth of French capital outlays. Whether the lines were financed by private entrepreneurs (as in Saxony and Prussia) or state legislatures (as in South Germany), the guiding assumption was that Germany's relatively undeveloped economy would not sustain a large enough volume of traffic to allow huge, western-style investments to amortize quickly.

We should be careful, however, not to underestimate the economic and technological impact of railroad construction in Germany, especially in countries like Prussia where development was the quickest. Prussian companies poured 150 million thaler into their lines by 1848, thereby inducing the modern, heavy industrialization of coal and iron as we have come to know it. In the 1840s alone, agriculture's share of total investment declined from 58 percent to 29 percent. Within the industrial sector itself, the investment share of producer goods (like metals, fuels, and industrial leather) doubled from 8 percent to 16 percent. The face of technology changed too as shallow, hillside mines yielded to deep shafts, charcoal iron gave way to coke iron, and hand-machining techniques bowed to heavy-duty machine tools.

To those who had dreamed of an aesthetic industrialization, these developments were unpleasant and very disillusioning. In Baden, the art and industry fairs continued into the 1830s. But the paintings and formal works of art had come to dominate the exhibits as businessmen, complaining that industry was treated as "peripheral,"[32] submitted fewer and fewer entries. The last unsuccessful exhibition was held in Karlsruhe in 1837. The organizing committee consoled itself with the sardonic observation that Württemberg was experiencing similar difficulties. Indeed the campaign to raise the aesthetic level of industry and industrialists was dying out there too. The last fair combining artistic and technological exhibits was held in Stuttgart in 1839. Afterwards the

32 Cited in Wolfram Fischer, *Der Staat und die Anfänge der Industrialisierung in Baden* (Berlin, 1962), 186.

directors of the Art School dissociated themselves from the movement, bemoaning "the filth and pressing masses"[33] that modern trends had produced. The exhibit of 1842 was devoted purely to industrial products. By this time Peter Beuth had also turned away from the unpleasing, ugly world of gaseous coking ovens, belching ironworks, and the exorbitant railroads that made them necessary. He grew more and more preoccupied with the art of antiquity and indulged his love for horses and the history of ancient horse-breeding cultures like Troy. His last accomplishment in office was the great Industrial Exhibit of 1844. It was the aesthetic alternative that greeted visitors there: products of the soil, the country factory, the instrument-makers bench, and the artist's casting furnace. After the exhibit closed its doors, Beuth asked to be relieved of his duties. The world no longer corresponded with his vision.

33. Cited in Gehring, "Das Wirtschaftsleben in Württemberg," 234.

Chapter 11

The Bourgeois Challenge

The competent, pragmatic First Minister of Hesse-Darmstadt, Baron Du Thil, had many reasons for looking askance at modern industry. Among them was the obvious fact that more mines, railroads, and industrial ventures meant more industrialists pressing the duke and his bureaucracy for political concessions. The industrial or *propertied* bourgeoisie *(Besitzbürgertum)* of Hesse-Darmstadt numbered about 850 in 1847, easily triple the figure of 1800. In Baden, Friedrich von Blittersdorf, a conservative official, made similar observations. "In the smaller German states," he wrote in 1839, "the civil servants and their families comprised all along the entire educated class of people and only in recent times has a middle class begun to form through the development of trade and industry." Indeed the number of factory owners in Baden had doubled in a decade: from 153 to 298. "But this class is still not numerous enough or sufficiently consolidated," he consoled himself, "in order to resist the civil service."[1] By 1847, however, the number had risen to 410. In neighboring Württemberg, William and his leading civil servants also worried about the political challenges which the new class of factory owners would present to their governors. Swelling from 200 or 300 in the early 1830s, the number of industrialists in Württemberg stood at 1,200 by the late 1840s. The largest concentration in Germany was

1. Cited in Loyd E. Lee, *The Politics of Harmony: Civil Service, Liberalism, and Social Reform in Baden, 1800-1850* (Newark, 1980), 187-88.

found in Rhineland-Westphalia, where over 10,000 members of the industrial bourgeoisie managed their businesses. There were more than 40,000 industrialists throughout the lands of the German Confederation at this time.

What were the social origins of Germany's pioneering industrial entrepreneurs? They were overwhelmingly Protestant, even in Catholic cities like Aachen or Munich. In most cases, they also migrated to embryonic industrial centers from other parts of their home region. Moreover, their education and capital came typically from the family shop, trading firm, or bank. In the textile branches, most entrepreneurs had a family background in trade, merchant banking, or putting-out manufacturing – 70 percent of textile factory owners, for instance, in Westphalia. From these origins came the market orientation necessary for a new venture. Those who established the first machine-building and metalworking factories, on the contrary, stemmed mainly from artisan families – 83 percent of new machine-tool factory owners, for example, in Saxony. In these cases, families passed along the technical skills necessary for a new venture.

Clearly, these were not typical families of the urban patriciate or artisanate. For, as explained in Part II, most merchants and handicraftsmen actually fought the coming of industry. The sons of these maverick bourgeois usually carried on the business and married into other local business families, as did the daughters. Once established in a town, entrepreneurial families tended to stay there, devoting considerable attention to acquiring social acceptability with the patriciate, scheming to penetrate or influence local government with its many benefits, but not ignoring party politics in the capital city where laws were often considered which could determine the future of industrialism.

The so-called cultivated bourgeoisie *(Bildungsbürgertum)* was also growing in numbers. Some partial sense of the pace is gained by considering enrollments in Prussian gymnasiums and universities. At 16,000 in 1820, they climbed to over 29,000 in the early 1830s. A half-century later, there were over 100,000 students in Prussian gymnasiums and universities – and 265,000 in Germany as a whole. Typically these aspiring bourgeois were the sons of clergymen or civil servants, but increasingly they were turning away from the traditional disciplines of theology and law to the newer fields of medicine and the liberal arts. And, like the propertied bourgeoisie, the *Bildungsbürgertum* sought to assert itself politically. "The disgruntlement and dissatisfaction which are becoming evident in this province," warned the Governor of the Rhineland in 1844, emanated mainly from the "educated groups which … desire to put their ideas … into practice at any cost." To this class belonged mostly "the lawyers, doctors, and merchants who hope by the means which they advocate to achieve a greater importance."[2] Although fragmented along regional, economic, religious, cultural, and party-political lines, a new social class was rising in German society by the eve of the great mid-century revolutions. Fifty years earlier, only the embryo of this elite had existed.

"We are the times,"[3] boasted a bourgeois publicist in 1834. This bold assertion reflected the common belief of the middle classes that modern times belonged to them. Businessmen and professionals were creating the new wealth and knowledge that would remodel social, economic, political, and national institutions. These "liberal" reforms included social parity with the nobility, representative bodies and constitutionalism, German economic integration, and a more genuine form of political unification than the moribund Confederation. Liberals possessed no enthusiasm for revolution. Violence would only disrupt the social order and threaten their own accomplishments. Accordingly, most German bourgeois were also reluctant to cooperate with lower orders in society which could make no matching natural claims to a share of political power. Despite the fact that the goals of middle class liberalism were limited, there was nevertheless a subversiveness to its politics and ideology that justified the wariness of the establishment.

The writings of David Hansemann, a successful wool merchant from Aachen, illustrate this point. After the Belgian uprising of August 1830, he penned a letter to Georg Maassen, the new minister of finance and a close political ally. "The Belgian Revolution is really the worst, stupid, unpolitical thing ever done by a people." Hansemann's dislike of mob violence was obvious, but he feared

2. Cited in Theodore S. Hamerow, *Restoration, Revolution, Reaction: Economics and Politics in Germany, 1815-1871* (Princeton, 1958), 60.

3. Cited in James J. Sheehan, *German History 1770-1866* (Oxford, 1989), 601.

that his own kingdom would suffer the same fate without bold parliamentary reforms. The transition to these institutions was begun during the Reform Era, but after 1820, Frederick William III had choosen to retain unlimited decision-making power, thereby sacrificing the unlimited *national* power that would result if government were opened to the majority. Hansemann was careful, however, to circumscribe his definition of "majority." He did not mean a numerical majority, but rather a qualitative majority whose education gave it "more insight" and whose wealth gave it "greater interest" in establishing "a firm, powerful, well-managed government." He was referring, of course, to the cultivated and propertied middle class: "the real strength of the nation." Parliament should cooperate with a monarch who retained far-reaching executive powers. Together they would sweep away medieval holdovers like tax exemption for the nobility and police powers; introduce modern practices like freedom of press and assembly; and build "a new, solid German federation in place of the lifeless creation of 1815." Hansemann envisaged a peaceful evolution from the Zollverein to a North German political union, for he felt Austria had been drawn too deeply into Balkan and Italian affairs to represent "the true national majority."[4] To his bitter disappointment, these views were not appreciated in high places, earning him nothing but the reputation of a dangerous dissident.

Friedrich Christoph Dahlmann paid a higher price for his moderate liberalism. Professor of history at the University of Göttingen, he helped author the Hanoverian constitution of 1833. Two years later, he published *Politics: Reduced to the Basis and Measure of Existing Conditions*. Like Hansemann, Dahlmann wanted the bourgeoisie to enjoy rights of political participation guaranteed in a constitution. The middle class was, after all, "the core of the population"[5] Also like Hansemann, the historian abhorred revolution, recognized the need for strong monarchical authority to assure progress, and longed for a Prussian-led unification of North Germany. Influenced by Hegel, however, Dahlmann had a more elaborate theory of the state and a far greater tolerance for historical

4. Citations from Alexander Bergengrün, *David Hansemann* (Berlin, 1901), 103-04, 109, 113, 115.

5. Cited in Sheehan, 598.

classes and institutions. He believed that the state embodied the spirit of unfolding conditions and grew organically from the contributions of both old and new classes – hence his call for a house of peers alongside a house of commons. Yet in 1837 this thoroughly moderate man was dismissed with Jakob Grimm and other members of the Göttingen Seven. Dahlmann had once argued against the right of a subject to resist his monarch. But now he took a stand: "I fight for the immortal king, the legal will of the government, when – with legal weapons – I resist what the mortal king does in violation of existing laws."[6]

Johann Gustav Droysen represented the extreme right wing of North German liberalism. Born in Pomerania and educated in Berlin, Droysen began his career teaching history at the University of Kiel in 1840. His first major publication concentrated on the wars of liberation, praising the partnership of the heroic German folk and the revamped Kingdom of Prussia. Droysen's respect for popular accomplishments and enlightened reform did not extend, however, to an advocacy of genuine parliamentarism. His next book, a very popular biography of Alexander the Great, argued that mighty Prussia had to subdue South Germany just as Macedonian warrior kings had imposed unity on the chaotic, self-governed city-states of Greece. Representative bodies were a necessary corollary of the modern state, but he rejected notions like the social contract and the separation of powers as "inherently senseless and illusory in practice,"[7] for they weakened the monarch who had to accomplish great feats. In fact, Droysen's preoccupation with the masculine mission of Prussia poisoned his impression of the non-military traditions of the South. Thus he compared the cultural atmosphere of Weimar with the "stagnant air in a room full of spinsters prattling about art."[8]

Interestingly enough, there were liberals in other parts of Germany who held essentially the same views about unification. Fifteen years before Droysen, Paul Pfizer, a Swabian writer, had argued that liberty within the German states would not guarantee

6. Ibid., 616.

7. Ibid., 600.

8. Cited in Hans Kohn, *The Mind of Germany: The Education of a Nation* (New York, 1960), 132.

unification – and might even delay its coming. It was better to encourage Prussia to champion the "Small German" *(Kleindeutsch)* cause – in other words, one that excluded Austria – then await the inevitable liberalization of the new nation-state. Heinrich von Gagern, a liberal leader in the diet of Hesse-Darmstadt, also saw the need for Prussian leadership.

But others disagreed. The most prominent standard bearer of liberalism in South Germany was Karl von Rotteck, professor of history and politics at the University of Freiburg. Co-author with Theodor Welcker of the famous *Staatslexicon* (Political Dictionary), Rotteck dreamed of transforming southwestern Germany into a bastion of individual liberty rivaling France, England, and the United States. This was far more important to him, in fact, than German unification. "I do not desire [national] unity without liberty, and I prefer liberty without unity to unity without liberty. [And] I reject unity under the wings of the Prussian or the Austrian eagle."[9] Rotteck's statement was typical of South German liberals who desired a far-reaching parliamentarism, but were extremely wary of either Prussian or Austrian hegemony.

To still others, however, Austrian leadership, or at least the cooperation of Austria and Prussia in a reformed confederation, was imperative. A "Large German" *(Grossdeutsch)* unification – in other words, one that did *not* exclude Austria – was favored by Catholic liberals and clergymen who feared religious persecution in predominantly Protestant North Germany. Moreover, imperialist-minded bourgeois viewed Austria as a "lantern for the East." Habsburg power could be a beacon for German expansion toward the Black Sea and eastern Mediterranean. Thus German liberals – like Germany itself – were divided and fragmented along many different lines of fissure.

The mix becomes even more complex when we add Austrian liberalism. First, there were no counterparts to great spokesmen of the German bourgeoisie like Hansemann, Harkort, and List. Austrian businessmen favored parliamentary reforms, but wisely chose to work behind the scenes where they could wield influence and avoid censorship. Perfectly content with the economic status quo

9. Ibid., 135.

in Austria's protected market, moreover, factory owners turned a deaf ear to those who advocated a national union of all Germans. Indeed some educated bourgeois in Vienna like Matthias Koch, a historian, J. N. Berger, a constitutional theorist, and Alexander Bach, a lawyer, advocated constitutional reforms for the German-speaking regions of the empire as a prelude to a break-away and merger with North Germans in a Greater German Reich (*Grossdeutschland*). The students of Vienna were also enthusiastic about this secessionist solution to Austria's nationality problem. For the most part, however, Austria's cultivated bourgeoisie agreed with the businessmen that Habsburg lands and Habsburg power in the German Confederation had to remain intact. The only open bridge between German and Austrian liberals, therefore, ran from the *Grossdeutsch* factions of the North to the politicized academic circles of Vienna.

The rise of the bourgeoisie – and the ideological assertions which accompanied this emerging new elite – were not ignored by conservative spokesmen. The most engaging of these was Friedrich Julius Stahl, a teacher of law at the Bavarian universities of Munich and Erlangen in the 1830s and the University of Berlin after 1840. Like Adam Müller and Friedrich Gentz before him, Stahl enlisted religious devotion in the struggle against subversion and unbelief. Unlike his predecessors, however, Stahl did not escape back into medieval times to shore up the sagging old order of guildsmen, pastors, and aristocrats. "Medieval principles and [modern] liberalism both have some truth in them," he wrote a friend in 1834, "and in my concept of the state, I have tried to weave them together."[10] Accepting the drive toward representative institutions and national unity as inevitable, Stahl sought ways to bolster monarchical authority in this age of transformation. Much like Rotteck, he saw king and parliament as dual centers of power. Unlike the great liberal, Stahl believed the monarch must be largely independent of elected politicians and free to appoint ministers, initiate laws, and build budgets. Gone, too, was the old conservative antipathy toward bureaucracy. Indeed he felt that monarchical authority would vanish without the competence and

10. Cited in Sheehan, 594.

expertise of bureaucrats on the side of the king. Thus Stahl's was a much more realistic brand of conservatism that anticipated the compromising necessities of the post-1848 period.

* * * *

Social change and ideological fervor were accompanied by serious political challenges within the leading states of the German Confederation. The situation in Prussia was especially acute, for the kingdom suffered from compound crises, one layered upon the other. First, the kingdom's business elite looked with increasing disfavor at a bureaucracy that seemed out of touch with modern times. "As thankfully as [David Hansemann] acknowledged [past favors]," writes his biographer, "as much as he sincerely revered men like Motz, Maassen, [and] Beuth … , protestations, at first faint, then gradually growing more vehement, against the conceit and self-satisfaction of the bureaucracy as well as its defective expertise in specific areas, mount throughout all of his commentaries on political and economic relations in Prussia."[11] Some were bothered by autarkical practices in the army, Mining Corps, and Overseas Trading Corporation *(Seehandlung)* which choked private initiative, while others objected to inadequate tariff and patent protection, increasingly irrelevant technological advice, stifling monetary policies, and Draconian restrictions against joint-stock corporations. "Men who are educated for state service," complained Joseph Mendelssohn, Berlin's leading banker, "do not know the fabric of industry and are not accustomed to it in as exacting a manner as is absolutely necessary."[12] Even railroad policy, once progressive, turned negative and controversial after 1844 as conservatives in the ministries grew afraid that industrial development was too rapid.

Placing unwanted additional pressure on a harried, beleaguered government was the reemergence of the nobility's opposition. The main centers of this blue-blood liberalism were in East Prussia around Rudolf von Auerswald, the Mayor of Königsberg, and in Westphalia around Georg von Vincke, son of the long-time provin-

11. Bergengrün, 82.
12. Cited in Brose, *Politics of Technological Change,* 238.

cial governor. Auerswald and his political friends agreed with the bourgeoisie that constitutional changes were imperative if Prussia were to stay abreast of the times, while "liberal" aristocrats like Vincke were driven more by the desire to retrieve lost estatist rights. With a similar mixture of motives, five of eight provincial diets (largely controlled by the nobility) passed resolutions in 1845 calling for parliamentary institutions.

Finally, there were a number of ugly confrontations in the provinces between haughty officers and indignant citizens. In Königsberg, for example, a lieutenant accused a young lawyer of insulting the king, then shot him dead in a duel. The entire citizenry sided with the deceased, demanding that the officer be banned from appearing in public. In Mainz and Coblenz, similar attempts were made to prohibit unpopular officers from entering clubs and casinos, while in Cologne, citizens protested after troops sent to restore order to a Kirmes festival killed one of the revelers. These incidents worsened military-civilian relations, heightened class tensions, and tarnished the image of Frederick William IV, the dreamy, idealistic monarch of Prussia since 1840.

The new king had grown to manhood during the Napoleonic era – harrowing years for Prussia, his father and mother, and the young crown prince. Frederick William emerged from this experience with a strong emotional bond to older, traditional institutions destroyed by the revolutionary beast. The adolescent lost himself in the romantic novels of Friedrich de la Motte Fouquè, a popular author who "derived his stories and characters almost exclusively from an imagined, dreamy, often fantastic notion of the Middle Ages, redolent with images of knights, damsels, rocky crags, dark forests, castles, and all the rest."[13] As he began to formulate a political agenda of his own in the 1820s, Frederick William thought of restoring the world of the Holy Roman Empire, of kings and loyal aristocratic retainers, of beautiful churches and religious devotion, of skilled craftsmen and simple, hard-working peasants. Artistically inclined, he longed to express his view of the world architecturally with the construction of villas, palaces, and churches.

13. David E. Barclay, *Frederick William IV and the Prussian Monarchy 1840-1861* (Oxford, 1995), 29-30.

"Accordingly," writes David Barclay, "it is impossible to separate or distinguish clearly among his aesthetic/architectural, religious, and political concerns." His reform program was an "all-encompassing work of art"[14] *(Gesamtkunstwerk)*. Paradoxically – and enigmatically – the crown prince was also attracted by certain aspects of his own unfolding epoch. He was a genuine Anglophile who appreciated English institutions and loved railroads. Despite his backward-looking ideas, therefore, many of his subjects expected great things of Frederick William IV. Advocates of parliamentarization could point to his love of English ways, while nationalists were enthused by his attachment to the old Reich.

Frederick William IV responded to the challenges of rule with a series of misunderstood and contradictory actions. His first years on the throne brought a loosening of censorship, appointment of liberals like Hermann von Boyen to high office, and the rehabilitation of old "demagogues" like Turnvater Jahn and Ernst Moritz Arndt. But when Theodor von Schön, the provincial governor of East Prussia, urged him to draft a constitution, Frederick William curtly refused, claiming that a "piece of paper" should never come between a patriarch and his subjects. Seeking to mollify public opinion in February 1847, however, he issued a written decree convening a representative assembly. The so-called "United Diet" was a cumbersome and unwieldy body, but the king's ordinance had promised it full budgetary rights. Prince William, the king's brother, warned him not to call the assembly, observing correctly that "the old Prussia is buried with the publication of this decree." The confused monarch ignored the advice – then seemed to remember it during his opening address. No power on earth, he reminded the delegates, would move him to adopt a "conventional, constitutional" relationship with his people – "not now, not ever."[15] Urged on by Hansemann and Vincke, the United Diet insisted on a clarification of its rights and demanded periodic sessions. When Frederick William refused, the defiant representatives voted against credits for railroad construction. Thus storm clouds gathered in the "new Prussia" as the decade approached its fateful ninth year.

14. Ibid., 24-25.

15. Citations from Heinrich von Treitschke, *Deutsche Geschichte im Neunzehten Jahrhundert* (Leipzig, 1899), 5: 607, 619.

The political climate in surrounding states was equally foreboding. A "spectacle of decorum and pliability"[16] in the 1830s, the Saxon diet was demanding and irreverent ten years later. The impatient legislators in Dresden insisted that soldiers take an oath of allegiance to the constitution and had the temerity to propose that the army substitute gymnastic training, popular among the most radical nationalists, for existing military education. In Mecklenburg, bourgeois landowners protested their discriminatory status in the diet, prompting a pained grand duke to complain that they all belonged "to the liberal party." In Hesse-Kassel, the elector was tempted to follow the Hanoverian example and overthrow the constitution, but was dissuaded by Prussian and Austrian leaders who feared violence. Tension was also mounting in Hanover, where the estates approved budgets begrudgingly and demanded public sessions. "We have resolved irreversibly," declared a pompous Ernst August, "never to allow public sessions." "So the Welf spoke his 'never' just a few days after King Frederick William called out his 'not now, not ever' to the United Diet – only a year [later] and the uncle, like the nephew, were to learn that not even kings can prescribe his way to the living God,"[17] wrote Heinrich von Treitschke dramatically.

Monarchical authority was also under assault across southern Germany. William of Württemberg received the hurrahs of the masses during his Silver Jubilee in 1841, but the cheering crowds belied a less pleasant reality. Indeed there was growing discontent with a king who was intolerant of parties, parliament, public criticism, and further progress. "Long experience" had convinced him of the "unfeasibility" of liberal demands for public trials, popular militias, and freedom of the press. "We can *never, ever* do without the censors," he told a surprised Prussian ambassador in 1842, "least of all in the constitutional states."[18] Friedrich Römer reaped the whirlwind of Swabian dissatisfaction with William, uniting parliamentary and extra-parliamentary opponents of the regime by the mid-1840s.

Grand Duke Leopold of Baden also grew tired of his diet's seemingly endless pressure for change. Turning to Friedrich von

16. Sheehan, 614.
17. Quotations are from Treitschke, 5:670-71.
18. Ibid., 673.

Blittersdorff in 1839, a bold effort was made to put parliament in its place. But public criticism and a series of liberal electoral victories eventually forced Blittersdorff's resignation. In 1846 Leopold appointed a new ministry under the conciliatory Johann Baptist Bekk.

Nor were absolutist tendencies absent from Bavaria. King Ludwig wheeled to the right after the shocking revolutions of 1830, appointing reactionary ministers like General Wrede and Karl von Abel, forming party alliances with the conservatives and the Catholic Church – even reviving odious terms like "subject" instead of "citizen." But when he fell in love with the beautiful dancer, Lola Montez, providing her with luxurious quarters and lavishing her with exorbitant gifts, the crazed monarch forgot himself as well as the moral discretion that was becoming increasingly necessary in a bourgeois age. "The dignity of monarchy suffers inestimably greater damage with such nonsense," reported a worried Prussian ambassador, "than with all that [was] instigated [years ago] by the Demagogues."[19]

The "dignity of monarchy" was also declining in Austria. The death of Francis in 1835 brought his mentally retarded son, Ferdinand, to the throne. As frequently occurs in such circumstances, a regency was quickly established to shield the monarchy from public embarrassment. The State Conference, as it was called, consisted of Archduke Ludwig, Archduke Franz Karl, Metternich, and his long-standing nemesis, Kolowrat. It soon became evident that the new arrangement was not working. For one thing, the royal relatives did not possess Francis's dispassionate resolve to squelch dissent. They were "too good-natured and too humane to ... carry on the old police pressure," remembered poet Franz Grillparzer, "and that was their ruin."[20] Adding to Austria's problems was the ongoing feud between Metternich and Kolowrat. For the notoriously reactionary conservatism of the former elicited a transparently opportunistic liberalism from the latter. In a move to block and frustrate his enemy, Kolowrat approved new organizations that would never have surfaced in the days of Francis. The

19. Ibid., 658.

20. Cited in C.A. Macartney, *The Habsburg Empire 1790-1918* (New York, 1969), 304.

Industrial Association of Lower Austria, a low-key lobby for businessmen and others who sympathized with the aims of industry, appeared in December 1839; Concordia, an organization of writers, actors, and artists, emerged in 1840, while no fewer than nine student clubs sprang to life in the following years, many overtly political. This trend accelerated in 1842 with the opening of the Legal-Political Reading Club, a gathering place for all bourgeois parties eager to change the system. Also represented there, however, were spokesmen for the noble opposition, especially those of Lower Austria and Kolowrat's homeland of Bohemia. In petition after petition in the mid-1840s, the estates of these provinces insisted on the restoration of their feudal rights. Much like their Prussian counterparts, the aristocrats championed a forward-looking liberalism which served to mask the fact that their gaze was really in the other direction.

Kolowrat's tolerance permitted the first real public political activity in Austria. Under Kaiser Francis, opposition politics had been nearly impossible. Criticism of the regime, not surprisingly, was forced down to the personal and private level where feelings and frustrations could be vented over a lunch or dinner with kindred spirits. If a conversational or friendship circle was well-connected to the court or bureaucracy, however, it stood a chance of engaging in practical party politics and intrigue. The dawn of more public expression and politicking witnessed not so much the proliferation of opposition political parties, therefore, as their rapid surfacing.

This phenomenon was illustrated well in the Legal-Political Reading Club, which was not so much "a political party directed … against the state,"[21] as Georg Franz believed, but rather a forum where the heads of a plethora of small factions and parties could openly discuss and debate their views. Represented there were four party groupings bridging state and society: Josephinian bureaucrats like bourgeois State Councilors Sommaruga, Pilgram, and Weiss; spokesmen of the Lower Austrian and Bohemian estates like Counts Schmerling, Doblhoff, and Thun; representatives of the

21. Georg Franz, *Liberalismus: Die Deutschliberale Bewegung in der Habsburgischen Monarchie* (Munich, 1955), 29.

cultivated bourgeoisie, above all lawyers and legal scholars like Bach and Berger; and finally, leaders "from the world of industry and finance"[22] who maintained a lower profile than the others. "The intellectual life of [Vienna] found [here] its focal point," writes one historian, "and simultaneously it was a barometer for the political mood of the capital." Pilgram, who eventually bolted from the organization, went much farther, describing the Legal-Political Reading Club as "a seedbed for the spread of propaganda."[23] Obviously, that it existed at all was a measure of how much politics was changing under the new regime.

The convening of the United Diet induced a similar transformation from private to public party politics in Prussia. To be sure, political life under the Hohenzollerns had not descended to the reactionary depths of Austria after 1815 – and controls were loosened in the mid-1820s and again in the early 1840s. But the fate of Johann Jacoby, a young physician from Königsberg, was a reminder of the necessity to keep opposition politics buried at the private level. Published in 1841, Jacoby's *Four Questions Answered by an East Prussian* declared that it was "an inalienable right" that "independent citizens" be granted the opportunity for "lawful participation in the affairs of the state."[24] The hapless businessman's son was arrested and put on trial for treason.

Jacoby's more prudent friends gathered regularly at Siegel's cafe to discuss their views more quietly and intimately. In Berlin, too, the years before the United Diet saw the business of political opposition conducted in the salons, reading rooms, cafes, and pubs. "These countless unsuccessful [oppositionist] forces," complained one writer, "[are] split up into many separate clubs [that only] do one another harm."[25] Not surprisingly, when the delegates of the United Diet descended upon Berlin, they sought out like-minded types in the cafes, restaurants, and hotel suites. But, as Treitschke correctly observed, there was potential in these preliminary meetings for the creation of "great all-Prussian parties" due to the fact that "the fis-

22. Ibid., 29.
23. Ibid., 29.
24. Cited in Sheehan, 624.
25. Cited in Dora Meyer, *Das öffentliche Leben in Berlin im Jahr vor der Märzrevolution* (Berlin, 1912), 45.

sure line of this division into parties *(Riss der Parteiung)* cut across all provinces in the same way."[26] Soon enough, men who knew little about one another discovered similarities and expressed themselves in the great public forum remarkably provided for them by their uncertain sovereign. It would take decades, however, before a political fragmentation born of authoritarian suppression evolved into a more orderly multi-party system in Prussia. Then, as now, this long period of fragmentation was in the nature of such transitions.

The process just underway in Austria and Prussia had been progressing for decades in Baden, Württemberg, and Bavaria. The early jumble of factions, sects, and free-standing deputies – accompanied, as we know, by parliamentary turbulence and unpredictability – had yielded somewhat by the 1830s to loose groupings or blocs. On the one side were those who could be counted upon to support the government; on the other side was the opposition.

Bavarian Chief Minister Karl von Abel ruled for a decade (1837-1847) before resigning in protest over the Lola Montez affair. His support came from an alliance of close-knit Catholic-conservative parties linked outside of parliament to the Eos circle and the theological faculty of the University of Munich. Protestant deputies from the Palatinate were the best organized opponents of Abel's policies, regularly meeting before important votes to orchestrate tactics. However, religious and regional differences divided the Rhenish members of the diet from other Bavarian liberals – who were themselves split along numerous lines of fissure. "Despite the strong resistance which the Abel ministry unleashed among [liberal] deputies ... " writes Helmut Kramer, "there was still no united opposition which followed definite leaders and acted according to common operational plans."[27]

A similar situation existed in Württemberg. The opposition possessed a number of prominent spokesmen – Friedrich Römer was clearly the most dreaded in debate – but the government's opponents were far too split up between Catholics and Protestants, city cosmopolitans and hometown burghers, and self-made businessmen and educated professionals to operate as a solid phalanx. For well

26. Treitschke, 5:615.

27. Helmut Kramer, *Fraktionsbinduungen in den deutschen Volksvertretungen 1819-1849* (Berlin, 1968), 27.

over a decade after William finally convened the diet in 1833, his ministers found consistent parliamentary backing from a coalition of civil servants led by Friedrich Ludwig Gmelin. Together "they represented a bastion of the bureaucracy which was thrust forward into the diet."[28] Not until the mid-1840s did Römer and his colleagues even begin to undermine this citadel of conservatism.

Only in Baden did monarchical authority gradually yield to parliamentary exegencies. Already, before Blittersdorff's last-ditch attempt to stifle the opposition (1839-1843), Grand Duke Leopold's ministers had faced determined opponents in the diet who coordinated their strategies in private meetings under a few recognized leaders like Karl von Rotteck and Johann von Itzstein. It was not until the more conciliatory regime of Johann Baptist Bekk, however, that more modern parties emerged. For, despite Itzstein's best efforts, the victory over Blittersdorff fragmented the opposition into three groups: a radical faction around Friedrich Hecker and Gustav von Struve and a left-center party under Karl Mathy, both eager to continue the fight for more parliamentary power; and a right-center group that was more moderate. To their right was a conservative party supportive of the government. Unlike Bavaria and Württemberg, these four parties sat together in the diet, negotiated parliamentary deals with other parties, and campaigned at election time with agreed-upon strategies. Within Baden's parties, however, it was still possible to detect the points of adhesion between formerly independent sects and friendship circles. Thus Karl Mathy bemoaned "those coteries"[29] of radicals who smeared him at election time.

Nationalist politics in German Europe also emanated from coteries of like-minded political friends. Thus the Hambach Festival of 1832 had been organized by a loose coalition of individuals, each with his own personal following. Afterwards, with ringleaders like Wirth and Siebenpfeiffer in jail or exile, Johann von Itzstein began to invite compatriots from the southwest to his private estate at Hallgarten for quiet deliberations on the national issue. Itzstein extended the discussion circle in the early 1840s to kindred

28. Hartwig Brandt, *Parlamentarismus in Württemberg 1819-1870* (Düsseldorf, 1987), 598.

29. Cited in Treitschke, 5:679.

spirits from East Prussia, Saxony, and the Rhineland. But here too, divisions soon opened. In October 1847, liberals like Mathy and Itzstein of Baden, Römer of Württemberg, Heinrich von Gagern of Hesse, and Hansemann of the Rhineland gathered at Heppenheim, agreeing that German unification should proceed from the Zollverein. Only a month earlier, radicals around Hecker and Struve had met in Offenburg to issue a call for the democratization of the German Confederation. While the Heppenheim conclave hinted at Prussian leadership, in other words, the Offenburg circle seemed to favor a Greater Germany, including a reformed Austria.

Political developments in the legal community closely paralleled the events culminating at Offenburg and Heppenheim. The reader will recall the controversy decades earlier between A. F. J. Thibaut and Friedrich Karl von Savigny over codification of German law. The former, a prominent jurist from Heidelberg, advocated codification as a step toward political unification, while the latter, professor of jurisprudence at Berlin, felt a national code would sacrifice regional and local traditions for ill-conceived, alien concepts. Savigny was convinced that German laws, for all their rich diversity, had been benignly influenced by Roman law, which he saw as a bridge between an orderly past and a hopeful future, while Thibaut viewed Roman law as the alien concept, preferring to base his new code on German legal rituals of the Middle Ages. Savigny's historical school prevailed until the mid-1830s, but after the dismissal of the Göttingen Seven in 1837, Thibaut's Germanist approach gained momentum. The impotence of the protesting university jurists, and worse, the government-imposed silence of the Prussian law faculties, steeped in their mystique of an autonomous jurists' estate that would resuscitate Roman traditions, exposed a gaping hole between theory and reality and incensed Savigny's opponents. Thus Jacob Grimm, a former protégé and victim of the firings, declared angrily that "the use of Roman law has, in practice, brought no advantage to constitutionalism and freedom."[30] Soon others like Anton Christ, a deputy in the Badenese diet, were calling for a uniform national code of laws, written in the German

30. Cited in James Q. Whitman, *The Legacy of Roman Law in the German Romantic Era: Historical Vision and Legal Change* (Princeton, 1990), 201.

language, and based entirely on German legal traditions. Another nationalist, Georg Beseler, fanned the flames higher in 1843 with *People's Law and Jurists' Law* , a direct assault on Savigny's school. The Germanist offensive climaxed with national conventions in Frankfurt and Lübeck in September of 1846 and 1847. Like Thibaut, the practicing lawyers who packed both congresses wanted legal unity to pave the way for political unification.

These developments excited Heinrich von Gagern, for he knew from observing politics in the nearby Palatinate that barristers were often "leaders of the people." And he fully appreciated the importance to middle class nationalism of "the public confirmation of the opinion of the lawyers."[31] Swirling around and below the bourgeois notables of unification politics, in fact, was a populist "movement of societies."[32] Still inspired by the famous "Turnvater" Jahn, for instance, the gymnastic clubs survived the crackdown of the reactionary Twenties (see Part II) and redoubled efforts to steel the bodies of young members for service to the nation. The gymnasts received new impetus from a war scare with France (1840) and Danish threats to the Duchy of Schleswig (1844-1846), expanding by 1847 to 250 clubs with around 85,000 members. Attracting mostly hard-pressed journeymen and apprentices, the movement became a trans-regional phenomenon with the great "Turnfest" held at Heidelberg in 1847. Typical features of these tournaments, observes Hans-Ulrich Wehler, were "hikes, torchlight parades, and festive banquets with fiery speeches, patriotic songs, and declamations – while the meeting towns were decorated with 'German' oak leaves and also, increasingly, with black, red, and gold flags."[33]

Even more popular were the singing clubs that spread from Switzerland and the southwest to other parts of Germany in the early 1800s. Gathering in forest clearings away from the threatening rumblings of early industrialization, choirs of fifty to one hundred small-town burghers raised their male voices in four-part harmonious songs like "The Watch on the Rhine," "Schleswig-

31. Cited in Michael John, *Politics and the Law in Late Nineteenth-Century Germany: The Origins of the Civil Code* (Oxford, 1989), 27.

32. See Dieter Düding, *Organisierter gesellschaftlicher Nationalismus in Deutschland (1807-1848)* (Munich, 1984).

33. Hans-Ulrich Wehler, *Deutsche Gesellschaftsgeschichte* (Munich, 1987), 2:404.

Holstein Embraced by the Sea," and "Deutschland, Deutschland Über Alles." It was, as one of the early leaders said, "decent, refreshing, patriotic publicity"[34] for the great nationalistic cause. But there was a definite egalitarian flair to the clubs. Thus Thomas Nipperdey reminds us of the then-popular saying: "The laughable barriers of social rank sink low before the power of song."[35] A movement with at least 100,000 backers by the late 1840s, the singing clubs also transcended their local origins with impressive nationwide festivals at Würzburg (1845), Cologne (1846), and Lübeck (1847) – the latter as a demonstration of solidarity for Schleswig-Holstein.

There were other important manifestations of this grass-roots nationalism in the decade before 1848. Thus thousands of patriots gathered near Detmold in 1838 for the ground-breaking ceremony of a monument *(Hermannsdenkmal)* commemorating Arminius's triumph over the Romans in the Teutoburg Forest. Thirty-thousand nationalist enthusiasts had assembled in Mainz the year before to participate in a Gutenberg Festival, and when it was repeated in 1840, "countless masses" came from eighty German towns and cities. Similar festivals and commemorations in the early 1840s for Schiller (Stuttgart), Dürer (Nürnberg), Jean Paul (Bayreuth), Mozart (Salzburg), Bach (Leipzig), and Goethe (Frankfurt) mobilized Germans in great numbers along the country's new railroads and improved highways. "This day gets its true significance," trumpeted the organizer of the Schiller Festival, "from the consciousness – manifested all around – that the whole of Germany helped to celebrate this festival [and] that all of those who participated and enjoyed themselves here were the representatives of the entire people."[36] It would not be long before this subterranean nationalism welled up to the political surface and inundated the startled rulers of the German Confederation.

34. Cited in George L. Mosse, *The Nationalization of the Masses: Political Symbolism and Mass Movements in Germany from the Napoleonic Wars through the Third Reich* (Ithaca, 1975), 138.

35. Cited in Thomas Nipperdey, *Deutsche Geschichte 1800-1866: Bürgerwelt und starker Staat* (Munich, 1983), 535.

36. Citations from Otto Dann, *Nation und Nationalismus in Deutschland 1770-1990* (Munich, 1993), 108.

Chapter 12

Social Change, Ideological Fervor, and Political Turmoil

The ascent of the middle classes to social and political prominence was accompanied by changes in German society of an even more radical nature. Indeed for every new factory, mine, or railroad of the early industrial revolution, Germany's enterprising businessmen had to recruit, train, and discipline a labor force. The Egells machine factory in Berlin employed 500 workers in 1847, for instance, while 1,200 wore the blue collar in Borsig's locomotive works. These operations were exceptionally large, of course, most typically employing no more than twenty or thirty hands. By the late 1840s there were around 170,000 factory workers in the Zollverein and probably over 300,000 when Austria and the rest of the Confederation is included. This figure swells to well over half a million, however, when we add the miners and railroad construction crews. Thus Germany's 40,000 industrialists had wrought a social revolution by mid-century.

What is known about the origins of this new working class? Contrary to popular impressions, Germany's first factory workers were not rural workers or peasants displaced from the land. Like the entrepreneurs themselves, in fact, they tended to migrate from the putting-out or handicraft branches related to the textile or metalwork required in the factory. Nor was the early proletariat a monolithic mass of unskilled machine-tenders. Factory work was highly differentiated, scaling downwards from the well-paid men who tooled and repaired machinery to the poorly paid men, women, and children who operated machines or performed simple tasks. Rural origins were more typical of the miners who sank their shafts deeper and deeper into the coal deposits of the Ruhr, the Saar, Saxony, Silesia, and Bohemia. The huge railroad construction gangs also recruited typically from the social flotsam and jetsam of the central European countryside.

Working and living conditions during the early industrial revolution corresponded more closely to the dismal image handed down to us over the generations. Twelve to sixteen-hour days in a seemingly endless succession of seven-day weeks was the rule. Wages for the vast majority of proletarians permitted subsistence living standards at best. Working by semi-automatic textile machines, moreover, was monotonous – and therefore dangerous. Even more hazardous, however, was the grueling job of puddling wrought iron next to a smoky, gaseous furnace, or chipping or hauling coal in hot underground shafts prone to explosions and cave-ins. Adding to the stress and exhaustion of industrial labor was the fact that it offered none of the mitigating circumstances of handicraft or rural labor. Hard work was year-round, not seasonal; holidays were rarely celebrated; recessions meant unemployment, not boredom on the job; and work was performed far away from home, not inside the patriarchal household. Nor did the smelly shanty towns and disease-ridden ghettos of the first industrial neighborhoods offer much relief from the job. Only the better-paid skilled workers managed to escape from these conditions into a more secure and respectable petty bourgeois existence. For the rest, hard times and miserable circumstances began the long, gradual process of shaping workers from different home towns and disparate backgrounds into a class with grievances to redress.

At first, workers sought solutions to their problems in the old ways. Popular protests had traditionally taken the form of local community actions against neighbors who had sinned or demonstrations against perceived outsiders like tax collectors, moneylenders, foreigners, or Jews. "Members of a guild, parish, or village," writes James Sheehan, "often saw these outsiders as the source of their discontent, violators of privileged territory, breakers of traditional codes, [or] disrupters of … the 'moral economy' on which local life was based."[1] One frequent type of protest was a carry-over from Early Modern popular culture known as "cat music" due to the screeching nocturnal crowds which gathered outside an offender's house, disturbing sleep in its mildest form, destroying the house and injuring its inhabitant in the most extreme cases. The first proletarian demonstrations were of this sort: cat music outside the factory; broken windows; sometimes even machine-smashing. In a variation on this traditional theme, railroad workers engaged in brief work stoppages to convey dissatisfaction with unfair wages or practices. Thus Prussian, Saxon, and Hanoverian crews engaged in thirty-three such protest actions between 1844 and 1847, most lasting only a few hours, but sometimes involving thousands of workers.

Even in these early years, however, some laborers went on strike in more peaceful fashion to press for concrete demands like higher wages, shorter hours, or safer working conditions. Recent research has uncovered sixteen instances of modern strikes between 1835 and 1847, most led by journeymen experienced in such matters. "For there was a fluid continuity," writes Hans-Ulrich Wehler, "between the presumably hundreds of journeymen's walkouts since the last third of the eighteenth century and the [first] strikes carried out by industrial artisans."[2] Nor was the political dimension lacking from these developments in the workplace. Throughout the industrializing portions of Germany, workers – mostly printers' journeymen, cigar workers, and other artisanal toilers who had tasted and rejected the new industrial style of work – began to form small, secret associations to fight back. On the foundation of these humble organizational beginnings, Stephan Born, a self-styled tribune of the people from Berlin, founded the "Brotherhood of the Workers." Its 18,000 backers, according to Born, were "putting society on notice" that inaction or indifference to the plight of the proletariat carried with it the price of "a terrible alternative." Small wonder that the Diet of the German Confederation banned journeymen's groups in 1835, strengthening the ruling in 1841 – or that Prussia extended the ordinance to

1. Sheehan, *German History*, 641.
2. Wehler, *Deutsche Gesellschaftsgeschichte*, 2:270

factory workers in 1845. The industrializing northern power wanted "to destroy dangerous labor organizations [and their] multitude of communist tendencies."[3]

Alarmist language like this reflected the widespread fear of workers among the upper classes. Concern for the dire social consequences of industrialization had underscored conservative criticism of the emerging new economic order, in fact, since the first years of the century. Thus Adam Heinrich Müller, a spokesman of Austrian conservatism, bemoaned the supplanting of noble artisans by depersonalized proletarians. Worried that man would sink to the level of a machine and society to that of a "bee-state" of workers and drones, Müller advocated a comprehensive reorganization of society with nobles, church, and guilds reacquiring their medieval privileges and industry drastically reduced "to its proper sphere."[4] In the 1830s, Müller was seconded by Catholic "socialists" like Franz von Baader and Joseph Jörg in Bavaria and Christoph Moufang in Hessian Mainz. All favored a corporatist restructuring of state and society which would curtail industrialism, redeem the workers, and enable all members of society to enjoy the fruits of property in accordance with their understanding of God's wishes. A Protestant Junker, Karl Rodbertus-Jagetzow, also believed the time was ripe for socialistic measures. Appalled that greedy industrialists were spawning the proletariat – a "populous race of barbarians in spirit and soul" – he felt the state should abolish private property and destroy its dangerous acquisitive spirit. A young Otto von Bismarck was also angered by capitalism. "Factories are enriching individuals," he wrote in 1848, "but raising a mass of badly nourished proletarians who are endangering the state with the insecurity of their existence."[5]

Most industrialists turned a deaf ear to such criticisms – or, if they listened, cited them as another reason to doubt the competence of a conservative establishment. But there were many notable exceptions. Thus Johannes Schuchard, a textile manufacturer from Barmen, worried about the revolutionary potential of industry's accelerating pace and scale. He sent a petition to Berlin

3. Ibid., 2:270, 268.
4. Cited in Brose, *Politics of Technological Change*, 52.
5. Rodbertus and Bismarck are cited in Wehler, 2:265-67.

in 1840 warning about "the commercial-industrial overexcitement which exists in England, promises palaces to us ... and [figures to provoke] a struggle of poverty against wealth."[6] As the work of Lothar Gall has shown, a not inconsiderable number of smaller businessmen in Germany agreed with Schuchard's views.[7]

Friedrich Harkort, Westphalia's great native son, was also worried by the violent threat of the burgeoning working class. Like his counterpart from Barmen, Harkort despised "that creation of value and wealth which is based on the sacrifice of human dignity and the degradation of the working class." The purpose of the machine, after all, was "to free men from animal servitude, not to fashion a more terrible bondage."[8] Unlike Schuchard, however, Harkort appreciated industrial growth and rejected any curtailment of its job-creating potential. Rather, he called on governments to reduce work hours, ban child labor, subsidize decent housing, facilitate sickness and disability programs, and further public education. Private individuals with the means could reinforce all of these efforts, moreover, as could workers' societies and workers' self-help efforts.

Gustav Mevissen of the Rhineland was another businessman who rejected the selfishness and indifference of his class. He had traveled throughout his home province in 1836, returning home worried and depressed about the materialism and smug self-confidence of the middle class. Like Harkort, Mevissen advocated government action to improve wages, working conditions, and workers' education. In 1842 he cooperated with other prominent Rhinelanders in founding the *Rheinische Zeitung*, an organ to promote these socially progressive ideas. Interestingly enough, a youthful Karl Marx became one of the paper's first editors that autumn.

The response of the cultured middle and upper class to the social problems associated with industrialization was also complex. As explained above, the industrial revolution did not occur automatically or inevitably – it was a hotly debated *political* question

6. Cited in Brose, 263.

7. See Lothar Gall, "Liberalismus und 'Bürgerliche Gesellschaft': Zu Charakter und Entwicklung der Liberalen Bewegung in Deutschland," *Historische Zeitschrift* 220 (April, 1975): 324-56.

8. Cited in Donald G. Rohr, *The Origins of Social Liberalism in Germany* (Chicago, 1963), 136.

that divided cultivated bourgeois and aristocratic fellow-travelers even more than it had the propertied bourgeoisie. For some, the prospect of social revolution was reason enough to erect barriers to industry's advance. In Bavaria, for example, Baron Öttingen-Wallerstein's anti-industrial policies of the 1830s found the support of Leo von Klenze, the neo-classical architect who headed the commission which recommended a return to the safer world of "prosperous mastercrafts-men" and "family-run workshops." Similar disillusionment with 'the pressing masses' emerged among the advocates of aesthetic industrialization in Baden and Württemberg, while in Prussia, Beuth and Schinkel also turned away from modernity's unfamiliar, frightening face.

Others rejected such negativism in favor of reformist, ameliorative agendas similar to those of Harkort and Mevissen. Thus Karl Biedermann, a young professor of philology and political science in Leipzig, cautioned his students not to overreact to socialist criticisms of industrial society. The accumulation of riches had indeed created abuses and injustices which only intelligent reforms could correct. He favored ideas like the graduated income tax, government aid to the poor, and private self-help and relief societies. Robert Mohl, an outspoken opponent of Württemberg's early hostility to industrialization, became an articulate spokesman of social reform by the 1830s. Professor of political science at Tübingen, Mohl wrote about the need for shorter hours, minimum wages, subsidized housing, and workers' savings plans organized by the state. Like many other social critics of the early industrial era, he was also attracted to the idea of resettling urban poor on the land. Mohl's program was representive of moderate liberal opinion in southern Germany. Thus he found ready support in Baden from Karl Welcker, sole editor of the *Staatslexicon* after Rotteck's death, and Karl Mathy, leader of the moderates in Baden's lower house. In fact, Mohl and Mathy co-authored an article for Welcker's publication. Urgent reform measures were necessary, they wrote, for the "higher purposes of the entire community."[9]

Enthusiasm for this social mission carried over into radical bourgeois circles in other parts of Germany. The activists whom Hecker

9. Cited in Rohr, 129.

and Struve assembled at Offenburg in 1847, for example, called for "an adjustment in the disparity between labor and capital." It was "the responsibility of society to elevate and protect labor." In Königsberg, moreover, a martyred Johann Jacobi insisted that officialdom "must begin at once to do something to relieve the distress of the working class." We should not overlook the fact, however, that middle class activists like Jacoby had no contacts with the masses, condemning, in his case, the "anarchist activities of a mob too lazy to work." Similarly, Hecker and Struve favored immediate democratic change and were prepared to take matters into their own hands, but they eschewed contact with "the great unwashed ... hungry mob"[10] and had no plans to mobilize it.

But some bourgeois activists were beginning to establish ties with those below them. In Cologne, for example, separate cliques gathered around Andreas Gottschalk, a physician with deep feelings for the plight of the proletariat, and Moses Hess, an editor of the *Rheinische Zeitung* dubbed by contemporaries the Communist Rabbi. Hess "drew comrades to himself," observes Hans-Ulrich Wehler, "spun a network of correspondents, and strengthened the political impulses of small groups of sympathizers on countless trips [throughout the province]."[11] Even Gottschalk and Hess, however, had no plans for an uprising of 'the great unwashed, hungry mob.'

Undoubtedly the most revolutionary and disturbing bourgeois response to the social crisis in industrializing Germany was penned by Friedrich Engels and Karl Marx in early 1848. Engels, the son of a textile manufacturer from Barmen, had served an apprenticeship with the family firm in England, observing there the sorry plight of the proletariat. Marx had studied at the Universities of Bonn and Berlin, written inflammatory articles for the *Rheinische Zeitung*, and lived the uncertain life of an exiled political emigré in Paris, Brussels, and London. In the next section we will discuss the significant intellectual development of Marx from a student curious about Hegel's world of ideas to a dangerous philosopher and revolutionary with a unique perspective on his own times – one that would have a powerful impact on posterity. The *Communist Manifesto* of

10. Above citations in Hamerow, *Restoration, Revolution, Reaction*, 65.
11. Wehler, 2:275.

Engels and Marx appeared too late in the 1840s to turn the continent upside down. But "no other modern movement or cause," observes Isaiah Berlin, "can claim to have produced anything comparable with it in eloquence or power."[12]

"A spectre is haunting Europe" began Marx and Engels, " – the spectre of communism." They laid this ghostly, revolutionary development, so truly haunting to the patricians of Europe, right at the doorstep of the bourgeoisie. For, in their view, the middle class of merchant and industrial capital, aided by those noblemen in the bureaucracy who understood the nature of the times, had spawned a new era, impressively dynamic and progressive in its economic and technological dimensions, yet one which threatened inevitable ruin for those privileged few who thus far were benefitting from it. We now follow Marx and Engels:

> Modern industry has converted the little workshop of the patriarchal master into the great factory of the industrial capitalist. Masses of laborers, crowded into factories, are organized like soldiers. As privates of the industrial army they are placed under the command of a perfect hierarchy of officiers and sergeants. Not only are they the slaves of the bourgeois class ... they are daily and hourly enslaved by the machine, by the overlooker, and, above all, by the individual bourgeois manufacturer himself. The more openly this despotism proclaims gain to be its end and aim, the more petty, the more hateful and the more embittering it is ... The proletariat, the lowest stratum of our present society, cannot stir, cannot raise itself up without the whole superincumbent strata of official society being [blown to bits] ... The development of modern industry, therefore, cuts from under its feet the very foundation on which the bourgeoisie produces and appropriates products. What the bourgeoisie therefore produces, above all, are its own grave diggers. Its fall and the victory of the proletariat are equally inevitable.

These threatening, provocative words appeared in print in February 1848. We should note, however, that Engels and Marx were well aware of other developments in contemporary society contributing to the ticking bomb which they believed would soon explode. For pre-industrial society was also coming unraveled. Again, the *Manifesto*.

12. Isaiah Berlin, *Karl Marx: His Life and Environment* (New York, 1959), 150.

> The lower middle class, the small manufacturer, the shop-keeper, the artisan, the peasant, all these fight against the bourgeoisie, to save from extinction their existence as fractions of the middle class. They are therefore not revolutionary, but conservative. Nay, more: they are reactionary, for they try to roll back the wheel of history. If by chance they are revolutionary, they are only so in view of their impending transfer into the proletariat; they thus defend not their present, but their future interests; they desert their own standpoint to place themselves at that of the proletariat. The 'dangerous classes,' the social scum, that passively rotting mass thrown off by the lowest layers of old society, may, here and there, be swept into the movement by a proletarian revolution; its conditions of life, however, prepare it far more for the part of a bribed tool of reactionary intrigue.[13]

As this passage makes very clear, Marx and Engels did not anticipate that revolutionary impulses would come from the rejected, passed-over strata of the pre-industrial order.

For the most part, however, they were wrong in this latter prognosis. For central European society was indeed caught up in a structural socio-economic crisis which threatened political insurrection. As we have demonstrated in Part II, peasant families throughout Germany struggled to make ends meet as agrarian reforms gave a percentage of the land to nobles as compensation. The new legislation also divided common land and, in isolated instances, redistributed strip farms, both of which had once provided a buffer against economic disaster. Again, noblemen and wealthy bourgeois received the lion's share of the spoils. The result for many families was destitution, lost farms, and emigration to cities and towns. But artisans also faced stiff competition from the first factories and those new handicraft shops which sprouted up in some states as a result of *laissez faire* legislation. Compounding these social difficulties was the fact that population was growing throughout the Confederation faster than agriculture, handicraft, or early industry could provide jobs for fathers and mothers who had little or no notion of family planning.

This ongoing structural crisis was exacerbated by cyclical problems as the 1840s unfolded. Many of these difficulties were related

13. Above passages cited in Max Eastman (ed.), *Capital, the Communist Manifesto, and other Writings by Karl Marx* (New York, 1959), 322, 328, 332, 333-34.

to a recession that worsened in England after mid-decade. England's problems quickly spread to the continent, undermining the commerce of Hamburg and Bremen, afflicting the crafts and industries of towns like Karlsruhe, Mannheim, and Offenbach, and putting tens of thousands out of work. The Austrian annexation of Cracow in 1846 made hard times worse for Silesian and Saxon manufacturers who had used the small republic to smuggle textile goods under Austria's high tariffs. Consequently, exports from the Zollverein of linen yarn fell by 40 percent between 1844 and 1847. The potato blight of 1845 – followed by the failure of both the potato and grain crops in 1846 – complicated matters even more. Usually net exporters of grain, Zollverein countries imported 165 million liters of rye in 1846 and another 250 million in 1847. But supplies were still so constrained that prices of foodstuffs rose 50 percent between 1844 and 1847. In Prussia, the cost of lower class daily staples like rye and potatos more than doubled. "Everywhere," writes Theodore Hamerow, "hunger, disease, and unemployment were arousing among the masses a mood of hostility toward the Restoration."[14]

One reaction to the double-edged sword of structural and cyclic social crisis was the great exodus which brought so many Germans to American shores. Overseas emigration rose from around 50,000 in the 1820s to 168,000 in the 1830s before swelling to 500,000 in "the hungry Forties."[15] Those who could not escape from their dilemmas by resettling abroad often depended on charity. Their numbers reached 10 percent in Hamburg and 20 percent in Cologne. Others slipped into a desperate life of begging, prostitution, traffic in children, poaching, wood stealing, crop robbing, or more violent crime. One contemporary estimated that a quarter of Berlin's population in the mid-1840s existed in this underworld of hunger, shame, and brutality. Another study of Hesse in 1846/47 found that one-third of the depressed farmers and town craftsmen could no longer support themselves. In extreme cases like Pforzheim in Baden, 70 percent of the workers had no jobs. Finally, as so often in such miserable

14. Hamerow, 77.
15. Ibid., 83.

situations of famine and malnutrition, disease raised its ugly head. Thus 50,000 died of typhoid, typhus, or other hunger-related sicknesses in Upper Silesia.

It should come as no surprise, moreover, that protests and riots grew more frequent in the 1840s. Undoubtedly the most famous of these was the revolt of the Silesian weavers in 1844. Years of technological advance and declining demand for linen had reduced once-proud craftsmen to wage earners dependent on the good will of putting-out merchants who were indifferent to the hard times of their workers. In June 1844, the angry, hungry weavers gathered in front of the mansion of one merchant and made the traditional demand of a present for their suffering. The rejection of this demand led to a cat music attack on the home, the calling out of regular troops, and the gunning down of eleven weavers. The so-called "potato rebellion" that rocked Berlin for four days in April 1847, is another notorious example. Incensed over the unfair price of basic foodstuffs, mobs plundered stores and markets, erected barricades to repel the attacks of infantry and cavalry called out on the second day, and even stoned the palace of Crown Prince William, the brother of the king, before order was finally restored. By far the bloodiest incidents, however, occurred in Cracow and West Galicia in February and March, 1846. Inspired somewhat by exiled revolutionaries – but basically uncontrollably eager to vent their long-suppressed emotions on someone above them – Polish peasants in these Austrian territories went on a killing spree. Armed with scythes and flails, they butchered and mutilated nearly 1,500 noblemen before troops could intervene.

It was out of this unraveling pre-industrial order that cadres of revolutionary socialists emerged quite separate and distinct from Marx, Engels, and their brand of thought. Socialist discussion circles and conventicles sprouted up inside the clubs and societies of the wandering journeymen or occasionally within the educational clubs founded for artisans by caring bourgeois. With a membership of 3,000 in 1847, the Berlin Handicraftsmen's Association "was ostensibly devoted to edifying lectures and uplifting entertainment," observes James Sheehan. "Its sponsors, largely moderate businessmen and progressive officials, would have been scandalized to learn that the *Handwerkerverein* was also functioning as what

Stephan Born called a 'training ground for up and coming revolutionaries.' "[16] Many of the most active dissidents did not risk underground political life in Germany, however, gravitating to the freer political atmosphere in Switzerland, France, Belgium, and England. Small crusading organizations came into being there, like the League of the Outlaws or the more famous League of the Just. Wilhelm Weitling, a tailor's son and frustrated journeyman tailor, was the main spokesman for the latter group. Inspired in equal parts by French radicalism and the gospels of Christianity, Weitling believed that the abolition of private property would lead to spiritual renewal and an earthly Utopia for the victims of industrialization. Marx could not stomach such an allegedly unscientific approach to revolution. After a stormy meeting outside Brussels in 1846, he lost his temper. "Ignorance," blurted Marx, "never yet helped anybody!"[17]

Wilhelm Hübner's *German Emigrants,* 1846.
Saying last good-byes at the cemetery, Germans leave for America.

16. Sheehan, 651.
17. Ibid., 652.

As 1848 neared, therefore, the lands of the German Confederation were threatened by three overlapping and interrelated crises. The industrial and cultivated bourgeoisie was growing in wealth, numbers, and political assertiveness. Upset with government programs that conflicted with or inadequately served business interests; angry with conservative regimes which ignored their intellectual talent and accomplishments; and basically frustrated, the middle class squared off for political struggle with the governing elites as tensions mounted. Industrialization had also created a new and troubling social question. Another lower class of workers and factory hands was quickly emerging in Germany – one which was beginning to protest and strike. As the proletariat became more active, the upper classes debated the issues and grew more and more afraid. But Germany was also plagued by other lower-class problems left unsolved from pre-industrial days – problems which were indeed getting worse as structural and cyclic socio-economic trends combined explosively in the 1840s. Certainly rivaling 1789 or 1989, 1848 would be a classic year of revolution. There were good reasons why.

These three crises were linked, however, to a fourth which would also surface in 1848/49. As we know, national enthusiasm was increasing throughout Germany. The movement clearly affected middle-class politics, but was also rooted lower in society among small town burghers and handicraftsmen organized in gymnastic clubs, singing societies, and single-issue organizations like that which raised funds for the *Hermannsdenkmal*. Germany's social crises of the 1840s were phenomena separate from nationalism – but they were also related. For the anxiety and uncertainty generated by this age of transformation found definite release in a nationalist cause which was seen as a panacea by many Germans. Like the ever more popular legend of Barbarossa, it was felt that Germany's time of troubles would end when the nation was again strong, united, and well-led.

Chapter 13

The Politics of Culture

It was almost twenty years since the Frederick William University of Berlin had opened its doors. By 1830 Humboldt's creation had attracted many of Germany's best minds: legal scholar Karl von Savigny; historian Leopold von Ranke; and the great master of philosophy and current rector of the university, Georg Wilhelm Friedrich Hegel. On this June day hundreds of students, professors, government officials, and well-wishers crowded into the Great Aula to hear Hegel present a Latin oration in commemoration of the tricentennial of the Augsburg Confession. Hegel had every reason to be confident. He had received the call to Berlin; his great works had appeared; admiring students and professorial disciples had flocked to his side. Prussia, his homeland for the past thirteen years, was a beacon illuminating the progressive path of the divine spirit. So Hegel proclaimed confidently that contemporary Protestant culture, with its view of God as self-conscious reason, and the modern Prussian state, which affirmed the freedom of man as a self-conscious rational being, together would allow history to progress peacefully without "unrest" or "rebellion."[1] There was no legitimate reason, he declared, for opposing the existing order.

As these remarks indicate, throughout the 1820s Hegel had drifted toward an accommodationist viewpoint. Increasingly he saw what was "real" in Prussia, in other words, as "rational." Even

1. Cited in John Edward Toews, *Hegelianism: The Path Toward Dialectical Humanism, 1805-1841* (Cambridge, 1980), 217.

before his death from cholera in 1831, factional lines had opened up between followers whose conservatism pleased the master and others whose discontentment with the status quo he frowned upon. Given the anxiety in high places after the revolutions of 1830, it was not surprising that one of the sycophants, Georg Gabler, received Hegel's chair, while another, Leopold Henning, advanced to full professor and edited the official organ of Hegelianism. The most influential spokesman of what came to be known as Right Hegelianism was Karl Friedrich Göschel, a judge whose Pietism ran so deep that it inundated all liberal interpretations of Hegel's thought. The corrupting influence of the flesh prevented man from perceiving the divine pattern until total comprehension occurred in the afterlife. Man's lot, therefore, was complete obedience to the divinely sanctioned order on earth. Göschel dismissed contemporary demands for individual freedom as "sinfulness." The purpose of the law was "to impose the divine will on a fallen world."[2]

The burden of advancing reformist or Centrist Hegelianism fell to Eduard Gans, a philosopher of law and Hegel's former colleague at the university; to Arnold Ruge, an unsalaried lecturer *(Privatdozent)* from Halle; and to a following of untenured academics, gymnasium teachers, and journalists. Gans saw no contradiction between the content of Christian religion and Hegelian philosophy, but unlike the accommodationists, he rejected the notion that the absolute spirit had become fully "actualized" in the state of Prussia. Indeed the unfolding of progress would continue as the ability to comprehend divine patterns spread outward from the bureaucracy to other intellectual elements in society which would be drawn into the state. The working class would also receive membership in the political community through social legislation and corporate reforms. For his part, Ruge sought to "feel the life impulse" and "embody the principle of development." Editing his own widely read journal, Ruge railed against the "sublime Brahminism" of Göschel and other "obscurantists," decrying their attempted "destruction of the genuine free spirit that has its form and existence in our state and its laws."[3] The progressive "principle of

2. Ibid., 225.
3. Ibid., 234.

development" as expressed by Gans and Ruge was representative of the mainstream of Hegelian thought as the 1830s drew to a close.

By this time, however, there was an opening to the Left that greatly accelerated the dissolution of the Hegelian school of philosophy. In 1835 David Friedrich Strauss rocked the intellectual world with his *Life of Jesus*. The book "deconstructed" Jesus by placing him in the context of ancient mythology. His conclusion that "the supernatural birth of Christ, his resurrection and ascension, remain eternal truths, whatever doubts may be cast on their reality as historical facts"[4] was bound to please neither the Right-Center Hegelian nor the orthodox Protestant establishments. For the latter saw him as a blasphemer, while the former renounced his implication that there was no divine substance to the dialectical workings of the absolute idea. Even more shocking was the publication of Ludwig Feuerbach's *The Essence of Christianity* in 1841. The argument here was bold and irreverent: God had not created man in his own image, but rather the reverse. Religion, Feuerbach told his readers, was to be found in "the dream of the human mind" not in "the emptiness of heaven." His purpose was to galvanize man for constructive work on earth by separating him from distracting preoccupation with perfection in the afterlife. He would convert "the friends of God into the friends of man, believers into thinkers, worshippers into workers, candidates for the other world into students of this world."[5]

As the Left readied to depart the Hegelian boat, Göschel and the Right began to shy away from the master's arguments and methods, leaving only orthodox Protestantism on this side. A conservative theologian, Ernst Wilhelm Hengstenberg, had predicted in 1836 that it would come to this. "Infidelity will gradually divest itself of any remnants of faith, just as faith will purge the remnants of infidelity from itself."[6] The breakup of Hegel's academic bastion quickened after the ascension of Frederick William IV in 1840. The new king agreed with Hengstenberg and other religious zealots in his entourage that the seeds of irreverence had grown

4. Cited in Sheehan, *German History*, 565.
5. Ibid., 566-67.
6. Cited in Toews, 250.

from Hegel's pantheistic system, not from the confusion of some of his followers. Hegel's chair at the university soon passed to the master's old enemy, Friedrich Wilhelm Schelling.

Friedrich Engels and Karl Marx, meanwhile, were completing the Left's abandonment of Hegel. Marx had come to study at Berlin in 1836 while the debate over Strauss's *Life of Jesus* was still raging. Within a year he had adopted Left Hegelianism as his new creed. Feuerbach's bombshell exploded with even greater effect. "We all at once became Feuerbachians,"[7] remembered Engels. With the completion of *The German Ideology* in 1846, the two left even Feuerbachianism behind in what was the first full exposition of Marxism. History advanced in dialectical fashion, but its motive force was not religious or ideological, but rather material. Historical transformation from one era to the next was driven by the struggle of opposing classes. This process of dialectical materialism would climax in the contemporary era with class warfare between bourgeoisie and proletariat. It was not the divine spirit which would be actualized in the present epoch, but rather the spirit of a bloody class revolution against an exploitative order. Marx and Engels had turned Hegel on his head.

* * * *

There were also those who wished to invert the literary world. Following the banning of the so-called Young German school by Baden and Bavaria in 1835, the Diet of the German Confederation proscribed them too. Karl Gutzkow, Heinrich Laube, Ludolf Wienbarg, Theodor Mundt, and Heinrich Heine were accused of attempting "to attack the Christian religion, undermine the existing social order, and destroy all discipline and morality."[8] The edict was another sign of the increasingly desperate mood which reigned in the German establishment as social and economic transformation spilled over into the political arena. While the connections between these authors were looser – and the threat they represented to authority slighter – than the governments supposed, we should not rush to belittle this admittedly overreactive move

7. Cited in Sheehan, 566.
8. Ibid., 579.

against the Young Germans. For it is certainly in the interests of authoritarian regimes to control subversive ideas. And these authors intended to subvert. "We young people who claim to continue and revive the tradition of German literature," wrote Gutzkow, "maintain a lively correspondence, prepare attacks and reciprocally correct one another, in short, we have a conspiracy, but this cannot be called a criminal one."[9]

What did these authors have in common? Mostly of lower middle class descent, they felt that previous literary traditions had been insufficiently committed to the great task of reforming state and society. We find Wienbarg castigating "the whole feudal-historical school" of the romantics "which would nail us alive to the cross of history." The Young Germans found nothing praiseworthy about peasant misery or aristocratic pretension. The Young Germans also saw classicism, like romanticism, as an escape from the challenges of the present into the comforting illusions of antiquity. "These former *grandees* of our literature lived in a sphere separate from the real world," wrote Wienbarg. "They existed in an enchanted, ideal world of their own, softly and warmly bedded, and like mortal gods looked down upon the sufferings and enjoyments of the real world ...".[10] Even Goethe, the greatest of the classicists, was not spared the rod of criticism. Thus Ludwig Börne, another essayist of this school, sternly rebuked the great one: "You had a good sword, but you were always only your own guardian." Heine was also critical, finding Goethe's works cool and lifeless, like statues "that cannot suffer and rejoice with us, that are not men but halfcasts of divinity and stone."[11]

To do justice to their political mission, the Young Germans typically wrote prose, not poetry, and essays, rather than novels or short stories. Wienbarg protested against "the tolerance of evil because it is legitimized by tradition," while Mundt rejected the conservative view "that the people are an impure and undignified substance, over whom an absolute ruler is enthroned, capriciously sending sunshine or rain." The middle class was generally favored over the

9. Cited in Ernest K. Bramsted, *Aristocracy and the Middle Classes in Germany: Social Types in German Literature 1830-1900* (Chicago, 1964), 302.

10. Wienbarg is cited in ibid., 304, 309-10.

11. Börne and Heine are cited in Sheehan, 573-74.

aristocracy, but not uncritically or without qualification. Laube admitted, for instance, "that the development of the revolution has become different from what we anticipated … as if the new were worse than the old, the merchant with his purse in his hand more disgusting than the old aristocrat with his genealogical tree."[12]

But occasionally the Young Germans employed verse to very dramatic effect. Undoubtedly the best example is Heine's angry eulogy to the Silesian weavers, with its curse against the Prussian motto of God, King, and Fatherland.

Their sombre eyes no tears are hiding;
They sit at their looms through set teeth chiding:
"Old Germany, we're weaving your shroud, and worse:
The warp and the woof of a threefold curse.
We're weaving, we're weaving.

"A curse on the God who ignored our wailing
When hunger gnawed and winds were railing;
In vain did we hope, and we waited in vain,
He mocked and befooled us and laughed at our pain.
We're weaving, we're weaving.

"A curse on the King to whom Croesus is kneeling,
And whose heart for our woes is dead to all feeling;
He takes our last farthings as taxes most meet,
And then shoots us down like dogs in the street.
We're weaving, we're weaving.

"A curse on the fatherland, false and faithless,
Where shame and infamy flourish scatheless,
Where every flower is broken in turn,
Where decay and corruption nourish the worm.
We're weaving, we're weaving.

"The shuttle flies along the loom,
Whilst day and night we weave the doom.
Old Germany, we're weaving your shroud, and worse:
The warp and the woof of a threefold curse.
We're weaving, we're weaving."[13]

12. Quotations here from Bramsted, 304, 309, 311-12.

13. The poem is translated in E. M. Butler, *Heinrich Heine: A Biography* (Westport, 1970), 177-78.

Prussian authorities banned the poem and confiscated it wherever it was found. But workers and artisans hid their copies and recited it for decades to come.

There was an outpouring of political poetry in the 1830s and 1840s. Count Anton Alexander von Auersperg raised more than a few eyebrows with his *Walks of a Viennese Poet* and *Rubble*, urbane poetic critiques of Metternich's oppressive system. Georg Herwegh's *Poems of a Living Man* and Heinrich Hoffmann von Fallersleben's *Song of the Germans* with its ode to "Germany, Germany, above all else" were also typical political poems. Herwegh was especially popular in the early 1840s "and this sudden fame went a little to his head," writes Jeffrey Sammons, "for he attempted to exploit Frederick William IV's putative liberality by presenting himself in person as the loyal opposition."[14] Herwegh was banished for his pains. Heine's revolutionary manifesto on the Silesian weavers' revolt was probably the best aesthetically of this genre. Its deadly serious tone, however, was not typical of Heine's political poetry. He usually employed sarcasm and satire, reflections of the futility, disillusionment, and defeat he felt writing from bitter exile in Paris. "He lampoons the King of Prussia and the King of Bavaria; he excoriates the German people for its political torpor and servility; he flays the greed and cruelty of the dominant classes and the wealthy."[15] We do no justice to Heine, of course, by confining him within political boundaries. As the works of E. M. Butler and Jeffrey Sammons ably demonstrate, his art was much more impressive than this, extending to love poems, nature poems, and novels that filled many volumes and inspired Germany's best composers. Heine was always larger than Young Germany.

A literary club in Berlin named, nonsensically enough, "The Tunnel over the Spree," provides us with another glimpse of the way that art and politics sometimes mixed. Founded in 1827 – but only coming into its own in the 1840s – this unusual group united leading civil servants, officers, businessmen, artists, actors, and writers in a love of poetry. This bond was supposed to be stronger

14. Jeffrey L. Sammons, *Heinrich Heine: A Modern Biography* (Princeton, 1979), 256.

15. Ibid., 259.

than politics, which was a forbidden theme, or rank and title, which were cloaked by having members adopt "Tunnel names." In the genre and themes which they chose, however, political preferences shone through. A young Theodor Fontane learned this quickly enough when his first reading, a tribute to Georg Herwegh, was not well received. Far more popular were the battle poems of Christian Friedrich Scherenberg. The folksy, backward-looking tone of his stirring ballads commemorating Ligny and Waterloo appealed ambiguously to conservatives proud of their state and comfortable in pre-industrial surroundings as well as liberals eager for new nationalistic beginnings.

Fontane soon adjusted to the subdued political culture of the Tunnel. His *Prussian Songs* of 1846 and 1847 adopted the genre of the ballad and the patriotic theme of Prussian military history. Woven into these eight poems about military heroes, however, was a subtle critique of the ruling establishment. Fontane, the liberal bourgeois, stressed individual greatness rather than praising a social and political system which he found objectionable. One of his subjects, Georg Derfflinger, had risen from obscure social origins to achieve great feats in the Thirty Years War. "All classes of society / Have their value as fighters / Even the hands of a tailor / Once grasped a hero's sword." The rest were noblemen, but they displayed a penchant for the individual initiative and timely action which only free spirits possess. Thus Marshall Schwerin ignores the Great King's orders and turns defeat into victory. General Zieten of the Husars also seems to overshadow Frederick the Great, who permits the weary veteran and master of the ambush to doze in his royal presence. "Let the old man sleep: / Through many a night / He stayed awake for us; / He guarded us long enough." Another, Leopold of Dessau, is served up as political inspiration for the present: "We are in dire need, / Despite all the good advice we are given, / And we almost blush / Before this man of action."[16] "Whenever Fontane introduces a reference to contemporary conditions," concludes Peter Paret, "he does so to contrast them with the past and finds them wanting."[17]

16. Citations from Peter Paret, *Art As History: Episodes in the Culture and Politics of Nineteenth-Century Germany* (Princeton, 1988), 69, 71, 73.

17. Ibid., 72.

Novelist Karl Immermann was another important literary figure from this period. Although he was Heine's friend and knew many of the Young Germans, Immermann was not really part of their school. The conservative son of a Prussian official, he had neither social origins nor radical politics in common with these men. Immermann belonged to a friendly clique of sophisticated aesthetes in Düsseldorf that included painter Wilhelm von Schadow, poet Friedrich von Uechtritz, and art historian Karl Schnaase. As a sensitive and cultivated bourgeois, nevertheless, he gives us a vivid, politically charged impression of class relations in a changing society. Immermann's most famous novel, *The Epigones*, surveys the gradual demise of an aristocratic family from the simple country Junker who expanded the estate, to his ostentatious son who squandered most of it, and finally to the grandson who strove above all to maintain the appearance of noble bearing and dignity amidst impending bankruptcy. The last duke falls into debt to a middle-class industrialist who gains title and control of the family property and converts it into a rural industrial venture, but lets the aristocrat live in the castle of his forefathers.

In this setting, Immermann is able to contrast two differing lifestyles and mentalities. Whereas the duke has elegant surroundings, appreciates art, and enjoys amorous adventures, the capitalist lives simply, calculates his earnings, plots business strategies, and has no time for women or art. In these scenes, Immermann warns compatriots from the propertied bourgeoisie that there were important lessons to learn from the nobility before it passed from the scene. Unlike advocates of aesthetic industrialization, however, Immermann does not seem to have sympathized with industrial development in any form. Toward the end of *Epigones* he worried that "the present speeds toward an avid mechanization with lightening swiftness: its passage we cannot hinder, yet we are not to be blamed if we fence-off a little green tract for us and ours and fortify this island as long as possible against the surge of industrial waves that rush by."[18] Immermann's magnum opus was therefore a classic statement on aristocratic decline and industrial transformation written from the detached, condescending vantage point of the cultivated bourgeoisie.

18. Cited in Bramsted, 65-66.

* * * *

Immermann's friend, Wilhelm von Schadow, returned to his Nazarene roots[19] in Rome for a few rejuvenating months in 1830. After he resumed his duties at the Düsseldorf Academy of Art, colleagues noticed a firmer resolve to infuse the school's painting with the true spirit of Christianity. Schadow gathered around him close disciples like Ernst Deger, Franz Ittenbach, and the brothers Andreas and Karl Müller in a concerted effort to realize the Nazarene dream of religious revival through art. The Artistic Society of Rhineland-Westphalia, a semi-official organization backed by provincial officials, academicians, and clergymen, played a prominent role in this aesthetic offensive, sponsoring scores of projects for Schadow's intimates as well as other students from the Academy. Their most famous works were the murals and frescoes which appeared in Castle Stolzenfels near Coblenz and the Apollinaris Church in Remagen. Both structures were Gothic, a medieval architectural style that was appropriately complemented by the angels, madonnas, and biblical scenes on the inside. Indeed the union of Gothic architecture and Nazarene painting epitomized official culture in the stormy aftermath of the revolutions of 1830 as church and state sought to buttress the establishment with cultural props.

Schadow's newborn zealotry eventually split the Düsseldorf School into two parties. On one side were disciples like Deger who flocked to the master; on the other were dissidents who longed for more realism and political engagement. The origins of the division can be traced to Karl Friedrich Lessing's *Royal Couple in Mourning*, which questioned the longevity of monarchy shortly before the fall of Charles X (see Part II). *Atelier Scene*, painted by six former students of the Academy in 1836, marked the beginning of a full-blown revolt. Dubbed "Siberia" to denote their banishment, the atelier is strewn with helmets, swords, dummies, statues, oversized canvases and easels, and other Nazarene paraphernalia.

One of the rebels, Wilhelm Heine, made a more serious statement with *Mass in the Prison Church* in 1837. Finished shortly after the dismissal of the Göttingen Seven, it portrays a dark jailhouse chapel packed with artisans, students, and young professionals.

19. For the Nazarenes, Part II.

The look of indifference or anger on their faces conveys the impression that neither the parson's stern sermon nor the presence of prison guards with weapons has intimidated the defiant "criminals." Wilhelm Hübner's *Weavers* is another good example of this politicized painting. Completed a few months before the Silesian weavers' revolt in 1844, it depicts a room full of desperate handicraftsmen vainly attempting to receive fair payment from a princely, insouciant merchant manufacturer. One weaver departs the chamber with clenched fists while a friend tries to soothe him, seeming to say: "Calm yourself, that man will get his comeuppance." The works of Heine, Hübner, and their friends paralleled the Young German literary movement so dear to the rebellious painters. It was no coincidence, moreover, that the *Rheinische Zeitung* in Cologne noticed "Young Düsseldorf" and praised its service to "the living, unstoppable progress of the spirit of history."[20]

Alfred Rethel was another member of the Academy who broke from the romantic, idealistic style of Wilhelm von Schadow. Like the works of Young Düsseldorf, his art was critically political. Exuding a longing for past greatness in present times, however, it retained much more of the characteristic historicism of the Düsseldorf School. Rethel came to the Academy as a boy in 1829, but was already developing his own unique brand of historical painting when he left as a young man in 1836. Themes quite different from the Nazarenes soon began to appear on his canvases: Hannibal's army crossing the Alps; Saint Boniface, the martyr, converting the Germans; a slain Gustavus Adolphus on the battlefield of Lützen. These works highlighted men of action who struggled, sacrificed, and died for worthy causes. Where, viewers might ask, were men like this today? Rethel's career prospects improved in 1840 when he received a commission to paint frescoes from the life of Charlemagne in the Gothic town hall of Aachen.

The young artist was soon embroiled in political controversy. Some thought that the subject of the frescoes should be the town, not an emperor, while others – most notably Wilhelm von Schadow, the Director of the Düsseldorf Academy – objected to the choice of

20. Cited in Hanna Gagel, "Die Düsseldorfer Malerschule in der politischen Situation des Vormärz und 1848," in Wend von Kalnein (ed.), *Die Düsseldorfer Malerschule* (Düsseldorf, 1979), 73.

Rethel himself. A personal audience with Frederick William IV finally cleared away these obstacles, but seven years of creativity had been lost before the painting began. The harshness of color which observers of the first panels noted was probably a window on his psyche after so much wasteful quarreling. If anything, however, Rethel's determination "to make up for the misery of the present by lovingly reflecting on the past"[21] was only strengthened by the delays. The first panel depicts the German Emperor Otto III kneeling in the crypt of Charlemagne two centuries after the great conqueror's death. Others from Otto's entourage descend from a ladder and move to praying positions. The embalmed corpse sits upright on an open Roman sarcophagus. Charlemagne holds the scepter and the orb with the imperial crown still on his head. Peter Paret describes the political impression which Rethel conveyed with this reverent scene: "The massive vertical of the emperor, before which the spiraling curve of the descending and kneeling men comes to a halt, gives powerful aesthetic expression to the underlying political myth of the corpse, emblematic of the imperial idea, towering over the living supplicant like another Barbarossa awaiting the day when at last he will rise to redeem the Germans."[22]

One of Theodor Fontane's Tunnel colleagues, Adolph Menzel, was also creating poignant political images at this time. Like Rethel, Menzel received his first career break around 1840 when he was teamed with Franz Kugler to illustrate the latter's history of Frederick II. The book responded to a growing curiosity about the Great King that was itself part of the larger Barbarossa phenomenon sweeping across Germany. Kugler's text paid tribute to Frederick's many accomplishments without ignoring the harshness and tragedy of his long rule. Menzel's drawings reinforced his partner's themes while simultaneously making an independent visual statement. Indeed the book's 376 wood engravings would do much more than the text to implant a lasting image of the Great One in the minds of nineteenth century Germans.

This image was in many respects bourgeois. Menzel's illustrations of Frederick's campaigns project an awareness of the harsh

21. Paret, 90.
22. Ibid., 90.

Wilhelm Hübner's *Weavers,* 1844. Social discontent in the Pre-March.

fact that war is often a necessary vehicle of progress; but storm, fire, and death motifs coupled with depictions of ruined towns, somber burial patrols, and battlefields heaped high with corpses captured the middle-class preference for peace and prosperity. Another engraving of a lone hand buttressing a crumbling stone wall sends a mixed message about the indispensable role of the king in repairing war's destructiveness, while a drawing of Frederick surveying the projected route of a canal underscores the positive theme of economic reform and technological progress. Like his colleague Fontane, however, Menzel believed that certain things were greater and more important than kings. He expresses this theme aesthetically in one of the final illustrations of Frederick as an old man sitting in front of the Potsdam palace, "its facade, which Menzel gives a more classicistic appearance than in fact it really had, already hinting at the coming of a new age, the towering pillars and the shrunken figure contrasting the continuity of the state with the transient existence even of a king."[23] The state would accomplish great feats in this new age, the book implies, if it had the courage and wisdom to follow in Frederick's reforming tradition.

* * * *

The German love of neoclassicism took root in the eighteenth century, then burst forth in full architectural bloom during the 1820s

23. Ibid., 49.

and 1830s. While there were many reasons for this, one important motivation was the need to draw on antiquity for political inspiration in the bleak authoritarian times of the Old Regime and Restoration. The Old Museum of Karl Friedrich Schinkel and the Glyptothek of Leo von Klenze are probably the best examples of neo-classicism's progressive impulse (see Part II). Schinkel and Klenze were far too creative, however, to limit themselves to one historical style. In fact, both strove throughout their careers to give birth to a new modern style which would do justice to the ancients by going beyond them. "Shouldn't it be possible," said Klenze, "to discover a new architectural style [which will evolve from the old] just like the Renaissance style developed out of styles known at that time?" For Schinkel, similarly, the challenge was "to conceive, in general terms, a pure style which does not contradict the best that every other style has achieved."[24]

Some historians believe that Klenze accomplished his goal with the completion of the Alte Pinakothek in 1836. This huge museum was actually a composite of many styles. The rounded arches of the windows which opened the exhibition rooms to the sky were Romanesque; the long facade with its row of pilasters seeming to disappear into infinity was Italian Renaissance; while the columned entrance and the sheer immensity of the building was classical Greek. The combination of size, symmetry, and homogeneity in the facade, together with the structure's purpose of displaying art to a wider public, gave a democractic aura to the Alte Pinakothek. For this reason it was widely imitated in France and England, most notably with the construction of the British Museum in 1854.

Schinkel came closest to achieving his grand stylistic synthesis in the Academy of Architecture, also finished in 1836. The inspiration for this building dated from 1826, when he had first seen English industrial architecture, marveled at its scale and ingenuity, but bemoaned its ugliness. British factories were "nothing but monstrous masses of red brick, built by a mere foreman, without any trace of architecture and for the sole purpose of crude necessity, making a

24. Both quotes from Dieter Dolgner, *Historismus: Deutsche Baukunst 1815-1900* (Leipzig, 1993), 38, 53.

most frightening impression."[25] The Academy of Architecture was red, square, and multi-storied like a factory, but its red and violet bricks, tiles, and unpainted terracotta owed more to the North Italian Renaissance than anything of recent British origin. Like a factory, moreover, its walls were divided into eight tall bays separated by vertical piers, but the effect here was borrowed from the pilasters of the Gothic profane, not the industrial revolution. The gently arching capitals over each window were a reminder of Schinkel's love for Greek antiquity. The master architect was very proud of this building, for it combined various styles in a new and colorful amalgam that pointed, like his neoclassical temples, to a future of change and promise.

Long before the Alte Pinakothek and Academy of Architecture opened their doors, however, the architectural synthesis which they represented had given way to a "struggle of the styles"[26] as highly politicized neo-Gothic movements arose to challenge the primacy of Neoclassicism. Some architects turned away from ancient models during the Napoleonic Wars, interpreting Gothic forms as an indigenous style vastly superior to alien architectural imports. The Gothic church with its buttresses, pointed arches, and towering steeples soon became associated with the spreading national awakening. Responding to the idea of completing work on the long unfinished cathedral in Cologne, for example, Joseph Görres wrote that it was "a symbol of the new Reich that we want to build."[27]

Ludwig of Bavaria and Crown Prince Frederick William of Prussia were also enthusiastic about the building project in Cologne, both entertaining vague notions about restoring German unity. But the Wittelsbachs and Hohenzollerns were more interested in the benefits that Gothic architecture could bestow on the dignity and prestige of their own two houses. Indeed the elegant towers and ramparts of Hohenschwangau near Munich, Burg Stolzenfels on the Rhine, and Schloss Babelsberg outside Potsdam bore stony witness to the righteous mystique of the divine right of kings.

To church hierarchies, on the other hand, the neo-Gothic revival was more important as an artistic means to buttress the

25. Cited in David Watkin and Tilman Mellinghoff, *German Architecture and the Classical Ideal* (Cambridge, Massachusetts, 1987), 110.

26. Dolgner, 13.

27. Ibid., 20.

faith in a secular age of revolution. The Apollinaris Church in Remagen – whose interior frescoes were painted by Schadow's Nazarenes – and the Mary of Mercy Church *(Mariahilfkirche)* in Munich are excellent examples of medieval forms replanted in modern times for proselytizing effect. On the Protestant side, Hamburg's Nikolai Church exaggerates the Gothic and conveys an air of confidence to an overshadowed secular world by extending the church tower 100 meters above the rest of the structure.

The wave of neo-Gothic town halls which spread across Germany in the 1820s and 1830s was a good indication, however, that the surrounding profane world had already found uses of its own for Gothic lines and forms. The Rathaus of Weimar, begun in 1837 by Heinrich Hess, is the best example of this phenomenon. The medieval sanctity of its triple-arched entrance and multi-piered facade accentuated the claim of the nation's older urban elites to autonomy and renewed prosperity. Surveying this complex return of medieval aesthetics, Goethe, the classicist, warned contemporaries about wanting "to call forth into reality the ghosts of previous centuries," while Peter Beuth, another lover of the Greeks, bemoaned the fact that so many were turning away from "the clear forms of antiquity."[28]

Neoclassicism faced other competitors in this struggle of the styles. The distinctive rounded arches of the Romanesque also reappeared after 1815, especially in the Rhineland where Carolingian traditions survived and provincials were eager to demonstrate their separateness from official culture in Berlin. Ludwig of Bavaria contributed to this revival with church construction after 1830 that was designed to enhance Munich's artistic status by diversifying its architecture. It was Frederick William IV, however, who did the most to popularize neo-Romanesque style. Convinced that Italian churches of the early Christian era incorporated the essence of Christian beliefs, the zealous Hohenzollern built the basilic Church of Peace *(Friedenskirche)* in Potsdam and the Church of the Savior *(Heilandskirche)* in nearby Sakrow. The gentle curves of the latter's arcade blended beautifully and organically with the surrounding woods and adjacent Havel, lending an aura of Christian

28. Ibid., 20; and Brose, *The Politics of Technological Change*, 117.

simplicity to the whole scene. The Church of Peace, built to house a twelfth-century mosaic from Murano, employed many of the same effects in its monastic setting on the water. As David Barclay observes, "[it] was to be the programmatic expression, in stone and glass, of Frederick William IV's vision of monarchy." The basilica "was supposed to symbolize the state's very essence," while the mosaic, with its central depiction of Christ as judge of the world, "evoked Frederick William's notion of his own ordination through the grace of God."[29] By constructing these churches, the king also wanted to nudge his dream of a revitalized Christian-Germanic Reich closer to reality.

The struggle over architectural style was sharpest, in fact, when artists and their sponsors sought to convey nationalistic messages. That Frederick William preferred neo-Romanesque to symbolize his vision of a restored Holy Roman Empire was perfectly in keeping with his romantic blend of piety and conservatism. Although Ludwig of Bavaria sponsored both neo-Romanesque and Gothic construction – as did Frederick William – his own memorial to the nation, the *Walhalla*, dedicated outside Regensburg in 1842, took the form of a Greek temple. Not without a fight, however. The king had wanted to combine Greek and Roman models, while another faction headed by Peter Cornelius, the famous Nazarene painter, hailed Gothic as "the great, glorious, genuine, original German building style."[30] It was Klenze who argued for a purely Greek design – and prevailed. The other great nationalistic project of the Pre-March, the *Hermannsdenkmal* in the Teutoburg Forest, was a victory for Cornelius's sentiments. When the cornerstone was laid in 1841, drawings called for an unmistakably Gothic hall as the massive pedestal for Arminius, the conqueror of the Romans. A cannon captured from the French at Waterloo was fired during the ground-breaking ceremonies, sending a clear message to Germany's modern-day enemies in the West. But Arminius's towering, armored figure was meant to communicate even more urgently with those at home. Would Germans respond to the image of the ancient warrior's raised sword by rising up themselves to forge a

29. Barclay, *Frederick William IV*, 25.

30. Cited in Thomas Nipperdey, "Nationalidee und Nationaldenkmal in Deutschland im 19. Jahrhundert," *Historische Zeitschrift* 206 (June, 1968), 553.

nation? In 1846, long before patriots would be able to gaze upon their mighty hero, work ground to a halt. Tough economic times had claimed another victim.

* * * *

Cultural trends before 1848 both reflected and were part of the political struggles of this turbulent period. On one level we observe sensitive artists and academicians reacting aesthetically and intellectually as German Europe industrialized, as the bourgeoisie and an embryonic proletariat emerged on the social and political stage, as the socio-economic order of peasants and craftsmen crumbled, and as a new nationalism stirred up old emotions. The break-up of the Hegelian School, the Young German challenge to older writers, the abandonment by Young Düsseldorf of Nazarene motifs, and the struggle of classical, Gothic, and Romanesque architectural styles mirrored the growing political polarization and fragmentation of Germany during the Pre-March era. Nationalistic trends also found artistic expression in monuments, buildings, painting, and poetry.

There was, however, a deeper meaning to these phenomena, for the cultural scene was often the only arena of political struggle and debate open under authoritarian regimes which brooked little or no criticism. The gymnasts and organizers of the Hambach Festival were forced underground or arrested, for example, but Rethel and Menzel employed patriotic motifs in their paintings, construction began on the Arminius Memorial, and the restoration of the Cologne Cathedral progressed. The censors and their supervisors remained vigilant in the official cultural-political arena too, of course, but they were usually more tolerant of opposition couched aesthetically than criticism voiced more directly and openly. Thus the Young Germans were banned and the Left Hegelians barred from academic life, while Young Düsseldorf was allowed to make many of the same statements on canvas. As experience throughout our century confirms, culture is often politicized, particularly when other outlets for criticism and dissent are blocked.

Part IV

ANSWERS TO THE GERMAN QUESTION

Fair weather seemed to grace the Fortress of Rastatt on 20 July 1849. Carl Schurz, a young officer in the rebel army holding the town, hurried to his post atop the highest tower of the citadel. Raising a telescope in one quick movement to his eye, Schurz began a routine observation of the surrounding country. To the east was the valley of the Rhine with its fertile fields and vineyards. An occasional church tower jutted upwards against the backdrop of the high hills and ridges that hid Baden-Baden from view. To the south he surveyed a flowering valley bordered by the Black Forest. To the north a plain stretched into infinity. Westwards one could spy the blue outlines of Alsace's distant mountains. "How beautiful is nature," thought Schurz, "in all its loving, generous goodness."[1]

A short journey away to the north was Bonn, the town of his university days. It was there, sixteen months earlier, that news of the fall of Louis Philippe had reached his ears. With the rest of the students he had gathered in the square, convinced that the political tremors from France would inevitably shake the earth throughout the Germanies. None could concentrate on lectures. Instead they flocked to the pubs and spoke of the coming day of democratic rights in the mighty new German Empire. And during that first revolutionary spring it had all come to pass – as if in a dream … .

1. Carl Schurz, *Sturmjahre: Lebenserinnerungen 1829-1852* (Berlin, 1972), 229.

Reality nudged the young man's shoulder. He must lower his glass and do his duty. In stark contrast to the natural beauty and bounty of the Rhineland in the distance were the nearby picket lines and encircling campsites of Prince William's Prussian soldiers. Cavalry patrols and horse artillery scurried about like spiders weaving sticky webs around their prey. Schurz and his six thousand compatriots knew they were trapped – and the Prussians among them knew they would be executed for treason if captured. But somehow emboldening rumors always made the rounds: General Sigel's rebel troops had defeated the Prussians in the Badenese highlands and would soon lift the siege; another revolution had broken out in France that would soon spread east to liberate Germany; the Hungarians had overwhelmed a combined Austro-Russian army and would soon join hands with beleaguered rebel soldiers in Baden. One day cannon fire was heard coming closer and closer to the fortress. Schurz and the other officers rushed to the tower to see Sigel's advancing columns with their own eyes. The cannon fire soon yielded to a demoralizing silence.

The only person to enter Rastatt on 20 July was a Prussian envoy bringing news that Sigel had been chased into Switzerland and that no other rebel troops were fighting on German soil. The rebels were allowed to send one scout outside the walls to ascertain the sobering truth of this message. Having seen Sigel's armaments stacked ignominiously on the Badenese side of the Swiss border, the downcast scout returned.

On 23 July the last of Germany's rebellious citizens laid down their weapons on the glacis and filed out of the gate. Prince William turned his back on the forlorn column of "traitors." All Prussians found in this force met the fate they expected. Schurz was not among the corpses, having escaped through a sewage canal to freedom and later fame in the United States.

The revolution which had begun with such fury, hope, and apparent success in March 1848 was over.

Chapter 14

The Revolutions of 1848 and 1849

The French people overthrew their king and established a republic in the last week of February 1848. Within days, travelers, teamsters, and speeding diplomatic couriers spread the word across France's eastern borders. The news ignited revolts in southwestern Germany where peasants, still smarting from a succession of lean years, seemed to know instinctively that victory was now in the air. The trouble developed first in small states which had ignored feudal emancipation. On 2 March, for instance, a throng of 30,000 irate peasants marched on Wiesbaden and forced Duke Adolf of Nassau to abolish serfdom. Trouble also erupted on the huge estates of the imperial nobility of Baden and Württemberg. Many of these former ruling families *(Standesherren)* had blocked the emancipatory efforts of reforming bureaucrats in Karlsruhe and Stuttgart, turning a blind eye to the growing resentment of serfs who knew their neighbors on state lands had received freedoms. The Niederstetten Castle of the Hohenlohes was torched on 5 March, while huge peasant mobs frightened the Fürstenbergs into capitulating on 8 March, the Leiningens on 10 March, and the Öttingen-Wallersteins on 23 March. Everywhere estate records and account books were destroyed, noblemen terrorized, and feudal privileges renounced. Not since the Peasant Wars of the early 1500s had such a wave of violence swept across rural Germany.

Events were also galloping forward inside the city walls of the West and South. Excited crowds ringed in the palace and diet building in Karlsruhe during the first days of March, demanding action on a long list of radical demands. The grand duke briefly contemplated clearing the streets by force, then wisely appointed liberal ministers and agreed to allow parliament to begin work on a new Badenese constitution. King William entertained similar thoughts of military action in Stuttgart before proclaiming reforms instead. The unhappy monarch forget his "never" and introduced a free press on 1 March, dismissed his ministers on 6 March, and appointed Friedrich Römer, the outspoken leader of Wurttemberg's opposition, prime minister a few days later. On the sixth, Ludwig of Bavaria decreed freedom of the press, ministerial responsibility to the diet, and an army oath of allegiance to the constitution. But the people of Munich, still angry over the king's affair with a self-exiled Lola Montez, demanded more. He abdicated in favor of his son, Maximilian, on 16 March.

In Frankfurt on 3 March, meanwhile, the Diet of the Confederation bent meekly with the revolutionary wind by announcing that each state was free to repeal the Carlsbad Decrees. Six days later, black, red, and gold were declared Germany's official colors, then on 10 March a majority of the delegates – acting independently of instructions – issued a call for representatives of the states to draft a new confederate constitution. Adding to the excitement and confusion was the fact that fifty-five leaders of the opposition, mostly elected officials from the Southwest, had met independently in Heidelberg five days earlier to prepare the groundwork for an all-German constitutional convention.

Nor were other parts of the Confederation spared the nightmare reality of mass hysteria and violence during those first weeks. In the royal forests of the Hunsrück, a small army of cat musicians felled trees, burned the forester's home, and chased away Prussian soldiers. In Grevenbroich County on the lower Rhine, poor peasants destroyed ditches that divided former common lands which they were sure had been unfairly taken away. Enraged artisans in Solingen terrorized merchant manufacturers who paid in truck or had dared to install machines. Eastern Westphalia was shaken by rebellious small landholders and landless peasants lashing out at market forces that seemed to benefit the rich and impoverish the small man. The violence spread through Saxony and Thuringia, where the Waldenburg Castle of Count Schönberg was burned to the ground, and to Prussian Silesia, where castle burnings prompted the mobilization of Count Brandenburg's Sixth Army Corps. In Bohemia, Galicia, and Hungary, moreover, nationalists sounded the bugle call of ethnic rights.

Simultaneous developments in Vienna magnified the shock of early March 1848. During the first days of the month, Austria's factionalized, fragmented opposition submitted a variety of petitions to the crown. The first came from the Industrial Association of Lower Austria which had the temerity to request an expansion of credit. The petition was denied, but when no one was arrested, others gained heart. The Legal-Political Reading Club and the students of the university came forward with bolder demands for liberal reform, while the Estates of Lower Austria, scheduled to convene on 13 March, produced two documents for debate that day. One, from the committee preparing the agenda, simply demanded more power to the estates, but another, written by the diet's radical leader, Alexander Bach, demanded reform of local government, freedom of the press, public trials, and estatist approval of taxes and budgets.

All Vienna knew 13 March would be "the day." Crowds began to form outside the diet building in the early morning, swelling with the arrival of a column of students (who marched from the university) and hundreds of workingmen observing "blue Monday" traditions of a day free from work. Before long the throng grew restive, broke into the building, and began destroying furniture. Troops commanded by Archduke Albrecht arrived in the early afternoon. The young and inexperienced Albrecht and his officers implored the mob to disperse, but were met with stones and bricks that knocked one of them unconscious. Finally, soldiers fired a volley directly into the mass of people, killing four and wounding scores more. Violence intensified on both sides, but the angry workers and students gained control of the streets, marched on the palace, made demands (which included the resignation of Metternich), and threatened to attack after nightfall. Poor Kaiser Ferdinand and the dukes and administrators who really ran the country debated whether to give in or crack down. Timid hearts – and Metternich's scheming rival, Kolowrat – prevailed before the deadline expired.

Mighty Prince Metternich tendered his letter and fled the country. The empire's beleaguered rulers also granted a pull-out of the troops, the formation of a civic guard, abolition of censorship, and – after additional pressure from the mob – a constitution.

The unimaginable news reached Berlin a few days later. Public order had been disintegrating there for days as large crowds defied dragoons sent to control them. Rocks, bottles, and insults were answered on one square with a point blank volley that killed two. Now reports of peasant violence in the Southwest, startling concessions in Frankfurt, and brooding, grumbling farm hands from Mecklenburg to the Mark Brandenburg were mixed with the electrifying word of Metternich's demise. Having dallied for two weeks with thoughts of change and promises of reform, Frederick William IV finally ignored hard-line advisers and succumbed to the worsening popular mood.

A huge crowd gathered before the royal palace on 18 March to hear a proclamation guaranteeing a free press, a constitution, and a Prussian-led unification of Germany. Suddenly alarmed by the presence of so many Berliners, Frederick William ordered the square cleared. Mysteriously, two shots rang out as the troops obeyed their sovereign. Although no one was killed, the people lost faith in promises and proclamations, scattered to their neighborhoods, and threw up formidable barricades. By morning nearly three-hundred soldiers and civilians were dead and the king had had enough. His soldiers were ordered to pull out, then the rebels forced king and queen to review the bodies of the dead in broad daylight. On 21 March, Frederick William donned the German tricolor and rode through the streets to cries of "Long Live the German Emperor!"[1] A new parliamentary era was about to begin in Prussia and in German Europe.

The March Days are almost without historical parallel. Only the whirlwind of incredible events in 1989 comes close by comparison. What had happened in 1848? It seems as clear now as it did to contemporaries that pressures had been building to the point of explosion for many years. "We lived then like people who feel under

1. Cited in Priscilla Robertson, *The Revolutions of 1848: A Social History* (Princeton, 1971), 123.

their feet the pressures of an earthwake," remembered novelist Gustav Freytag. "Everything in the German situation seemed loose and unstable, and everyone declared that things could not remain as they were." Composer Richard Wagner remarked to a friend in 1846 that people were mentally ready for revolution. "The new Germany is ready, like a bronze statue which requires only a single blow from a hammer in order to emerge from its mold."[2] We have seen that other artists were sensitive to the same realities. Germany in the 1840s was in the midst of the last great crisis of the old socio-economic order. Population had been growing for over a generation with few factors to mitigate the menacing pauperization of society. Agrarian reforms had exacerbated the problem by providing opportunities for some by sacrificing the old securities of others. Industrial legislation had had a similar effect on artisans and craftsmen already hard-pressed to preserve the vanishing world of the guilds. Early industrialization opened the curtain on a new set of social and political problems, moreover, as the proletariat emerged on the scene and the bourgeoisie grew in numbers and assertiveness. Additional tremors resulted after mid-decade when Germany sank into the depression which was spreading from England and western Europe. The rising tide of nationalism was both a reflection of these social and economic problems as well as a challenging, unsettling factor in its own right. The most explosive ingredients to the mixture, however, were a waning popular respect for monarchs – epitomized by the Lola Montez scandal – and a deep-seated fatalism in ruling circles. "I am an old physician and can distinguish between temporary and fatal diseases," Metternich told a guest in 1847, "and we now face one of the latter. We'll hold on as long as we can, but I have doubts about the outcome."[3] The eroding legitimacy of Germany's leaders, together with their paralyzing resignation to the coming deluge, translated into hesitation and weakness in March 1848. From one end of the Confederation to the other, the masses sensed this, were emboldened by it, and quickly prevailed.

* * * *

2. Citations in James J. Sheehan, *German History 1770-1866* (Oxford, 1989), 656-57.

3. Ibid., 657.

There were three immediate effects of the early spring eruption of 1848. First came the so-called "March ministries." Throughout German Europe, terrified kings and dukes granted ministerial portfolios to leaders of the liberal opposition movement: David Hansemann and Ludolf Camphausen in Prussia; Johann Stüve in Hanover; Ludwig von der Pfordten in Saxony; Heinrich von Gagern in Hesse-Darmstadt; Karl Mathy and Karl Welcker in Baden; Friedrich Römer and Paul Pfizer in Württemberg; and Gottlieb von Thon-Dittmer in Bavaria. After a delay of a few months, Alexander Bach entered office in Austria. Second, the new men scurried to remove the root causes of the recent peasant *jacquerie* . By summer, Hesse-Darmstadt, Hesse-Kassel, Baden, Württemberg, Bavaria, and Austria had followed Nassau in sweeping away the remnants of serfdom. Progress in this direction also came to Brunswick, Hanover, Thuringia, and Saxony.

Third, liberal and democratic parties moved quickly toward creation of a new Germany. The deliberators at Heidelberg on 5 March formed a committee to summon "trusted men of all the German peoples" to a more representative congress. The preparatory group issued invitations to hundreds of present and past members of state and local elected bodies. Three weeks later nearly 600 men of the opposition filed into Frankfurt's Roman Hall where once the Holy Roman Emperors had been crowned. But the awe they must have felt in these hallowed medieval surroundings quickly yielded to the reality of modern parliamentary life. Radical factions led by Friedrich Hecker and Gustav von Struve insisted on a complete break with the existing order. They envisioned the assembly as a provisional government that would abolish hereditary monarchy, proclaim a republic along American lines, issue revolutionary decrees, and eventually prepare the way for national elections. Moderates around Heinrich von Gagern agreed on the need for electoral legitimacy for German institutions, but vehemently opposed the idea of accelerating a revolution which had already generated frightening scenes of social violence and destruction of property. The Germans, he said, were not ripe for a republic. It was time to work with kings who were making changes, not abolish institutions that had stood the test of time. The moderate majority established a watchdog committee to monitor the Diet of the German Confederation and oversee the exodus of its reactionary members. But the main task of the "Pre-Parliament," as this meeting came to be known, was to draft procedures for all-German elections in May.

The movement now began to suffer from a common revolutionary malady: political polarization and unwillingness to compromise. For Hecker and Struve, convinced that the people would follow them, issued a call to arms. They traveled throughout Baden appealing to angry peasants, unemployed workers, and confused soldiers with a rousing refrain that mocked Gagern: "Who is *unripe* for the Republic?"[4] By mid-April they had gathered about four thousand followers. Georg Herwegh, living in exile in Paris since his ill-advised interview with Frederick William IV, raised a "German Legion" of jobless emigres and marched home to join Hecker and Struve. "As they marched through the valleys with their black-red-gold banners beating against the scythes which were almost their only weapons," writes Priscilla Robertson, "they looked as if they had come out of the Thirty Years' War."[5] It was soon over. Regular troops of Baden's liberal regime defeated the poorly equipped rebel army on 20 April before Herwegh's colorful column had crossed the border. Armed with their intimidating blades, the poet's German Legion survived one skirmish with soldiers of Württemberg's new order before taking flight into Switzerland. Already drifting toward extreme, irreconcilable positions before March – witness the competing meetings at Offenburg and Heppenheim in 1847 – the opposition movement had taken less than a month to polarize into warring camps.

The May elections were another defeat for the Left. The Heidelberg electoral law provided for fairly democratic voting, but restricted the selection of candidates to "mature, independent" citizens. This was widely interpreted to mean *men* of property, wealth, and social standing. Most states adopted indirect balloting procedures, moreover, which further increased the likelihood that electors would choose notables as candidates. About three-quarters of the representatives who took their seats in Frankfurt's St. Paul's Church on 18 May were civil servants, judicial officials, lawyers,

4. Cited in Robertson, 170.
5. Ibid., 172.

professors, journalists, and physicians – and most of these were of moderately liberal persuasion. Another tenth of the delegates were businessmen who saw eye to eye with the cultivated bourgeoisie on many issues. Thus only a minority could be expected to pick up the fallen cudgel of radicalism.

This is not to say that the delegates presented anything like a united front. For political fragmentation – another classic menace to young parliamentary experiments – immediately reared its ugly head. Almost 800 men were elected representing a wide variety of states, regions, and localities; different religious beliefs; and contrasting political convictions. Some had public political experience – mainly the South Germans – but most did not. Entering the political stage for the first time, the typical deputy had experienced politics in the private friendship circles that functioned as political parties in the authoritarian milieu of the Pre-March. While there were contacts with other factions and cliques in and out of government, suspicion of outsiders mounted outside the friendly confines of the intimate circle. It is also easy to understand that many of the individuals who surfaced in 1848 were extremely proud of themselves – a vanity heightened by the widespread awareness that history was being made. Cooperation with others would be difficult. All of these circumstances mitigated against a quick and easy transition to a smoothly functioning party system.

Indeed it was out of the question. In a manner reminiscent of the Prussian United Diet, new parliamentarians tended to drift skeptically from restaurant to hotel in search of kindred spirits. It took a few weeks before the amorphous mass of individual politicians began to yield to loose groupings. By September, nine clubs (named after the locales where they met) were discernible: the liberals had five; the conservative Right, one; and the democratic Left, two. A final political club was formed by Catholics to represent their church and faith, while radical women with short hair and cigars broke convention to form "a noisy support group for the Frankfurt left."[6] Inside the clubs, members could orient themselves to the particulars of upcoming debates in the plenum. Voting discipline was rare at first.

6. Catherine Prelinger, *Charity, Challenge, and Change: Religious Dimensions of the Mid-Nineteenth-Century Women's Movement in Germany* (New York, 1987), 109.

The clubs, in fact, were not really parties, but rather party blocs or coalitions. Belonging to the conservative Cafe Milani, for instance, were aristocratic reformers close to Georg von Vincke, leader of the United Diet in 1847, and conservative social reformers around Joseph Maria von Radowitz, an adviser of the Prussian king. Uniting them was the desire to limit the constitutional competence of the Frankfurt Parliament. The "Kasino" was the largest liberal club, joining over 150 North German moderates who formed behind the separate standards of distinguished men like F. C. Dahlmann, Jacob Grimm, J. G. Droysen, and Gustav Mevissen. Franz Raveaux, a social activist from Cologne, and Karl Biedermann, a liberal journalist from Leipzig, brought their followers into the *Württembergischer Hof*, a left-liberal club of 70 or 80 delegates, mainly from the southwest, who favored a strong central government. Perhaps a quarter of the delegates continued to wander from club to club, however, while another quarter never sufficiently overcame their suspicions and egos to declare membership in any club.

Brilliant leadership is mandatory but rarely present in such times of confusion. How can fledgling parliaments full of inexperience be expected to produce the type of poise and control normal for long-established elites? It is always ironic that the legacy of illegitimate authoritarianism to those who would estabish freer practices is a plague of polarization, fragmentation, and inexperience – forces that enervate the new regime and strengthen the case for a return to the recently discredited old order. It was no different in the German Europe of 1848. The first day of debate deteriorated into a free-for-all as speakers tried to speak above one another and the chatter and calls from the gallery. Some order resulted on 19 May with the election of Gagern to the chair. But not even his skills could prevent the assembly from becoming what Herwegh derisively labeled the talkative "Parla- Parla- Parlament."[7]

Gagern was probably the most experienced politician of the liberal movement. Along with his brother, Friedrich, he had left the world of study and discussion for the politicized fraternities of the liberation period. There had been little time to dwell on the

7. Cited in Sheehan, 678.

pathetic squelching of that movement, for Gagern soon joined other oppositionist deputies in the Hessian Diet. Decades of parliamentary debate and maneuver against Baron Du Thil's autocratic administration was an education in politics that nearly everyone else who was seated at St. Paul's Church lacked. Remarkably, he had not allowed these dark years to jade him. Gagern was by nature a conciliator for whom it was always "easier to love than to hate,"[8] as he put it. But there were other factors at work in and around him that would make conciliation difficult in the polarized world of Frankfurt. Like so many other liberals, Gagern was a man of means, the scion of a family of Imperial Knights of the Holy Roman Empire. Cooperation with leftists and tribunes of the masses would not come naturally. "I will have no mob rule," he declared. The death of Friedrich, moreover, opened an unbridgable gap with extremists who advocated force – his brother had commanded the Badenese units which defeated Hecker and Struve, but paid for the victory with his life. Only if reason and moderation were the order of the day would Heinrich von Gagern be the man of the hour.

During May and June of 1848, Gagern's leadership was put to the test, for the Frankfurt Parliament quickly divided over the same issue that had torn asunder the Pre-Parliament: the nature and extent of central or national authority. Although outnumbered, radicals and democrats led by Saxon populist Robert Blum were the first to form a club, the *Deutscher Hof,* and press the question of national parliamentary sovereignty. The conservative "Cafe Milani" parties were the next to close ranks in staunch opposition to such proposals. As the liberal delegates "argued back and forth in confusion"[9] and groped toward organizations of their own, Gagern came forward with a compromise resolution which recognized Frankfurt's sovereignty in principle while reserving real authority in practice to the states. The mild nature of the proposal showed how much the former *Burschenschaftler* had mellowed with age, but politically it was shrewd enough to find a majority.

8. Both citations here from Robertson, 150.

9. Helmut Kramer, *Fraktionsbindungen in den deutschen Volksvertretungen 1819-1849* (Berlin, 1968), 77.

The demand for real executive authority persisted, however, and by late June parliament was again deadlocked in angry, seemingly interminable debate. Gagern now proposed a "bold stroke" to end the impasse. Archduke Johann, a Habsburg of allegedly democratic stripe, would assume the office of Imperial Regent and appoint a cabinet independent of parliament. The powers of the Diet of the German Confederation would transfer to the regency. The motion passed.

Gagern had demonstrated again his knack for clever parliamentary politics. The choice of a Habsburg appealed to Austrians, Catholics, and *Grossdeutsch* enthusiasts, while the creation of a national cabinet coupled with the Archduke's reputation as a friend of the people won over much of the Left. Even *Kleindeutsch* advocates like Gagern himself, moreover, favored some form of wider union or federation with Austria. But the limits of what had been accomplished were soon painfully evident. In July the new government demanded recognition of its authority by the armies of the states. Beginning to recover now from the shock of March, kings realized that the coming of the March ministries had not altered the fact that monarchs, not ministers, commanded the loyalty of the soldiers – and that abandonment of this power would be foolhardy. The sovereigns also knew that the letter of the law favored them, for transfer of the diet's powers to Frankfurt had not changed the fact that power under the Confederation had rested exclusively with the states. Thus Austria, Prussia, Bavaria, and Hanover refused to transfer the allegiance of the troops to Archduke Johann's government. When the demand was read in Potsdam, in fact, Prussian guardsmen refused to swear the new oath, issuing three cheers for Frederick William instead. This was perhaps some small consolation for Hecker in exile and Struve in jail, for they had known from the start that power is rarely yielded willingly. It must be taken.

The Frankfurt Parliament was a paper tiger dependent on the good will of the states. The eruption of the Schleswig-Holstein controversy that year demonstrated this conclusively. When Denmark annexed Schleswig in March, Holstein revolted and requested military aid from Prussia. Acting on behalf of the German Confederation, Prussian troops campaigned against Denmark throughout the spring and summer. By August, Frederick William was eager for peace because Russia and England were unhappy with the prospect of a Danish defeat. Without consulting the Frankfurt Parliament – which had assumed the rights and responsibilities of the diet in July – Prussia signed an armistice at Malmö on 26 August. The treaty provoked heated opposition from patriotic deputies in Frankfurt who had waved nationalist banners for months in anticipation of extending German power to the North Sea. In a close vote on 5 September between fairly evenly balanced radical and moderate blocs, the Parliament condemned the armistice. Moderation prevailed on 16 September, however, and the vote was reversed. This parliamentary vacillation of a seemingly fickle majority triggered mob violence in the city by lower-class residents who had heard sterner rhetoric from St. Paul's all summer. Two conservative deputies were brutally murdered before Prussian and Hessian troops could rescue the helpless parliamentarians. It had been a humiliating display of division, indecision, and impotence.

A similar constellation of forces was bringing down the parliamentary experiment at the state level. In the Habsburg lands, ethnic nationalism prevailed initially in Bohemia, Hungary, and Italy. Ferdinand's generals had been confident all along, however, that order could be restored with force. In June 1848, Field Marshal Alfred von Windischgrätz "proved his mettle by shooting down the revolution in Prague,"[10] while General Josef Radetsky pacified northern Italy in July. Croatian irregulars under the brutal Joseph Jellacic advanced to the gates of Budapest in September before withering artillery fire drove them back across the border.

Meanwhile in Vienna, the Imperial Diet had convened to deliberate a new constitution. The work was slowed by social differences between sophisticated, educated Viennese and illiterate peasants; language barriers between Germans, Poles, South Slavs, and Italians; and ethnic suspicion and hostility. All of these problems were compounded by a nearly total ignorance of parliamentary procedures. Making matters worse, most of the peasant delegates went home after feudal payments and labor obligations

10. Robertson, 224.

remaining from serfdom were abolished in August. Mistrustful of the pro-Frankfurt orientation of the liberal Viennese delegation, moreover, the Czechs bolted in October. The timing was opportune, for at the end of the month Radetsky and Jelacic crushed the revolution in Vienna. The Croatian's battle-hardened brutes slit the throats of gaily uniformed young men from the Student Legion, while Windischgrätz ordered the summary execution of Robert Blum, founder of the leftist *Deutscher Hof* who had traveled to Vienna to embolden the city's defenders. Eager to reestablish Austria's preeminent position in Germany, the general wanted to teach the Frankfurt Parliament a lesson in power politics. Austria's own intimidated parliament was dissolved, then reconvened in the Moravian town of Kremsier.

Frederick William was quickly exhausting his small reserve of patience for constitutional monarchy by this time. It had been hard enough to cooperate with the March ministry of Hansemann and Camphausen, men who treated the king respectfully but had little appreciation for his backward-looking political vision. However, elections to the constituent assembly had complicated matters by returning a democratic majority which was not content with the new ministers' moderate conception of limited monarchy. Rallying around Benedict Walldeck, a popular Westphalian peasant leader, and Johann Jacoby, the martyred East Prussian, parliament pushed for elimination of noble ranks, titles, and privileges; creation of a plebeian militia; and parliamentary control of the army. The assembly also wanted to dilute the monarch's veto power and remove "king by the grace of God" from the draft constitution. Worse still was the escalating pattern of mass meetings, riotous demonstrations, and street violence. The armory was raided, the assembly building surrounded repeatedly by threatening crowds, "and night after night was made hideous with Berlin's special contribution of 'cat music' in front of the houses of reactionaries: a shrieking, whistling, squeaking, bellowing, grunting, howling, miauling, hitting of kettles and shouting up the downspouts."[11] From the king's perspective, there was a downward, deteriorating slide from the ministries, to the diet, to the streets. Finally in early

11. Ibid., 137.

November, 13,000 soldiers marched into the city from Potsdam and restored order. The government was entrusted to Count Friedrich Wilhelm von Brandenburg, the leathery corps commander from Silesia. The diet was sent packing to a nearby town, then dissolved a month later.

Events in Frankfurt, Vienna, and Berlin that autumn had made it frightfully clear that a unification of Germany negotiated with the most powerful states was *the most* that nationalists in St. Paul's could expect. An appeal to the masses was one alternative that the moderate parties in control of the national assembly never seriously considered. Thus separate congresses of guild masters and journeymen met in Frankfurt that summer in an attempt to enlist parliament's support for radical handicraft legislation. But the delegates were too committed to the emerging industrial order, too wary of the lower classes, and too preoccupied with drafting a German constitution to listen to these pleas. So the liberals would broker unification.

The first attempt came in late October when Anton von Schmerling, a liberal nobleman from Lower Austria who headed the Archduke's cabinet after the September riots, cobbled together a majority for a proposal that would have incorporated Bohemia, Moravia, and the German provinces of Austria into a *Grossdeutsch* state. Inspired by the conquest of revolutionary Vienna, Austria's new chief minister, Felix von Schwarzenberg, replied boldly that the Habsburg empire was indissoluble. The so-called Kremsier Declaration undermined Schmerling and brought Gagern to the head of Frankfurt's shadow government.

Johann's new premier journeyed to Berlin for a personal interview with Frederick William in late November. Only decisive action to solve the national question, he warned the king, could prevent renewed popular violence. If the Hohenzollern ruler became the hereditary emperor of a German state tied loosely to Austria, a second revolution could be averted and Prussian interests well served. Frederick William replied politely that such a crown would have to be offered by the other German princes to be acceptable. Knowing this could be arranged, Gagern left Berlin hopeful. Privately, the king was torn between a desire to fulfil his own "youthful dream" of uniting Germany and indignation at the prospect of accepting "an invented crown contrived of dirt and clay."[12]

While Frankfurt's moderates sought a deal with the old elites, democrats reached down to the grass roots in search of countervailing power. The March revolutions had ended a period of surveillance and suppression which dated back to the Carlsbad Decrees of 1819. When Metternich's coercive system was suddenly lifted, there was a veritable explosion of organizational activity. Literally thousands of Democratic Clubs, Constitutional Associations, People's Associations, Clubs of the Fatherland, German Associations, Loyalist Leagues, and Pius Associations sprang to life all over Germany and Austria. The Parliamentary Left convened two "Democratic Congresses" in an unsuccessful bid to tap this potential base of support. Held at Berlin in early November, the second of these was "so noisy that the president asked for a brace of pistols to keep order rather than his bell."[13] Its suppression by the army prompted leftists like Franz Raveaux of the *Deutscher Hof* to redouble their efforts. On 21 November they founded the Central Association for the Preservation of the Victories of March. Within a few months there were 950 local branches claiming around 500,000 members. By establishing an organizational link between Frankfurt's leftist parliamentary coalition and the electoral base, the so-called "Central March Association" had many attributes of a modern political party.

Jonathan Sperber's research on the Rhineland in 1848/49 lets us take a closer look at this new movement. Many of the democratic clubs there recruited marginal, disaffected shop owners, guild masters, journeymen, and farmers whose petty-bourgeois grievances translated naturally into demands for a republic. Their longing for a radical break was also related to the absence of deep monarchical loyalties in the Prussian Rhineland and the Bavarian Palatinate, both of which had been merged rather artificially into new kingdoms in the Napoleonic era. Religious differences further intensified the republican opposition, for Catholics in Cologne or Aachen chafed under Protestant rule imposed from Berlin, while

12. Cited in David E. Barclay, *Frederick William II and the Prussian Monarchy, 1840-1861* (New York, 1995), 192.

13. Robertson, 137.

Protestants in Kaiserslautern or Speyer similarly rejected intolerant Catholic policies formulated in faraway Munich. The rank and file of these clubs "did not express themselves in articulate or written form," writes Sperber, "but in jeers and catcalls on the streets, in slogans chanted during riots, and in acts of violence or hostility toward symbols of the state."[14]

The nationalistic bias of the democratic clubs was a symptom of this opposition to the states. For the future nation state was seen as a kind of panacea that would supercede the Berlins and Munichs and end their reign of oppression. Because Catholics and Protestants envisioned the new nation in confessional colors, however, a divisive wedge was driven into the movement. In the Prussian Rhineland, for instance, Catholics alarmed by the anti-clericalism of Protestant agitators formed "Christian-Democratic" clubs or "Pius" associations named after the Pope. Along the lower Rhine in Baden, Catholic suspicions of what awaited them if Protestant revolutionaries swept into power had the same effect. There were 400 Pius Associations with over 100,000 members in the Diocese of Freiburg alone by the autumn of 1848. Democrats drummed up the most recruits in regions like the Palatinate where there were overwhelming Protestant majorities. The Central March Association had established 120 branches in this small Bavarian enclave by early 1849. With Dresden, it lay at the center of the revitalized democratic movement.

In December 1848, Gagern stepped down from the cabinet to rally St. Paul's around his *Kleindeutsch* unification plans. When debates began in January, about half of the Frankfurt Parliament backed him, primarily North German Protestants and other moderate liberals. Opposing Gagern was an unstable coalition consisting of Schmerling's small Austrian delegation; conservative Catholics fearful of losing Habsburg protection for the church; and leftist club members eager to impose democracy on all of German Europe. As the winter wore on, both sides became deadlocked. Schwarzenberg broke the impasse in March by dissolving the Kremsier Diet and rejecting the compromise proposals for German

14. Jonathan Sperber, *Rhineland Radicals: The Democratic Movement and the Revolution of 1848-1849* (Princeton, 1991), 470.

unification that it had formulated. His *fait accompli* essentially terminated all chance that Austria would be included in a German state. The left now struck a constitutional deal with Gagern: in return for democratic concessions – universal manhood suffrage, curtailment of states' rights, and a weakening of the emperor's veto power – it agreed to a smaller Germany with the Hohenzollerns as hereditary heads of state. Bells and cannons sounded the jubilant news all over Germany.

On 3 April 1849, a large delegation from Frankfurt offered the crown of imperial Germany to Frederick William IV inside the Royal Palace of Berlin. The king had struggled within himself for months in anticipation of having to make up his mind. He was also pressured by reactionaries at home and abroad who advised a firm stand, and ministers like Brandenburg who believed it would be unwise to sacrifice Prussia's golden opportunity to steal a diplomatic march on Austria. Three weeks before the parliamentarians arrived, Frederick William seemed to have decided. To the aging patriot Ernst Moritz Arndt he wrote:

> What is offered me? Is this birth of the hideous labor of the year 1848 a crown? The thing which we are talking about does not carry the sign of the holy cross, does not bear the stamp 'by the grace of God' on its head, is no crown. It is the collar of servitude, by which the heir of more than twenty-four rulers, electors, and kings, the head of 16,000,000, the master of the most loyal and bravest army in the world, would be made the bondservant of the revolution ... The revolution is the abolition of the godly order ... the setting aside of legitimate order, it lives and breathes its deadly breath so long as bottom is top and top is bottom.[15]

The king's public reply to the delegation on 3 April was less pointed and more polite. But it was clear enough that he would not accept a crown from below.

To his credit, Gagern did not abandon the cause. As the weeks passed in April 1849, he and kindred spirits from the different German lands engineered another round of petitions, speeches, and resolutions. By the end of the month, twenty-nine states had approved the Frankfurt constitution and the Hohenzollern regency.

15. Cited in Robertson, 165.

Only Bavaria, Saxony, and Hanover balked. But this impressive campaign of moderation and reason failed when Prussia declared its opposition to the new constitution and Austria and Prussia both ordered their delegates in St. Paul's to return home. Most did. Gagern and other liberals who stayed behind, attempting to concentrate on the daily agenda as compatriots packed bags, presented "a sad spectacle," one recalled, "of inconsolable confusion, uncertainty, and depression."[16] Archduke Johann delivered the final blow in mid-May by forcing Gagern's resignation and appointing new men to terminate central authority and dissolve the assembly. Things had gone too far for the "democratic" Habsburg.

The left opted to fight. Days before the Imperial Regent acted against Gagern, democrats rose up in Dresden, the Palatinate, and Baden. Southwestern rebel leaders quickly conspired with Franz Raveaux to invade the right bank of the Rhine and protect the radicals still meeting in St. Paul's. The invasion was a fiasco. Without a military force of their own, the 136 die-hards of the rump parliament had to comply when city authorities in Frankfurt demanded they leave. Arriving in Stuttgart, the harried leftists asked for asylum and made preparations for national elections in August. But Württembergian troops forced them to disband on 18 June. By this time, Prussian regulars had "shot down the revolution" in Dresden, wielding the deadly, rapid-firing needle gun for the first time. Soon thereafter Prussian regulars occupied the Palatinate, then crossed over into Baden. The main rebel forces there fought bravely at Waghäusel on 21 June, but were easily defeated. Only the doomed defenders of Rastatt were left.

* * * *

The leaders of Germany's revolutions were not unfamiliar with the kinds of challenges facing today's young democratic experiments. Polarization, fragmentation, and inexperience took a heavy toll. While it is uncertain whether any of these classic obstacles to democratic progress could have been surmounted in 1848 and 1849, in the end it was another foe of novice state builders that buried the cause. The Frankfurt Parliament was impotent. The Left

16. Cited in Sheehan, 706.

knew this, but when it tried to take power in April 1848, and again in June and July of 1849, it was crushed by superior external force. As would occur in Poland (1863), Czechoslovakia (1939), Hungary (1956), and other places in other times, democracy did not collapse from within so much as it was conquered from without.

Chapter 15

A New Realism for a New Era

The conservative establishment had survived revolutionary shocks in 1848/49. While some advisers at the top urged their sovereigns to turn the clock back to Metternichian times, repressing pressures for change with soldiers and sermons, others knew this would be inadvisable. "The old times are gone and cannot return," said one of the Prussian ministers. "To return to the decaying conditions of the past is like scooping water with a sieve."[1] Better to make some concessions to the spirit of the times while preserving healthy measures of royal authority and bureaucratic control than to hold fast to absolutism, provoke another revolution, and be swept away. Despite whimsical feelings for the old order, therefore, a more pragmatic approach to politics began to pervade the chancelleries of Berlin and Vienna.

The new chief minister in Prussia since November, Count Friedrich Wilhelm von Brandenburg, embodied this new realism. Having protected the nobility from rioting peasants in March 1848, the commander of the Silesian Sixth Corps knew from experience that counter-revolutionary policies could not ignore the root causes of the people's anger. Rather than reversing the peasant emancipation of the revolutionary diet, therefore, Brandenburg's administration implemented it with the stipulation that noblemen receive compensation. Two decrees of March 1850, facilitated the transition to free farming for about 640,000 peas-

1. Cited in Sheehan, *German History*, 710.

ants, nearly triple the number of serfs liberated by the legislation of Stein and Hardenberg. Before this, the down-to-earth soldier had restored corporate privileges to the guilds and established special industrial councils that allowed master craftsmen to monitor factories. "The events of the years 1848 and 1849 have taught us," declared one conservative backer of this policy, "that the artisan class desires not political but social improvements."[2] Characteristically, however, Brandenburg did not believe it was practical to ban new factories with the result that the industrial revolution moved forward with rapid strides. By 1860 there were 2,000 large-scale factories in Prussia with fifty workers or more.

Rebel troops assaulted by Prussian regulars at Waghäusel, June 1849.

Another concession to moderate liberals was the promulgation of a constitution which provided for upper and lower chambers with budget rights. In its final form, the lower house was elected on an ingenious plutocratic suffrage which granted a third of the seats to wealthy Prussians who paid the top third of the taxes, and so forth, with the last third of the seats going to the vast majority of people paying little or no taxes. Despite its blatant favoring of men of property, the constitution and the three-class suffrage won only grudging acceptance from the king. With great reluctance in

2. Cited in Theodore S. Hamerow, *Restoration, Revolution, Reaction: Economics and Politics in Germany, 1815-1871* (Princeton, 1958), 230.

January 1850, Frederick William IV finally swore allegiance to a "piece of paper."

Brandenburg's successor, Otto von Manteuffel, presided over Prussia's young parliamentary era until October 1858. Accustomed to practical politics as Minister of the Interior under Brandenburg, the new man had to balance numerous conflicting forces in the state. Thanks to the spadework of Günther Grünthal, we now have some orderly sense of what struck contemporaries as the "chaotic muddle"[3] of Prussian parliamentary politics in the 1850s. At the beginning of Manteuffel's tenure, the diet had already evolved from a plethora of small circles of friendly, like-minded deputies to three or four very loose groupings or blocs, each of which formed around two or three dominant personalities. As the decade unfolded, however, controversial issues and votes induced a fragmentation into ten distinct parties and three groupings of independents.

Some parties were more significant than others, of course. The three-class franchise allowed a party around Ludwig von Gerlach and Friedrich Julius Stahl a considerable number of seats. Although Stahl, as we know, could be very pragmatic, this group essentially represented the rights and privileges of the landowning nobility. On many – but certainly not all – issues, these conservatives were supported by Frederick William IV. Another aristocratic party led by Moritz August von Bethmann Hollweg, a legal scholar from Bonn, favored an English-style accommodation with modern times. The king's brother, Prince William, and his liberal-minded wife, Augusta, sympathized with this group. To their left was a cluster of oppositionist factions that defended parliamentary rights, rule by law, and economic progress. Georg von Vincke, the liberal aristocrat of United Diet fame, and Friedrich Harkort, a well-known businessman from the Ruhr, led these parties. Prussian Catholics, mostly from the Rhineland, formed another large coalition in the diet. The main purpose of the Catholic party was to ward off discriminatory threats to their church. On other issues, the aristocratic wing around Wilderich von Ketteler sided with the Junkers, while middle class deputies under Peter and August

3. Cited in Günther Grünthal, *Parlamentarismus in Preussen 1848/49-1857/58* (Düsseldorf, 1982), 397.

Reichensperger backed the parties of Bethmann Hollweg, Vincke, and Harkort. Manteuffel attempted to broker these conflicting interests and agendas, not allowing any one bloc – or its royal sympathizers – to undermine bureaucratic control.

The negotiated political balance of this decade probably warrants discarding the label of the Reactionary Fifties. To be sure, the Right won victories. The king persisted in creating an appointed House of Lords which weakened to some extent the political position of the diet. "As an elite bastion of aristocratic privilege and monarchical sentiment," observes David Barclay, "it was to play a crucial role in the history of the Prussian-German state until the monarchy itself collapsed in 1918."[4] The nobility also warded off legislative threats to its tax exempt status while restoring rights, abolished in 1848, to entailed estates, local police authority, and control of local government. At the same time, however, Manteuffel forged ahead with his predecessor's hated program of peasant emancipation. The chief minister also thwarted an ambitious conservative crusade to resuscitate the defunct provincial diets and undercut the lower chamber in Berlin. Frederick William had wanted these corporatist bodies restored, but Manteuffel prevailed with his view that they were not appropriate to the modern age of commerce, scientific agriculture, and industry. Prussia should "hang on to the past but look to the present and thereby repudiate [reactionary policies]."[5] The kingdom's railroad and banking elites still complained bitterly about unwanted competition from state lines and hostile anti-capitalist policies that hindered business expansion. But Manteuffel's administration won grudging nods of approval from lobbying businessmen when it dismantled the state's mining regulations, sold the gigantic industrial assets of the Overseas Trading Corporation *(Seehandlung)* into private hands, and prevented the conservative parties from squelching "commandite" banks which guaranteed limited liability for major investors. Together with these hard-fought business victories, Prussia's ongoing promotion of the Zollverein (see below) was perhaps the best sign that Gerlach, Stahl, and the reactionaries were not as dominant as historians once thought.

4. David. E. Barclay, *Frederick William IV and the Prussian Monarchy, 1840-1861* (Oxford, 1995), 249.

5. Ibid., 264.

Prussia's halting political progress brought it more into line with backsliding developments in the central and southern states. Between 1815 and 1830, rulers in the Third Germany had granted constitutions and established diets in response to political exigencies and popular pressures. Well before 1848, however, monarchs here had grown weary of parliamentary bickering and oppositionist attempts to encroach on royal prerogatives. Now, therefore, kings and grand dukes exploited the post-revolutionary weakness of their political adversaries. New constitutions granted during Europe's year of revolution were revoked in Hanover, Saxony, Württemberg, and Baden. Sovereigns turned to tough administrators like Wilhelm Friedrich von Borries (Hanover) and Baron Joseph von Linden (Württemberg). Maximilian II of Bavaria was the only ruler to retain his March Ministry well into the 1850s, but even here there was a turn to authoritarianism after mid-decade. In none of these states, on the other hand, was the principle of representative government abandoned. Like Prussia, they incorporated diets into the new conservative arrangements, accepting parliamentary institutions as an unavoidable aspect of modern times.

In Austria, too, there was a new, hard-headed realism. Knowing that the monarchy needed a real sovereign, Count Felix zu Schwarzenberg facilitated the abdication of feeble-minded Emperor Ferdinand and the ascension to power of Francis Joseph, the competent son of Archduchess Sophie. The new minister was also aware of other imperatives. Because the peasants were finally content, it made no sense to risk their wrath by rescinding emancipatory legislation. Similarly, the revolutionary principle of equality before the law would stay on the books, for it removed a lower class grievance and made the state more resilient. For a time, in fact, Schwarzenberg kept up liberal constitutional appearances. Alexander Bach retained a ministerial portfolio, Anton von Schmerling was brought into the cabinet, and Count Philipp Stadion, Governor of Galicia since the Polish uprising of 1846, was entrusted with the task of preparing a constitutional draft full of freedoms and concessions.

This was one appearance, however, which was deceiving. The Kremsier Diet, dissolved in March, 1849, was never reconvened. Months became years, yet Stadion's constitution was not implemented. By 1851 it was becoming apparent that neither Francis

Joseph nor Schwarzenberg felt it was necessary that Realpolitik include abandonment of absolutism. "Today we have taken a long step forward," the emperor wrote his domineering mother in August. "We have thrown our constitutional stuff overboard."[6] The infamous New Year's Eve Patent followed a few months later. "Gone were the elaborate array of representative institutions, the separation of judicial and administrative bureaucracies, the promise of national autonomy and linguistic equality, jury trials, and much else that Stadion, Schmerling, and the other reformers had tried to create."[7] With this series of decrees, Austria had bolstered the powers of the crown. Simultaneously, however, the empire had driven a wedge between itself and the constitutional countries of south-central Germany. Liberal public opinion there began to reconsider the old suspicions of Prussia.

* * * *

Even during the darkest reactionary years of Kaiser Francis, Austrian economic policy had retained a certain pragmatism. The guilds were given every opportunity to make a case against the evils of industrialism, but still it went forward, protected from foreign competition in a huge domestic market. This trend accelerated after 1848. Schwarzenberg's economic expert was Karl Ludwig Bruck, an artisan's son from Elberfeld who migrated to Triest, founded a successful shipping company, and later served with the Austrian delegation in St. Paul's Church. Although he resigned for political reasons in 1851, Bruck's policy of moderate tariff reductions, closer relations with the Zollverein, free internal trade, state railroad construction, and liberal banking facilitated a commercial and industrial expansion that lasted until the disruption of the Crimean War (1853-56) and the crash of 1857. Between 1849 and 1854, the value of imports doubled and exports more than tripled. The empire's formidable cotton textile industry expanded from 800,000 spindles in 1834, to 1,400,000 in 1852, and 1,800,000 in 1861. The railroad network grew rapidly from 1,620 kilometers in 1848 to 5,400 in 1860, while steam engine

6. Cited in C. A. Macartney, *The Habsburg Empire 1790-1918* (New York, 1969), 453.

7. Sheehan, 723.

capacity increased impressively from 100,000 horse power in 1850 to 330,000 in 1860. Not surprisingly, the output of pig iron moved upward too: from 198,000 tons in 1847 to 313,000 tons in 1860. Prussia and the Zollverein were racing ahead somewhat faster, and England and France still enjoyed a great lead. But there should be no doubt about the solidity and soundness of Austrian industry.

Under Brandenburg and Manteuffel, Prussia permitted the guilds some legal and political amenities. Like Austria and most states in the Zollverein, the land of the Hohenzollerns hesitated one last decade before opening the door to full-fledged industrial freedom (see below). Meanwhile throughout the Germanies, new forces of production pushed hard against the last resistant sinews of the old economic order. Buoyed by the commercial prosperity of the Zollverein, whose trade nearly doubled between 1850 and 1857, railroad promoters had a heyday. The most important remaining links in the all-German rail network were completed as kilometers of track increased from 5,820 in 1850 to 11,300 in 1860. Steam engine capacity (h.p.) expanded from 260,000 to 850,000 during this dynamic decade, while pig iron production took off from 229,000 to 529,000 tons. Cotton spindlage stood at 625,000 in 1834 and 900,000 in 1852 – still considerably behind Austria – then catapulted past the Danube Monarchy to 2,235,000 by 1861. A more isolated comparison between Austria and Prussia shows the two powers fairly even: Prussia had more railroad track (5,760 vs. 5,400 kilometers) and pig iron output (395,000 vs. 313,000 tons); but Austria's cotton textile industry dominated (1,800,000 vs. 675,000 spindles).

Qualitatively (i.e. in terms of technological improvements), the 1850s was also a breakthrough decade. The steam engine statistics cited above convey some impression of the transition from simple manufacturing to mechanized production. This transformation was particularly evident in textiles, the engine of the industrial revolution. In the competitive cotton industries of Bavaria, Württemberg, and Baden, for instance, nearly three-quarters of all spinning was performed with self-acting mules by the mid-1860s. The automatic nature of the device enabled unskilled, inexpensive operators to tend many machines with hundreds of spindles each, thereby tremendously increasing labor productivity. Mule spinning put pressure on weaving establishments, which installed power looms by the tens of thousands in the 1850s. Like mule spinning, the automatic loom allowed a low-paid worker to operate three or four machines and produce about twenty times more than he could on a hand-drawn device. In the iron industry, cheap, abundant coke increasingly supplanted charcoal as the blast furnace fuel. In the burgeoning regions of the Saar, the Ruhr, and Silesia, for example, coke pig iron soared from 25 percent of output in 1850 to 76 percent in 1860. The Coppee coking oven, an innovation which spread to German Europe from Belgium, accelerated this process. The efficient new technology halved the sulfur content of coke and greatly improved the usefulness of the pig iron produced, thus undercutting charcoal iron's qualitative advantage. Finally, the machine tools which worked Germany's iron and steel into final products underwent a revolutionary development. The mechanization of production required metal parts made with increasing precision. The milling machines and rotating, turret lathes which began to make their way to central Europe from the United States allowed far greater tolerances than metal craftsmen working arduously with files could achieve. In certain branches like small arms manufacture, precision machine tools permitted an evolution toward the mass production of interchangeable parts underway across the Atlantic. Prussia's needle gun was one of the first deadly results of these new methods.

These economic and technological changes acted as strong integrative forces. Entrepreneurs eager to learn about the latest trends in metallurgy or mechanization paid the competition a visit, while mechanics and engineers eager to market their skills moved from region to region in response to the best offers. When credit was unavailable in Karlsruhe or Berlin, one turned to the Darmstädter Bank, the Credit Anstalt in Leipzig, or the Schaffhausen Bank in Cologne. Such inter-connectedness induced a fifty-fold increase in the number of banknotes circulating in the Zollverein between 1845 and 1865. Nor were these links restricted to northern Germany. Thus bankers from Cologne, Breslau, and Hamburg participated in the financing of Austria's long railroad line from Vienna to Passau. The railways obviously reinforced these integrative trends, shortening the long Berlin-Vienna trek, for instance, from weeks to days. Mail moved just as quickly, while the telegraph lines which followed the wrought iron tracks could actually bring *instantaneous* word of delays or other urgent business. As we would expect, the new velocity of comunication augmented its volume: the number of letters mailed annually in Prussia, for example, doubled from 1850 to 1860; the number of telegrams rose eleven-fold. With communication and transportation improvements making Germany, essentially, a smaller place, it should come as no surprise that the German love of organizations carried over to the national level. Between 1856 and 1862, engineers, economists, lawyers, gymnasts, marksmen, and singers formed All-German organizations. In these ways, industrialization was drawing German Europe – and Germans – closer together.

The international politics of industrialization, on the other hand, tugged Germans in opposite directions toward the competing poles of Austria and Prussia. Karl Ludwig Bruck, part of the liberal facade which Schwarzenberg built onto his first cabinet in November 1848, never lost his Rhinelander's enthusiasm for a *Grossdeutsch* unification of all German lands. He wanted to realize these dreams economically and had worked hard at Frankfurt for a grandiose tariff union joining the Habsburg realms to the Zollverein. Bruck returned to his agenda as Austrian Minister of Commerce in October 1849, publicly proposing the same type of merger. Prior to this, he had secured approval for dismantling Austria's prohibitive tariff system and removing all remaining trade barriers between Austria and Hungary. The empire's tariff wall still towered above the Prussian-led customs union, but Bruck hoped his scheme would appeal to textile and iron producers wanting more protection, especially in southern Germany. The wily minister also knew that his ideas fit nicely with Schwarzenberg's power politics. "Only by the establishment of the Austro-German customs union," argued Bruck, "can Austria secure her proper position as leader in German affairs: so long as she is not a member of the Zollverein, all material interests gravitate toward Prussia."[8]

The plan was foiled by Rudolf von Delbrück, Bruck's counterpart in Berlin. The Prussian Minister of Commerce was a free-trader

8. Cited in W. O. Henderson, *The Zollverein* (Chicago, 1959), 211.

who maintained close ties to agricultural, banking, commercial, and light manufacturing groups whose export interests were better served by lower tariffs. With Saxony, Bavaria, Württemberg, Baden, Nassau, and both Hesses leaning toward Vienna in 1851, Delbrück negotiated the entry of Hanover and neighboring states to the Zollverein, thus gaining long-sought access to the sea. He then announced the early termination and renegotiation of the Zollverein. Eager to retain contacts with Hanover, and fearful of the loss of lucrative Zollverein revenues, the south-central states wavered. There was also Russian pressure to maintain the Zollverein as a means to ward off any attempt by Napoleon III to lure the Third Germany into closer ties with France. Schwarzenberg's death in April 1852, was the final blow to an Austro-German customs union, for, as Delbrück recalled, "the creative power and the ruthless energy behind these plans had been extinguished."[9] By the end of the year, Austria had to admit defeat as the Zollverein was renegotiated from Berlin without Habsburg participation.

After returning to office in 1855, Bruck renewed his efforts with the same disappointing results. Free trade groups in northern Germany remained stronger than the protectionists, while Austrian and Bohemian industrialists continued to lobby effectively at court with dire predictions of economic collapse if tariffs were lowered. There were only a few consolations. In 1857 a monetary agreement controlling the exchange rate of the Prussian thaler, the South German florin, and the Austrian florin was completed. And earlier, a commercial treaty lowering many tariffs between Austria and the Zollverein went into effect. But the arrangements seemed to benefit traders and industrialists in the North. For the Zollverein's share of Austrian imports increased from 17 to 34 percent, while the portion of Austrian exports going to the Zollverein rose more slowly from 29 to 32 percent. Like domestic politics, economic developments in the 1850s favored Prussian leadership.

* * * *

Compensating somewhat for these setbacks to Vienna's position was its successful reestablishment of the German Confederation.

9. Ibid., 219.

The liquidation of the Frankfurt Parliament in May 1849, had made this a theoretical possibility, but Schwarzenberg knew that the moment was inopportune. Despite victories over revolutionary forces in Italy, Bohemia, and Austria, Hungary remained defiant. Prussia, moreover, had rallied all of Germany behind its own unification scheme. The brain child of Joseph Maria von Radowitz, a leading conservative at St. Paul's and a close friend and adviser of Frederick William IV, these plans called for Prussian executive powers in a league of princes connected loosely to the people by a plutocratically elected parliament. Soon after Hungary's defeat in August 1849, however, Schwarzenberg secured the opposition of Tsar Nicholas to Prussia's Union Constitution. Always wary of Prussian aggressiveness, Bavaria deserted first, followed by Württemberg and some of the middle states, Saxony, and Hanover. The Austrian minister exploited this momentum by convening a rump session of the Confederation attended by these deserter states in May 1850.

Baden and twenty-five smaller states still clung to the Prussian Union. Elections were held to the Reichstag of this embryonic state in January 1850, and in March, hundreds of delegates gathered in Erfurt. The bulk of these subdued parliamentarians were moderate and right-wing Kasino liberals like Friedrich Dahlmann who had sat in St. Paul's and were now desperate to salvage something of 1848. Heinrich von Gagern was also among the assembled. But when their constitution was presented to a Congress of Princes in May, fourteen of the twenty-six states, intimidated by Austria and Russia, broke ranks. "The Union project was already mortally ill," concludes David Barclay, "and its death pangs would ruin Radowitz's career and bring Central Europe to the brink of war."[10]

Indeed, Frederick William IV and his brother, the martial Prince William, were prepared to fight rather than accept a return to the Austrian-led Confederation. Support at home soon crumbled, however, for the conservative parties were appalled at the prospect of waging war against Austria, the traditional defender of conservatism, while Brandenburg, Manteuffel, and the other ministers quickly determined that discretion was the better part of valor.

10. Barclay, 202.

"Let God in His mercy prove that William, Radowitz and I are wrong!", cried Frederick William. "I believe that we are not."[11] In November 1850, reason prevailed. Prussia abandoned its moribund unification scheme at Olmütz and agreed to cooperate with Austria in the reestablishment of the Confederation. This occurred at Dresden the following spring.

Austria's victory brought early dividends. In 1851, the reader will recall, the rulers of south-central Germany fell into line behind Bruck's plan of an Austrian-led customs union. The old days of Austrian predominance seemed to have returned. But Schwarzenberg's death and Delbrück's intimidating renegotiation of the Zollverein on Prussian terms quickly restored diplomatic fortunes to Berlin. In the process it became apparent that the presidency of the Zollverein was as powerful in German affairs as the presiding chair in the Confederation. Regardless of persistent official thinking in South Germany about the prudence of standing by Austria, moreover, the New Year's Eve Patent undercut much *public* sympathy for the Habsburgs in constitutional lands of the Third Germany which had more in common with Prussia.

The outbreak of the Crimean War in 1853 did further harm to Austria's position. The new chief minister, Karl Ferdinand von Buol, forgot the Habsburgs' debt to Russia – the Tsar's army had crushed the Hungarian revolt in 1849 – and pursued a pro-western policy throughout the conflict. This tack did little to impress the British and French while costing the Danube Monarchy the friendship of Russia – indeed Moscow was astonished and outraged by what it considered outright betrayal. Conservatives throughout the German Confederation worried by the specter of Bonapartism in France were also disappointed that Vienna seemed to side with Paris, while the leaders of key states like Bavaria and Saxony who simply wanted to avoid military conflict were frightened by Austrian brinkmanship. Frederick William IV, on the other hand, doggedly maintained his kingdom's neutrality against the conservative parties, which preferred that he join hands with Russia, and the party of Bethmann Hollweg, which pressured him to back England and France. Advocates of neutrality throughout the Germa-

11. Ibid., 212.

nies appreciated Frederick William's determined stand. By comparison with Viennese ingratitude, moreover, Prussia's neutrality seemed like friendship to Moscow. When the war ended in 1856, Prussia's star shone more brightly in German Europe.

These were twilight years for Frederick William IV. His lofty plans for modern-day absolutism a memory, his dream of converting the kingdom into an "all-encompassing work of art" reduced to a few inconsequential sketches, Prussia's king lived more and more in the past. Aged well beyond his sixty-two years, he finally suffered an incapacitating stroke in October 1857. Prince William received temporary authority to govern, but for twelve months nothing in Prussia really changed. Soon after William took his oath as Regent in October 1858, however, it became evident that a new era had begun.

* * * *

The reputation of William, Prince Regent of Prussia, had changed dramatically in the 1850s. The executioner of Rastatt, hated enemy of revolutionaries, and staunch, uncompromising opponent of liberalism appeared to have made his peace with modern times by the early years of the decade. Insiders were not surprised. Even before 1848 they had seen him in the company of liberal courtiers and practical businessmen and had noticed his openness to railroads, needle guns, rifled steel cannon, and innovative battlefield tactics. As military governor in Coblenz after 1849, the "leathery practitioner," as William described himself, opened the court to men of the new age like Moritz August von Bethmann Hollweg. Indeed the king's brother was more thoroughly reconciled to constitutional realities than the monarch himself. When Frederick William's illness made it impossible for him to rule, therefore, liberals rejoiced. These sentiments were reinforced when William dismissed the old ministers and replaced them with Bethmann Hollweg and Pre-March liberals like Rudolf von Auerswald. The Regent who had backed Radowitz and suffered the "humiliation" of Olmütz also spoke of the need to make "moral conquests in Germany by means of wise domestic legislation, the elevation of morality, and the use of unifying means like the Zollverein."[12] Liberal optimism seemed justified.

12. Cited in Sheehan, 863.

For all his practical adjustments to political exigencies, however, William remained above all else a military man. When he swore allegiance to the constitution that autumn, in fact, Prussia's first soldier was already greatly worried about the battle readiness of his army. The burgeoning industrial revolution was generating new technologies as well as new anxieties in commanders worried about the obsolescence of their weapons. One of the Prince's close military advisers, Albrecht von Roon, was also worried about an outmoded military organization unchanged since Napoleonic times. Mobilization plans called for militiamen to join regular army units in wartime. Roon believed that organization and fighting effectiveness could be enhanced by increasing the number of line regiments and drastically curtailing the role of the militia. In order to increase the reliability of troops during domestic troubles, moreover, he recommended an extension of service – and the attendant indoctrination – from two to three years. William considered Roon's memorandum for over a year before approving it in September 1859.

There was good reason to hurry forward with military reforms that summer, for dramatic events were unfolding in Italy. Count Camillo Cavour, Prime Minister of Piedmont-Sardinia, had formed a clever alliance with Napoleon III which called for military assistance in the event of war with Austria. When the inevitable hostilities came in June, the allies won bloody battles at Magenta and Solferino that forced a tearful Francis Joseph to sue for peace. A united Kingdom of Italy under the House of Savoy was proclaimed in 1860.

The Italian campaign highlighted all that was wrong with the Danube Monarchy. Expenditures during the Crimean War had forced the state to raise taxes, sell railroad assets, cut the army budget, and push its weak credit to the limit. As a result, a loan to cover the war in Italy went only 40 percent subscribed despite onerous official pressure on banks. Like power-hungry, financially strapped monarchs in other times, the Habsburgs were forced to learn about the public financial disadvantages of authoritarianism. Unable to afford more than twelve badly equipped corps, the Habsburgs could only send nine south, for the others were required to guard against internal revolts. One of the nine, an unreliable corps comprised of Hungarian units, had to be kept in reserve, then sent home, while 15,000 Hungarians and Croats – 6 percent of the army in Italy – deserted in the first battle. The commanders were also unfortunate products of the old order: Francis Joseph, who had no experience; and Count Gyulai, who was "an almost inconceivably incompetent commander."[13] Their delays, hesitation, and lack of resolve contributed to the June defeats. Finally, the Diet of the Confederation, backed by Prussia, refused to intervene in the war, while England and Russia, sobered by warfare in the Crimea, ignored Vienna's warnings about Napoleonic aggression. The entire political, military, and diplomatic system in Vienna had failed.

Even before the climactic battles, the emperor's ministers had implored him to quiet the widespread denunciation of the establishment by introducing timely reforms. That summer Bruck advocated far-reaching constitutional change and guarantees of freedom of enterprise as ways to solidify the regime and sway public opinion in Germany. Francis Joseph agreed to a new business code which abandoned the guilds (1859), but contented himself with vague promises of new political institutions. When nothing substantial materialized in 1860, further unrest prompted the so-called October Diploma. "We shall indeed have a little parliamentary government," he wrote his mother, "but the power remains in my hands."[14] But after these announcements failed to procure loans from the financial bourgeoisie, the beleaguered monarch turned to Anton von Schmerling. The old 48er exacted the grudging concession from Francis Joseph in February 1861, that Austria would receive a parliament to vote on taxes and other legislation. The lower house of the so-called Imperial Council would be selected by diets of the various crownlands – 85 of the 343 deputies, for instance, from Hungary – while the upper chamber was a bastion of the grand nobility and the crown. Although the emperor retained exclusive rights in matters of defense and foreign affairs, the coming of the Imperial Council marked the definitive end of absolutism in German Europe.

13. Macartney, 491.
14. Ibid., 499.

Unconstitutional rule by kings was also buried in Prussia by the 1850s, but events in the "New Era" greatly strengthened this tendency. Parliamentary elections in November 1858, returned less than a third of the conservative deputies, while Georg von Vincke's liberal factions secured 195 of 352 seats. William's new cabinet included moderate party politicians who had led the struggle for economic concessions before 1858. Now they continued the "negotiated settlements"[15] of previous years by cooperating with former diet colleagues to eliminate one grievance after another of the commercial and industrial bourgeoisie. New Era ministers accommodated business interests by removing the last restrictions on mining, abandoning the unpopular state purchase of railroad companies, and accelerating the approval of new private lines. The controversial tax exempt status of Junker estates came to an end and the guilds lost their last legal props. To the applause of dominant free-trade groups, moreover, the minister of trade opened negotiations with France for most-favored-nation arrangements. An important sign of the growing bourgeois stake in the new order was the establishment of a bank consortium in 1859 to underwrite government loans. It was the allure of this same sort of service that drove a resistant Francis Joseph into parliamentary concessions after the Italian war.

During the same years, however, another concern gradually began to shift public attention to more divisive issues. Albrecht von Roon became minister of war in November 1859 on the strength of his proposals for army reorganization. A few months later, his measures were received cooly in the diet by Vincke's liberal coalition. Some deputies remained attached to the militia as a symbol of the great reform era of Stein and Hardenberg. Weightier objections were raised to the annual expense of seven million thaler on new line regiments and the three-year service, monies which were needed for roads, river improvement schemes, and other productive investments. Not wanting to disrupt relations with William's moderate ministers, the liberals approved the budget with the stipulation that Roon delay implementation of his bill.

15. James M. Brophy, *The Accommodation of Capital: The Railroad Industry and Political Culture in Prussia 1830-1870* (Columbus, forthcoming 1997).

When William and his anxious generals raised the new regiments anyway, the diet called foul and criticisms grew more acrimonious.

Despite mounting tension by late 1860, however, Vincke's factions still refused to reject the budget. On the contrary, there were signs that they would consider army reform more "palatable and acceptable"[16] if William did something to make the "moral conquests" in Germany promised at the onset of his regime. Vincke's coalition was clearly engaged in another round of hard negotiating. And the object of their pressure was to enlist Prussia as an agent of German unification. Karl Twesten, one of the more independent members of the opposition, expressed these sentiments well in 1861. "If some day a Prussian minister would step forward ... and say ... 'I have moved boundary markers, violated international law, and torn up treaties, as Count Cavour has done,' gentlemen, I believe that we will then not condemn him ... [rather] we will erect a monument to him."[17]

In June 1861 a faction determined to confront the government over these issues broke away from Vincke's "old liberals" to form the "German" Progressive Party. Given the absence of any evidence that Prussia was solving the German question, they charged that the substitution of regular army units for the beloved militia would only facilitate reactionary purposes at home. The Progressives won 104 seats later that year, then in early 1862 joined 48 men of the Left-Center in proposing an itemized budget that would have prevented the government from continuing unauthorized miltary expenditures. Angered and affronted by this challenge to his prerogatives as king and head of the army, William dismissed his moderate ministers, appointed hard-liners, and called for new elections. The famous constitutional conflict was underway.

The nationalistic overtones of the Prussian crisis were clearly overpowering the sound of other issues. The same harsh notes of Germanic excitement, in fact, could be heard rising in feverish crescendo throughout the Confederation. For the fighting in Italy

16. Cited in Michael Gugel, *Industrieller Aufstieg und bürgerliche Herrschaft: Sozioökonomische Interessen und politische Ziele des liberalen Bürgertums in Preussen zur Zeit des Verfassungskonflikts 1857-1867* (Cologne, 1975), 95.

17. Cited in Theodore S. Hamerow, *The Social Foundations of German Unification 1858-1871* (Princeton, 1969, 1971), 2:171.

had unleashed the greatest wave of patriotic fervor in Germany since the revolutions of 1848/49. Among bourgeois patricians, this was evidenced by the founding of the Nationalist Society at Frankfurt am Main in September 1859. Worried by a hostile European atmosphere which had triggered two recent wars, hundreds of prominent businessmen and professionals from Prussia, Hanover, Saxony, and other parts of the Confederation agreed on the urgent necessity of "a stable, strong, and permanent central government of Germany." Given Austria's defeat and record of reactionary policies, Germany should look to Berlin for political and military leadership. Every German should support Prussia insofar as its tasks "coincide with the needs and tasks of Germany, and insofar as it directs its activity toward the introduction of a strong and free common constitution for Germany."[18] Eventually peaking at 25,000 members, the Nationalist Society was a measure of the sympathy which Prussia had earned in Germany since the revolutions.

The patriotic wave of 1859 was also in evidence during the centennial celebrations of Schiller's birth that November. The poet and playwright who had wanted his art to prepare Germans for freedom and unity now smiled from the grave as countrymen from Bremen to Innsbruck marched in his honor. Everywhere these festivals were conducted in a highly charged political atmosphere. In Munich, five hundred students made a bonfire of their torches in a city square to the accompaniment of patriotic songs. In Frankfurt, a huge mock-up was made of Germania crowning Schiller with a laurel wreath and emblems of the different Germanic tribes. In Berlin, democrats rioted with police. Over 500 cities and towns celebrated Schiller's birthday – workers, guildsmen, gymnasts, riflemen, singers, and village people from miles around paying homage to a man who made them feel German. "Only the nobility and the military were said to be hostile, which was understandable, as Schiller was a symbol of freedom and national consciousness."[19]

The enthusiasm carried over into the new decade. All-German festivals of gymnasts (Leipzig), marksmen (Frankfurt), and choral

18. Ibid., 1:316.

19. George L. Mosse, *The Nationalization of the Masses: Political Symbolism and Mass Movements in Germany from the Napoleonic Wars through the Third Reich* (Ithaca, 1975), 87.

societies (Nürnberg) were held, each attracting crowds of about 100,000. All three created national organizations in 1861 and 1862, with the gymnasts building an imposing following of 134,000. From the beginning, these movements exhibited obvious partisan sympathies for a democratic unification from below without the aid of kings and princes. Neither the Habsburgs nor the Hohenzollerns had many supporters, as the Nationalist Society learned when it attempted unsuccessfully to make inroads. The great national festivals were all held outside Austria and Prussia, while many speakers alluded enthusiastically to the "Third Germany."

There was widespread sympathy, moreover, for arming the people. The riflemen who gathered at Frankfurt in July 1862, for example, raised cheers for the Swiss and American sharpshooters who were seen as representatives of nations that knew how to fight for freedom and unity. In Berlin a few months later, patriots formed the Defense League of Arminius and approached the Nationalist Society for a loan to purchase weapons. That the request was denied goes without saying, for bourgeois notables were as alarmed as the authorities by the specter of the nationalist mob in arms. Indeed, memories were still fresh of the crazed nationalist who the year before had taken shots at Prussia's king because he had not "done enough for German unity."[20]

William's response to this incident was a remarkable sign of the times. When other states urged him to crack down on a Nationalist Society allegedly to blame for such excesses, William replied curtly that it would be wiser to fulfill the just demands of the German people. In making their own unification proposals, therefore, the leading German states were on a kind of tiger ride. The first initiatives, interestingly enough, came in the area of legal reform. Since the polemic between Savigny and Thibaut in 1815, nationalists had viewed codification of Germany's diversity of laws and standardization of its contrasting legal systems as a step toward political unification. These demands radicalized with the Germanist congresses of 1846 and 1847 and the Frankfurt Parliament of 1848. The febrile intensification of nationalistic passion in the late

20. Cited in Otto Pflanze, *Bismarck and the Development of Germany: The Period of Unification, 1815-1871* (Princeton, 1990), 151.

1850s, however, made once-dreaded proposals attractive to the middle-sized states. For if legal reforms were implemented by the German Confederation, its political stock would soar and its institutions would gain in longevity, thus thwarting the efforts of nationalists who abhorred Germany's federal structure. With this strategy in mind, representatives from Bavaria, Saxony, Württemberg, and other smaller states gathered at Würzburg in November 1859 to discuss adoption of common (i.e. confederate) civil and criminal laws and the creation of a German supreme court. Austria cleverly supported these plans. The actual work of codifying civil and commercial laws was begun by committees of the Confederation in February 1862.

A plan for political unification was penned by Count Friedrich Ferdinand von Beust, Minister President of Saxony, in October 1861. His scheme envisioned an executive power shared by Austria, Prussia, and a Third German state; a revamped diet alternating between Austrian and Prussian leadership; and a representative chamber elected indirectly by state parliaments. Although complex, it had the advantage of accommodating important state interests, opening government to the people, but avoiding democratic rule. Austria, realizing that Beust's German state would act as a break on Prussian ambition, responded favorably to Beust's initiative with a revised and less complicated version of his plan.

Anton von Schmerling, the spirit of Habsburg diplomacy at this point, had not forgotten his *Grossdeutsch* agenda. Mindful of 1848's descent into chaos, however, he planned to manipulate and control nationalist forces. Black-red-gold flags appeared in Vienna; articles on the Habsburg's German mission were planted in the press; and Archduke Charles's statue was inscribed "to the tenacious fighter for Germany's honor."[21] There was a political echo in the North when Julius Fröbel, another veteran of 1848, formed the Reform Association to oppose Nationalist Society propaganda. With high hopes of reasserting itself in Germany, Austria presented its unification scheme to the Diet of the Confederation in August 1862.

Prussia responded defensively to these various initiatives. Realizing that it would be hamstrung in Beust's federal state, Berlin

21. Cited in Macartney, 535.

countered in December 1861 with a version of its old Union plan reworked slightly to insure the approval of Baden, Prussia's only ally in the South. With Napoleon III as a neighbor, Karlsruhe looked to the Prussian Army for protection. Otherwise, Berlin sought to parry blows with what had always been its best move: economic policy. While boycotting the Confederation's legal reform efforts, for instance, Prussian ministries forged ahead with a commercial code which they planned to present to the Zollverein. In March 1862, moreover, Prussia concluded a "most-favored-nation" treaty with France. Given Napoleon's free trade arrangements with England, this meant a lowering of Prussia's moderate tariffs – with transparent political motives, for Austria was still too accustomed to higher tariffs to follow suit. Acceptance of the treaty by other members of the Zollverein would make "the economic severance of Austria from the rest of Germany an accomplished and enduring fact,"[22] as an irate, insightful Austrian minister put it that spring. Hoping to build popular momentum in this direction, Berlin presented the commercial treaty to its recalcitrant diet in August 1862. The Prussian deputies approved the resolution in a landslide, also sanctioning the administration's strategy of making the treaty with France a *sine qua non* for renewing Zollverein arrangements due to expire in 1865. Such pressure would be extremely difficult to resist for countries like Saxony whose economy had become almost fully integrated with Prussia's since 1834.

The Progressives and Left-Center in Berlin looked favorably upon these developments. Were these not indications that hard, tough negotiating had compelled the government to take initiatives in the German question? The Left's political base was certainly growing stronger. Elections in March had defiantly returned 229 oppositionist deputies – a 65 percent majority. The hapless conservative parties had shriveled to eleven seats, a mere 3 percent. His electoral strategy failing, William, king in his own right since the previous year, lashed out at his opponents. "War to the death against the monarch and his standing army has been vowed," he wrote angrily, "and in order to reach that goal the Progressivists

22. Cited in Henderson, 291.

and democrats and ultra liberals scorn no means." The opposition "will be able to develop an officers' caste of their own which ... are to be won for the revolution." As Eugene Anderson observes, "one can still hear the pen stab the paper and the ink explode."[23]

Paradoxically, however, William's anger weakened his hold on the throne. With neither the understanding nor the necessary temperament for party politics, with even his hard-liners chagrined by the persistence of parliament, an exasperated, anxious king was ready to threaten abdication – or even to step down – before yielding to the diet. It was August 1862.

* * * *

Otto von Bismarck became Minister-President of Prussia one month later. With this event, the New Era began to yield to a new epoch. After mistakes and miscalculations in 1862 and 1863, Bismarck maneuvered himself into a position of power *vis-è-vis* the diet by 1864. As late as the summer of 1866, however, he had found no end to the long-standing impasse. As we shall explore in much greater detail in the final chapter of this part, foreign crises would finally offer a way out. Prussia and Austria waged a successful war against Denmark in 1864, then fought one another in 1866 for the supremacy of German Europe. Prussia's victory enabled her to unify northern Germany in 1867. When the northern and southern states united militarily against France in 1870, a powerful "Second Reich" with semi-parliamentary institutions was the political result. In Austria, meanwhile, a string of military defeats had opened government to the liberals and allowed the empire's most outspoken subject nationality, the Hungarians, to achieve autonomy.

Before delving into these developments, however, we turn first to social and cultural trends in the 1850s and 1860s. Readers should keep in mind that all topics analyzed in these two subheadings occurred simultaneously with – and were in many ways related to – the political events handled in the last chapter of the book.

23. Quotes from Eugene N. Anderson, *The Social and Political Conflict in Prussia 1858-1864* (Lincoln, 1954), 106-07.

Chapter 16

Social Change in Town and Country

Prenzlau, northeast of Berlin in the Ückermark, was a town of around 6,000 in the mid-1860s. Soldiers from its army base participated in the successful war against Denmark. A host of small industries, shops, and stores serviced the army, the towns-people, the surrounding lake country, and nearby farm lands. Among these small businessmen, producers, and artisans were three brothers of the Brose family who worked leather: two made shoes, while the third crafted boots and gloves. Together they lived a marginally secure petty-bourgeois existence in the encroaching shadow of the leather goods factories.

Prenzlau was a fairly representative Prussian town at the time of the Danish War. There were thirty cities in the kingdom with over 20,000 inhabitants, led by Berlin with over 600,000; Cologne with about 125,000; and Königsberg with around 100,000. Urbanites were much more numerous than a half century earlier, but they represented only 10 percent of the population. In Germany as a whole, the figure for big cities was 7.5 percent. More typical were the scores of middle-sized towns like Prenzlau, Cottbus, Frankfurt am Oder, Siegen, Neuwied, and Cochem. Ranging between 2,000 and 20,000 people, they accounted for around 27 percent of all Germans. The railroads reached most of these boroughs during the 1850s and 1860s, enabling them to play a crucial intermediary role between the big cities and the countryside. The bulk of the

German population – about 64 percent – lived in country villages surrounding these small-to-middling towns.

Death struck William Brose, the glover, in the autumn of 1864. With five young children, his grief-stricken widow now faced a difficult decision. Stay in town and hope to find security through remarriage – or emigrate to America where a sister was prepared to receive her. Finally the decision came. What few possessions she had were sold to pay for the long train journey over Berlin to the coast; steerage space for six to New York City; and another arduous rail trip deep into the American midwest. The surviving brothers said their goodbyes at the station that November. Worn down by the trek and a life of odd jobs in Wisconsin, my great-great-grandmother – whose name nobody in the family remembers – died two years later.

Her story is an instructive point of departure for our discussion of German society after mid-century. Bearing and raising children, cooking for the family, and tending to household chores like hauling water and cleaning left wives little time for leisure activities. This was especially the case if the family business was in a putting-out network. In shoemaking, for example, women often inserted eyelets or performed final polishing of factory-made shoes at home, while the last steps of metal working, furniture making, candlestick production, and garment making often involved women working in their homes. In those few hours a mother had to spare, moreover, she might also do porcelain painting or other types of design work on dishes, buttons, or country pottery. In the Prussia of 1861, about 1,400,000 women "assisted relatives" outside the framework of formal employment. These numbers were significant, representing around 23 percent of all females over 14 and about 16 percent of Prussia's total workforce.

Despite the arduous nature of their existence, women of the lower middle class in Germany were proud of their existence above the domestic servants, factory hands, seamstresses, cleaners, barmaids, and prostitutes. Indeed the life of a glover's wife would be one that most girls who left the villages for work in towns and cities aspired to have. Yet, for all of Germany's industrial and scientific progress, we must remember that this was still a very precarious life – death or a freak accident could quickly hurl one down society's slippery slope. Thus my family's tragedy would visit hundreds of homes in Prenzlau in 1866 after victorious soldiers returned from another campaign – this time in Austrian Bohemia – with the deadly cholera.

The story of William Brose's widow is representative in other respects, for emigration remained a very important part of the German social experience. Germans had begun to cross the Atlantic in the late 1700s, but it was not until the "Hungry Forties," when 500,000 pulled up stakes, that great numbers were involved. "Bid farewell to country and village," penned Wolfgang Müller von Königswinter in 1842: "The house that gave you life, the mountain, the field, the river in the valley, that loving grave in the churchyard / Clutch one last fistfull of dirt for heart and memory / A free new Fatherland beckons across the sea!"[1] Carl Wilhelm Hübner captured these sentiments on canvas a few years later in his poignant *Farewell of the Emigrants*. Weary from life before the journey begins, a married couple and two dazed children stand by ancestral graves seeking strength for the departure. In the background we see friends and neighbors who have stopped at the edge of the village, wondering, perhaps, if they would be leaving soon.

As the 1840s gave way to the 1850s, numerous factors worked to accelerate the pace of emigration. Special organizations were founded with their own newspapers and publications catering to Germans who were already tempted to leave. Governments throughout the Confederation established counseling bureaus and subsidized travel costs in a pragmatic effort to promote emigration and relieve pressure on society. By the 1850s, elaborate cross-Atlantic networks of families and friends also existed to ease the uncertainty, insecurity, and anxiety of risking such a long passage. The underlying socio-economic causes of emigration, moreover, were still present. Both the artisan and the peasant faced stiff, sometimes brutal competition in the ugly new world of industry and market capitalism. A million and a half Germans wandered overseas in the 1850s and 1860s, most drawn to the rich farmland and highly touted small business opportunities of America.

1. Printed in Wend von Kalnein (ed.), *Die Düsseldorfer Malerschule* (Düsseldorf, 1979), 344-46.

Among these were many defeated handicraftsmen who could no longer survive economically in the old country. In Baden alone during the 1850s, for instance, 15,000 guild masters departed. Most were bitter that no political remedy had been found for the threat of factories and industrial technology. Hopes had been buoyed after the conservatives' return to power in 1849. Prussia, Hanover, Saxony, Baden, Württemberg, Hesse-Darmstadt, Nassau, and Bavaria introduced corporate reforms which seemed to promise a return to guild control of production. Hanover and Württemberg also passed tough municipal residency requirements designed to curb competition from migrants. But the promise of these measures was hollow, for none was designed to stop an industrialism that had grown too important to state finances and military establishments. With Austria leading the way in 1859, the pretense of earlier legislation yielded to the harsh new reality of freedom of enterprise.

The Habsburg initiative was followed quickly by Nassau (1860), Saxony (1861), Baden (1862), and Württemberg (1862). Prussia eased its guild laws in 1861, moreover, then turned a blind eye as the industrial councils (which were supposed to regulate the factories) disappeared one by one – the last in 1864. To combat these adverse trends, a German Union of Handicraftsmen was founded at Weimar in September 1862. Its leaders cried out for "a life-and-death struggle against this plague and fraud of liberal industrial conditions."[2] But their pleas and petitions had no effect. The 'plague' of free industrial enterprise spread to an avalanche of smaller duchies after mid-decade as well as to Hesse-Darmstadt in 1866 and Bavaria in 1868. Thirty German states had abandoned the guilds by 1869.

While the German Union of Handicraftsmen flailed away ineffectually at industrialism, the "social priest," Adolf Kolping, devised means of aiding artisans that had a more lasting impact. Having learned the shoemaking trade as a youth in Cologne during the 1830s, the sensitive and deeply religious Kolping had trouble adapting to what struck him as the intemperance and immorality of the workshop milieu. He turned to the priesthood, therefore,

2. Cited in Hamerow, *Restoration, Revolution, Reaction*, 245.

determined that his would be a social ministry. Kolping founded a journeymen's union at Elberfeld in 1847, and within a few years, others were opened in the surrounding area. Perhaps most important to the wandering artisans was the network of over 350 hostels which spread throughout the Rhineland, southern Germany, Austria, and Switzerland during the 1850s and 1860s. Here the movement's 60,000 members could find cheap room and board, instruction in reading and writing, weekly lectures in historical, semi-political, and religious themes, and of course a chapel for mass, confession, and communion. There were also reading rooms well-stocked with newspapers and general reading matter. The combination of food, lodging, and a positive emphasis on self-help and education made the Kolping Associations popular among Catholics and non-Catholics alike. Thus August Bebel, later to become leader of the Social Democratic Party of Germany, recalled that the reading rooms helped quench his thirst for political information. "For clubs of a purely social nature I had neither money nor inclination."[3] There can be no doubt that Bebel was also attracted by the thinly veiled anti-capitalistic politics of a movement that strove to provide shelter for the small man from Germany's industrial storm.

Hermann Schulze, Mayor of Delitzsch in Prussian Saxony, was just as concerned about the plight of small producers and their families. A left-liberal at St. Paul's Church, "Schulze-Delitzsch" was determined to carry liberalism's failed political potential into the social realm. In 1849 and 1850, he founded a mutual aid society to provide poor townsmen with sickness benefits, a cooperative association of cobblers to buy shoe leather, and a bank that pooled the savings of ten artisans. By the late 1850s, these precedents had grown from one small town into a national movement of eighty co-op banks and hundreds of consumer and raw materials-purchase cooperatives. The "urban banks" were particularly innovative. Limiting their business to members in a single town, they often provided loans against the co-signature of a friend or relative. After another decade of rapid growth, the Schulze-Delitzsch cooperatives boasted over 300,000 members. Relying on one another

3. August Bebel, *My Life* (Chicago, 1912), 36-37.

and the economic power of capitalism, Delitzsch's craftsmen had taught Germany that industrialization need not destroy them.

Industrialism also left an indelible mark on agriculture and the rural population. We have seen that early industry was heavily dependent on the countryside for raw materials, fuel, and water power. This dependency gradually eased after 1850 as coal continued to replace charcoal; the first synthetic dyes competed with moad, madder, and older dye crops; and steam engines increasingly supplanted water wheels. In fact, agriculture grew more dependent on industry as industrial cities grew into essential markets for farms; banks became a vital source of farm credit; and railroads emerged as the essential transporter of crops and farm purchases. "Tools for planting and harvesting, Sunday suits and special dresses, prepared foods and household ornaments, family photographs and pocket-watches, colloquial expressions and table manners – all these products of the urban world slowly seeped into German towns and villages."[4]

In the process, however, farmers from the marginal peasant to the latifundium owner grew anxious as the perception spread that control over their livelihoods was slipping into other hands. Unseen bourgeois financiers decided on loans in faraway offices; agents of rich investors determined railroad rates in a seemingly arbitrary fashion; and a welter of confusing market forces whose tentacles stretched across oceans controlled prices and manipulated the terms of trade. Meanwhile, agriculture's position in the German economy, once dominant, continued its downward slide. At 46.5 percent of net social product in 1850, it had fallen to 41.6 percent by 1867. This was indeed a new era.

Politics and market forces combined in other ways to generate anxiety in the countryside. The agrarian reforms of the Pre-March had largely finished the task of dividing the commons, but the more complicated process of enclosure whereby scattered strips of land in the various fields surrounding villages were consolidated into modern farms had barely begun. Only Mecklenburg, Schleswig-Holstein, and the extreme Northwest had enclosed-style agriculture. After the revolutions of 1848/49, however, pragmatic reformers

4. Sheehan, 765.

in Brunswick, Hanover, and Baden promoted enclosure, while elsewhere in Germany this productive rearrangement of holdings advanced piecemeal until aggressive Prussian legislation of 1872. As enclosure spread during the third quarter of the century, intense pressure mounted on small- and middle-sized farmers (who may or may not have enclosed themselves) to emulate their more entrepreneurial neighbors. Indeed the logic of enclosure was to exploit its possibilities by substituting crop rotation for fallow techniques, chemical fertilizers for manure, and steam equipment for farm animals. Generally speaking, this was done more aggressively in northern and eastern Germany than in the west and south, but even the Junkers of Prussia and Mecklenburg were sometimes reluctant to change. The usual result was bankruptcy. Nor was modernization always a panacea, for some pioneers lacked the business savvy to survive capitalism's challenges. By the 1880s, for instance, two-thirds of the noble estates in eastern Prussia were in the hands of bourgeois commoners. Thus enclosure legislation and technological change combined with the new uncertainties and loss of control discussed above to create harsh realities and sometimes insurmountable challenges for farmers. "Endowed at last with complete control over his holding, better educated, brought by the railway into touch with distant markets, the peasant was waking from his sleep,"[5] wrote John Clapham. But obviously it could be a deadly slumber from which some peasants – and noblemen – never awoke.

Political developments were even harder on the owners of the smallest farm plots. As we know, the revolutions and their aftermath definitively ended the era of serfdom. Throughout the Confederation, frightened revolutionary regimes and their hard-headed conservative successors rushed through emancipation legislation. Everywhere, however, the nobleman was compensated by payments from peasants that burdened them all their lives. Measured in the currency of the post-1871 Empire, the cost of freedom amounted to 210 million marks in Hanover, 30 million in Brunswick, 72 million in Baden, and 7.5 million in tiny Saxe-Altenburg.

5. J. H. Clapham, *Economic Development of France and Germany 1815-1914* (Cambridge, 1966), 215.

The totals for Prussia and Austria were much higher. For the small man on the land, these payments often combined with taxes, new market forces, and competition from modernized farms to drive him below the margin of profitability.

Typically the struggling peasant and his wife tried to supplement family income with domestic weaving, simple handicrafts, or work on other farms and construction sites. Even when forced to sell their cherished plots, farmers attempted to stay near the land with full-time employment as village laborers or cleaning women. But for hundreds of thousands in the 1850s and 1860s, the day came for packing up everything and moving on.

> The state freed the peasant from the burdens of the past [notes Theodore Hamerow], but it could not protect him from the dangers of the future. His safety lay in flight. The masses of the overcrowded countryside began to desert their fields in a mighty internal migration which within the lifetime of one generation completed the urbanization of Germany. They descended on the blast furnaces of the Ruhr, the textile mills of Saxony, the coal mines of Silesia. They doubled and tripled and quadrupled the size of cities like Düsseldorf, Leipzig, and Breslau. They became the 'industrial reserve army' which [Karl] Marx analyzed in ... *Das Kapital* ... .[6]

Unlike earlier decades when the bulk of internal migration had exited the Southwest, departures after the 1850s came mainly from the northeast. Censuses after 1900 showed only one-in-three residents of the area stretching from Brandenburg to Memel who had remained in his or her place of birth. Quite often towns like Prenzlau were a stepping stone to final employment in burgeoning industrial cities and regions like Berlin or the Ruhr. And sometimes the peasant did not stop until he reached the Bismarcks, Kings of Prussia, and New Mecklenburgs of the United States.

* * * *

Prenzlau published its first address book in February, 1866.[7] Listing the occupation or status of every adult except housewives, it provides a fairly accurate breakdown of the labor force. Nearly a third

6. Hamerow, 227.
7. *Wohnungs-Anzeiger der Stadt Prenzlau nebst deren Vorstädte* (Prenzlau, 1866).

of Prenzlau's gainfully employed – with family members perhaps 35 percent of the overall town population – were innkeepers, shopowners, mastercraftsmen, journeymen, or non-guild artisans like the Broses. There were 2,200,800 artisans and shopowners in the states of the Zollverein in 1861 – and easily more than three million if Austria is included – representing with their families between 15-16 percent of the population. Over a fifth of Prenzlau's workforce – with wives and children perhaps 18 percent of all Prenzlau residents – were designated simply as "workers." Most of these labored in the hat, shoe, glove, and clothing factories that one would expect to find in a garrison town.

The accelerating industrial revolution had spawned unskilled proletarians in all German cities and towns by the 1860s. Blue-collar working families ranged from a low 2.76 percent of the population in Königsberg, to 7.06 percent in Berlin, 13.41 percent in Essen, and a high of 27.29 percent in Bremen. There were 541,000 industrial workers in all of Prussia in 1861 and well over a million if the rest of Germany and Austria is included. This was easily double the figure of the late 1840s. By the early 1870s there were 1,281,000 industrial workers in Prussia whose proportion of the workforce had grown from 6.8 percent in 1861 to 12 percent – and with family members to about 10-11 percent of the population.

Common to the worker's experience were his or her dependence on wages, a dearth or lack of property, a one-sidedly subordinate position to the owner, strict job discipline in a central factory or work site, the complete separation of work from home and family, and the dismal quality of housing with its attendant negative effects on family life and gender relations. Slowly at first, then more quickly as industrialization accelerated, these commonalities began to forge a new social class. "A rigid anchoring in slums despite all the moving about," writes Hans-Ulrich Wehler, "the narrow radius of social contacts fixed by this [situation], the intimacy of so many communing on the street and in courtyards, the mutuality of the pub – as a substitute living room, as a place to exchange opinions, as a clearing house for information of all sorts – all of these constraining circumstances of life had the social-psychological effect … of creating, despite all the differences, a common basis of life. And these commonalities [of private life] combined in a wider network with common experiences on the job to form a genuine proletarian social milieu."[8]

Within the industrial labor force, however, there were vastly differing subcultures that greatly affected the economic and political response of workers to their workplace environment. Where strong patriarchal traditions carried over from the artisan's shop to the factory – as they did among hatters, cobblers, glovers, and tailors – employees remained relatively docile. Similar factors operated in machine-tool plants which had often evolved from handicraft manufacturing, demanded high skills, and paid well. Although little training was involved and guild connections were non-existent, moreover, the high wages of metallurgical workers combined with the grueling work day to dampen labor activism.

Unrest among workers sprung typically from subcultures other than these. Among printers and typesetters, cigar makers, and ship builders, handicraft traditions actually promoted strife and trade unionism, for journeymen in these trades where guilds were weak or non-existent had learned bargaining and striking techniques which they brought into industry. Formerly respectful and cooperative, moreover, miners began to protest and strike in the 1860s as small hillside operations which had featured fraternal self-help yielded to deeper, more dangerous mines owned by self-made capitalists who ignored traditional practices and routines. The old cooperative patterns deteriorated further as new hands streamed in from the crowded countryside. The typical textile operative and railroad construction worker were also part of this flood from the land. In both cases, the depth of exploitation could trigger tumultuous protests, although quite often these took on rural, pre-industrial forms like the late-night cat music.

We have seen that labor organizations like Stephan Born's Brotherhood of the Workers were already on the scene before 1848. The revolutions disrupted this beginning, however, as conservative regimes regained power and finished the business of cracking down in the early 1850s. With labor leaders in jail or exile and freedom of association severely limited, organizational initiatives from below were not seen during the remainder

8. Hans-Ulrich Wehler, *Deutsche Gesellschaftsgeschichte* (Munich, 1995), 3:150.

of this decade. It was not until 1862 that labor activism began to revive (see below). The task of organizational activity in the meantime fell to that minority of the middle class which did not ignore social issues.

The most ambitious efforts occurred on the liberal side as scores of worker educational associations were founded throughout Germany. These clubs attempted to teach journeymen and proletarians the virtues of self-reliance. While politics as such was forbidden, there was a definite bias in reading matter, the themes of guest speakers, and the political leanings of club leaders toward liberal goals like freedom of speech, assembly, association, and enterprise. Hermann Schulze was also an avid supporter of the workers, arguing that his cooperative movement was the best means of aiding them. Co-ops took a hands-on approach to self-help, taught respect for private property and the laws of economics, and promised to integrate blue-collar workers into the established order. Like so many members of the cultivated and propertied bourgeoisie who were socially aware and active at mid-century, the Mayor of Delitzsch envisioned alternatives to big business and heavy industry that contrast with our stereotypical images of industrialization. However, unlike many frustrated reformers of earlier decades – witness the now-forgotten drive toward aesthetical industrialization – he actually implemented his dreams.

Catholic social activists also began to organize industrial workers. The first attempt came at Regensburg in 1849 when clerics in the town's Pius Association set up a workers' club to compete with liberal educational efforts. Named after Saint Joseph, the patron saint of labor, this club featured religious teachings as well as a fund to support widows and sick or disabled workers. Catholic efforts were more visible in the Ruhr with the founding of eighteen clubs for factory workers and miners claiming perhaps 5,000 members by the mid-1860s. The priests and mastercraftsmen who headed these organizations encouraged members to abandon vulgar habits like swearing, card playing, and drinking, attend mass after work and communion on Sundays, and visit the bedsides of sick or injured comrades. Club meetings featured dues collection, songs from the choir, a sermon from the priest, and perhaps an opportunity for the workers themselves to ask a question or express an opinion. Like Kolping, club leaders believed that religious fundamentals were central to any genuine solution to social problems. Catholic social teaching did more than encourage docility and passivity, however, for it also gave the leaders a certain activism as they made demands on factory and mine owners, provided club benefits, and emulated the mutual aid programs of the Schulze-Delitzsch cooperatives. Oftentimes, moreover, club activities like the funeral procession for victims of mine accidents exuded a definite air of resentment against present social conditions. "One is reminded here," observes Klaus Tenfelde, "of the powerful demonstrations of the suppressed workers during the years of the Anti-Socialist Laws [after 1878] when ... the burial of some [Social Democratic] party leaders and friends was used for the expression of silent protest."[9]

Liberal organizational activities intensified in the early 1860s. As we shall see, elements within the Nationalist Society grew disillusioned with the prospects of Prussian leadership as the constitutional conflict escalated in Berlin. While some liberals were revolted by the idea of mass support, others saw this as a mandatory part of the parliamentary struggle. Thus Rudolf von Bennigsen, one of the Society's founders from Hanover, warned in January 1862 that popular backing was the only way to avoid being torn asunder by "clerical and political reactionaries on the one side and the threatening workers' question on the other."[10] Schulze-Delitzsch, another charter member, was even more adamant in this respect. A Prussian Diet Deputy and spokesman for the Society's left wing, it was he who appeared before the Frankfurt Shooters' Festival in June. The rather cool reception granted him there helps to explain the subsequent leftist bid to mobilize the workers educational associations. "After the Summer of 1862," concludes Christian Gotthardt, "the honorables of the Nationalist Society turned to the workers clubs, promised ideological and logistical

9. Klaus Tenfelde, *Sozialgeschichte der Bergarbeiter an der Ruhr im 19. Jahrhundert* (Bonn, 1977), 392.

10. Cited in Christian Gotthardt, *Industrialisierung, Bürgerliche Politik und Proletarische Autonomie: Voraussetzungen und Varianten sozialistischer Klassenorganisationen in Nordwestdeutschland 1863 bis 1875* (Bonn, 1992), 129.

support for their educational efforts, and expected in return the workers' and journeymen's adherence to [the Nationalist Society's] national-political program."[11] As the radical trend continued that October with the advocacy of the Frankfurt Constitution of 1849, liberals at the local level founded new clubs and won new recruits. "The workers eagerly joined the societies which the liberals helped them to form," recalled August Bebel, member of a Saxon club, "and regarded the liberal leaders as their most devoted friends."[12] Over 225 clubs were founded between 1860 and 1864 alone. Membership, always difficult to determine, stood somewhere between 25,000 and 50,000 in the mid-1860s.

As liberal and Catholic organizers sought to spread their principles among industrial workers, a third ideology entered the competition. Throughout 1862 liberal workers had sought more influence in the Nationalist Society, only to be sent away by condescending bourgeois who wanted mass support but would not stoop to a genuine alliance. After a Saxon labor delegation failed to win liberal approval for an independent congress of workers in February 1863, indignant club members turned to Ferdinand Lassalle. The self-styled socialist author, philosopher, and attorney from Leipzig accepted their offer, then articulated his views in an open letter to the city's workers in March.

Unlike the self-help, *laissez faire* solutions of the liberals, Lassalle advocated state-financed factories and workshops managed communally by the workers themselves. These producer associations would break proletarians' ironlike dependency on wages and enable them to advance to a rightful place in the social order. To assure state assistance, workers had to push for universal suffrage, then use their votes as leverage. Lassalle followed this journalistic fanfare with a series of now-famous secret negotiations with Bismarck. The sly aim of these talks was to convince the Minister President that workers with votes would represent a valuable weapon against the liberal opposition in Berlin. Although intrigued, Bismarck was too clever himself to be tricked by a slight of hand. "What was there that Lassalle could have offered or given me [when] he had noth-

11. Ibid., 129.
12. Bebel, 44-45.

ing behind him?"[13] The agitator from Leipzig was undaunted by this setback, establishing the General Union of German Workingmen in May 1863. By the following summer the new political organization numbered around 4,500 members drawn mainly from Saxony, Rhineland-Westphalia, Hanover, and Bremen.

The liberal and socialist initiatives of 1862/63 induced the Bishop of Mainz, Wilhelm Emmanuel von Ketteler, to issue his own programmatic statement. Ketteler was one of a limited but growing number of Catholic clergymen who sought solutions to social problems in the ideas of St. Thomas of Aquinas. This medieval theologian had believed that every man had a God-given right to share in the fruits of the land. Only through ownership of or access to material things would he be able to care for his family, develop his potential, and achieve his destiny. It followed that no individual or social class could abuse or monopolize property at the expense of other community members. Thus the social function of property limited not only the use of property, but the right of property itself. Published in March 1864, Ketteler's *The Labor Question and Christianity* took a Thomistic approach to the great driving issue of the day. Like liberal and socialist leaders, he was convinced that only cooperative or communal labor institutions could assure industrial workers the benefits of property and rescue them from social oblivion. Without the humbling influence of Christianity, however, selfishness would come to the fore and ruin the cooperative movement. Thus Ketteler advocated "Christian" labor organizations that would combine the "material and moral protection" of the Catholic worker clubs, the "cooperative self-help"[14] principles of Schulze's movement, and the negotiating functions of English trade unions. Because the liberals and socialists were too preoccupied with strictly political solutions to social problems to place any faith in trade unions, Ketteler therefore became one of the first in Germany to favor this spreading English form of labor organization. It is important to note the theoretical nature of this program, however, for freedom of association in the political realm (to which unions were usually relegated) did not exist in most states of the German Confederation.

13. Cited in Georg Brandes, *Ferdinand Lassalle* (New York, 1925), 218.

14. Citations from Eric Dorn Brose, *Christian Labor and the Politics of Frustration in Imperial Germany* (Washington, 1985), 31.

While these ideological and political controversies raged, the workers themselves began to take initiatives. In 1862 printers journeymen formed associations in Leipzig and Berlin to represent themselves before employers. The days were over, noted the young Berliners, when they would "trustfully place our fate in the hands of our principals."[15] A similar trade-union-like organization was founded for printers' employees from nine cities of the middle Rhine at Frankfurt in 1863. The most dramatic sign of labor's dawning new era came at Leipzig in 1865 when 800 printers' journeymen struck against their "principals." Both the printers of Leipzig and sympathetic cigarmakers who supported the action founded national trade unions in the aftermath of the strike. As we shall explain below, however, the real take-off point for German unionism awaited legislation in 1868/69 that legalized trade unions and strikes throughout Prussia and northern Germany in the newly formed North German Confederation.

15. Cited in Ulrich Engelhardt, *"Nur vereinigt sind wir stark": Die Anfänge der deutschen Gewerkschaftsbewegung 1862/63 bis 1869/70* (Stuttgart, 1977), 181

Chapter 17

The View from the Atelier

The Düsseldorf Academy of Art was torn asunder by the revolutionary social and economic changes transforming town and country. While its zealous, arch-conservative director, Wilhelm von Schadow, promoted religion through art (see below), younger talents broke with him and seceded. On this side of the school were socially concerned artists like Carl Wilhelm Hübner, whose depictions of struggling handicraftsmen and emigrants were powerful appeals for meaningful action. Hübner's political friend, Johann Peter Hasenclever, was similarly affected by the ongoing social transformation. He was probably the first German artist, however, to direct his attention away from the artisans and peasants and toward the struggling industrial proletariat.

Hasenclever's *Workers Stand Before the Magistrates* is set in the exquisite rococo conference room of a Rhenish town hall. On the left, six workers have entered the room with written demands. They are dressed in the best clothes that they possess, but only one looks deferential while the others, especially the petition-bearer, are determined and defiant. On the right, twenty-two patrician city councilors glance up from their deliberations with looks of anger, surprise, and fear. One portly magistrate dressed appropriately in a gold vest wipes sweat from his brow with a white handkerchief. The two adversarial classes of society are divided by rays of sunlight that stream through storm clouds into the room. As a servant rushes to close the tall double window, one of the workers points threateningly to a mob in the square being harangued by an agitator. When Karl Marx saw Hasenclever's courageous, class-conscious proletarians in 1853, he exclaimed that the artist had recreated "in full dramatic vitality that which the journalist can only analyze."[1]

The painting was inspired by similar events which occurred in Düsseldorf in October 1848. Thus *Workers Stand Before the Magistrates* is also part of the rich artistic legacy of Europe's year of upheaval. Indeed this Rhenish district capital spawned a great deal of art related to revolutionary developments. The *Düsseldorfer Monthly*, a satirical magazine with a serious political agenda, boasted in Andreas Achenbach one of the most talented graphic caricaturists in nineteenth-century Germany. His illustrations and cartoons cut with a rapier wit to the quick of conservative establishments. One engraving entitled *Charitable Contributions for Silesia* depicted Prussian soldiers dragging coffins to bury the suppressed lower classes of that depressed province. Another showed Metternich collapsing on his chair in shock after hearing the news of revolution in Vienna. Achenbach's most memorable woodcut, *Current of the Times*, presents Louis Phillip with all his money in England. As the deposed French monarch reclines to his right on a sofa, a torrent of angry rebels streams leftward past his island exile, pushing, shoving, and trampling horrified continental monarchs and ministers. Achenbach's use of black shading for the rioting people made their shouting faces and outstretched arms blend into an impersonal mass of ruthless surging energy. The image could not have been more frightening to an upper class already paralyzed by the uprising of what seemed to be dark subterranean forces.

The unrestrained violence of the lower classes frightened the middle class as well as the aristocracy, dividing well-to-do patricians from unprivileged commoners just as Hasenclever had done in his painting. We can pursue this theme further in the work of Adolph Menzel. His pre-1848 paintings displayed dissatisfaction with the staus quo and a noticeable longing for the dawning of a new era. Consistent with these sentiments, the artist responded positively to the apparent fall of the old order. Present in Berlin

1. Cited in Kalnein, *Düsseldorfer Malerschule*, 331.

shortly after the street fighting, Menzel began work on *The March Casualties Lying in State*. The picture reproduces the moving scene on the square of the Gendarmenmarkt when thousands of Berliners from all classes viewed the stacked coffins of the 183 civilians killed four days earlier. Menzel, as he later recalled, had taken up brush "with pounding heart and in high enthusiasm for the ideas in the service of which the victims had fallen." Yet it would remained unfinished. While aesthetic reasons may have played a role – Menzel, unlike Achenbach, often included too much realistic individual detail to control his crowd scenes – politics also contributed. For as Berlin's deteriorating law and order moved him to the realization that the March events "had been a lie or stupidities," recalled a colleague, he "turned the picture to the wall and ... no longer wished to lay a hand on it."[2]

Alfred Rethel's *Another Dance of Death* reflects the same middle class disillusionment with the revolutions of 1848. Completed shortly before the Dresden uprising of May 1849, the series of six woodcuts employs the medieval motif of death appearing as a skeletal harbinger of doom. The bony champion rides toward town with a pruning hook over his shoulder, frightening some of the more prudent country people who hurry out of his way. But the petty bourgeois burghers are misled by Death's rousing egalitarian rhetoric into a hopeless and bloody revolt. The final panel shows the mounted skeleton departing over a demolished baricade as an artillery crew stands at ease in the background. One dying fighter looks Death disbelievingly in the face. Robert Reinick's accompanying verse drew the obvious but somber conclusion: "See, he has unmasked himself! / As victor, high on horseback, / The mockery of decay in his eyes, / The hero of the red republic rides away."[3] *Another Dance of Death* was Rethel's warning to the traditional handicraft classes threatened by industrialism that the revolution's worthy goals – constitutional government and national unification – had been taken too far in a radical, communistic direction.

The defeat of the revolution granted the Nazarenes an Indian Summer of favor and fading influence. Wilhelm von Schadow

2. Citations in Peter Paret, *Art as History: Episodes in the Culture and Politics of Nineteenth-Century Germany* (Princeton, 1988), 101.

3. Ibid., 112.

directed his students to devote redoubled energy to the mythical, religious, and historical themes which he was sure would contribute to the nation's spiritual and political recovery. He received renewed encouragement until his retirement in 1859 from bureaucrats in Berlin who wanted to maintain control over a changing society. During the decade after the great mid-century revolutions, Schadow's truest disciples brought the great opuses begun in the 1830s and 1840s to an end: the frescoes in the Apollinaris Church in Remagen; the murals of Castle Stolzenfels near Koblenz; and the friezes of the Royal Palace in Dresden. One follower, landscape painter Johann Wilhelm Schirmer, transplanted Schadow's cause to the newly founded Art Academy of Karlsruhe. Like the master, he was determined to wage war against the "realistic direction of our times" and make sure that "all art and science serves the church."[4] Typical of his later works was *The Four Times of Day* (1856) which weaves the biblical story of the Good Samaritan into beautiful natural settings far away from modernity's sins and corruption.

The leftist coteries of the Düsseldorf School, meanwhile, drifted into exile and decline. Police harassed Lorenz Clasen, editor of the *Düsseldorfer Monthly*, into early retirement in 1850. He left town for an obscure, unproductive existence in Leipzig where he later died. Andreas Achenbach abandoned his satirical engravings and turned to sea- and landscapes almost totally devoid of political message. Only the oft-repeated theme of man mastering the storm hinted at his deeply buried hope for a democratic Germany. A fellow illustrator at the magazine, Benjamin Vautier, produced even more innocuous paintings like *An Arrest*. This street scene concentrates on the psychology of gossiping, pitying neighbors who look down a narrow alley as a man is led away. There is nothing to prevent the viewer from concluding that the distant, dejected fellow and his weeping wife deserve their fate. Ludwig Knaus, another leftist who had broken with Schadow, also found a market for harmless idylls like *The Golden Wedding Anniversary*, a celebration of love, marriage, and village tradition.

In other paintings by Knaus, however, the anger and social voice of Young Düsseldorf lived on past the disappointments of 1848/49.

4. Cited in Kalnein, 135.

In *Card Cheats*, for instance, two devilish old regulars at a local tavern have succeeded in parting a naive farmer from his money. The look of defeat and doom on the young man's face as his daughter, sent too late from home to fetch him, looks on, poignantly captures the mood of dispair which swept much of rural, small-town Germany at mid-century. *Funeral Procession in the Forest*, which made Knaus's reputation when it was exhibited in Berlin, projects the same powerful emotions. He depicts two journeys to oblivion – one that has ended and one not far from its terminus – as children accompany casket bearers past a hungry vagabond.

With the escalation of political conflict in Prussia during the early 1860s, Knaus's critical politics came closer to the surface. *His Majesty Traveling,* painted in 1867, shows the inhabitants of a hamlet receiving William I. The villagers are aware of the historic moment, but obviously expect nothing good or merciful from their royal visitor. Only a dog and the blissful children seem impressed. "The face of the sovereign, who wears a gray officers coat and a cap on his head, exudes coldness, unkindness, contempt for humanity, and restrained malice,"[5] observes Wolfgang Hütt.

Such irreverence did justice to the Düsseldorf tradition of Clasen, Hübner, Hasenclever, and Achenbach. By this time, however, middle class factions and parties in Germany were increasingly unsure whether they should reject the Hohenzollerns – or worship their success.

Twenty years after painting the casualties of March 1848, Adolph Menzel felt this ambivalence. Although well established in Berlin, he accompanied the Prussian armies which defeated Austria in 1866, drawn more to the field hospitals than to the headquarters. "Among the results of this expedition are studies in pencil and watercolor of the naked corpses of soldiers, which in their merciless objectivity are unequalled in the art of the nineteenth century."[6] Four years later Menzel stayed behind as Prussia sent troops westward for the climactic campaign against France. His artistic contribution to this historic moment was *The Departure of William I to Join the Army*. Interestingly enough, the sovereign's

5. Wolfgang Hütt, *Die Düsseldorfer Malerschule 1819-1869* (Leipzig, 1964), 144.
6. Paret, 156.

carriage and bodyguard of plumed mounted guardsmen are in the middle distance of this painting. In the background protrudes City Hall's red brick tower – a symbol of *civilian* institutions – while in the foreground, well-dressed people line the street. Most are cheering for William, but some turn to walk away or are engaged in other pursuits. The hard-working burghers and patricians of Berlin and Germany, Menzel seems to say, are the basic substance and foundation of the new empire.

A few months later, the artist's friend, Theodor Fontane, congratulated Menzel and sent him a poem commemorating the triumphant return of the soldiers from France. As the men pass the statue of Frederick the Great, Fontane has the Great One lean down and whisper: "Good evening, gentlemen – *now it is enough*."[7] Clearly the writer's feelings were also mixed about the great events of 1870.

* * * *

Theodor Fontane's career by this time had turned from poetry to journalism, history, and historical novels. Employed periodically by a government newspaper during the 1850s, he finally acquired a permanent position with the *Kreuzzeitung* in 1860. The editors of this conservative paper were impressed with a series of essays Fontane had begun on the history of noble families in the garrison towns and country stretches within a day or two of Berlin. The first of five volumes of his *Wanderings through the Mark Brandenburg* appeared in 1861. The choice of this subject reflected the tempering, sobering effect on the author of events since 1848. One had to cast a wary eye on common people prone to violence, question the realism of middle class politicians, and attempt to appreciate and learn from the history of an old, persevering elite. Fontane still believed that the bourgeoisie would be "a brisk and free breeze in the sails of our ship of state." But Prussia also needed "the saving anchor, whose iron prong in the sands below holds us firm when the breeze threatens to turn into a storm,"[8] he wrote in metaphoric reference to Ludwig von der Marwitz, a die-hard Junker from the Reform Era.

7. Ibid., 158.
8. Ibid., 161.

The deeper Fontane's wanderings allowed him to peer into the Junker mentality, however, the more he gravitated back to earlier prejudices against their class egoism. While researching the second volume in 1862, for instance, he ate in plain traveling clothes at the table of one noble family. "Actually it is quite immaterial how one appears before such ladies and gentlemen," he wrote, "[for] an abyss divides us, and no patent pump on earth can fill it."[9] The *Wanderings* would continue to occupy the poet-historian until the 1880s, but already by 1863, he had begun work on another project which sought to express his shifting, maturing political convictions.

Johann Peter Hasenclever's *Workers Stand Before the Magistrates*, 1848. Art and the Proletarians.

Finally appearing fifteen years later, *Before the Storm* was the first of those many historical novels that would make Fontane famous. The story was set in eastern Prussia prior to Napoleon's invasion of Russia. A group of estate owners and patriots leads an unauthorized assault on a French-held garrison and fails. Through one of the characters, a young bourgeois law student who fights bravely, is captured, and executed, Fontane demonstrates that the aristocracy has no monopoly on chivalry and courage and that the middle class deserves upper class respect. The fact that civilians initiated the attack was important to Fontane's wider critique of German

9. Ibid., 162.

society after the defeat of Napoleon III. Indeed the spreading official patriotism of the 1870s, with its emphasis on unquestioning acceptance of the state, lent a timely quality to *Before the Storm*. Its emphasis on the importance of civil society reinforced the message of Menzel's *Departure of William I to Join the Army*.

Friedrich Spielhagen's novelistic flurry of the 1860s lent added weight to the assault on aristocratic pretensions. Like Fontane, he found employment in an assortment of non-creative positions in order to survive, including a stint as tutor for a noble family in Pomerania. It was here that the egalitarian, democratic-minded Spielhagen absorbed knowledge about the class he later pilloried in successive novels. *Problematic Natures* (1862) introduced readers to Dr. Oswald Stein, a family tutor whose intellect, manners, and physical prowess are clearly superior to the bluebloods around him. Despite these qualities, however, he is treated as a non-entity. "There must be tutors, just as there must be laborers in the arsenic mines," declares one haughty aristocrat, "although I, for one my part, would like to be neither the one nor the other." Victory in a duel against a nobleman only makes matters worse for Stein as the deceased's class compatriots now shun and insult the "problematic" bourgeois. Other novels like *The von Hohensteins* (1865) and *In the Rank and File* (1866) mocked the nobility's unproductive life of leisure. In the former, for instance, young Wolfgang von Hohenstein, as yet unspoiled by aristocratic ways, contrasts the industriousness of middle-class men and women with his father's new fiancée. "How luxuriously Madame President leaned back in the swelling cushions, how lazily her satiated, white hands played with the long ears of the lap-dog, how often the work of the young lady paused, if one could call her frivolous tinkling on the piano, work."[10] In numerous passages like this in his novels, Spielhagen advanced the notion that the nobility, although still very powerful, was innately inferior to a middle class which would someday assume its rightful place.

The confident, proselytizing side of bourgeois thinking was epitomized by Gustav Freytag's classic, *Debit and Credit* (1855). The

10. Citations from Ernest K. Bramsted, *Aristocracy and the Middle Classes in Germany: Social Types in German Literature 1830-1900* (Chicago, 1964), 158, 188.

massive educational novel presents three alternative developmental paths for the individual: the pretentiousness, laziness, and overindulgence of the aristocracy; the deceit and manipulative behavior Freytag attributed to Jews; or the wholesome, hard-working life of the German burgher. Of course, there is never really any choice, for the reader is advised from the outset "to seek the German people where it is to be found exercising its diligence, namely at work." Accordingly, we trace the rise of young Anton Wohlfahrt from apprentice clerk, to manager, and finally to partner in a respectable Breslau wholesale firm. The founder of the business, T. O. Schröder, educates Wohlfahrt to the meaning and mission of the modern era. "Only since our cities have grown up have there been civilized states in the world, only since that time has the secret been revealed that free labor alone makes the life of the peoples great and sure and enduring." The vista he opens up for his protégé is of the ascendant bourgeoisie and its code of industriousness supplanting noblemen and their antiquated notions of the meaning of honor. Freytag is quite explicit about this changing of the social guard. Thus at one point in the book an aristocrat proposes a toast to the success "of a German business where work is a joy, where honor has its home."[11] Nor should these themes surprise us, for the author was co-editor of *Grenzboten*, a liberal journal in Leipzig, and an active member of the Nationalist Society. The message of Freytag's novel, in other words, was a highly politicized one.

The literary structure of *Debit and Credit* was designed to correspond with its propagandistic themes. The "realistic" style coming into vogue in the 1850s stressed the significance of detail and the literal meaning or "transparency" of words, as Russell Berman describes it. Educated, enlightened authors could assume that readers had achieved similar levels of sophistication and were therefore capable of understanding the meaning of words, appreciating the importance of details, and penetrating beyond all of this, importantly, "to perceive the general law encoded in the particular detail which only the untrained might misperceive as accidental."[12] This was, in fact, the careful, studied approach that readers of the day

11. Ibid., 114-115.

12. Russell A. Berman, *The Rise of the Modern German Novel: Crisis and Charisma* (Cambridge, Massachusetts, 1986), 80.

took to *Debit and Credit*. Conrad Alberti, a novelist of the 1880s, declared that "any German with the slightest claim to being cultured has read the novel one, two, even three times."[13] The particular details of the book that the reader must order are the minute daily operations and routines of the firm of T. O. Schröter. The code or fundamental law behind the empirical details which readers were invited to discover was nothing short of a "blueprint for an aggressive economic modernization." And the key to this unfolding material progress was the *desire* to accumulate objects of exchange coupled with the necessary *asceticism* to prevent middle class acquisitiveness from leading to societal collapse. Thus the "social strategy" of bourgeois emancipation and domination "generates the aesthetics of [literary] realism."[14] The book's specific style, in other words, served the economic and political agenda of the author.

Published two years later, Adalbert Stifter's *Indian Summer* contrasted with *Debit and Credit* in content, style, and political message. A school inspector in Linz whose liberalism and confidence in progress had been undermined by the jolting experience of 1848 in Vienna, Stifter tells the story of a young hiker, Heinrich Drendorf, seeking shelter from a storm in the mountains of Upper Austria. He finds the orderly estate of Baron Risach, an enobled bourgeois who invites him inside. Risach appears to be a champion of culture and progress. He possesses an impressive library; his fields are a model of scientific agriculture; and he seems to look brightly into the future. "What will it be like when we can send messages across the whole earth with the speed of lightning, when we ourselves will be able to reach the most diverse places on earth with alacrity in the shortest of times, and when, with the same speed, we will be able to transport great shipments?" In the course of his plodding novel, however, Stifter makes it clear that Risach's estate is actually an escape from the impending chaos and entropy of the modern world. He dislikes its bureaucratization, overconsumption of goods, and shoddy workmanship. Risach prefers the ancient Greeks to modern men, "as if the seriousness of their being and their respect for themselves disallowed the excesses that later ages considered

13. Katherine Roper, *German Encounters with Modernity: Novels of Imperial Berlin* (London, 1993), 2.

14. Quotes from Berman, 80, 90-91.

attractive." His remedy for the disintegration of modern times is a stultifying, machine-like order where things are never out of place. Stifter reinforces his anti-modern message with stylistic devices like long sentences without punctuation, as if commas would somehow interrupt order and begin the process of collapse. He also dictates the story in the first person, avoiding the give and take of dialogue and thus impeding the sophisticated exchange of meaning between author and reader so important to literary realism. The odd punctuation and "authoritarian mode of address,"[15] argues Berman, were stylistic precursors of modernistic novels which questioned the benefits of industrialism in the decades before 1914.

While *Indian Summer* was a stylistic departure in its day, doubts about Germany's social and economic transformation were not uncommon to the literature of this period. Writers like Berthold Auerbach, Friedrich Hebbel, Gottfried Keller, and Wilhelm Raabe glorified life in villages and small towns, usually portraying big cities as places one had to escape to find redemption. Raabe's *Hunger Pastor* (1864) is typical of this genre. The protagonist is born in a small town, studies theology, and comes into his own in a poor village parish on the Baltic. The book was also full of sympathy for the ephemeral era of handicraft production, opening with a moving description of the boy's father, a talented cobbler who loves his work, but dies prematurely. Even Gustav Freytag's *Debit and Credit*, otherwise an apotheosis of capitalism, exhibits a preference for development within traditional bounds. The company of T. O. Schröter is a patriarchal family business more typical of the past than the future. Excessive growth and accumulation is painted blackly as something desired only by the alien Jew. Industrialism's literary reception, so full of controversy and ambiguity, yields valuable evidence for historians seeking to understand this era, for understanding, shaping, and coping with their times was exactly what agents of contemporary culture were trying to do.

In conclusion we turn to another popular novel of the mid-nineteenth century, Joseph Viktor Scheffel's *Ekkehard*. Published initially in 1855, it was reprinted in 1862, then went through a hundred editions by the mid-1880s. Scheffel, like Fontane, was a gifted historian

15. Quotations from ibid., 125-26, 128, 132.

who preferred to present his evidence in a more readable fictional medium. *Ekkehard* is based on the medieval chronicles of the Monastery of St. Gall. It tells the story of a Swabian monk who falls in love with a duchess, fights against the invading Hungarian horsemen of Attila, then repairs to a mountain retreat to chronicle the epic tale. Unlike Fontane, Spielhagen, or Freytag, however, there is no obvious political message to Scheffel's work. And yet, as Peter Paret observes, the story-like innocence of *Ekkehard* was itself politically significant. Until mid-century, the Middle Ages had been expropriated as powerful symbols in the cause of politics: by conservatives and religious zealots who wanted to establish a bulwark against all change; as well as by nationalists who wanted to reestablish a German state. But Scheffel "domesticated" the period and "took away its power to impose chiliastic demands on the present." This "embourgeoisment of the Middle Ages," suggests Paret, may help to explain the remarkable popularity of the book. For after 1870, with the German Question settled and unification achieved, "it was no longer necessary to tap medieval sources for inspiration."[16] *Ekkehard* was not a call for commitment and struggle, but rather a device for celebrating what had been achieved.

Hermann Grimm, a prominent Goethe scholar at the University of Berlin in the 1870s, commented explicitly on these shifting political and historical emphases in German literature.

> Before Germany became united and free and stood politically on its own feet, [he wrote], the goal of our historical work was to submerge ourselves in the past, from which … we dared to derive a better present for ourselves. All historical works bore the secret motto: things cannot possibly remain as they are in Germany … [But now] we possess a present that far surpasses our desires. Its offerings are no longer, as before, merely something to be hoped for or attained, but something to be held fast, developed, and exploited. In the dawn of this new day, we see past ages in a different light. We no longer search in them for weapons to help us win our freedom. Rather, now that the battle for freedom has been won, we search for that which will strengthen our new position and secure our possession of the goods we have gained.[17]

16. Paret, 147.

17. Cited in Peter Uwe Hohendahl, *Building a National Literature: The Case of Germany* (Ithaca, 1989), 197, 187.

Like the sculptor in Friedrich Spielhagen's *Storm Tide* who turns a sedate statue of Homer into a proud Germania by switching heads, the countenance of the times – and of literature – was changing. It was a Janus face, however, for clearly there were those in the world of culture, just as in the everyday workaday world, who fought against these trends.

* * * *

In 1854 King Maximilian II of Bavaria invited Leopold Ranke, professor of history at the University of Berlin, to deliver a series of private lectures in Munich. Having studied with Ranke in the 1830s, the Wittelsbach sovereign wanted him to draw some general lessons from the history of modern times, employing detail only as examples were necessary. Maximilian's invitation to Ranke reflected the scholar's status as the most productive and best known historian in Germany, and probably all of Europe. Indeed since *History of the Latin and Teutonic Nations* appeared thirty years earlier a steady stream of impressive tomes had flowed from Ranke's pen: a history of the popes; a comparison of the Turkish and Spanish monarchies; a history of Germany during the Reformation; and nine volumes on Prussia since the Great Elector. All of these works focused on diplomacy and high politics during the Early Modern Era. They analyzed the interplay between universal, centralizing forces like Catholicism and Habsburg empire-building and distinct "particularistic" cultures struggling for independence – the same tensions which had played themselves out during the cataclysmic era of the French Revolution and the wars of Napoleon. A common theme of these histories, therefore, was the process of nation-building which had preoccupied the Thuringian-born historian since the dramatic, heady, idealistic days of his youth in the 1810s. The same interest lay at the core of Ranke's ongoing research into the rise of nation-states in England and France. These projects consumed most of his time for the next fifteen years, finally appearing in the late 1860s.

The methodology that Ranke employed – and had preached to a generation of students by the 1850s – was as famous as the length and breadth of his publications. The theoretical deductions and generalizations which had characterized the history of the French Enlightenment and the historical philosophy of Hegel yielded in his seminars to an inductive, empirical quest for general truths. One had to discover, amass, and categorize documentary evidence, analyze it objectively and dispassionately, and cull from "the precise establishment of the particular ... the understanding of the general." Ranke was well aware that he strove for an ideal of objectivity rarely if ever realized in practice, but he believed deeply that historians had to pursue this ideal or risk ruining the scientific basis of the discipline. "I have wished," he wrote in his English History, "to extinguish my own self, as it were, and to allow only things to speak." This attempt to divorce one's own passions and prejudices from the analysis made it advisable to study periods remote from the present, but it should be possible to apply the same methods successfully to contemporary history, rigorously avoiding "the influences of transitory personal interests and opinions." Whatever his focus, the historian "must gain an independent point of view from which the objective truth, a general view, opens out more and more."[18]

Ranke intended his comments on objectivity as a warning to younger historians whose works were embroiled in the controversy and drama of the German Question (see below). The old master himself looked askance at these political developments, pleased that some kind of nation-state was forming, but unhappy that Bismarck was tampering with monarchical principles and diluting the Prussian state with German institutions. Undergraduates at the university were more cause for concern, for they were turning away from his classes to attend more exciting, politically charged lectures. Ranke's last course in 1871 had to be canceled because of low enrollment. As the present grew increasingly disappointing, the septuagenarian lost himself in the Greek classics he had studied as a young man. "These hours raised me out of the orbit of views which dominate the modern world into higher and, as it were, purer regions."[19] Like others before him, Ranke returned in old age to an antiquity which was once a powerful symbol of

18. Citations from Leonard Krieger, *Ranke and the Meaning of History* (Chicago, 1977), 248, 269, 271.

19. Ibid., 292.

progress, but had now dissipated into nostalgia for lost or partially realized visions.

Friedrich Karl von Savigny had been another pioneer of Germany's empirical historicism. But, like Ranke at the end, he had good reason to be disillusioned about present times. A giant on the law faculty at Berlin since 1810, Savigny devoted a career to the idealistic notion of a society held in balance by jurists. Professors of jurisprudence – not judges, lawyers, or bureaucratic codifiers – would know how to appreciate local and regional differences, preserve legal traditions, and rule through their scholarly treatises on what was wise and fair. The model for this autonomous jurists' estate was Rome's early imperial period when emperors like the great Hadrian had respected the institution of the law. Savigny's vision for a new era of Roman law began to fade in the 1830s and 1840s with the injustice done to the Göttingen Seven and the subsequent onslaught of the Germanists (see Part III). And, if the latter's day passed with their inability to shape legal and political unity for German Europe in 1848, the 1850s brought no solace. For a younger generation began to abuse the "true" legacy of ancient Rome. Historians of the law like Theodor Mommsen and Rudolf von Jhering undermined the image of Roman morality and nobility with their emphases upon its commercial energy and capitalist drive. Other young scholars turned to Roman law as the underpinning for that national code of laws Savigny had always opposed. Worse still, some were so caught up in the present that they rejected the ancient past as any source of inspiration for political or legal change. Thus Bernard Windscheid, later architect of the German Civil Code (1896), wanted to discard antiquity, relegating it to a purely aesthetical role: "When the authority of [Roman law] is put aside in Germany, then ... the lecture halls of the teachers of Roman law shall truly fill; and the rising generation shall ... learn, not contempt for national law, not the foolish exaltation that bends all law to the measure of Roman concepts – but what one learns from antiquity, what beauty is."[20] Savigny closed his eyes on this disappointing world in 1861.

20. Cited in James Q. Whitman, *The Legacy of Roman Law in the German Romantic Era: Historical Vision and Legal Change* (Princeton, 1990), 228.

Jacob Burckhardt, professor of history at the University of Basel, was another alienated scholar at mid-century. One of Ranke's most gifted students, Burckhardt devoted his first book, *The Age of Constantine* (1853), to the fall of ancient civilization and the emergence of a new western culture. The young man finished his best known work, *The Civilization of the Renaissance in Italy*, seven years later. In this comprehensive cultural history, Burckhardt offered a portrait of the individualistic and humanistic impulses that gave rise to Europe's modern era. Like Ranke, he believed that historians had to divorce themselves from present cares and controversies and use the evidence to feel their way into other times. "My starting point has to be a vision," he wrote a friend, "for instance, historical vision issuing from the old sources."[21] Burckhardt turned his back on modern times much earlier and more emphatically than Ranke, however, lamenting in 1848 how "discouraged" he was "with the nineteenth century." Accordingly, he chose serene and sleepy Basel, a throwback to another era, over the industrial rumblings and democratic tremors of bigger cities and towns. In his imagination, similarly, Burckhardt removed himself to older civilizations allegedly superior to contemporary Europe. While the Renaissance was midwife to modern times, it had nevertheless achieved more by freeing art from political and religious controls. The late nineteenth century worried him by comparison. "We have entered an era of wars in which many aspects we believed formed part of our intellectual life will be thrown overboard as intellectual luxury."[22]

Only in a historiographical sense was Burckhardt a harbinger rather than a critic of modernity, for he departed from Ranke's brand of political history to write cultural history. This choice grew out of his love for poetry and landscape painting as well as the linguistic emphases of Jacob Grimm and August Boeckh, two of Burckhardt's professors at Berlin. He was also more open to the possibility that research could lead to more than one historical "truth." "The same studies that have served this work," he wrote

21. Cited in the editor's preface (p. x) to Jacob Burckhardt, *The Civilization of the Renaissance in Italy* (New York, 1960).

22. Both citations from Felix Gilbert, *History: Politics or Culture: Reflections on Ranke and Burckhardt* (Princeton, 1990), 65, 73.

in an introduction, "might easily, in other hands, not only receive a wholly different treatment and interpretation, but might also lead to essentially different conclusions."[23]

Burckhardt's mature tolerance for other historical opinions reflected the growing tendency in his day toward politicized scholarship. We have already discussed how Johann Gustav Droysen, professor of history at Kiel, devoted his study of the Wars of Liberation and his biography of Alexander the Great to the proposition that Germany would rise to greatness under Prussian leadership. After 1855 Droysen argued stridently in his unfinished *History of Prussian Politics* that Hohenzollern rulers had pursued policies since the fifteenth century that were in the best interests of Germany. Ludwig Häusser of Heidelberg advanced the same theme between 1855 and 1857 with a four-volume history of German Europe in the decades before the Congress of Vienna. The most unabashed champion of Berlin's destiny was Heinrich Sybel, a student of Ranke who taught at the University of Munich. "The historian who seeks to withdraw to an elegant neutrality inescapably becomes soulless or affected," he wrote in 1856. Modern times demanded scholars who were committed to political goals. The time for "objective, impartial historians devoid of blood and nerves"[24] had passed. The chorus of pro-Hohenzollern historians in Germany during the mid-1850s so worried Count Rechberg, Austrian plenipotentiary at Frankfurt, that he warned Vienna about the growing influence of this "Prussian school."

But Austria's power was far too great – and memories of the Holy Roman Empire still too dear – for the shrill advocates of Borussia to go unchallenged. One of the first voices raised in opposition was Joseph Alexander von Helfert, a Viennese bureaucrat whose historical work sought to heighten awareness of Austrian national identity. Another was Onno Klopp, a school official from Hanover who published a biography of Frederick the Great which castigated Prussia's predatory instincts. Klopp and other writers favored a decentralized German state and found much to praise in

23. Cited in Paul K. Conkin and Roland N. Stromberg, *The Heritage and Challenge of History* (New York, 1971), 81.

24. Cited in George G. Iggers, *The German Conception of History: The National Tradition of Historical Thought from Herder to the Present* (Middletown, CT, 1968), 117.

central Europe's federal traditions. Wilhelm Giesebrecht's *History of the German Imperial Epoch* (1859) generated even more controversy with its portrayal of early medieval Germany as a golden era. For Heinrich Sybel lashed out at Giesebrecht's naivete and was attacked in turn by Julius Ficker, a history teacher in the Tyrol who admired the old Empire's religious foundations as well as its delegation of authority to towns and local communities. Small wonder that Ranke, who had taught both Giesebrecht and Sybel, admonished historians to be objective and advised young scholars to distance themselves from contemporary topics.

This tug of war between feuding historians would be decided on the battlefields of Königgrätz and Sedan. Prussia's defeat of Austria in 1866 and France four years later enabled those who had touted Berlin's historical destiny to dominate the historiographical field for over a century. The classic statement of this position was Heinrich von Treitschke's five-volume *German History in the Nineteenth Century* which began to appear in 1879. The Saxon-born liberal was famous for his unilateral advocacy of Prussian Great Power interests long before he accepted a post at the University of Berlin in 1874. His massive and artistic history treated Austria and the Confederation as forces of inertia and resistance which Prussia had to overcome to achieve its mission in Germany. From Treitschke's vantage point, developments had progressed ineluctably along a linear path from the earliest days when the Mark Brandenburg was powerless, to the glorious time of Frederick the Great, the impressive Reform Era, the Prussian-led Customs Union, and finally to unification. Commenting on the opening of the Zollverein in 1834, for instance, he wrote of "a new link, strong though conspicuous, welded into the long chain of events leading the margravate of the Hohenzollerns onward towards the imperial crown. The eagle eye of the great king looked down from the clouds, and from a remote distance could already be heard the thunder of the guns of Königgrätz."[25] "This was not *a* German history," notes Andreas Dorpalen, "but *the* history; it became the gospel of German patriotism, to be taken on faith and not to be

25. Heinrich von Treitschke, *History of Germany in the Nineteenth Century*, translated by Eden and Cedar Paul, (New York, 1919), 5:461.

pedantically dissected, and as such it made its way into thousands of German homes."[26] Like Scheffel's *Ekkehard*, Treitschke's *German History* was a celebration. That the book did not appear as frequently in homes south of the Main River, or receive favorable reviews in the Austrian press, goes almost without saying.

* * * *

1857 marked the advent of what music historians have dubbed "the war of the romantics." Franz Liszt, Orchestral Director in Weimar, conducted his *Faust* Symphony in September of that year, followed by a performance of *Dante* in November. One month after these premiers came *Battle of the Huns*, the eleventh symphonic poem conducted by the Hungarian-born piano virtuoso in recent years. This flurry of performances elicited angry responses from outraged opponents, who spoke of "impure harmony," "gratuitous ugliness," and "no originality, only glitter." One critic charged that Liszt "dosed the listener with a sort of vision-promoting medicine," while another preached the need "to teach temperance at a ginshop door."[27] The composer's new style of music had clearly touched a raw nerve.

The opposition to Liszt boasted some of the biggest names in German music. One of the most influential was Eduard Hanslick, Vienna's prestigeous critic and author of *On Musical Beauty*. Shortly before the second edition of this book appeared in 1858, Liszt had introduced his symphonic poems with their attempt to capture musically the mood or emotion of well-known stories and dramas. This experiment disgusted Hanslick, a firm believer that music inhabited an autonomous sphere quite separate and distinct from the other arts. Because music was not a language, wrote Hanslick, a symphonic "poem" was a contradiction in terms. In the performing world, Liszt's enemies were found among the followers of Felix Mendelssohn-Bartholdy and Robert Schumann. Accomplished and innovative composers in their own right, both had nevertheless adhered to the rules of form, tempo, key and harmony established by the great masters. As if to emphasize their

26. Andeas Dorpalen, *Heinrich von Treitschke* (New Haven, 1957), 223.

27. Citations from Alan Walker, *Franz Liszt: The Weimar Years 1848-1861* (New York, 1989), 361; and Eleanor Perènyi, *Liszt: The Artist as Romantic Hero* (Boston, 1974), 324.

membership in this old school, both were leaders in the cult-like Bach revival of the 1830s and 1840s. Mendelssohn initiated this return to the classics with a spectacular presentation of the *St. Matthew Passion* in 1829, while Schumann used the pages of his *New Journal of Music* after 1834 to advance the notion that "a step back would perhaps be a step forward." Schumann followed Bartholdy to the grave in 1856, but their backward-looking "progressive" cause was continued by Clara Schumann, the composer's wife and a well-known concert pianist; Joseph Joachim, a talented violinist; and Johannes Brahms, a young pianist and gifted, promising composer. "Johannes is the true Apostle," Schumann had written in 1853. Brahms and Joachim publicly condemned Liszt and his "so-called New German School" with its "new and unheard-of theories" in 1860. Their manifesto denounced his creations "as contrary to the innermost spirit of music."[28]

Indeed Liszt's stylistic and structural innovations produced a new, heady kind of musical wine. He occasionally departed from the eight-tone diatonic to the full twelve-tone chromatic scale, creating rare sounds and evoking strong emotions with unusual chords. Liszt's orchestral arrangements also surprised audiences with their colorful use of multiple harps and double-basses, unique massing of drums, cymbals, and gongs, and employment of strange instruments like the bass-clarinet. Harder to appreciate were his glaring polyphonic combinations of contrasting melodies, odd time signatures and uneven rhythms, and frequent modulations of key. Thus one of Liszt's students recalled with pride how he had made an old school musician "sick with fear"[29] by demonstrating how to move from F-sharp minor to C-major in one bar. Perhaps the greatest innovation of the symphonic poem was a single-movement structure which fused the separate movements of the traditional sonata into one. Making this possible was the technique of "transforming" or varying one musical idea throughout the piece. As an admiring biographer observes, Liszt's leading themes "are twisted, unwound, rewoven like a serpent's coil."[30] The combined effect of

28. Citations in Arnfried Edler, *Robert Schumann und seine Zeit* (Düsseldorf, 1982); and Walker, 349-50.

29. Cited in Walker, 332.

30. Perènyi, 316.

so much newness was overwhelming to many listeners, prompting those unused to and intolerant of its effects to demand abstention.

Although he mocked his critics privately, Liszt wisely left the task of counterattacking them to others. And the public champion of the new music, without a doubt, was Richard Wagner. The brilliant but egomaniacal composer had rushed onto the musical scene in the 1840s and 1850s with *Rienzi*, *Tannhäusser*, and *Lohengrin*, operas he described as "music of the future." While these masterpieces anticipated and, to some extent, informed Liszt's musical departures, the embattled innovator in Weimar was more teacher than student. At work on the last part of his famous *Ring of the Niebelungs* trilogy in 1857, for instance, Wagner became so preoccupied with Liszt's symphonic poems that he put on-going work aside to begin writing the score of a new opera, *Tristan and Isolde*.

This composition began an intensification of Germany's new sound which would culminate fourteen years later in *Siegfried*, the final opera of the *Ring* trilogy. Wagner pushed chromatic harmonies, counterpoint, polyphony, and modulations to extremes, testing players and taxing audiences. He also added more trumpets, trombones, and tubas to the orchestra, creating such a din with his brass that the most audible singers had difficulty being heard. The recapitulation of musical ideas was much more pronounced too, witness *Tristan and Isolde* 's thirty motifs "restlessly emerging, developing, combining, separating, then again reuniting, growing, diminishing, finally clashing, embracing and well-nigh engulfing one another,"[31] as Wagner described them. These excesses and lack of proportion prompted Friedrich Nietzsche – surely a perceptive observer – to speak about alarming tendencies in the music. "He came to see Wagner's work," writes Robert Gutman, "as a stupendous effort to assert and dominate, bringing together anything and everything – the neurotic, the ecstatic, the magnificent, the clamorous, all thrown pell-mell within the prodigious frame of grand opera – an art so determined to convince at any cost that all means, course and refined, were used to create effects."[32]

31. Cited in Jack M. Stein, *Richard Wagner and the Synthesis of the Arts* (Westport, 1973), 145.

32. Robert W. Gutman, *Richard Wagner: The Man, His Mind, and His Music* (New York, 1968), 353.

The creations of Liszt and Wagner were in many ways products of the time. Revolution, suppression, political crisis, war, and conquest drew both men to heroic and tragic tales which they attempted to express musically – stories which corresponded, certainly, to the psychological needs of some German Europeans between 1848 and 1871. Wagner's operas were full of martial enthusiasm, witness Lohengrin's raised "German sword for the German land," or Wotan's emboldening words: "Where bold spirits stir, I openly foment war."[33] Performed in November 1857, moreover, Liszt's *Hèroïde funèbre* was a musical monument to the fallen of all wars and revolutions. "It is for art to throw its transfiguring veil on the tomb of the brave," he wrote, "to encircle the dead and dying with its golden halo, so that they may be the envy of the living."[34] Similarly, *Battle of the Huns* memorialized the slaughter at Catalanian Fields as Attila clashed with Theodoric for the capture of Rome. Most of his symphonic poems, in fact, portrayed heroes faced with a dilemma or overwhelming odds. Much more than their stories, however, it was the music of Liszt and Wagner which captured the spirit of the times. Eduard Hanslick was wrong, for the daring and controversial "music of the future" was indeed a language which expressed as well as any written words the change, transformation, dynamism, and sheer energy of the age.

The promise that many traditionalists had seen in Johannes Brahms was realized in the 1860s and 1870s. Appropriately enough, the young musical purist from Hamburg settled in Vienna where so many of the great masters had lived. There his greatest works unfolded. The death of his mother and the fighting between German states moved him to complete *A German Requiem* in 1866. This solemn choral work expressed the theme of reconciling the living to death. Its seven orderly, symmetrical movements were linked by a few recapitulated musical ideas. "If I want to retain the same idea, then one should recognize it clearly in every transformation, augmentation, inversion," he wrote of the *Requiem*. "The opposite would be idle playing around and always a sign of impov-

33. Ibid., 308, 426.
34. Cited in Walker, 324.

erished inspiration."[35] His *Symphony in C-minor* was underway by this time, but not performed until 1876. A tempestuous work designed to mirror life's conflicts, this first symphony seems to signal the onset of catastrophe until a horn solo intones salvation in the final movement. "Then the broadly flowing, hymn-like Allegro proclaims its triumph over all fear and pain,"[36] writes Karl Geiringer. Brahm's *Second Symphony* was composed more quickly in the summer of 1877 during a vacation in the Carinthian village of Pörtschach. Its majestic, romantic D-major movements and light instrumentation for flutes, oboes, and clarinets exuded "rippling streams, blue sky, sunshine, and cool green shadows,"[37] according to one conductor. The progression to third "B" – Bach, Beethoven, and Brahms – now seemed secure.

Even Wagner paid compliments. After hearing Brahms perform some of Händel's variations, for example, he said "one sees what can still be done with the old forms in the hands of one who knows how to deal with them."[38] This was a grudging admission, perhaps, that the old forms were still necessary. Wagner would probably have agreed that the rhythms and harmonies of this older sound offered predictability and security to audiences – sophisticated enough to understand it – who were worried by the revolutionary nature of the times. Thus Brahm's symphonies and choral works were just as much a product of the epoch as the "music of the future." Each was written in a different key, but played together they expressed the polyphony and counterpoint of conflicting forces in a changing society.

* * * *

Austria's military defeats of 1859 and 1866 marked not only the end of a centuries-old era of Habsburg dominance in Italy and German Europe, they also signaled the beginning of different, somewhat freer times at home. The Danube monarchy had risen to

35. Cited in Leon Botstein, "Time and Memory: Concert Life, Science, and Music in Brahm's Vienna," in Walter Frisch (ed.), *Brahms and His World* (Princeton, 1990), 9.

36. Karl Geiringer, *Brahms: His Life and Work* (New York, 1982), 254.

37. Ibid., 129.

38. Ibid., 83.

the challenge of Napoleon and survived revolutionary shocks in 1830 and 1848. Throughout these decades of martial victory and political resistance, the architectural image of Vienna continued to serve as a showcase for Austrian absolutism. Its baroque and Gothic structures, surrounded by an awesome glacis, were a permanent reminder of the system's long tenure, power, and legitimacy. Changes undertaken in the 1850s also corresponded to the reactionary purposes of soldiers and statesmen who could never forget 1848. The obsolete glacis would be replaced by a ring-like boulevard broad enough to permit artillerymen to lay down a deadly pattern of fire should the mob ever rise again. The political liberalization of 1860, however, brought architectural renewal that matched the aspirations and visions of the emperor's parliamentary partners. The "Ring Street" that emerged in the 1860s and 1870s was a monument in stone to the new political direction in Vienna.

Twenty-five meters wide, polyhedral in shape, and many kilometers around, the *Ringstrasse* would accommodate scores of public and private structures before its completion. Most important to the liberal magistrates who now governed the city of Vienna, according to Carl Schorske, were the four buildings which represented liberal values. Shared political power was on display in the Imperial Council, municipal autonomy in City Hall, higher learning in the University of Vienna, and dramatic art in the Burgtheater. The latter was finished in early baroque style "commemorating the era in which theater first joined together cleric, courtier, and commoner in a shared aesthetic experience." The University's style was Renaissance befitting its status as a "citadel of secular rationalism," while City Hall was Gothic "to evoke its origins as a free medieval commune, now reborn after a long night of absolutist rule."[39] And appropriately enough, the parliament building was done in the classical Greek style understood throughout the West as an architectural symbol for freedom, independence, and self-rule. Its designer, Theophil Hansen, placed the eight Corinthian columns of the building's acropolis-like portico on second-story level to accentuate the illusion of height. All four

39. Carl E. Schorske, *Fin-de-Siècle Vienna: Politics and Culture* (New York, 1981), 37-38

buildings were situated on an arc in close proximity to one another, and thus were in easy view of the baroque Hofburg, especially parliament, which was directly across the street. The strategic positioning of these structures, as well as the expropriation of four distinct historic styles, exuded the confidence and optimism of a liberalism which seemed to know that it would master the future.

One year into the reign of Maximilian II, King of Bavaria, travelers began to depart from Munich's Central Train Station. Here too there were signs that its architect, Friedrich Bürklein, wished to master the future, but his confidence was joined by an unmistakable anxiety. For the building was finished in a mixture of the Romanesque and Gothic. Trains entered and departed through five rounded portals that were graced by a stained-glass rose window over the middle arch. On the inside, towering twenty meters above the tracks, were twenty-four wooden arches which supported the superstructure. Rows of half-timbered windows running parallel to the tracks allowed beams of light to enter from high above. Clearly travelers were meant to be in awe of the basilica-like structure, not the smoking, chugging engines dwarfed far below. Traditional architectural styles and building materials were supposed to contain and control technology. Munich's Central Train Station was a good example of the later, anxious stage of the movement toward an "aesthetic industrialization."

This was not the architectural reception that Maximilian professed to favor for modernity. A year after the station opened, he announced a competition for a new architectural style corresponding to the spirit of the times. Unlike Schinkel, Klenze, Hansen, and his father, Ludwig I, Maximilian did not favor classical Greek designs. Bavaria had been a semi-parliamentary state for over three decades and therefore needed no architectural stimulation for or celebration of liberal values. The fundamental idea of the new epoch he defined as a striving for freedom, in particular, the unchaining of all moral and physical forces. Maximilian invited architects to find an appropriate expression for this unfolding of the human spirit and opening up of technological potential. Somewhat contradictorily, however, he suggested that it would be purposeful "not entirely to lose sight of the so-called Old German or

Gothic architecture."[40] His agenda, apparently, was somehow to revive this style and transform it into a symbol of modern times.

Maximilian Street (1853-1863) and its accompanying buildings and bridges were the most representative expression of the king's new architecture. Twenty-three meters wide, the parkway ran eastward nearly 1700 meters from Max Joseph Plaza over the Isar. Midway it widened for about 400 meters into an impressive "forum" flanked on the north by the government building of Upper Bavaria and on the south by the National Museum. These and other structures along *Maximilianstrasse* were finished in a style which even the trained eye could hardly distinguish from Gothic. Behind the multiple piers and pointed-arch windows of their facades, however, was something structurally new. External features like piers, which had once supported buildings, now yielded their function to iron trusses and beams. By using more glass in the Gothic facade – as August von Voit had done in Munich's Glass Palace exhibition hall in 1854 – these skeleton-like supporting structures could have been exploited to produce a transparent or porous effect along the street which might have realized the king's dream of a "free" style for the industrial age. As it was, admitted Maximilian in 1860, the attempt to enliven Gothic architecture had succeeded only in awakening "the spirit of Medieval Germany" while not doing justice "to the modern requirements of our people." He died in 1864, upset that architecture had made no unique contribution to the nineteenth century and worried that its future belonged to a "subjective eclecticism"[41] dictated arbitrarily by political taste.

The contributions of his son, Ludwig II, seemed to confirm these worst fears. Bavaria's famous Dream King was not on the throne for long before his foreign policy hopes were dashed. Vacillation between neutrality and a pro-Austrian stance was disastrous in 1866, while pro-French sympathies were totally out of place in 1870. Ludwig's absolutist pretentions were also problematic in what was becoming a parliamentary state along English lines. These setbacks and frictions combined with the king's shy, lonely

40. The invitation is printed in August Hahn, *Der Maximilianstil in München: Programm und Verwirklichung* (Munich, 1982), 19-21.

41. Citations in Hans Hermann Wetcke, *Die andere Tradition: Architektur in München von 1800 bis Heute* (Munich, 1982), 55-56.

disposition and personal maladjustment to create a longing for escape. The rugged hilly landscapes southwest of Munich proved the perfect setting for those romantic castles the world has come to know. All three afforded easy passage to another dimension: the Gothic Neuschwannstein, patterned after the Wartburg, into the world of minstrels and early Germanic legend; the rococo Herrenchiemsee into the majestic epoch of Versailles and the Sun King; and the isolated Linderhof with its Venus Grotto into the shadowy, alienated world of Wagnerian opera. As the reader will know, Ludwig II eventually found his ultimate escape in the cold, dark waters of Lake Starnberg in 1886.

In Berlin, meanwhile, the seat of the Hohenzollerns passed through its New Era and Wars of Unification. This period witnessed a construction boom featuring a plethora of styles and stylistic mixtures. One of the most unique was the new City Hall (1861-69). Its blend of the Romanesque and Renaissance, tall clock tower patterned after London's Parliament, and colored stone contrasted with nearby palaces and recalled the day when burghers ruled. The Bourse (1859-63) was also done in a variety of styles. Its internal grand hall, twenty meters high, was supported by a base of Ionic columns which yielded at second-story level to an arcade of Corinthian columns. The facade incorporated the same mix of columns in a massive Baroque structure. The early and late classical features, combined with the architectural symbol of absolutism, enunciated a maturing liberalism's need to make compromises with the old order. The National Gallery (1865-69) made a similar statement. Erected on Museum Island close to the Old Museum, its rich Roman motifs contrasted gently with Schinkel's elegant Greek edifice, seeming to describe the inevitable progression from the purity of liberal ideals to the hard reality of political give-and-take, conquest, and empire.

* * * *

What can be said in summary about 'the view from the atelier' during the 1850s and 1860s? Through his upper window the artist looked down on a dramatic and climactic period of German history. Occasionally, outside developments were influenced by his art – usually, in turn, it was colored by them – but always the perceptive observer could learn through art to understand, appreciate, and adjust to the times. The dominant cultural theme or leitmotif between the 1840s and 1870s was change versus order. Painting, literature, historiography, music, and architecture shaped and were shaped by these opposing forces. Culture reflected separate but related struggles between revolution and the old political order; conservative and liberal parties; bourgeoisie and nobility; the corporate economy and industrialism; federalism and nationalism; and Prussia versus Austria. Germans were tugged backwards and forwards and between polar opposites before reaching a balance of sorts in the 1870s. If readers seek cultural symbols that best epitomize the resolution of these conflicts, they need only visit Museum Island in Berlin or walk along Ring Street in Vienna, for the eclectic combination and juxtaposition of styles captures the progressive yet essentially compromising nature of the precarious new equilibrium.

Chapter 18

The Division of German Europe and the Bismarckian Synthesis

Berlin's Hotel Royal provided posh accommodations for the upper classes of Europe. Serviced by their own teams of chamber maids, waiters, porters, and butlers, its spacious luxury suites offered court-like surroundings for visiting dignitaries who could entertain, lobby, or merely enjoy a splendid view of the governmental quarter. In July 1859, the curtains of one room were pulled back to let in fresh air and light for a bed-ridden guest. The wrinkled furrow of his brow was a sign of obvious discomfort. "His Excellency, the Ambassador, will see you now." The butler's voice coming from the door at the end of the entryhall to the suite served as a warning to get composed. The tall, slightly balding man reached for his newspaper and pretended to be reading.

Hans Viktor von Unruh walked into the room and seated himself on a chair beside the bed. "Herr von Bismarck, I was sorry to hear that you were not well." "Always well enough to receive *you*, Unruh. But you know," he said in a raised voice signaling a quick start to the business at hand, "I believe this newspaper pains me more than the quack who treated my knee in St. Petersburg." With that Bismarck hurled the conservative *Neue Preussische Zeitung* to the foot of the bed in agitation. "Why that paper hasn't a trace of Prussian patriotism – its pushing for Prussian support of Austria against France and Italy!" "Many fear, Herr von Bismarck, that after a French defeat of Austria it will be Prussia's turn like 1805 and 1806," replied Unruh politely.

Now the real monologue began. Unruh listened patiently as Bismarck explained that history never really repeated itself in this way; that even if it did, preventing the continued bondage of "the real Germany" to Austria was of greater consequence; and that most of the small and middle-sized states would "dance to the Austrian piper" because their petty existence was less threatened in Vienna than in Berlin. One thing was certain: Prussia was completely isolated in Germany. "There is but one ally for Prussia."

"And which ally is that?" asked Unruh curiously. "The German people!" responded Bismarck emphatically. Unruh drew back in his seat with a startled look on his face. Bismarck quickly surmised the reason, then continued. "Well, what did you think? I am the same Junker as ten years ago when we got to know one another in the diet. But I would have no eyes to see or head to think if I could not recognize clearly the realities of the situation."

Unruh liked what he was hearing. "Herr von Bismarck, if you can do this, even if it goes against your personal inclinations, if you can so quickly size up Prussia's dangerous situation and apply the appropriate remedy with such assurance, then I would much rather have *you* as a Prussian minister."[1]

For a moment, neither man talked. The only sound was Bismarck stroking his mustache like a cat after its meal. The discussion soon ended and Unruh left the room.

* * * *

The ambassador and the businessman had known each other since the United Diet of 1847. Then the nobleman was fresh from his estates and the parochial world of the country squire. The man Unruh greeted in the Hotel Royal, on the other hand, was definitely not the same Junker, Bismarck's assurances notwithstanding. To be sure, eight years in the foreign service – first as Prussian envoy to the Frankfurt Diet, now as William's ambassador in St. Petersburg – had not lessened his love of dogs, horses, and trees; nor would he

1. For Unruh's recollection of the meeting, see Willy Andreas (ed.), *Bismarck: Die gesammelten Werke* (Berlin, 1924), 7:37-39.

ever feel quite as relaxed and content as he did out of the big city. But his political program had undergone some striking changes. Unruh must at least have sensed this or would not have come.

Munich's Central Train Station, 1849. Aesthetic Industrialization.

Even in the early years of his political career, Bismarck had displayed the opportunistic characteristics of a maverick, but in essence, his politics differed little from the conservatives around Leopold von Gerlach. Like the general who stood so close to the king, he was preoccupied with mastering the revolution, buttressing the crown, and preserving the social and political world of the nobility. In foreign affairs this meant solidarity with Austria and Russia, the old stalwarts of the Holy Alliance. By the early 1850s, however, Bismarck sensed the need to adjust to new realities. Revolutionary forces were defeated in Germany, while to the west, Louis Napoleon had also suppressed the Left. Within the Confederation, moreover, Schwarzenberg wanted nothing of the old cordiality between Vienna and Berlin. Not long after assuming his duties at Frankfurt in 1851, therefore, Bismarck began a determined campaign to promote Prussian expansion at the expense of Austria. An alliance with authoritarian France; or with Russia and France; or better still, the appearance of doing these things, would gain Prussia leverage against Austria. Catering to moderate liberal opinion in Germany was another clever means to this end, for in

Frankfurt Bismarck had quickly learned to distinguish between petty rulers who wanted only to preserve their states, and the cultivated and propertied bourgeoisie who were tempted to look toward Berlin for leadership. This experience was reinforced by the Erfurt Parliament (1850) where the squire had come to appreciate the willingness of reasonable "national" liberals to bargain for German unity. As evidenced by an exchange of letters in 1857, Gerlach was not as flexible as his protégé. Unable to travel the same road, the two parted political ways.

The New Era should have blessed Otto von Bismarck. The Regent and his servant both wanted to fortify the crown's political position in Prussia and to strengthen Prussia's image in Germany. And both had made remarkable adjustments to reality in the new age. The man who had warned Frederick William IV against convening the United Diet now selected ministers from his brother's parliamentary opposition. To play this game more successfully, William could have used a man who had "effected the transition from a conservative party politician to that peculiar type [of minister] that the transition from monarchical and bureaucratic absolutism to the party-political, parliamentary system produced and promoted in other countries besides Prussia." This type, continues Lothar Gall, was "the relatively independent cabinet minister who walked a tightrope between the two systems."[2] But William balked at Bismarck's headstrong independence and reputation for recklessness. Making matters worse, Queen Augusta, who sometimes exerted influence on her husband, despised the man whose Machiavellian unscrupulousness clashed with the liberal political culture of her native Saxe-Weimar. Rather than advance him to the Foreign Ministry, therefore, the royal couple put him in "cold storage on the Neva,"[3] as the new ambassador quipped. Except for the occasional return home, Bismarck had to watch from afar as the Italian War passed without any advantages accruing to Prussia – or to himself.

Transfer to Paris in 1860 was a similarly cruel fate for the man who had once toyed with the idea of a Franco-Prussian alliance. Still very far from the center of power, Bismarck could only hope

2. Lothar Gall, *Bismarck the White Revolutionary*, translated by J. A. Underwood, (London, 1986), 1:138.

3. Cited in Pflanze, *Bismarck*, 1:136.

that the escalating constitutional conflict would soon necessitate the presence of a strong man in Berlin. He finally received the call in September 1862. Worried that William would pass the reins to Crown Prince Frederick, a man who relished the chance to work with "Progressivists," Albrecht von Roon convinced a reluctant king to meet with Bismarck.

As his carriage completed the long, wooded approach to Castle Babelsberg, outside Potsdam, the pensive man inside knew that his destiny would probably depend on questions asked and answers given. When asked if he would execute the army reorganization, even against the will of parliament, Bismarck answered "yes." Having anticipated a hard bargaining session, William was relieved and impressed. "Bismarck judged man and mood with complete accuracy," concludes Otto Pflanze. "Despite his doubts about the wisdom of the course [William] was following, he assumed the role of a feudal vassal come to learn his lord's will."[4] So the king decided to continue the struggle and Bismarck became Minister President of Prussia. Faced with an entrenched parliamentary opposition, wrote William to a resisting Augusta, "I could not hesitate – nor would my conscience and my sense of duty any longer allow me to hesitate – to set against this unflinching resolve one equally unflinching."[5]

Bismarck entered office extremely confident and full of himself. The party politicians and speech-makers would not hold out for long, he predicted, especially when presented with dazzling foreign policy initiatives and victories. It soon became evident, however, that the new man had sorely underestimated the complexities of the situation. The promise of bold steps in Germany failed to impress a diet budget committee already convinced that change had to start at home. His tactless reminder that it was "not by means of speeches and majority resolutions that the great issues of the day will be decided – that was the great mistake of 1848 and 1849 – but by iron and blood"[6] was quickly used by the opposition to brand him a warmonger. His fading chances of reaching a compromise on army reform were dashed when William himself refused

4. Ibid., 1:176.
5. Cited Gall, 1:203.
6. Ibid., 1:204.

to yield significantly on the issue of three-year service. With little room to maneuver, Bismarck vented his frustrations in the only direction he could: assaulting the diet with one vituperative outburst after another, including an unfortunate personal attack against Victor von Unruh. In May 1863, a large majority declared that it had "no further means of communicating with this ministry ... All further discussion only strengthens our conviction that between the crown's advisers and the country there exists a gulf that cannot otherwise be filled than by a change in personnel and furthermore a change in the system."[7] There was only one consolation in all of this: the diet's threatening language had angered the king, thus strengthening his determination to retain Bismarck. The adroit minister president used this confidence to exact a Draconian press decree and begin purging the bureaucracy of liberal deputies. Thus relations deteriorated even more as spring turned to summer.

Foreign policy developments compounded Bismarck's difficulties. In October 1862, the Nationalist Society lurched to the left by declaring its advocacy of the Frankfurt Constitution of 1849. Whereas earlier the Society had emphasized German unity above all else, the ugly drift of events in Prussia had convinced some of its leaders that Berlin could not be trusted to fight liberalism's battles. Austria's initiative to reform the Confederation along *Grossdeutsch* lines was also gaining momentum that autumn. Bavaria, Württemberg, Saxony, and Hanover agreed to an Austro-Saxon plan (see above) that was designed to contain and neutralize Prussia. Simultaneously, Julius Fröbel's Reform Association picked up thousands of new members across southern Germany. Indeed to many, Vienna's liberal credentials were now more legitimate than Berlin's. Only by threatening the smaller states with retaliation was Bismarck able to defeat the proposal in January. He accompanied this crude intimidation with a warning that the only viable means to achieve German unity was the creation of a national parliament chosen directly by the people. While this was also frightening to many of the petty rulers who feared for their sovereignty under such an arrangement, it was hardly a credible position for a man locked in bitter struggle with his own diet.

7. Ibid., 1:227.

With Bismarck groping in desperation, Anton von Schmerling pressed Austria's advantage. The competent minister of the interior convinced Francis Joseph to present the empire's unification scheme to William personally in Bad Gastein. All the princes in the Confederation were to congregate in Frankfurt to consider the scheme in August 1863. Bismarck managed to convince his sovereign not to attend, but when the Austrians persisted, sending the King of Saxony to speak with William, the Prussian head of state wavered. An emotional two-hour meeting which saw Bismarck angrily threaten to resign was required to keep the king on course. "Even the history of Byzantium scarcely provides such a picture of decrepitude and confusion as is offered by the present regime in Prussia," barked the organ of the Nationalist Society. The Diet of the Confederation overwhelmingly approved Austria's Federal Reform Act in September, but meekly added the proviso that Prussia must approve. Still playing to an elusive liberal audience, Bismarck vetoed the plan, adding that only a "true national representative body founded on the direct participation of the entire nation" was qualified to mediate between the interests of the states. With that, Schmerling's campaign collapsed. But the bourgeoisie was still unimpressed. "This bare-faced attempt by the Bismarck ministry to turn the jealousy that [Prussia] feels toward Austria into a fresh prop for its shaky existence," fired the Nationalist Society, "will come wretchedly to grief."[8]

It had been a shaky first year for Otto von Bismarck. But there was still reason for optimism. For one thing, the failure of the Federal Reform Act lessened Schmerling's influence and opened doors for his rival, Count Johann von Rechberg. The foreign minister was uncomfortable with Schmerling's nationalistic appeals and disagreed with policies that antagonized Prussia. Rather, Germany's two Great Powers should cooperate to ensure survival in Europe's hostile atmosphere. The escalating situation in Schleswig-Holstein was particularly worrisome. In March 1863, Denmark reopened the issue by taking steps to annex Schleswig, thereby seeming to threaten Holstein as well. Immediately German patriots howled that something must be done to protect these northern provinces.

8. Ibid., 1:233, 235.

The sudden death of the Danish king in November complicated matters further by producing a rival claimant, Friedrich von Augustenburg, a German nobleman who proclaimed himself the Duke of Schleswig-Holstein. At this point the Nationalist Society continued its radical leftist journey by issuing an incendiary appeal for patriotic associations across Germany to gather money and weapons for the new "duke." The princes, as "sons of the common Fatherland," were warned to back Augustenburg's claim. The people of the lesser states would "pardon and forget many wrongs" but never forgive "betrayal of their honor and freedom to foreigners." Eager to add another petty kingdom to their number in the Confederation, Third Germany joined the growing chorus for Augustenburg. Here indeed was a situation ready made to order for a man of Bismarck's manipulative instincts. "By himself the individual can create nothing," he said accurately. One must "wait until he hears God's footsteps resounding through events and then spring forward to grasp the hem of his mantle."[9] Bismarck would try to play Austria and the patriots off against one another to Prussia's advantage.

In late November 1863, Prussia and Austria declared Denmark in violation of the London Treaty of 1852. This series of agreements had obligated Denmark to retain a loose personal union through its monarch with Schleswig and Holstein, or to consult with the duchies before changing their constitutional status. Simultaneously, Vienna and Berlin branded the Nationalist Society's support of Friedrich von Augustenburg as "revolutionary." The states of the Confederation were urged to make similar declarations. These actions were the surprising work of Bismarck. Many observers had expected him to play a liberal hand again by championing the popular rival claimant to the duchies. Instead he cleverly opposed a Denmark roundly hated by Germans, but in a way that chastised the diet majority in Frankfurt, undercut the Nationalist Society, and split Austria from Third Germany only months after they had stood united against Prussia.

Secretly, Bismarck aspired to wage a joint war on Denmark, annex Schleswig and Holstein to Prussia, and finally impress the liberal opposition at home. If Austria, influenced by Rechberg, agreed

9. Citations in Pflanze, 1:80, 239.

to the annexation, this would strengthen Prussia and keep nationalist opponents in Germany divided and off balance. If Austria listened to Schmerling's "Greater German" advice and objected, war would remove Austria and its German confederates from Prussia's path. While it seems clear from numerous remarks that Bismarck wanted to proceed with this Danish strategy, there were still nagging doubts about the likely response of the Prussian Diet. Would the Left abandon its principles and approve the necessary war credits? If not, how would the war be financed? The promising bank consortium formed in 1859 had fallen apart as the constitutional crisis worsened. Bismarck knew that the footsteps of God were sometimes muffled. In which direction were they leading?

War broke out between Denmark and Austria and Prussia in January 1864. Hoping in vain for Swedish assistance or intervention from other powers, the bulk of Denmark's outmanned armies were soon forced to retreat into southern Jutland. Only the formidable trench fortifications of Düppel in eastern Schleswig held out. As the war had approached, Bismarck asked parliament to approve war credits, but the motion was defeated by a huge majority. One Progressive spokesman, Rudolf Virchow, criticized the minister president's policy as a conservative alliance with Austria to preserve an unacceptable status quo in Germany. "He is no longer the man who joined us with the feeling that he was going to accomplish something with an energetic foreign policy,"[10] quipped Virchow in mocking reference to Bismarck's "iron and blood" appeal of 1862. Its war chest nearly depleted, Prussia forced a cease-fire with a bloody assault on the Düppel trenches in April. When the Danes proved intransigent at the negotiating table, Prussia brought the fighting to an end by seizing the strategic island of Alsen in June. Denmark ceded the duchies to Austria and Prussia in October 1864.

The war was over, but its aftermath proved once again how extremely difficult it was to predict – let alone to master – the outcome of a dynamic situation. For one thing, the victors now faced the problem of dividing their spoils. This would have been manageable had Rechberg survived, but Francis Joseph accepted his resignation that same autumn. The foreign minister had wanted to

10. Cited in Gall, 1:245-246.

perpetuate cooperation with Prussia in order to deal with pressing domestic problems (see below) and present a united monarchical front to Napoleonic France. This policy was undercut by climactic negotiations in the Zollverein over Prussia's two-year effort to ratify its free trade treaty with France. Needful of allies in the constitutional conflict, Bismarck wanted to veer from this anti-Austrian course and make tariff concessions to Rechberg. But it was too late. Led by Rudolf von Delbrück, the Prussian Ministry of Trade had forced one state after another to accept the treaty or abandon the lucrative Customs Union. Rechberg's fall brought his rival, Anton von Schmerling, to the fore again. As Bismarck warned the king, this would mean *Grossdeutsch* initiatives in Vienna to sway the small and medium-sized German states, including support for Augustenburg's cause in Schleswig-Holstein. Indeed throughout the winter, friction between Vienna and Berlin over the duchies brought relations to the brink of war. Adding to Bismarck's worries was the fact that parliament ignored his "urgent wish" for an end to the constitutional conflict in January 1865, opting instead to continue fighting "the Bismarck system without regard for the [Danish] victory swindle."[11]

The immediate crises would pass by late summer. Thus Schmerling resigned because of Hungarian developments; Austria and Prussia agreed in the Gastein Convention to share administration of Schleswig-Holstein; and Prussian ministers managed to amass a war chest, without help from the parliament, by selling state properties. But these were only stopgap measures. Well aware of the pressing need for long-term solutions, Bismarck had seriously reconsidered his political options throughout these months. In the process, he underwent a kind of political metamorphosis. The maverick conservative had assumed since the late 1850s that Prussia's internal and external opponents could be easily manipulated. Commercial concessions to the bourgeoisie, lip service to the idea of representative institutions, and bold statements about Prussia's German mission would somehow accomplish the Lesser German goal which had eluded liberal politicians in 1848/49. These separate factors "could be incorporated as self-contained elements in

11. Cited in Pflanze, 1:277.

an essentially conservative overall picture," writes Lothar Gall. The experience of the Danish War and its aftermath, however, convinced Bismarck that only a more revolutionary combination of the same elements would bring victory over Austria and an end to the statemate in Prussia. "Now he found himself with no choice but to yoke them together in a way that gave him reason to fear that he might be putting himself in the position of the sorcerer's apprentice, who summons up forces that, applied to a particular objective, eventually elude control to an ever-increasing extent."[12] This fear of losing control cautioned Bismarck against rushing into a seemingly inevitable war with Austria in 1865. Before William's chief minister stood a fair chance of controlling the situation, he knew that three conditions must be fulfilled: the Prussian political and military elite had to be determined to fight Austria; other European powers must remain neutral or actually join Prussia; and German public opinion had to be impressed that Prussia was fighting for the unification and liberalization of Germany.

Events escalated toward war during the fall and winter. A congress of German parliamentary deputies met at Frankfurt in October 1865, to condemn the Gastein Convention as an unpatriotic slap to Augustenburg, while the Nationalist Society convened there for the same purpose later that month. Bismarck wanted to punish the Frankfurt City Senate for condoning the meetings, but when Austria refused in early 1866, he informed Vienna threateningly that it had to choose between an "upright alliance" and war "to the knife." Both sides mobilized briefly in February after the Austrian governor in Holstein permitted a pro-Augustenburg rally, then a lull ensued which Bismarck used to negotiate with Italy. Shortly after an alliance with Italy was completed in April, he announced radical plans to transform the German Confederation into a federal state with a legislature elected on the basis of universal manhood suffrage. When unsubstantiated reports of Italian troop movements near the Austrian border reached Vienna in late April 1866, Austria mobilized its army, followed quickly by Italy and Prussia. The two German Powers were on the verge of their first military clash since the Seven Years War a century earlier.

12. Gall, 1:263.

What is perhaps most remarkable about Bismarck in the last weeks of peace was the marginal ability of the sorcerer to control forces around him. In fact, few of his "prerequisites" were fulfilled before the tocsin sounded. William, torn between martial enthusiasm and feelings of guilt about fighting a brother monarch, needed the minister's daily attention to stay in line. Conservative cliques around Queen Augusta and the Gerlachs intrigued to keep the peace. Few politicians in or out of Prussia, moreover, took his egalitarian federal reform proposals seriously. The popular humor magazine, *Kladderadatsch*, captured the mood in liberal circles with a tongue-in-cheek announcement that it was shutting down. "We have been dealt a hard blow ... The Bismarck cabinet appeals to the German nation and supports itself upon the people! Hahahaha! Who's laughing? All Europe and adjacent parts of the world! We aren't up to such competition."[13] Signals from abroad were also mixed and difficult to decipher. While England and Russia were unlikely to intervene in central Europe, Napoleon III was determined to gain from a war in Germany. The only solid achievement for Bismarck was an Italian alliance that pledged southern armies to march on Austria if war broke out in the north by July. Significantly enough, this was the *only* condition identified by Helmuth von Moltke, Chief of the Prussian General Staff, as a prerequisite for success in an isolated war with Austria and its German confederates. Given his other causes for concern, the confidence of the military must have been great consolation for Bismarck as spring wore on to summer.

The unresolved controversy in Schleswig-Holstein triggered hostilities in June 1866. In what amounted to a declaration of war, Austria proposed that the Diet of the German Confederation decide the duchies' fate. The strong possibility of a vote for Augustenburg sent Prussian troops across the border to seize Holstein, which had been administered by Austria since the Gastein Convention. Vienna responded by eliciting approval from the Frankfurt Diet for mobilization against Prussia, whereupon Berlin proclaimed the Confederation dissolved. Two days later on 16 June, ancillary Prussian forces marched on Hanover and Hesse-Kassel, managing – with

13. Cited in Pflanze, 1:321.

some difficulty in Hanover – to defeat their forces before they could unite with the Bavarians. Ludwig's forces now lapsed into a state of demoralized inactivity, later to be overrun by Prussian units moving south from Hanover. Only the army of Saxony, 32,000 strong, slipped south to join Austria. By occupying that kingdom, however, Prussia took command of the western passes into Bohemia. Through these quick, decisive actions, Moltke had prevented the troops of Austria's formidable coalition from concentrating against him. Odds which had caused the minister president great consternation were now considerably narrowed. But Bismarck could not take much credit for reports of quiet along the Rhine. For if the upcoming campaign in Bohemia dragged on without quick resolution, Napoleon would know how to turn Bismarck's disingenuous promises of territorial compensation to account.

Moltke had concentrated his forces in the South by systematic use of railroad lines. His plan of attack called for three powerful armies to descend in a west-to-east arc from Saxony (Army of the Elbe), Lower Silesia (First Army), and Upper Silesia (Second Army); converge in north-central Bohemia near Jicin; and destroy the Austro-Saxon armies. The most recent historian of the early summer campaign, Geoffrey Wawro, argues convincingly that the Austrian chief, Ludwig August von Benedek, was a dithering incompetent who possessed no experience or aptitude for army command. He dawdled for three weeks in the fortified town of Olmütz while matters came to a head in Germany and Moltke's armies concentrated at the mountain passes. "Pretty boys, mostly," observed one town official. "They had a fine time, attending concerts and cavorting round town."[14] Aghast, the emperor finally ordered Benedek to break camp and march northwest toward the enemy. The Hungarian-born general now struggled in the direction of Jicin, hoping to overwhelm his opponent's divided forces separately before a trap could be sprung.

An opportunity presented itself as the Prussian Second Army nearest to Benedek streamed through the eastern passes in three columns. In fighting near Trautenau on 27 June, one column was

14. Cited in Geoffrey Wawro, *The Austro-Prussian War: Austria's War with Prussia and Italy in 1866* (Cambridge, 1996), 124.

bloodied, while at Skalice, he had three entire corps within striking distance of a badly outnumbered second column. Choosing not to give battle, Benedek continued westward with the bulk of his troops. The Second Army proceeded to blast through the passes, easily routing a formidable flanking force with the deadly needle-gun. Shocked, Benedek halted his march. This delay – and Prussia's new weapon – enabled Prussia's Elbe and First armies to overrun Austro-Saxon advance units near Jicin and cross the Iser River. Dazed and demoralized by these setbacks, Benedek retreated to an indefensible hilly salient north of Königgrätz, apparently attempting to cross the Elbe River before the converging 221,000 Prussians crushed him. But, to the amazement of subordinates, Benedek gave no orders to march; nor to dig in – he simply did nothing. Two days "passed idly," recalled one officer. "There was no discussion whatsoever of converting our campsites … into a *real* position where one could fight a battle."[15] Finally, late in the night of 2 July, Benedek came to his senses and hurried defensive deployment orders to his sleeping army corps.

A few hours later, in the rainy morning darkness of 3 July 1866, the Elbe and First armies attacked. Prussian fortunes ebbed during the first engagements as successive assault waves were decimated by massed Austrian artillery – the only antidote in the campaign to the Prussians' rapid-firing infantry rifle. With the Prussian Second Army still hours away at midday, Benedek had an opportunity to counterattack with 215,000 soldiers against Prussians inferior in number. Eager subordinates had begun the assault on the right flank, in fact, and urged Benedek to commit his entire force while there was still time. But the indecisive Austrian could not bring himself to move up his massive reserve to join the counterattack. Rather, he ordered the attacking units back into line. In the midst of this confusing, demoralizing maneuver, the Elbe Army began to break through Benedek's left flank and the Prussian Second Army finally engaged Benedek's right. Both assaults were supported by cannon firing from *higher* ground.

The situation now deteriorated quickly. Advance units of the Second Army captured Chlum Heights to Benedek's rear. From

15. Ibid., 204.

this hill, the startled Prussians gaped at the massed infantry, cavalry, and artillery of the Austrian reserve, some 47,000 strong, dressed in the traditional white of Austria. "From our bird's-eye perspective we looked down on them," recalled one artillery officer, "and they looked like beautiful white stones with which children play … The view surprised me so that, forgetting everything else, I cried out: 'God! How beautiful that looks!' But [my superior] pulled me up and said: 'This is no time for admiring pretty things. Get your batteries up here!'"[16] This was a timely command, for Benedek now ordered half of his reserve to retake Chlum. Prussian cannon and needle guns mowed them down, heaping bodies in grisly mounds and inflicting 10,000 casualties – one fourth of Austria's terrible losses that day. Only suicidal rear guard cavalry charges and courageous artillery heroics allowed Benedek's battered, defeated, and thoroughly demoralized army to escape total destruction. The war was over.

Seldom in history has so much depended on the outcome of a day's battle. In the Treaty of Prague finalized that August, Vienna conceded the dissolution of the German Confederation and Austrian exclusion from German affairs. Moreover, Francis Joseph assented to Prussian annexation of Schleswig-Holstein, Hanover, Hesse-Kassel, Nassau, and the city of Frankfurt am Main. Saxony would join the powerful new North German Confederation uniting Prussia and all German states north of the Main. Bismarck halted the process of Prussian expansion at this river primarily to avoid provoking France, but secretly, Bavaria, Württemberg, and Baden were forced to sign offensive and defensive military alliances with Prussia. The new confederation, like the South German states, would also march in wartime under the Prussian General Staff. "The world is collapsing!"[17] shouted Papal Secretary of State Antonelli, shocked by the sudden demotion of the Vatican's Habsburg ally. But no territory was taken from Austria – nor, to Napoleon's angry disappointment, was any given to France. Despite Bismarck's "halt on the Main," therefore, another conflict seemed likely.

16. Cited in Gordon A. Craig, *The Battle of Königgrätz: Prussia's Victory over Austria, 1866* (Philadelphia, 1964), 138.

17. Ibid., 170.

The reaction of Prussian conservatives was similar to Antonelli's, for in the aftermath of Königgrätz Bismarck was ready to make peace with the liberals. "The power of the monarchy in Prussia must be supported by a powerful army," he told the Crown Prince on 4 July, "but it must go with the opinion of the nation."[18] Bismarck had known this in the Hotel Royal when he met with Unruh, but four frustrating years in office had given him a much deeper appreciation of the dictates of the times. When war broke out in 1866, it had been seven years since the state had been able to borrow money from its wealthy bourgeois elite. This stood in stark contrast to the relatively normal first years of constitutionalism in the 1850s when the debt had expanded from 158 to 290 million thaler. Now, with state mines, ironworks, and railroad stocks sold; tax surpluses from the good years spent; and the huge war chest exhausted, where would Prussia find the necessary funds for war against its fuming archenemy in the west? Without a return to orderly parliamentary rule of law, moreover, how could Prussia hope to enjoy legitimacy in its vast new annexed territories, let alone in strategic provinces like the Rhineland and Westphalia? With these considerations in mind, William asked the diet in early August for retroactive approval of monies spent since 1862. The king wanted this "indemnity in respect of the period of administration without a legal budget" to affect an "indispensable understanding" between government and parliament. He hoped that "with this [Indemnity Bill] the conflict that has prevailed hitherto will be brought to a close for all time."[19]

By that crucial summer, significantly enough, many liberals were ready to grasp the olive branch that had been offered to them. Indeed the constitutional struggle had taken a heavy toll on the Prussian opposition. For years they had been hounded and intimidated, their newspapers censored, their businesses passed over for government contracts, their principles held up to ridicule by a formidable political foe. Understandably, unity had not been easy to maintain. Parliamentary deputies came under pressure, especially after 1864, from local constituencies and chambers of

18. Cited in Pflanze, 1:328.
19. Cited in Gall, 1: 310.

commerce eager to show their patriotism in wartime. "The well-to-do bourgeois are politically stunted," complained Unruh, himself a businessman. He felt they lacked the "political nerve" to square off with Bismarck. These rifts had grown by 1866, a fact which was confirmed during the elections of early summer as the Conservatives rose from 28 to 142, while the Progressives and Left Center declined from 253 to 148. There can be no doubt, moreover, that the stunning military victories of June and July gave liberals reason to reassess the worth of a once-maligned establishment. The famous remarks of Gustav Mevisssen, whose liberal credentials were rooted in the Pre-March and the Revolutions of 1848/49, are still worthy of quotation. After observing the victory parade through the Brandenburg Gate, he described his sentiments: "I cannot shake off the impression of this hour. I am no devotee of Mars; I feel more attached to the goddess of beauty and the mother of graces than to the mighty god of war, but the trophies of war exercise a magic charm upon the child of peace. One's eyes are involuntarily riveted on, and one's spirit goes along with, the unending rows of men who acclaim the god of the moment – success."[20]

These factors help to explain the overwhelming vote of approval (230-75) for the Prussian Indemnity Bill in September 1866. Loans of 30 million thaler to finance uncovered war expenses soon followed.[21] It was a sign of the intensity of the constitutional conflict, nevertheless, that half of the liberals refused to make peace. In their minds, the struggle had not been "brought to a close for all time." This would become clear enough during the upcoming months as Bismarck sought to create his new political order north of the Main.

* * * *

Austria had initiated a new political system five years earlier. The February Patent of 1861 called for an Imperial Council of 343 delegates selected by all of the provincial diets. While wide-ranging powers were retained by the monarch, parliament possessed the

20. Cited in Pflanze, 1:291, 331.

21. See Ernst Klein, *Geschichte der öffentlichen Finanzen in Deutschland (1500-1870)* (Wiesbaden, 1974), 125.

all-important right to approve new taxes. Within months, however, the Imperial Council dwindled to its 203 Cis-Leithanian members as Hungarians, Transylvanians, Croatians, Tyrolians – and later – Czechs refused to participate in an assembly that denied them ethnic autonomy.

Despite the simplifying ramifications of these defections, business was not easy to conduct in "Schmerling's Theater," the derisive term which Viennese reserved for the theatrics that characterized Austria's young parliamentary era, for the remaining western representatives in the Council were divided along many fronts. One pitted opponents against advocates of the Patent. The supporters of the changes, the so-called "Constitutional Party," possessed a solid majority with 118 seats, but were themselves split into three regional coalitions which subdivided further into little parties surrounding individual personalities. To outsiders, there appeared to be no organization or leadership. Vienna's *New Free Press* complained that each deputy "spoke, made and defended proposals and interpellations, and voted as he saw fit – a leader was nowhere to be found." A new deputy seeking party friends was completely frustrated. "But I was told: watch out, they belong to the Greater German, the others to the Greater Austrian Party, they are Autonomists, those are Federalists, Centralists, Democrats, and I don't know what else. As God is my witness, I still don't know to this day whether or not a well-ordered political party exists in this house."[22]

By 1863, however, a certain system was emerging from the disorder. Lending some coherence and effectiveness to the council's work was the parliamentary experience which many members brought from the Frankfurt, Vienna, and Kremsier diets of 1848/49. Ministerial empathy also aided the liberal movement. Like King William in 1858, Francis Joseph had filled his cabinet with bureaucratic noblemen who wanted Austria to carry on in an enlightened tradition. Anton von Schmerling was a graduate of this "Josephinian" school, as was Ignaz Edler von Plener, the minister of finance. Acting as a bridge to the ministries – and eventually to one another – was the presence of thirty-seven civil servants in the

22. Citations in Georg Franz, *Liberalismus: Die Deutschliberale Bewegung in der Habsburgischen Monarchie* (Munich, 1955), 240.

Council. There were also thirty-eight lawyers among the deputies who soon established links to fellow professionals with similar training and mentality.

Perhaps most important of all was a minimal liberal program that united most factions, parties, and ministers of the "left" on certain key issues. One was the belief that German-speaking subjects had a natural right to rule other peoples in the empire. Another prevalent view – even among the Greater Germans who wanted to preserve Austria's preeminence in Germany – was the need for financial retrenchment and fiscal responsibility. Plener and the Imperial Council fought hard to reduce deficits in the early 1860s and succeeded over the outraged protests of the army which suffered most from these cuts. Military funding was slashed from 179 million gulden in 1860 to 80 million in 1866. Even Francis Joseph could not move Plener to allocate funds for equipping the army with rapid-firing breechloaders which the enthusiastic Emperor had seen tested in April 1865. Only 1,840 of the new rifles were on hand by Königgrätz – with the known results. Ironically, Prussia may have prevailed in Bohemia by forcing through army rearmament and postponing an accommodation with liberalism until the war was won.

Defeat now led to a dramatic political reorganization of the Austrian Empire. With Austro-Prussian relations deteriorating rapidly in 1865, Francis Joseph had abandoned Schmerling's Germanocentric policy and begun to negotiate concessions with the recalcitrant Hungarians. It was this change of course that prompted his minister's resignation. Austria's weakened state after Königgrätz underscored the need to complete these talks and eliminate a source of internal dissension and external vulnerability. Formalized in May 1867, the historic compromise created a "Dual Monarchy" of Austria-Hungary. Francis Joseph was the common head of state of Austrian and Hungarian kingdoms that were further connected by joint ministries for war, foreign affairs, and finance. Otherwise, Hungary was autonomous, including its own diet with power of the purse in Budapest. Liberals in Austria's Imperial Council received many concessions themselves, including far-reaching civil liberties which had been withheld in 1861. But they condemned the agreement with Hungary as a "domestic

Königgrätz,"[23] sentiments echoed for opposite reasons by the remaining subject nationalities. In retrospect it is clear that the deal was necessary if a revamped empire was to recover from the debacle of 1866. Indeed, as we shall see, the emperor and his Austrian entourage were not yet ready to concede Germany to the Prussians.

Nor were the vast majority of Bavarians. For three years after the war, however, the kingdom's liberal political leadership moved in this direction. Ludwig II was certainly not the prime mover. The unhappy monarch largely withdrew from public duties after 1866, leading a Bohemian life in Berg Castle and dreaming about his grandiose building projects while cruising Lake Starnberg in a steamboat named "Tristan." On the advice of Richard Wagner, however, he dismissed Ludwig von der Pfordten, the moderate who had dominated Bavarian politics almost without interruption since 1848, and replaced him with Chlodwig von Hohenlohe-Schillingfürst, the favorite candidate of the Bavarian Progressives. Three years earlier this predominantly Protestant "Club of the Left" had split away from the dominant (and largely Catholic) liberal coalition in the diet to further the *Kleindeutsch* program of the Prussian Progressives and the Nationalist Society. After Königgrätz, foreign policy differences between leftists and moderates mellowed as Greater Germany faded into obscurity. Now, with roughly a two-thirds majority, Hohenlohe pressed for liberal domestic legislation and a closer alignment with the North German Confederation.

Three issues heightened tensions in 1867/68. First was the publication of Prussia's secret military alliances with the South German states. While liberals defended these treaties – even proposing army reform along Prussian lines and encouraging Baden and Württemberg to follow suit – many others saw them as unacceptable encroachment on Bavaria by unpopular North Germans. Second was an education bill which sought to curtail church control of schools. To Protestants and Catholics of liberal persuasion, Pius IX's recent Syllabus of Errors (1864) had demonstrated a shocking backwardness and disqualified the church as a reliable educator. Loyal Catholics, on the other hand, saw the liberal proposal as a devilish threat to true religion. Third, liberal legislation against the

23. Cited in Macartney, *The Habsburg Empire*, 555.

guilds in January1868 was anathema to petit bourgeois Catholics who were hard-pressed by factory competition and aware, perhaps, of the social message of Kolping and Ketteler.

These intertwined, highly emotional foreign and domestic controversies erupted during free elections held for a new parliament of the Zollverein in February 1868 (see below). The Progressives and their allies won only 12 seats in Bavaria, while the Union of Bavarian Patriots seized 26 (54 percent). The unpopularity of liberal policies was confirmed in November 1869 during diet elections which, despite a more restrictive suffrage, threw 80 of 154 seats (52 percent) to the Patriots. Absolutist pretensions aside, Ludwig had no choice but to dismiss Hohenlohe in January 1870. Friends of Prussia had good reason to be wary.

Events in Württemberg were unfolding in much the same way. After reigning for nearly half a century, King William finally died in June 1864. Parliamentary relations during his last decade had remained essentially unchanged from those first heady, confident years on the throne, for William found in Baron Joseph von Linden a tough administrator and clever politician who knew how to prevent leftists in the diet from influencing affairs of state. By 1856 the wily first minister had built up a Government Party of submissive civil servants and beholden local officials who backed his proposals and kept the angry, frustrated Progressives at bay. With the ascension of William's effete and dissolute son Karl, however, the situation quickly changed. Neither willing nor able to maintain his father's tight grip, the indifferent monarch abandoned censorship and lifted restrictions on rights of assembly and association. A voting reform followed in 1868 granting universal, direct, and secret manhood suffrage.

The king's chief minister was Baron Karl von Varnbüler, a realistic politician with a Bismarckian sense for steering his ship through parliamentary narrows. This remained relatively easy between 1864 and 1868, for the older, limited suffrage had returned the Government Party with roughly half of the seats. The Progressives, moreover, had split asunder amidst Germany's nationalistic controversies of the mid-1860s into three groupings: the German Party, which favored alignment with the North German Confederation; the Reinburg Club, a heterogeneous coalition of liberal Protestant bourgeois and conservative Catholics with only their anti-Prussianism in common; and the People's Party, a left-oriented group which pursued the elusive dream of a Third Germany. By walking a tightrope between guarding Württembergian independence and pragmatically cooperating with the new power in Berlin, Varnbüler was easily able to manipulate the various progressive factions and find majorities.

But diet elections in July 1868 complicated the politics of ministerial survival. Contested under a broader suffrage, they boosted the People's Party (and a closely aligned faction known as the Greater Germans) to prominence with 45 seats (51 percent), while the German Party received 12 mandates and the Government Party only 32. The Reinburg Club had been absorbed into the other parties. These results jeopardized Varnbüler's policy of appeasing Prussia at a very delicate time, for he wanted diet approval of a budget which provided for the Prussian army system, including needle guns and spiked helmets. Matters reached a head in March 1870 when the diet rejected this budget and Varnbüler's cabinet resigned. Along with Hohenlohe's resignation that winter, the dramatic developments in Stuttgart were a sign of advancing parliamentarism in southern Germany. They were also an added indication of how much controversy Prussia could generate in the South four years after Königgrätz. In neighboring Baden, Baron Franz von Roggenbach, long an advocate of Prussian leadership, drew the bleak conclusion that "division and partisanship of every kind have erased the last traces of the movement for national unity and given the upper hand for a long time to come to centrifugal currents."[24]

Only Baden, in fact, seemed relatively reliable from the purview of Berlin. Since ascending the throne in 1852, Grand Duke Frederick had been sympathetic to the Prussian cause in Germany. As crown prince in the 1840s, he had drunk deeply of Lesser German ideals in the classrooms of historians Ludwig Häusser (Heidelberg) and Friedrich Dahlmann (Bonn). When Baden's liberals aroused themselves to new political activism in the late 1850s, moreover, Frederick demonstrated his willingness to cooperate with the parliamentary majority. In 1860, for instance, he revised a Condordat

24. Cited in Pflanze, 1:408.

negotiated with the Vatican after anti-clerical protests from the diet. And in 1866 Frederick suppressed his preferential feelings for Prussia after the liberals, badly divided, finally sided with Austria and the Confederation. The liberal factions reunited around *Kleindeutsch* policies after Königgrätz, then pressed forward with military and anti-clerical reforms applauded by northern Protestants. Church and lay Catholic leaders attempted to mobilize farmers and small townsmen against the ruling party in Karlsruhe, castigating secular schools, civil marriage, freedom of enterprise, and pro-Bismarckian foreign policies as the work of godless, uncaring, Protestant city dwellers. But pro-Prussian candidates won 53 percent of the vote in the Zollverein elections of 1868 despite the fact that Catholics comprised a majority of the population in Baden. Liberals retained 55 of 63 seats in the diet.

Southern Germany possessed fifty years of parliamentary experience by the late 1860s. Political parties had evolved from tiny clusters of deputies grouped around scores of notables to two or three larger, disciplined, relatively modern party groupings or coalitions. The violent nationalistic clashes of the mid-1860s and the coming of general manhood suffrage in 1868 weakened and disrupted the liberal and progressive parties and generated new populist challengers, but these developments did not destroy workable party systems. This result ensured reasonably efficient government, for, after decades of resistance, heads of state had finally yielded to the necessity of setting policy in accordance with parliamentary majorities. South German parliamentarism was significant in the wider sense that it helped to shape and define perceptions throughout German Europe of the spirit of the times. In other words, events in Munich, Stuttgart, and Karlsruhe reminded rulers in Vienna and Berlin that their own political course of compromise and concession was somehow unavoidable and in keeping with the Zeitgeist.

* * * *

Following diet approval of the Indemnity Bill in September 1866, Otto von Bismarck took an extended vacation on the Baltic island of Rügen as a guest of Prince Wilhelm Malte von Wylich Putbus. Important matters of state followed him there. Max Duncker, a

Progressive and political adviser for Crown Prince Frederick, had drafted a constitution for the North German Confederation, while high-ranking subordinates in the Foreign Ministry had prepared a second document. In what have come to be known as the Putbus Dictates, Bismarck critiqued these drafts and unveiled his own conception of the new state. For five months after his return to Berlin in December, the minister-president negotiated with heads of state, generals, and parliamentarians from northern Germany. His complicated original design would be altered in some of its details from the blueprint dictated on Rügen, but its essential character was not substantially changed. Because this basic structure would be carried over into the German Empire in 1871, we should examine it closely.

Bismarck once said that the best training for a politician would be a circus act under a juggler. In the North German Confederation, he sought to juggle various contending forces without making a mistake that would send everything crashing to the ground. As a Prussian minister in his kingdom's hour of victory, it was important to assure Berlin a powerful position. Accordingly, the extensive powers of the "presidency" of the Confederation (e.g. foreign policy, war and peace, army affairs) went to the Prussian King, while command of the confederate army was bestowed on the Prussian General Staff. Moreover, the so-called Federal Council (*Bundesrat*), an upper legislative chamber appointed by the princes, afforded a significant place to Prussia with 17 of 43 seats. This was enough to prevent any other state from acquiring the two-thirds majority required for constitutional amendments. The historical force of particularism was far too important in Germany, however, to allow Prussia a *dominant* position in the new federal structure – especially if the wary and vigilant South German states were to be coaxed into membership. Hence legal jurisdiction and matters of religion and education were left to the states. Bismarck also conceded the Federal Council a central role in the legislative process and stipulated that federal laws required only a simple majority, thus limiting Prussia's veto power to constitutional issues.

Balancing the presidency, the upper chamber, and the particularism of the states was the centralizing force of the nation. Bismarck called for an Imperial Diet *(Reichstag)* elected on the basis of universal manhood suffrage that would also play a central law-making role. All domestic legislation signed by William and the Federal Council required majority passage in the diet. Because the competency of the Confederation was so much wider than the defunct Frankfurt Diet, the deliberations of North Germany's elected officials were genuinely important. Matters of business and labor, customs and commerce, currency and banking, transportation and communication, as well as all tariffs and indirect taxes were determined centrally. So, too, was the confederate budget, including monies for the military. After the searing experience of the constitutional conflict, Bismarck and the generals wanted to remove the army budget from the Prussian Diet. Accordingly, the draft constitution of the Confederation proposed that army size and funding be fixed at 1 percent of the population and 225 thaler per soldier. After considerable wrangling with the constituent diet, however, Bismarck agreed that the so-called "iron budget" would require legislative approval after 1871. Perhaps most important of all, the minister-president consented without a struggle to parliamentary approval of all new loans. In the last analysis, therefore, it was the *national* superstructure that made Bismarck's work appear so revolutionary to conservatives of the old stripe. "Pressure," writes Otto Pflanze, "would be met by counterpressure: the nation against the dynasties, the confederation against Prussia, Reichstag against Bundesrat, parliament against parliament, centralism against particularism, the centripetal against the centrifugal."[25] In the event of conflict with the Imperial Diet, of course, the opposite set of checks would prevail.

With the work of the constituent diet completed, regular elections in August 1867 returned 297 deputies to Berlin. Men from Hamburg, Hanover, the Mecklenburgs, and East Elbia mixed with legislators from Saxony, Thuringia, Hesse, and the Rhineland. There was ample experience with parliamentary politics and commitment to party-political principles, however, to bridge most local and regional differences. Thus tiny parties and uncommitted deputies claimed only 40 seats, while the so-called "federal-constitutionalists," a party with regional priorities comprised mainly of Saxons

25. Ibid., 1:348.

and annexed Prussians, secured a mere 22. The legislative fulcrum of the Imperial Diet was formed by four larger parties which together claimed 165 votes. In the center were the Free Conservatives (36), Old Liberals (15), and National Liberals (84). All accepted the settlements of 1866/67 and were prepared to move with Bismarck toward incremental improvements. To their left were the Progressives (30), dissatisfied with the outcome of their struggles and determined to push toward a more thorough parliamentarism. Although Bismarck continued to see the typical party as "a kind of parliamentary joint-stock company" that loosely joined disparate factions, and Heinrich von Treitschke complained about a Reichstag "honey-combed with intriguing cliques,"[26] it was nevertheless clear, for the most part, that the splintering and fragmentation of the early parliamentary days of the 1840s and 1850s had been overcome.

The impressive legislative accomplishments of the first North German Reichstag and its successor, the first diet of the German Empire, were perhaps the best proof of this. A national currency, a central bank, a standard set of weights and measures, a unified postal system, a liberal all-German industrial code, and elimination of the last internal toll barriers completed the institutional framework for a modern, capitalistic economy begun by progressive bureaucrats in the early 1800s. The modern business order received further impetus from laws legalizing bills of exchange, freeing corporations and joint-stock banks from the restrictive practice of bureaucratic approval, and sanctifying rights of private property. The antiguild and strict trade union provisions of the industrial code made the new establishment even more acceptable to wealthy men fearful of Germany's struggling working class. Along with the creation of the Reichstag itself, these reforms and enactments were more than tactical sops to a subdued bourgeoisie by a triumphant Bismarck. They were, writes Lothar Gall, "the expression in political terms of a highly realistic understanding of the way things were going economically, socially and politically; it was much more a consummation of something for which the time

26. Citations, respectively, in James Retallack, *Notables of the Right: The Conservative Party and Political Mobilization in Germany 1876-1918* (Boston, 1988); and Dorpalen, *Heinrich von Treitschke*, 183.

was ripe than the manipulative creation of an individual."[27] Unlike the Conservatives, Bismarck had a keen sense for the Zeitgeist.

The times were far too dynamic and upsurging, however, for all societal forces to be suspended in equilibrium, even by a juggler of Bismarck's insight, perception, and skill. Indeed the first years of the North German Confederation (and the Empire which soon followed) were marked by gender, racial, class, and religious tensions which did not augur well for domestic peace in upcoming decades. Before turning to the final events leading to the creation of the German Empire, we should first direct our attention to these forces of disequilibrium.

Affecting millions, Protestant-Catholic problems were probably the greatest threat to North Germany's surface stability in the late 1860s. We have already observed the disruptive influence of religion in the South as issues of church autonomy, denominational schooling, and secular marriage divided communities and parties. Coming in an age of cultural, scientific and technological progress, Pius IX's assault on the "errors" of modern society in 1864 exacerbated confessional relations. Lying deep below the surface, however, were three centuries of prejudice and violence between Catholics and Protestants. This deeper animosity was very evident after war broke out between Catholic Austria and Protestant Prussia in 1866. Riots and desertions accompanied Prussia's call to the colors in Rhineland-Westphalia where some reservists had to be taken at gunpoint to their induction stations. When "news of … Prussian victory came in," recalled one Westphalian Catholic, "then nothing could be felt but doubt, scorn, and bitterness."[28] The subsequent division of Germany along the Main River left northern Catholics depressed and extremely apprehensive about the future of their church and faith.

Wilhelm von Ketteler's tract, *Germany after the War of 1866*, attempted to shake Catholics from their fatalism. The highly influential Bishop of Mainz warned against that "crippling world view which believes the world is coming to an end if God doesn't direct it

27. Gall, 1:314-15.

28. Cited in Jonathan Sperber, *Popular Catholicism in Nineteenth-Century Germany* (Princeton, 1984), 157.

in accordance with our short-sighted human insights."[29] However painful it might be, God's decisions were wise. Catholics should discover the holy wisdom in the seemingly unfortunate turn of events and use these divine insights to good ends. In a subtle rejection of the Pope's *Syllabus of Errors*, Ketteler hinted that the new constitutional arrangements unfolding in the modern world north of the Main were to be exploited by Catholics for the ultimate benefit of the cause. His fellow Prussian bishops responded to this message during the 1867 Reichstag campaigns by encouraging their parishioners to elect "reliable, insightful and pious men" and "upright and forthright adherents of our holy religion."[30] The results were a mixture of success, confusion, and failure as Catholics voted in great numbers, but often with no direction for candidates who were not "adherents of our holy religion." The disappointing outcome led to redoubled organizational activity and more serious discussion of founding a new Catholic party.

Developments in Rome soon undercut these defensive efforts. For in 1869 Pius IX convened a Vatican Council to deliberate – and accept – the doctrine of papal infallibility. The reaction from the Protestant side was immediate and extreme. A Viennese newspaper published a report about a deranged nun allegedly imprisoned under terrible conditions in Cracow. "Suddenly the all-too-familiar convent atrocity stories multiplied across Europe," writes Margaret Anderson. "The German Journalists' Convention meeting in Vienna proclaimed it a 'debt of honour for every thinking man to enter the lists' for the abolition of cloisters, the expulsion of the Jesuits, and the revocation of Austria's concordat with the Vatican." In Bavaria, Hohenlohe sent a circular to the governments of Europe proposing co-ordinated resistance to papal infallibility, while in Berlin-Moabit a mob ransacked a Dominican chapel. The Progressives of Berlin followed the infamous "Moabit Cloister Attack" with a series of meetings "demanding 'for the sake of religious peace' the expulsion of all monastic orders – 'hotbeds of superstition, fornication, and sloth.' "[31] The Vatican Council seemed oblivious to these

29. Cited in Heinz Hürten, *Kurze Geschichte des deutschen Katholizismus 1800-1960* (Mainz, 1986), 128.

30. Cited in Sperber, 160.

31. Margaret Lavinia Anderson, *Windhorst: A Political Biography* (Oxford, 1981), 124-25.

shocking events, proceeding by July 1870 to accept the new dogma. German Catholics, meanwhile, intensified efforts to rally faithful burghers, peasants, artisans, and industrial workers for this unfolding "struggle of culture" *(Kulturkampf)*. Even before the bishops left Rome, in fact, the first programs for a new Catholic party were published in Münster and Cologne.

Simultaneously, Germany's accelerating industrialization generated social tensions of a different sort. The reader will recall that workers were forming trade union-like committees by 1865 which went on strike against employers. The first modern strikes dated back to the mid-1840s and 1850s when about 10 occurred per year. The trend now increased, with 23 strikes in 1864; another 30 in 1865; and crescendoing to 152 in 1869 and 362 in 1872. Some of these were sizable affairs. Thus 1,500 miners walked out near Essen in 1868, and a formidable 21,000 in 1872. Nine hundred cigar workers struck in Leipzig in 1869, and 6,500 metal workers in Chemnitz in 1871.

The strike movement, not surprisingly, was roundly condemned by the upper classes. One Silesian owner compared the strike wave to the revolutions of 1848 when "a plague, a contagious disease infected the people." The official *Norddeutsche Allgemeine Zeitung* referred to strikes as "the most distinct and discernible symptom of [our] social sickness."[32] In keeping with Bismarck's pragmatic willingness to adjust to reality, however, the Confederation legalized trade unions and strikes (as long as there was no accompanying disturbance of the peace) in July 1868.

The political parties responded quickly. Lassallean Socialists established a national trade union organization in Berlin that autumn. For years central leadership of the General Union of German Workingmen had ignored trade unionism in favor of more direct political strategies. Local organizers from industrial towns in Hanover and Saxony finally prevailed, however, with pragmatic arguments about the recruiting advantages of an alliance with the emerging unions. The Socialist initiative was followed days later by the founding of another association under the tutelage of Max Hirsch and Franz Duncker, two Prussian Progressives. The Lassal-

32. Citations in Engelhardt, *"Nur vereinigt sind wir stark"*, 113-14.

leans boasted a membership of 50,000 by spring, while the so-called Hirsch-Duncker trade unions claimed 30,000.

The advent of strikes and trade unions polarized relations between the classes. For decades, liberals had proudly claimed to speak for more than the bourgeoisie. This assertion jibed with reality in the early 1860s as hundreds of thousands of artisans and workers gathered under progressive banners in cooperatives and educational clubs. While liberals maintained cordial ties with the prospering Schulze-Delitzsch co-ops after 1866, relations soured, however, with the labor associations. August Bebel, working-class leader of the Saxon clubs, steered the movement toward the anti-Prussian People's Party forming in Württemberg and other southern states. In 1869, then, he united most of the club membership and over two-thirds of the Lassalleans in a separate Social Democratic party to champion workers' rights. The Hirsch-Duncker trade unions failed to bridge the widening gap, for the National Liberals saw striking unions as a plague, while the Progressives never genuinely accepted them. Moreover, the Social Democrats, after initially doubting the wisdom of founding unions, threw their support to the Lassallean trade unions after absorbing the remainder of this party in 1875. Seemingly deserted by the middle class, meanwhile, the workers' educational clubs declined precipitously in membership before finally disbanding in 1869.

Class relations in the Catholic camp developed along similar lines. Journeymen's leagues, miners' associations, and workers' clubs had formed under socially concerned priests after mid-century, but these were clearly not trade unions. Nor did most members of the Catholic clergy and upper classes approve of them. Typically, socially established Catholics were wary of "popular tribunes who promise the proletariat mountains of gold," as one put it. "Today there's a strike here, tomorrow there; instead of working, they're drinking in the tavern. Just look at the workers. Aren't they dressed better than before? Don't they eat better than before? Isn't their situation continually better?" In fact, Bishop Ketteler was nearly alone in his advocacy of trade unions. He presented his ideas for interconfessional Christian trade unions to the Conference of Prussian Bishops in September 1869, calling for a "new Kolping" to lead the organization, push for social reforms, and become an "apostle of peace between capital and labor."[33] But the bishops refused to endorse any social measures beyond charity. Catholic workers would remain torn for decades between class interests that favored joining unions and religious loyalties to a socially conservative church under siege.

Adding to the mounting tension in Germany was the gradual reemergence of anti-Semitism. Much older than anti-Catholicism, this mix of racial and religious prejudice was deeply embedded in German-gentile culture. As observed in Parts I and II, it could flare up violently in times of national crisis and economic hard times like the French invasions and postwar depression. In most states until 1848/49, moreover, Jews were subjected to legal discrimination and a ghetto existence. One fleeting by-product of that revolutionary year was the "emancipation" of the Jews. Liberals deplored the alleged selfish exclusivity and alien traits of Jewishness, but assumed that legal emancipation would integrate them into the national fold and remove their supposedly unpatriotic traits. But Frankfurt's emancipatory legislation triggered a nasty anti-Semitic backlash led by mastercraftsmen who barely distinguished between liberals and Jews and saw freedom of enterprise as a Jewish conspiracy. One xenophobic guild circular lambasted Jews as hated "strangers who were nowhere at home and who have no heart for the people where they live."[34] With the return of reactionary regimes came a resumption of the old discriminatory practices, but popular anti-Semitism did not submerge into dormancy. Rather, it stayed active during the frenetic industrialization of the 1850s. The migration from rural areas, where anti-Jewish sentiments were strongest, to towns and cities, where Jews tended to congregate, afforded rabble-rousers an opportunity to preach their irrational hatred against "foreigners in our midst" who allegedly prevented Germans from earning a decent living. The liberal resurgence of the 1860s made matters worse, for it brought not only a flurry of free enterprise statutes (see above), but also renewed legislation to emancipate the Jews.

33. Cited in Brose, *Christian Labor* , 34, 43.

34. Cited in Shulamit Volkov, *The Rise of Popular Antimodernism in Germany: The Urban Master Artisans 1873-1896* (Princeton, 1978), 216.

Baden (1862), Württemberg (1864), Austria (1867), the North German Confederation (1869), and finally the German Empire (1871) removed discriminatory laws from the books, thereby provoking anti-Semitic outbursts from petit bourgeois Germans alienated by modern developments. The Great Depression which followed the stock market crash of 1873 allowed these passions to intensify. Anti-Semitic fanatics grew increasingly preoccupied with solving the so-called "Jewish Question."

These years also witnessed the rebirth of a women's movement in northern Germany. The radical revolutionary interlude of 1848/49 had projected some remarkable women into leading political roles. Louise Aston, famous before the revolution for her advocacy of atheism and free love, was exiled for her participation in the March uprising in Berlin. Luise Otto-Peters of Leipzig, editor of *Women's News,* was a pious German Catholic who condemned Aston's alleged unfeminine ways, but was no less insistent on advancing women's rights. Inspired by her paper's motto – "For the empire of freedom I recruit female citizens"[35] – women from all parts of Germany formed intimate circles to hear it read aloud. The suppression of *Women's News* in 1852 forced Otto-Peters into political retirement, but in early 1865 she decided to resume political activity. With the help of other interested women in Leipzig like Auguste Schmidt and Henriette Goldschmidt, she established the Association for the Education of Women. The new organization expanded that October into the nationwide General Union of German Women, which grew slowly but steadily to 11,000 members by 1877.

The immediate objective of the General Union was the right of professional work for women. "Work, which will be the basis of the new society, is the duty and the honor of the female sex," Otto-Peters wrote in 1866. "We therefore claim the right and the duty to work." Closely related to this goal was the need for women's educational opportunities. Accordingly, the General Union petitioned the Reichstag to facilitate the expansion of women's educational and employment opportunities and generally, to enhance the legal position of women. By exiting the private sphere and making a

35. Cited in Prelinger, *Charity, Challenge, and Change*, 106.

valuable contribution in a public world dominated by men, these dedicated feminists wanted to earn for women the right to vote – the "capstone"[36] of the whole effort, as Otto-Peters put it in 1872.

Underlying the philosophy of the General Union was a concept Ann Taylor Allen describes as "spiritual motherhood." The gender-specific maternal qualities of women had to permeate society in order to affect a cultural transformation into the new society. The change of heart to a gentler way of doing things would begin with the woman's contribution to child-rearing and early formal education. This strategy explains the emphasis placed by the General Union on improving wives' property and guardianship rights, educating females, and opening the teaching profession to them. With suffrage rights, presumably, the peaceful maternal revolution would carry over into national, or even international, politics.

The policy implications of "spiritual motherhood" were clear as early as 1866 in a speech Henriette Goldschmidt delivered to the Leipzig Association for the Education of Women. Saddened by the killing of the Austro-Prussian War, she exhorted her colleagues to overcome the antagonisms caused by men. "We women are created not to hate, but to love."[37] The talk, which was published in Otto-Peters' journal, *New Paths*, must have raised eyebrows among male army officers wedded to a different mentality. A few years after the defeat of France, for instance, Helmuth von Moltke said that "perpetual peace is a dream, and not a pleasant one at that." For war belonged to a "[divine] ordering of the world" that allowed "the most noble human virtues to develop – courage and self-deprivation, faithfulness to duty, and willingness to sacrifice one's life." Without war, he concluded, "the world would wallow in materialism."[38] The vastly different world views of Goldschmidt and Moltke were evidence of mounting gender friction in the Era of Unification.

* * * *

36. Citations in Ann Taylor Allen, *Feminism and Motherhood in Germany, 1800-1914* (New Brunswick, 1994), 97, 109.

37. Ibid., 101.

38. Cited in Roger Chickering, *Imperial Germany and a World Without War: The Peace Movement and German Society 1892-1914* (Princeton, 1975), 392-93.

In early 1869, full of dispair, Baron Georg von Werthern, Prussian envoy in Munich, wrote to Bismarck. The cause of Prussian leadership in Germany had deteriorated with the rise of South German particularism since 1866, he claimed. Germany had been Prussia's for the taking after Königgrätz, but this golden opportunity had been let slip by not marching on Vienna and imposing rights of conquest. Now costly sacrifices appeared to be the only way to regain what had been squandered. The chancellor's reply is now a classic, still instructive for the glimpse it affords into his modus operandi. "I also hold it probable that violent events would further German unity. To assume the mission of bringing about a violent catastrophe and take responsibility for the timing of it, however, is quite another matter. Arbitrary interference in the course of history, motivated on purely subjective grounds, has never achieved any other result than to shake down unripe fruit. That German unity is not at the moment a ripe fruit is in my opinion obvious … We can put the clocks forward, but time does not on that account move any faster, and the ability to wait while the situation develops is a prerequisite of practical politics … We can look forward to the future with repose and leave to our successors what remains to be done."[39]

Bismarck wanted to complete the "unification" of Germany as much as the hungry generals and impatient National Liberals. A number of factors had prevented this in 1866. French fear of an even greater German colossus across the Rhine had prompted Prussian counsels to halt at the Main. There was also a perceived need to pause in order to consolidate huge territorial annexations and adjust to new confederate relations. South German particularism and anti-Prussianism reinforced the wisdom of waiting for all-German bonds to strengthen gradually. After three years, however, these ties seemed weaker, not stronger. Northern liberals wanted to sweep the Zollverein elections (1868) and use the new economic parliament to affect a political union. But 49 of the 85 delegates elected in the southern states were determined opponents of these designs. Although northern deputies outnumbered the southerners, Bismarck wisely refused to force through a vote

39. Cited in Pflanze, 1:447.

for Lesser German unification. Diet elections in Württemberg (1868) and Bavaria (1869) strengthened the centrifugal forces of South German patriotism. Given these circumstances, Bismarck was prepared to wait five, ten, or even twenty years to absorb the South – by which time it might indeed be his successors who accomplished "what remains to be done."

Patience was Bismarck's greatest asset. As 1869 yielded to 1870, however, preemptive action – if it could be cleverly staged – grew more and more attractive. For France, anxious to reverse the verdict of 1866, was reequipping its infantry with rapid-firing rifles, expanding the army (with reserves) to over a million men, and negotiating military alliances with Austria and Italy. Prussia countered with Russian talks aimed at neutralizing Austria, should it march; military discussions to coordinate strategies with the increasingly unreliable southern states; and a refitted and vastly superior artillery. Adding to the pressure on the chancellor was northern liberal criticism of his commitment to nationalism as the time for Reichstag renegotiation of the army's "iron budget" drew near.

Then, through the welter and cacophony of events, Bismarck began to hear the faint sound of God's footsteps. In February 1870, Spain offered its throne to Prince Leopold of Hohenzollern-Sigmaringen, heir to the Catholic branch of the Prussian royal family. Bismarck had known of the plan for almost a year, seeing it at first as an excellent way to distract Paris from graver matters. But by early summer the affair had escalated into a crisis as France overreacted to the specter of a Hohenzollern on its southern flank. When Paris insisted that Berlin renounce Leopold's candidacy, William agreed in order to keep the peace. A second demand that he renounce the candidacy for all time, however, drew the monarch's polite refusal. After asking the General Staff if the army were ready, Bismarck, at Bad Ems with William, altered the communique to make the rejection blunter and undiplomatic. The famous Ems Telegram was seen by France as a national insult that deserved cold hard steel in response. Both sides mobilized their armies in mid-July 1870.

Unlike 1866, when most German rulers sided with Austria, Bismarck's provocative diplomacy had given the army a great advantage, for the French army expansion was not completed. Still, their commanders anticipated assembling a force of nearly 400,000 men that would advance across the Rhine, join Austrian and South German armies, crush the upstart Prussians, and reorganize German Europe. Instead, French troops were caught in a huge traffic congestion caused by inferior general staff work and a radial pattern of railroads which forced all reservists to travel through Paris to reach the eastern frontier. With only 200,000 soldiers at the front, French commanders decided to improvise a defensive strategy. The Austrians now waited for a more opportune moment to intervene in the war, while the governments of Bavaria and Württemberg were swept by a wave of anti-French patriotism into honoring their military alliances with the North.

Meanwhile in early August, 310,000 German soldiers, transported efficiently on east-west railways planned and constructed under the vigilant eye of the Prussian General Staff, crossed into Lorraine. On 1 September at the decisive battle of Sedan, Napoleon and one of his two armies were pounded mercilessly into submission by 500 artillery pieces. An even larger force was surrounded at Metz and starved into surrender on 29 October. The victorious Germans now besieged Paris where a republic had been proclaimed to carry on the fight. After all attempts to free the capital from outside had failed, 90,000 defenders of Paris tried to penetrate German siege lines. The failure of this escape – and an ongoing, brutal bombardment – forced the defenders to capitulate.

On 18 January 1871 – one day before the attempted breakout – William, Bismarck, and 500 German officers gathered in the famed Hall of Mirrors at Versailles to proclaim the creation of the German Empire. Three months of intense negotiation and wrangling had preceeded the ceremony. Baden was eager to join the expanded Confederation, and Württemberg agreed after minor concessions, but proud Bavaria exacted a higher price. Its diplomatic corps and army would maintain a separate existence, the latter submitting to Prussian command in wartime, while the competence of the Bundesrat was extended to include declarations of war. In return for a bribe of 300,000 marks per year, moreover, Ludwig II invited William to accept the imperial title. A bitter argument now ensued between Bismarck and his sovereign over whether or not the wording of the title should give emphasis to

William's legitimate position as King of Prussia. Grand Duke Frederick of Baden took it upon himself to end the standoff with a greeting in the Hall of Mirrors in the name of all the princes: "Long live his imperial and royal majesty Emperor William!"[40]

* * * *

Sixty-five years had passed since the abolition of the Holy Roman Empire of the German Nation. Its memory, fused with a variety of contemporary political agendas, did not fade through six decades. Free corps students wore its colors in 1813, carried its banner to the Wartburg in 1817, and again at Hambach Castle in 1832. The ardent dream of restoring it motivated thousands of gymnasts, marksmen, and singers in the bleak epoch of the German Confederation. Greater German parties from Austria and "Third Germany" factions from the South-Central states wore the emotional emblem of the old empire in 1848 and again in the 1860s. In the end it was Prussia, the German land with the least attachment to the Holy Roman Empire during its last century of existence, which restored imperial glory to Germany. But the Second Empire was at best a consolation to those who remembered 1806, for it had taken a German civil war and the division of German Europe to accomplish. Notwithstanding medieval pomp in the Hall of Mirrors, moreover, the Kaiserreich looked forward to a new era, not backward to the old. Industrialization and social change began to alter state and society in the decades after 1815 – and these ongoing modern developments were reflected in the institutions, politics, tensions, and culture of the Second Empire. It would last until 1918.

40. Cited in William Carr, *The Origins of the Wars of German Unification* (New York, 1991), 208.

Select Bibliography

Works in English

Allen, Ann Taylor. *Feminism and Motherhood in Germany, 1800-1914*. New Brunswick, 1994.

Anderson, Eugene N. *The Social and Political Conflict in Prussia 1858-1864*. Lincoln, 1954.

Anderson, Margaret Lavinia. *Windhorst: A Political Biography*. Oxford, 1981.

Barclay, David E. *Frederick William IV and the Prussian Monarchy 1840-1861*. Oxford, 1995.

Beck, Hermann. *The Origins of the Authoritarian Welfare State in Prussia: Conservatives, Bureaucracy, and the Social Question, 1815-70*. Ann Arbor, 1995.

Berlin, Isaiah. *Karl Marx: His Life and Environment*. New York, 1959.

Berman, Russell A. *The Rise of the Modern German Novel: Crisis and Charisma*. Cambridge, 1986.

Billinger, Robert D., Jr. *Metternich and the German Question: States Rights and Federal Duties, 1820-1834*. Newark, 1991.

Blanning, T.C.W. *The Origins of the French Revolutionary Wars*. New York, 1986.

______. *The French Revolution in Germany: Occupation and Resistance in the Rhineland 1792-1802*. Oxford, 1983.

Bramsted, Ernest T. *Aristocracy and the Middle Classes in Germany: Social Types in German Literature 1830-1900*. Chicago, 1964.

Brandes, Georg. *Ferdinand Lassalle*. New York, 1925.

Brophy, James M. *The Accommodation of Capital: The Railroad Industry and Political Culture in Prussia 1830-1870*. Columbus, forthcoming 1997.

Brose, Eric Dorn. *Christian Labor and the Politics of Frustration in Imperial Germany*. Washington, D. C., 1985.

______. *The Politics of Technology in Prussia: Out of the Shadow of Antiquity 1809-1848*. Princeton, 1993.

Broyles, Michael. *Beethoven: The Emergence and Evolution of Beethoven's Heroic Style*. New York, 1987.

Bruford, W.H. *Culture and Society in Classical Weimar 1775-1806*. Cambridge, 1962.

Burke, Peter. *Popular Culture in Early Modern Europe*. New York, 1978.

Butler, E. M. *Heinrich Heine: A Biography*. Westport, 1979.

Carr, William. *The Origins of the German Wars of Unification*. New York, 1991.

Clapham, J. H. *Economic Development of France and Germany 1815-1914*. Cambridge, 1966.

Craig, Gordon. *Germany 1866-1945*. New York, 1978.

______. *The Battle of Königgrätz: Prussia's Victory over Austria, 1866*. Philadelphia, 1964.

Diefendorf, Jeffry M. *Businessmen and Politics in the Rhineland, 1789-1834*. Princeton, 1980.

Dorpalen, Andreas. *Heinrich von Treitschke*. New Haven, 1957.

Duffy, Christopher. *Austerlitz 1805*. London, 1977.

Dunlavy, Colleen A. *Politics and Industrialization: Early Railroads in the United States and Prussia*. Princeton, 1994.

Epstein, Klaus. *The Genesis of German Conservatism*. Princeton, 1966.

Frevert, Ute. *Women in German History: From Bourgeois Emancipation to Sexual Liberation*. Oxford, 1989.

Frisch, Walter (ed.). *Brahms and His World*. Princeton, 1990.

Gagliardo, John G. *Germany under the Old regime 1600-1790*. London, 1991.

______. *Reich and Nation: The Holy Roman Empire as Idea and Reality, 1763-1806*. Bloomington, 1980.

Gall, Lothar. *Bismarck: The White Revolutionary*. Translated by J. A. Underwood. London, 1990.

Geiringer, Karl. *Brahms: His Life and Work*. New York, 1982.

Gilbert, Felix. *History: Politics or Culture: Reflections on Ranke and Burckhardt*. Princeton, 1990.

Gray, Marion W. *Prussia in Transition: Society and Politics under the Stein Reform Ministry of 1808*. Philadelphia, 1986.

Gutman, Robert W. *Richard Wagner : The Man, His Mind, and His Music*. New York, 1968.

Hamerow, Theodore S. *Restoration, Revolution, Reaction: Economics and Politics in Germany 1815-1871*. Princeton, 1958.

______. *The Social Foundations of German Unification 1858-1871*. 2 vols. Princeton, 1969-1971.

Hauser, Arnold. *The Social History of Art*. New York, 1951.

Henderson, W. O. *The Zollverein*. Chicago, 1959.

Hertz, Deborah. *Jewish High Society in Old Regime Berlin*. New Haven, 1988.

Herzog, Dagmar. *Intimacy and Exclusion: Religious Politics in Pre-Revolutionary Baden*. Princeton, 1996.

Hohendahl, Peter Uwe. *Building a National Literature: The Case of Germany*. Ithaca, 1989.

Holborn, Hajo. *A History of Modern Germany*. 3 vols. New York, 1959-69.

Hughes, Michael. *Nationalism and Society: Germany 1800-1945*. London, 1988.

Hull, Isabel V. *Sexuality, State, and Civil Society in Germany, 1700-1815*. Ithaca, 1996.

Iggers, George G. *The German Conception of History: The National Tradition of Historical Thought from Herder to the Present*. Middletown, CT, 1968.

John, Michael. *Politics and the Law in Late Nineteenth-Century Germany: The Origins of the Civil Code*. Oxford, 1989.

Kamenetsky, Christa. *The Brothers Grimm and Their Critics: Folktales and the Quest for Meaning*. Athens, OH, 1992.

Kisch, Herbert. *From Domestic Manufacture to Industrial Revolution: The Case of the Rhineland Textile Districts*. New York, 1989.

Knight, Frida. *Beethoven and the Age of Revolution*. London, 1973.

Kohn, Hans. *The Mind of Germany: The Education of a Nation*. New York, 1960.

Kraehe, Enno E. *Metternich's German Policy: The Congress of Vienna, 1814-1815*. Princeton, 1983.

______. *Metternich's German Policy: The Contest with Napoleon, 1799-1814*. Princeton, 1963.

Krieger, Leonard. *Ranke and the Meaning of History*. Chicago, 1977.

Lee, Loyd E. *The Politics of Harmony: Civil Service, Liberalism, and Social Reform in Baden, 1800-1850*. Newark, 1980.

Lüdtke, Alf. *Police and State in Prussia, 1815-1850*. Translated by Pete Burgess. Cambridge, 1989.

Macartney, C.A. *The Habsburg Empire 1790-1918*. New York, 1969.

Malia, Martin. *Alexander Herzen and the Birth of Russian Socialism*. New York, 1965.

Manceron, Clause. *Austerlitz: The Story of a Battle*. Translated by George Unwin. New York, 1966.

Moran, Daniel. *Toward the Century of Words: Johann Cotta and the Politics of the Public Realm in Germany, 1795-1832*. Berkeley, 1990.

Mosse, George L. *The Nationalization of the Masses: Political Symbolism and Mass Movements in Germany from the Napoleonic Wars through the Third Reich.* Ithaca, 1975.

Paret, Peter. *Art As History: Episodes in the Culture and Politics of Nineteenth-Century Germany*. Princeton, 1988.

Peppard, Murrary B. *Paths Through the Forest: A Biography of the Brothers Grimm*. New York, 1971.

Perènyi, Eleanor. *Liszt: The Artist as Romantic Hero*. Boston, 1974.

Pflanze, Otto. *Bismarck and the Development of Germany: The Period of Unification, 1815-1871*. Princeton, 1990.

Prelinger, Catherine. *Charity, Challenge, and Change: Religious Dimensions of the Mid-Nineteenth-Century Women's Movement in Germany*. New York, 1987.

Price, Arnold H. *The Evolution of the Zollverein*. Ann Arbor, 1949.

Robertson, Priscilla. *The Revolutions of 1848: A Social History*. Princeton, 1971.

Rohr, Donald. *The Origins of Social Liberalism in Germany*. Chicago, 1963.

Roper, Katherine. *German Encounters with Modernity: Novels of Imperial Berlin*. London, 1993.

Rothenberg, Gunther E. *The Art of Warfare in the Age of Napoleon*. Bloomington, 1978.

Sabean, David Warren. *Property, Production, and Family in Neckarhausen, 1700-1870*. Cambridge, 1990.

Saine, Thomas P. *Black Bread – White Bread: German Intellectuals and the French Revolution*. Columbia, SC, 1988.

Sammons, Jeffrey. *Heinrich Heine: A Modern Biography*. Princeton, 1979.

Schmitt, Hans A. "Count Beust and Germany, 1866-1870: Reconquest, Realignment, or Resignation?" *Central European History* 1 (1968): 20-34.

Schorske, Carl E. *Fin-De-Siècle Vienna: Politics and Culture*. New York, 1981.

Sheehan, James J. *German History 1770-1866*. New York, 1990.

Sorkin, David. *The Transformation of German Jewry, 1780-1840*. New York, 1987.

Shorter, Edward Lazare. "Social Change and Social Policy in Bavaria, 1800-1860." Ph. D. dissertation, Harvard University, 1967.

Simon, Walter M. *The Failure of the Prussian Reform Movement, 1807-1819*. New York, 1971.

Smith, Bonnie G. *Changing Lives: Women in European History since 1700*. Lexington, KY 1989.

Sperber, Jonathan. *Popular Catholicism in Nineteenth Century Germany*. Princeton, 1984.

______. *Rhineland Radicals: The Democratic Movement and the Revolution of 1848-1849*. Princeton, 1991.

Stein, Jack M. *Richard Wagner and the Synthesis of the Arts*. Westport, 1973.

Toews, John Edward. *Hegelianism: The Path Toward Dialectical Humanism, 1805-1841*. Cambridge, 1980.

Vaughan, William. *German Romantic Painting*. New Haven, 1994.

Volkov, Shulamit. *The Rise of Popular Antimodernism in Germany: The Urban Masters 1873-1896*. Princeton, 1978.

Walker, Alan. *Franz Liszt: The Weimar Years 1848-1861*. 2 vols. New York, 1989.

Walker, Mack. *German Home Towns: Community, State, and General Estate 1648-1871*. Ithaca, 1971.

Warrack, John. *Carl Maria von Weber*. London, 1968.

Watkin, David, and Mellinghoff, Tilman. *German Architecture and the Classical Ideal*. Cambridge, MA, 1987.

Wawro, Geoffrey. *The Austro-Prussian War: Austria's War with Prussia and Italy in 1866*. Cambridge, 1996.

Whitman, James Q. *The Legacy of Roman Law in the German Romantic Era: Historical Vision and Legal Change*. Princeton, 1990.

Works in German

Aretin, Karl Otmar von. *Bayerns Weg zum souveränen Staat: Landstände und konstitutionelle Monarchie 1714-1818*. Munich, 1976.

______. *Heiliges Römisches Reich 1776-1806: Reichsverfassung und Staatssouveranität*. 2 vols. Wiesbaden, 1967.

Bachem, Karl. *Vorgeschichte, Geschichte und Politik der Deutschen Zentrumspartei*. 9 vols. Cologne, 1927-1929.

Becker, Josef. *Liberaler Staat und Kirche in der Ära von Reichsgründung und Kulturkampf: Geschichte und Strukturen ihres Verhältnises in Baden, 1860-1876*. Mainz, 1973.

Beenken, Hermann. *Das 19. Jahrhundert in der deutschen Kunst*. Munich, 1944.

Beer, Adolf. *Die österreichische Handelspolitik im neunzehnten Jahrhundert*. Vienna, 1981.

Bergengrün, Alexander. *David Hansemann*. Berlin, 1901.

Best, Heinrich. *Interessenpolitik und nationale Integration 1848-49: Handelspolitische Konflikte im frühindustriellen Deutschland*. Göttingen, 1980.

Bibl, Viktor. *Kaiser Franz: Der letzte Römisch-Deutsche Kaiser*. Leipzig, 1937.

Birker, Karl. *Die deutschen Arbeiterbildungsvereine 1840-1870*. Berlin, 1973.

Böhme, Helmut. *Deutschlands Weg zur Grossmacht: Studien zum Verhältnis von Wirtschaft und Staat während der Reichsgründungszeit 1848-1881*. Cologne, 1966.

Börsch-Supan, Eva. *Berliner Baukunst nach Schinkel 1840-1870*. Munich, 1977.

Brandt, Hartwig. *Parlamentarismus in Württemberg 1819-1870*. Düsseldorf, 1987.

Buchwald, Reinhard. *Schiller: Leben und Werk*. Wiesbaden, 1959.

Dann, Otto. *Nation und Nationalismus in Deutschland 1770-1990*. Munich, 1990.

Dolgner, Dieter. *Historismus: Deutscher Baukunst 1815-1900*. Leipzig, 1993.

Düding, Dieter. *Organisierter gesellschaftlicher Nationalismus in Deutschland (1808-1847): Bedeutung und Funktion der Turner- und Sängervereine für die deutsche Nationalbewegung*. Munich, 1984.

Edler, Arnfried. *Robert Schumann und seine Zeit*. Düsseldorf, 1982.

Eisenberg, Christiane. *Deutsche und englische Gewerkschaften: Entstehung und Entwicklung bis 1878 im Vergleich*. Göttingen, 1986.

Engelhardt, Ulrich. *"Nur vereinigt sind wir stark" : Die Anfänge der deutschen Gewerkschaftsbewegung 1862/63 bis 1869/70*. Stuttgart, 1977.

Fiege, Gertrud. *Caspar David Friedrich in Selbstzeugnissen und Bilddokumenten*. Hamburg, 1977.

Fischer, Wolfram. *Der Staat und die Anfänge der Industrialisierung in Baden 1800-1850*. Berlin, 1962.

Franz, Georg. *Liberalismus: Die Deutschliberale Bewegung in der Habsburgischen Monarchie*. Munich, 1955.

Friedrichs-Friedlaender, Carola. *Architektur als Mittel politischer Selbstdarstellung im 19. Jahrhundert: Die Baupolitik der bayerischen Wittelsbacher*. Munich, 1980.

Gall, Lothar. *Bismarck Der Weisse Revolutionär*. Frankfurt, 1980.

______. "Liberalismus und 'Bürgerliche Gesellschaft': Zu Charakter und Entwicklung der Liberalen Bewegung in Deutschland." *Historische Zeitschrift* 220 (April 1975): 324-56.

______. *Der Liberalismus Als Regierende Partei: Das Grossherzogtum Baden Zwischen Restauration und Reichsgründung*. Wiesbaden, 1968.

Gehring, Paul. "Von List bis Steinweiss: Aus der Frühzeit der Württembergischen Industrialisierung." *Zeitschrift für Württembergische Landesgeschichte* 7 (1943): 405-44.

______. "Das Wirtschaftsleben in Württemberg unter König Wilhelm I (1816-1864)." *Zeitschrift für Württembergische Landesgeschichte* 9 (1949-1950): 196-257.

Götschmann, Dirk. *Das Bayerische Innenministerium 1825-1864*. Göttingen, 1993.

Gollwitzer, Heinz. *Ludwig I. von Bayern: Königtum im Vormärz, eine Politische Biographie*. Munich, 1986.

Good, David F. *Der wirtschaftliche Aufstieg des Habsburgerreiches 1750-1914*. Vienna, 1986.

Gotthardt, Christian. *Industrialisierung, Bürgerliche Politik und Proletarische Autonomie: Voraussetzungen und Varianten sozialistischer Klassenorganisationen in Nordwestdeutschland 1863 bis 1875*. Bonn, 1992.

Grünthal, Günther. *Parlamentarismus in Preussen 1848/49-1857/58*. Düsseldorf, 1982.

Gugel, Michael. *Industrieller Aufstieg und bürgerliche Herrschaft: Sozioökonomische Interessen und politische Ziele des liberalen Bürgertums in Preussen zur Zeit des Verfassungskonflikts 1857-1867*. Cologne, 1975.

Hahn, August. *Der Maximilianstil in München: Programm und Verwirklichung*. Munich, 1982.

Hahn, Hans-Werner. *Wirtschaftliche Integration im 19. Jahrhundert: Die hessischen Staaten und der Deutsche Zollverein*. Göttingen, 1982.

Horsetzky, Adolf von. *Kriegsgeschichtliche Übersicht der wichtigsten Feldzüge seit 1792*. Vienna, 1914.

Hubrig, Hans. *Die patriotischen Gesellschaften des 18. Jahrhunderts*. Weinheim, 1957.

Hürten, Heinz. *Kurze Geschichte des deutschen Katholizismus 1800-1960*. Mainz, 1986.

Hütt, Wolfgang. *Die Düsseldorfer Malerschule 1819-1869*. Leipzig, 1964.

Ibbeken, Rudolf. *Preussen 1807-1813: Staat und Volk als Idee und Wirklichkeit*. Cologne, 1970.

Kalnein, Wend von (ed.). *Die Düsseldorfer Malerschule*. Düsseldorf, 1979.

Kiesewetter, Hubert. *Industrialisierung und Landwirtschaft: Sachsens Stellung im regionalen Industrialisierungsprozess Deutschlands im 19. Jahrhundert*. Vienna, 1988.

Klein, Ernst. *Geschichte der öffentlichen Finanzen in Deutschland (1500-1870)*. Wiesbaden, 1974.

Koselleck, Reinhard. *Preussen zwischen Reform und Revolution: Allgemeines Landrecht, Verwaltung und soziale Bewegung von 1794 bis 1848*. Stuttgart, 1967.

Kramer, Helmut. *Fraktionsbindungen in den deutschen Volksvertretungen 1819-1849*. Berlin, 1968.

Löhde, Walter. *Friedrich Schiller im politischen Geschehen seiner Zeit*. Munich, 1959.

Megerle, Klaus. *Württemberg im Industrialisierungsprozess Deutschlands: Ein Beitrag zur regionalen Differenzierung der Industrialisierung*. Stuttgart, 1982.

Meyer, Dora. *Das öffentliche Leben in Berlin im Jahr vor der Märzrevolution*. Berlin, 1912.

Na'aman, Schlomo. *Der Deutsche Nationalverein: Die politische Konstituierung des deutschen Bürgertums 1859-1867*. Düsseldorf, 1987.

Nipperdey, Thomas. *Deutsche Geschichte 1800-1866: Bürgerwelt und starker Staat*. Munich, 1983.

______. "Nationalidee und Nationaldenkmal in Deutschland im 19. Jahrhundert." *Historische Zeitschrift* 206 (June 1968): 529-85.

Rürup, Reinhard. *Emanzipation und Antisemitismus: Studien zur "Judenfrage" der bürgerlichen Gesellschaft*. Göttingen, 1975.

Schnabel, Franz. *Deutsche Geschichte im Neunzehnten Jahrhundert*. 3 vols. Freiburg, 1933-1937.

Schumann, Dirk. *Bayerns Unternehmer in Gesellschaft und Staat, 1834-1914*. Göttingen, 1992.

Siemann, Wolfram. *Vom Staatenbund zum Nationalstaat: Deutschland 1806-1871*. Munich, 1995.

Slokar, Johann. *Geschichte der österreichischen Industrie und ihrer Förderung unter Kaiser Franz I*. Vienna, 1914.

Srbik, Heinrich Ritter von. *Metternich: Der Staatsmann und der Mensch*. 2 vols. Munich, 1925.

Stamm-Kuhlmann, Thomas. *König in Preussens grosser Zeit: Friedrich Wilhelm III. der Melancholiker auf dem Thron*. Berlin, 1992.

Strach, Hermann (ed.). *Geschichte der Eisenbahnen der Oesterreichisch-Ungarischen Monarchie*. 2 vols. Vienna, 1898.

Tenfelde, Klaus. *Sozialgeschichte der Bergarbeiter an der Ruhr im 19. Jahrhundert*. Bonn, 1977.

Treitschke, Heinrich von. *Deutsche Geschichte im Neunzehnten Jahrhundert*. 5 vols. Leipzig, 1879-1897.

Valjavec, Fritz. *Die Entstehung der politischen Strömungen in Deutschland 1770-1815*. Düsseldorf, 1978.

Vogel, Barbara. *Allgemeine Gewerbefreiheit: Die Reformpolitik des preussischen Staatskanzlers Hardenberg (1810-1820)*. Göttingen, 1983.

Wetcke, Hans Hermann. *Die andere Tradition: Architektur in München von 1800 bis Heute*. Munich, 1982.

Wiest, Helga. *Die Entwicklung des Gewerbes des rechtrheinischen Bayern in der Frühzeit der deutschen Zolleinigung*. Munich, 1970.

Winter, Eduard. *Romantismus, Restauration und Frühliberalismus im österreichischen Vormärz*. Vienna, 1968.

Wehler, Hans-Ulrich. *Deutsche Gesellschaftsgeschichte*. 3 vols. Munich, 1987-95.

Wilhelmy, Petra. *Der Berliner Salon im 19. Jahrhundert (1780-1914)*. Berlin, 1989.

INDEX

A

B

C

D

E

O

P

R